W9-BJN-711

Government at the Grass-Roots

Government
at the
Grass-Roots

Second Edition

George S. Blair
Claremont Graduate School

PALISADES PUBLISHERS
Pacific Palisades, California

Published originally as *American Local Government*
by Harper & Row, Publishers.

Second edition, Copyright © 1977
by Palisades Publishers

Library of Congress Catalog Card Number: 76-24095

International Standard Book Numbers:

0-913530-07-7 (paper)
0-913530-08-5 (cloth)

Palisades Publishers
P.O. Box 744, Pacific Palisades, California 90272

Printed in the United States of America

Contents

Preface

American local government usually has been analyzed segmentally. Various books are devoted to some aspect rather than the whole design of our pattern of local governments. Thus, we have books concerning city government, county government, rural government, urban government, or government of metropolitan areas. While the form and practice of city and county governments will be emphasized, this book encompasses all major types of local governmental units—counties, cities, townships, towns, school and other special districts—and includes a chapter on governmental patterns and problems in metropolitan areas.

In addition to this comparative treatment of the several types of local governmental units, further aspects of this book differentiate it from other currently available texts. A major difference lies in the strong emphasis here on local government structure. The author believes that processes must take place within a structural setting and the forms of local government are described at some length. A second difference concerns the discussion of major governmental processes at the local level. Several chapters are devoted to a comparative description of the legislative, executive, judicial and administrative functions rather than giving them superficial treatment in discussing alternative patterns of government. Third, local government theory has been woven into the discussion throughout the book. Current literature in this field in both book and article form is surprisingly void of such discussion and a frame of reference is desirable in discussing problems of contemporary change and proposals for local government reorganization. A fourth difference relates to the internal treatment of the material. We have attempted to avoid overworked cliches and stereotypes in considering governmental structure, processes and services, and have drawn from relevant materials and writings in a number of social sciences.

The material in this book organizes itself logically into four parts—the setting, politics and structure, processes, and policies and problems. The first four chapters present the setting of American local government in the twentieth century. Local politics and structures of local government are described in Chapters 5 through 9. Governmental processes are discussed in Chapters 10 through 13, and policies and problems of local government are treated in the final six chapters.

This writer holds certain value judgments about American local government. The first is a belief in the tradition and values of local self-government. In current times, both the theoretical justification and practical significance of local government are often challenged. One purpose of this book is to rechallenge the challenges through an analysis of their content and implication to American local government. A second value judgment is a belief that institutions of local government currently need strengthening in our federal system. Intergovernmental cooperation is a fine thing and is on the increase at both federal-local and state-local levels. But cooperation implies voluntary relationships, not forced or mandatory administrative requirements. Further, there is a difference between local assistance in setting goals and establishing programs and local administration of centrally-determined goals and programs. A third belief is the premise that local governments and their institutions are too often resistant to reforms and change that are both needed and desirable. Local government can be effective government only if the local communities meet the needs of their citizens effectively.

We should like to acknowledge our appreciation and give proper credit to the many students and practitioners of local government who have helped us as critics and in supplying information. Unfortunately we cannot name them all because of their number, but three students deserve special mention. They are Dr. David L. Martin, now of Auburn University, and Jeanne Solak, for their assistance with Bureau of the Census materials; and Cynthia Short, for her assistance in typing the manuscript. Appreciation also is expressed to my wife Gloria, who provided constant encouragement and understanding during the long period of research and writing. My son David and daughter Becky also deserve thanks for the fewer demands they made during this same time.

While it is conventional to do so, it is also quite proper to add that the responsibility for debatable conclusions—and any errors of fact—are mine alone.

Claremont, California   G.S.B.

Chapter 1

Tradition and Values of Local Government

Units of American local government have experienced a longevity significantly greater than that of the thirteen original states as states or of our national government. The tradition of local government was firmly embedded in the American colonies and the values of such entities in the success of democratic government in the United States has never seriously been questioned.

The general acceptance of American local government in the late eighteenth century is implicit in the Constitution, which was ratified by the thirteen states starting in 1787. This document establishing our federal system recognizes only a two-tier scheme of government in the United States, and thus does not consider the question of how power should be distributed between the states and their political subdivisions. This seeming oversight, however, reveals the framers' intent that the creation and supervision of local units were and should remain entirely the concerns of the states. Local governments had proven their necessity and desirability in colonial times for such purposes as judicial, militia, taxing, and administrative centers. It thus was presumed that the states would not only utilize existing units of local government but also would establish additional units to serve state purposes as well as to supervise affairs in smaller communities.

The reasonableness of this interpretation of the intent of the framers of the Constitution is borne out by policies advanced in the Northwest Ordinances of 1785 and 1787. These laws were enacted by the Continental Congress under the Articles of Confederation as a blueprint for the general pattern of government in the western territories. The Ordinance of 1785, commonly called the ''Land Ordinance,'' provided for the survey and sale of these lands. The Ordinance of 1787 provided for governmental organization of the territory, including the creation of counties and townships as units of local government. This Act also guaranteed the sanctity of private contracts, abolished the age-old law of primogeniture, prohibited slavery and involuntary servitude, and contained a rudimentary statement of human rights.[1] Most of the humanitarian provisions of this Ordinance became part of the Constitution in its first amendments, and subsequent Congresses traced the course of new states by the provisions prescribed in this basic Act.

DEFENSE OF LOCAL DEMOCRACY

Democracy is not an easy concept to explain adequately. As defined in *Webster's Collegiate Dictionary,* it is "government by the people; government in which the supreme power is retained by the people and exercised either directly (absolute, or pure democracy), or indirectly (representative democracy) through a system of representation." Government by the people in the United States, however, means more than simply government by the majority. Certain basic rights are guaranteed to all the people whether they are members of the current majority or members of groups within the minority. Thus, our system of democracy reflects four basic principles—majority rule, minority rights, political equality, and regular election.

According to Robert MacIver, a Scottish sociologist,

> Democracy is not the rule of "the masses" nor is it something for "the masses" only. Democracy is not the enthronement of mediocrity, to the disadvantage of the elite, the enlightened, the cultivated. Democracy is the political liberation of all men from the chains of power.

For MacIver, democracy provides the way of liberation both from mass intolerance and from the ruthlessness and corruption of power. It gives equal rights to all persons, and by doing so it breaks all barriers of education, culture, and opportunity, that formerly set people apart, as preordained inferiors and superiors.[2]

The rationalization of democracy in a local government is largely the same as that for democracy in general and cannot be developed very adequately in only a few paragraphs. It is commonly accepted that the core concepts of democratic theory evolve around the nature of the individual citizen from which the concept of the state in which a person lives is developed. This sequence of roles is in sharp contrast to other systems of government that explain the nature of the state first and then construct the concept of the individual around his life and duties as a citizen of the state. Two central threads of the democratic theory are the Greek contribution of the capacity of a human to reason and the Christian concept of a person as a creature of God. Embracing the doctrine of the rationality of the individual,

Christianity developed the theory of equality, a basic tenet of democratic dogma.

Beginning with these concepts of the quality of humankind, the tenet of freedom developed logically. Within the limits of action not harmful to other people, democratic theory holds that a person is free to will and determine his own public and private activities. The qualification on this freedom, that an individual's actions must not harm others, is an important concept leading to the establishment of sanctions and communities to enforce them on errant members of society. Thus, the citizen became a member of a civil community and was a shareholder of its power because he has the right and duty to participate in its political processes.

Democratic theory also embraces a preference for the method by which community decisions or will is registered. In terms of procedure, this method may be described in simple terms as a process of ratification by the electorate following discussion of the issues at hand. As principles for a machinery of government, Charles Wilson states that the spirit and methods of democracy imply three such guides. First, political decisions must be taken by a system in which all citizens can share. Second, political decisions must be made only after discussion and vote. And third, political decisions must be made so that a process of continuing public political education is carried on.[3] Since universal discussion and consent are highly impracticable, if not impossible, in modern society, the concept of representative democracy rather than direct democracy is both desirable and acceptable as a meaningful adaptation of democratic theory in local as well as in central government.

Institutions of American local government are designed to meet these three fundamental requirements of functioning democracy—participation, discussion, and education. Our local governments across the nation enable their citizens to share in political decisionmaking and in the administration of carrying out policies so determined. They provide the media of discussion to inform the citizen and the machinery to enable him to register his voice of consent or disapproval. Also, these governments and their agencies operate in the public eye to further the continuing political education of the voters. Since the citizen may truly share in the local political process, the democracy of local government in action is its own best justification and rationalization. The effectiveness of citizen sharing, however, is in part a function of size of the community. The voice of the citizen may be heard with less clarity and fall on less receptive ears in large units of local government. A cynic might be prompted to say that if the citizens rule, they have little to rule over since a small unit of government has control over only a limited range of affairs. A local government large enough to control a wide range of affairs is so big that the citizens' role is that of largely ratifying decisions made for them.

It would be theoretically possible to design a system of democratic central government without democratic local governments within the larger community. But such a plan would be extremely difficult to adapt into a community previously governed under an alternative system or to institute as a first experiment in self-government in a new nation. It is also possible that the theoretically perfect system would fail miserably in actual application. Thus, we can conclude that democratic local governments are not only a desirable counterpart of democratic national government but that they are necessary and vital partners in and to the larger community.[4] In an alliterative sense, a good case may be made that a Leviathan state requires its Lilliputian communities to enlist the interest of its citizens and to carry out the services of the government.

VALUES OF LOCAL GOVERNMENT

The case for the affirmative concerning the values of local self-government has been very convincingly made by two foreign observers of the American scene. Following his visit to the United States, French statesman Alexis de Tocqueville wrote:

> Yet municipal institutions constitute the strength of free nations. Town meetings are to liberty what primary schools are to science; they bring it within the people's reach, they teach men how to use and how to enjoy it. A nation may establish a free government, but without municipal institutions it cannot have the spirit of liberty.[5]

The second foreign observer, James Bryce, an Englishman, based his arguments for local self-government largely upon his reflections of the American and Swiss systems that he had observed. He described small communities as the "tiny fountain heads of democracy." In commenting on local government in the United States, Bryce stated, "These examples justify the maxim that the best school of democracy and the best guarantee of its success, is the practice of local self-government."[6]

Americans, however, are not immune from lauding the values of their local governments. A staff report to the President's Commission on Intergovernmental Relations in 1955 stated that "Local governments are to total government what basic tissues are to the human body. Without them, government would have no vitality." In a similar vein, the staff report added, "The counties, cities, towns, villages, and boroughs serve as training schools for the leaders of government and in the affairs of local government are tried those who aspire to State and National office."[7]

A highly important virtue of local self-government accrues from the important services these units provide through officials who are selected by, are close to, and know the problems of the citizenry of the community.

Through these processes of approving services to be rendered, choosing persons to administer them, and checking upon the performance of these people in office, the vital democratic processes of participation, discussion, and political education are in visible operation to both the officeholder and constituent alike.

Evolving from the conditions described above, the positive concept of community becomes meaningful to the citizens within its boundaries. A sense of common interest in community affairs arises from the many opportunities for local service, and it becomes a common duty of the citizens to see that their representatives perform efficiently and honestly. Although a popular song would have us believe that "anywhere I hang my hat is home," studies of sociologists underscore the direct and indirect values if alienation from the local political process is to be avoided. Such alienation sometimes occurs among recent migrants to urban centers who do not identify themselves with their new and larger communities, or among lower class constituents who are greeted by the disinclination of the local governors to accede to their concerns promptly or effectively. As a result, the responsibility for controlling the local government is abdicated to others.[8]

A third positive virtue in local government is the "schoolroom of democracy" concept. Service in local government not only trains men and women to work for others but to work with others since government at any level involves a large measure of compromise. Service in local institutions often serves as a springboard for service in branches of state and national government.[9] The political career of Barry Goldwater, Sr., which led to the United States Senate and a presidential nomination, began as a city councilman. Hubert Humphrey was mayor of Minneapolis before serving as United States Senator, Vice-President, and presidential candidate. A second aspect of the "schoolroom of democracy" concept results from the wide citizen participation in government possible at the local level. The existence of many boards, commissions, offices, and committees provides opportunities for participation by a larger number of citizens and helps generate a feeling of actual sharing in the processes of community self-government.

A fourth contribution of local governments is their role as administrative agencies of the state. Many programs and services provided by city and county governments result from the carrying out of policies prescribed by the state government, and in some cases even those of the national government, as with county agricultural agents, welfare administrators, and civil defense directors. Local application of centrally-determined policies results in modification of these more general goals to conditions, social and economic needs, and cultural patterns of localities. The role of the administrative unit of the state is important in another way because state policies are often established after consultation with local administrators or upon recommendations of committees or commissions that include representatives from local governments.

A fifth positive benefit of local self-governing institutions is their contribution to the development of local centers of thought and action. According to Arthur E. Morgan, educator and public official, "for the prevention and transmission of the fundamentals of civilization, vigorous, wholesome community life is imperative." Unless people live and work in the intimate relationships of community life, he believes a truly unified nation or community of mankind cannot emerge. If a person does not love his neighbor whom he knows, how can he love the human race, which is but an abstraction? In short, if an individual has not learned to work with a few people, Morgan does not believe he can be effective with many. He continues by stating, " . . . the small community has supplied the lifeblood of civilization, and neglect of it has been one of the primary reasons for the slowness and the interrupted course of human progress."[10] Many small units of local government would not be recognized as communities in the sense Morgan uses the term while some neighborhoods in large cities would be so identified. The key test of community, according to Morgan, is an attitude and action pattern of common attention to matters of common concern rather than a pattern of action in which citizens respond and act in highly individualistic ways.

These statements concerning the values of local self-government are commonly accepted, but they have not gone completely unchallenged. Some persons feel that democracy cannot be served effectively by outworn or outdated forms or units and that such obsolete institutions must be scrapped and replaced by new ones better fitted to our modern pattern of living. Arthur C. Millspaugh, political scientist, advanced this argument more than forty years ago when he wrote,

> Few facts have been found and few principles have been established regarding the role of 'local self-government' in the drama of democracy. Here, indeed, is a rich and almost unpenetrated field awaiting exploration. Localized democracy has tremendous emotional support. Many impartial students give it their benedictions. It has been the subject of some obituaries. Its praises have been sung, but its values have not been scientifically determined. Until they are, it is doubtful whether the concept of local self-government deserves any large place in a realistic political science. The concept, once vitally related to facts, may at present be worse than irrelevant to the ideal of popular government. It may now be merely another example of "degradation of the democratic dogma."[11]

The Committee for Economic Development offered a similar indictment of local government recently. The Committee found American institutions of local government to be under severe and increasing strain. While they had been well designed, by and large, to meet the simpler needs of earlier times, many small local governments are poorly suited to cope with new burdens imposed on all governments by the complex conditions of modern life. Since adaptation to change has been so slow, so limited, and so reluctant, the Committee believes that the future role—even the continued viability—of these institutions is in grave doubt.[12]

A third critical voice is that of political scientist William Anderson who has skillfully countered the major political arguments for small local governmental units. Concerning the "school of self-government" concept, Anderson suggests that the school needs both a new teacher and a new curriculum and that many of its "classrooms" are merely experiences in parochialism, parsimony, and extravagance. The principle of keeping government close to the people is not always complemented by the demands of these same people for new and improved public services. Anderson points out that the standards of efficient administration in terms of minimum population requirements, economic support, or accommodation to geographical features may run counter to the political tenets of very small governments.[13] Anderson, however, is a staunch supporter and defender of local government and his plan for a "rationalized" system of local governments is discussed in some detail in Chapter 2.

Other critics point out the extensive gap between the theory and the practice of American local government. While citizens, practitioners, and writers almost uniformly applaud the ideas of grassroots government, an apparently strong case can be made to show the failure of such units to practice it. Voting statistics support this criticism since actual voter registrations seldom total more than three-fourths of the potential number and voter participation in local elections often amounts to less than half the registered total. However, even such substantiating evidence for this hypothesis might lead to drawing unwarranted conclusions. Possibly the core of the local self-government concept is the psychological fact that the opportunity to participate exists, rather than the quantitative response to this opportunity as demonstrated by the turnout on election day. The odds of being heard certainly are more favorable in a typical local government than in a government at a higher level, and general acceptance of the idea that "my voice is effective when I choose to use it" should not be too strictly measured against the frequency of its use as an indicator of its basic importance.

Strong dangers to participatory local government, however, may result from a national government being overly internationalized in its outlook and policy emphasis and from an increasingly professionalized bureaucracy. The first threat is largely one of neglect—sufficient attention and funds may not be allocated to the domestic needs of citizens in their communities to alleviate or solve their pressing problems due to a concern for the many problems of international affairs. The second danger may result in the conversion of policy matters into administrative questions to avoid the possible pitfalls of working through the local political process. As professionalization increases, some local officials act as members of their respective professional organizations employed by a community rather than as employees of the community who secondarily hold membership in a professional organization. One writer has described professionally-staffed administrative agencies as the "New Machine" that runs the cities.[14]

IMPORTANCE OF LOCAL GOVERNMENT

Pluralism is a necessary feature of a citizen's interest in his government. There are many factors that determine an individual's interest in the several units of local government in which he is a citizen (most persons are residents of at least three governmental units—a county, a school district, and either a city or a special district) as well as his interest in his state and national governments. Particularly since World War II, the American citizen has seen the spotlight of public interest and attention focused increasingly on the serious problems of national and international affairs. The shift in popular interest from the local area to the national and international scenes was not sudden or unwarranted. Certainly, the problems of national security and international peace deserve serious consideration by all citizens as are the many attendant national problems arising from the interactions of big government, big business, big labor, and big interest groups. Many of these non-local institutions and agencies are under serious challenge, due in no small part to self-inflicted wounds resulting in and from Vietnam, Watergate, the energy crisis, and others. Unfortunately, most of the suffering is borne at the local level.

It is much more than a nostalgic sentiment or romanticized yearning for the good old days, however, that prompts this writer to believe in the continued importance of strong units of local government. Perhaps "atoms of democracy" is a better phrase than "pillars of democracy" to describe the place of local units in our federal system. The term atom represents a basic unit of matter; in a political sense, the local community represents the basic unit of government. The Lincoln-coined phrase "Government of the people, by the people, for the people" still may accurately describe the citizen's role in the affairs of his local government, while his role in higher levels of government becomes more one of choice and ratification rather than of participation and consent.

Although we often hear much about the march of power from the city hall and county courthouse to the state capitol, the obligations of local governments continue to increase and the services they provide grow in both number and importance. Public education, public health, protection of person and property, recreation, water supply, and sewage disposal facilities are truly vital services and each is still supplied principally by local governments. The functions of both city and county governments have expanded markedly in recent years as new or increased services are offered in such diverse program areas as hospitals, recreation, housing, renewal, airports, libraries, planning, and zoning.

Further evidence of the importance of local governments is the increasing budgets to provide these services. There is a possible fallacy in equating quantity with quality, but the continued growth of local governmental expenditures attests to the acceptability of these services by the citizens who demand and pay for them. In 1974, the total annual expenditures of local governments reached an all-time peak of $124.7 billion, a seventeenfold increase since 1929.[15]

The fact that local government is big business also is shown by the 8.6 million full- and part-time workers on its payrolls and the yearly expenditure of over $70 billion for their services in 1974.[16] While this expenditure represents a new high and is a considerable amount, it should not be forgotten that many of the "citizen-politicians" at the local level receive little or no compensation other than the satisfaction that comes from serving one's neighbors and community. Many of these local employees are amateurs in governmental administration, but their service in a way offsets services that must increasingly rely on the use of experts and career public servants at the higher levels. Since the concept of democracy implies the type of citizen interest and service found at the local level, local governments may still be described as the bulwark of American democracy.

Another argument for the importance of local government may be built around the nature of the problems they face now and probably will in the future. While problems of water supply, public health, education, care for dependents of all kinds, transportation, and urban renewal, for instance, cannot compete with international problems for the interest of the citizen, nevertheless it is essential that approaches to solve or ameliorate these kinds of local problems be determined—hopefully—within the framework of local democratic institutions. The single factor of population mobility raises problems which all three levels of government are attempting to meet, but it is in the day-by-day operations of local governments that the problems must be met head-on. Whether more people are moving into or leaving a particular community, the problems of adjustment in expanding or curtailing services, in finding new revenue sources, in responding to citizen needs and demands, are tremendous and must be solved largely within the local area with the sympathetic understanding and assistance of higher levels of government.

The increasing concern of our state and national governments in developing programs to meet local problems and pressures is further testimony to the importance of these local communities in our governmental system. As local problems become common to many places, they become more important and pass from local to higher governmental levels for action. They become a state or national concern because of their significance to an increasing number of local communities, rather than because they are basically statewide or nationwide in scope.

In the immediate years ahead, citizens may continue to focus their major attention on higher levels and to take their local governments largely for granted. However, this emphasis may not last and there already are indications that citizens are increasingly concerned about problems in their neighborhoods, communities, and cities. But even if the activities of local governments remain somewhat obscured, their underlying importance will also remain. The reasons for this rather paradoxical condition have been aptly phrased in these words:

> No incumbent mayor or city councilman will ever sign a treaty of peace ending all war; no city engineer will ever build a hydrogen bomb; no police chief will ever command a victorious United Nations army; but these local officials . . . will determine whether the several communities in which we live will remain relatively civilized and decent.[17]

NOTES

1. R. H. Nelson and J. J. Wuest, *The Primary Sources of American Government,* Putnam, 1962, pp. 45-49.
2. Robert M. MacIver, *The Ramparts We Guard,* Macmillan, 1950, pp. 42-43.
3. Charles H. Wilson (ed.), *Essays on Local Government,* Basil Blackwell, 1948, p. 16.
4. For an insightful analysis of local government theory, see Anwar Syed, *The Political Theory of American Local Government,* Random House, 1966; and Wickwar W. Hardy, *The Political Theory of Local Government,* University of South Carolina Press, 1970.
5. Alexis de Tocqueville, *Democracy in America,* Vol. I, Vintage Books, 1954, pp. 63-64.
6. James Bryce, *Modern Democracies,* Vol. I, Macmillan, 1921, pp. 131-3.
7. Advisory Committee on Local Government, *Local Government,* a report to the Commission on Intergovernmental Relations, Government Printing Office, 1955, p. 9. While the Commission did not repeat this flowery phrasing in its *Report,* its general acceptance of this philosophy seems apparent.
8. Three informative and illuminating articles that elaborate upon this thesis are: Robert C. Angell, "The Moral Integration of American Cities" in Paul K. Hatt and Albert J. Reiss, Jr. (eds.), *Cities and Society,* rev. ed., The Free Press, 1957, pp. 617-30; Basil G. Zimmer, "Participation of Migrants in Urban Structures," *American Sociological Review,* 20 (April, 1955), 218-24; and Morris Axelrod, "Urban Structure and Social Participation," *American Sociological Review,* 21 (February, 1955), 14-18.

9. B. Dean Bowles, "Local Government Participation as a Route of Recruitment to the State Legislatures in California and Pennsylvania, 1900-1962," *Western Political Quarterly,* 20 (September, 1966), 491-503.

10. Arthur E. Morgan, *The Small Community,* Harper, 1942, pp. 3, 19.

11. Arthur C. Millspaugh, *Local Democracy and Crime Control,* Brookings Institution, 1936, p. 69.

12. Committee for Economic Development, *Modernizing Local Government,* Committee for Economic Development, 1966, p. 8.

13. William Anderson, *The Units of Government in the United States,* Public Administration Service, 1945, pp. 40-41.

14. For a discussion of this point, see Theodore L. Lowi, *The End of Liberalism, Ideology, Policy and the Crisis of Public Authority,* Norton, 1969, pp. 200-206.

15. Bureau of the Census, "Governmental Finances and Employment at a Glance," Government Printing Office, January, 1976, p. 4.

16. *Ibid.*

17. Stephen K. Bailey, H. D. Samuel, and Sidney Baldwin, *Government in America,* Holt, Rinehart and Winston, 1957, p. 455.

Chapter 2
Types and Numbers of Local Government

Although the basic structure of local government presently reflects the forms that developed during colonial days, extensive changes have occurred over the years in numbers, functions, and size of local units. In 1972, at the time of the latest official count of governments, there were 78,218 units in the United States. While this total sounds large, the number for the nation as a whole has been declining in recent decades. The decrease is accounted for by the consolidation of many school districts and a small drop in townships. The number of counties has remained almost constant, while both municipalities and non-school special districts have numerically increased.

WHAT IS A LOCAL GOVERNMENT?

No commonly accepted definition exists of what a local governmental unit is in the United States. While scholars have difficulty in defining a local government the matter is a simple one for most citizens. They know that our government is like all Gaul—divided into three parts—national (or federal), state, and local.[1] Thus, it follows that a local government is the government of some particular local community.

The Bureau of the Census has developed a more complete definition of a local governmental unit. While this definition is usually not described in full, its utility is accepted by all. It includes three general criteria which a local unit must meet to qualify as a government. The first holds that a unit must have existence as an organized entity with essential corporate powers. Second, a unit must possess governmental character. Third, a unit must enjoy substantial autonomy as evidenced by fiscal and administrative independence subject only to requirements of state law and supervision.[2]

The Criterion of Autonomy

The criterion of substantial autonomy is probaby the most essential characteristic of a local government, since this implies a major degree of independence from external control. As creatures of the state, all local governments are subject to state control in at least certain areas and in the exercise of certain powers. However, substantial autonomy exists if the unit has a reasonable degree of independence in administrative and fiscal affairs.

Administrative independence is related primarily to the method by which the members of the local governing body are selected and to the functions they perform. Thus, an agency with a popularly-elected governing body or one with a governing body composed of representatives from two or more state or local governments is considered to be an independent unit of government. Similarly, this status of independence is achieved if the unit has an appointed governing body that performs functions differing from those exercised by and are not minutely specified by the creating government or governments.

The status of fiscal independence for a unit is met by the presence of one or more of the following powers: (1) the right to determine its own budget without review or major modification by another unit; (2) the right to prescribe the taxes to be levied for its support; (3) the right to fix and collect charges for services rendered; and (4) the right to incur debt without review by another local government.[3]

The Criterion of Entity Existence

To exist as a corporate entity, a local government must embrace both area and population—that is, it must be created to serve a citizenry existing in a known location. Similarly, it must be identifiable in that its corporate name distinguishes it from other existing units. To serve its citizenry, the unit must have some form of organization and be empowered to exercise certain essential public powers. These include the rights to a distinguishing name, to sue and be sued, make contracts, acquire and dispose of property, and to perpetual succession, subject to the possibility of deorganization by the state.[4] Commonly, local governments are identified by state law as municipal corporations, public corporations, or as bodies corporate and politic.

The Criterion of Governmental Character

There are three essential features of governmental character that identify a unit of local government. The first relates to its officeholders and requires them either to be elected by the citizenry of the unit or to be appointed by other officials who are popularly elected. Second, the unit must bear a high degree of public responsibility and accountability. This requirement is met if it reports periodically to its citizenry or if its records are open to inspection by the public. The third characteristic implies the responsibility for performing one or more functions of a governmental nature such as health, safety, and welfare.

A second and briefer definition of a local government has been formulated by William Anderson. He identifies as a local government any agency which has a

> resident population occupying a defined area that has a legally authorized organization and governing body, a separate legal identity, the power to provide certain public or governmental services, and a substantial degree of autonomy including legal and actual power to raise at least a part of its own revenues.[5]

Thus, the Anderson definition embodies seven essential characteristics.

THE PATTERN OF GOVERNMENT

Although American states vary widely in physical size and population, the types of local governmental units found within them follow a fairly common mold. The four major types of units entrusted with public responsibilities at the local level are counties, municipalities, townships (and towns), and special districts. Many states create special districts for school purposes rather than entrust that function to some general purpose unit. These school districts are so significant that some treat them as distinct from other types of special districts. However, this distinction seems more one of traditional convenience than one of logic or meaningful difference. In citing numbers of local units below, the categories used by the Bureau of the Census will be followed but school districts are discussed as merely one form of a single-purpose special district.

Local governments may be discussed conveniently in a small number of categories, but the units within a single category may exhibit wide variations in size, population, and functions performed. Townships are an interesting illustration. The term is used to embrace towns in the New England states, the rural township of midwestern states, and incorporated municipalities in such states as New Jersey and Pennsylvania. Thus the term identifies such differing communities as Warren, Maine (a small town), Homewood Township, Kansas (a rural township), and Upper Darby, Pennsylvania (a municipality of over 90,000 population). However, the differences in local governments in the fifty states are actually far less than might be expected in our federal system which permits each state to design its own system of local government.

Counties

The county is the most territorially inclusive local unit. Numbering more than 3,000, the county exists in every state but Connecticut and Rhode Island.[6] However, this governmental land division is known as the parish in Louisiana and borough in Alaska. Since these units differ more in terminology than in purpose and function, the term county will be used to include the Alaskan borough and the Louisiana parish.

There is a wide range in the number of county governments among the states. Texas with 254 has the greatest number, while Delaware and Hawaii with three each have the fewest. The average number per state is sixty-one, with twenty-five states exceeding this number. Generally speaking, the average is exceeded by midwestern and southern states while northeastern and western states have fewer than the average. In terms of population, counties range from a low of less than 200 in Loving County, Texas, to more than seven million in Los Angeles County, California. The average population of counties is about 60,000. However, 127 counties—only 4.2 percent of the total number—account for about half of the total population while the smallest 305 counties, a tenth of the total, embrace less than one percent of the whole population.[7]

Municipalities

Called by many names including cities, boroughs, and villages, municipalities are the most important general-purpose units of local government in the United States and exist in all fifty states. Although not as inclusive in territory as counties, municipalities exercise more powers and provide more services than those rendered by county governments. As incorporated communities, municipalities operate under local charters that are either prescribed or approved by state legislative action or prepared under a self-executing home-rule provision.[8] Functionally, municipalities perform some operations as state instrumentalities and some because of the benefits to be derived primarily by the local residents.

While municipalities exist in all fifty states, the number of incorporated communities range from a high of nearly 1,300 in Illinois to one, the city of Honolulu, in Hawaii.[9] Three states—Pennsylvania, Iowa, and Ohio—have over 900 municipalities, and twelve others have over 500. On the other hand, seven states have fewer than fifty municipalities, with only eight operating in Rhode Island.

The spread in population of municipalities is also considerable. Only about 150 of them have populations of over 100,000, with New York City being the largest with 7.8 million. The majority of municipalities are small; they contain fewer than 1,000 inhabitants.

Townships and Towns

Local governmental units classified as townships exist in twenty-one states, largely in the central, north central and northeastern sections of the nation. In the six New England states and in some areas of New York and Wisconsin, they are more commonly known as towns, while in fourteen states, in addition to most of New York and Wisconsin, the unit is identified usually as the township. Both township and towns were primarily established to serve rural communities and most of them still fulfill this function. Of the approximately 17,000 units of this category, only a tenth have populations of over 5,000. However, both in New England and in areas adjoining urban centers in other states, the township is becoming increasingly like municipalities, in both governmental form and services provided.

The three types of units comprising this category of local governments—the New England town, the rural township, and the urban township—are briefly described at this point to indicate their major differences. The town is the traditional and most important unit of local government in New England. The term as now used includes rural areas known as plantations in Maine and locations in New Hampshire, as well as the small town that is more celebrated in literature. In terms of numbers, Rhode Island with thirty-one has the smallest number while Maine with 472 has the greatest. In the less densely populated sections of New England, the town still operates as a unit of rural local government; it is organized simply and performs only a limited number of governmental services. In more urban sections, the town provides more services and has powers similar to those of municipalities.

The rural township as a unit of government exists in fifteen states with more than 1,000 found in each of ten of them—Illinois, Indiana, Kansas, Michigan, Minnesota, North Dakota, Ohio, Pennsylvania, South Dakota, and Wisconsin. Except around urban centers, these units are rural in nature, supply few functions, and are simply organized. The influence of the congressional township system used in surveying these states is evident in the size of townships in parts of several states. The congressional township was uniformly an area of thirty-six square miles, while the average township area in Kansas is just over and that of Indiana townships is just under this figure. [10]

Towns and townships adjacent to more highly urbanized areas are themselves increasingly becoming units of urban government. The necessity for this development is apparent from the size of some townships, since almost 300 have populations of at least 25,000. [11] Excluding New England such large townships are found especially in Pennsylvania, New Jersey, Indiana, Illinois, and Michigan. In some states all municipal territory is excluded from township jurisdiction while in others only larger cities are excluded. In a third group of states, such densely populated clusters, even though incorporated, remain within the township for certain governmental purposes.

Special Districts

Special district governments exist in all states except Alaska and are the most numerous of all types of local governments. Special districts total about 40,000, of which approximately 16,000 are independent school districts with the rest—about 24,000—serving a variety of single or limited purposes ranging from air pollution control to the supply, storage, conservation, or maintenance of water.[12] Twelve states have over 500 school districts and the same number have over 800 other types of special districts. The three major types of special districts other than school are those for fire protection, soil conservation, and urban water supply. They account for more than a third of all non-school special districts. In addition to the independent school districts, the Bureau of the Census recognized about 1,500 other school systems which operate as part of a state, county, municipal, or township government, or as an agency of a group of school districts.

The two basic types of special districts—school and non-school—have had a contrasting pattern of development in recent years. Since 1942, the number of independent school districts has declined by about 85 percent as school reorganization and consolidation has expanded. On the other hand, non-school districts have increased about fourfold. Problems generated by and benefits resulting from the creation of special purpose districts are considered in detail in Chapter 9.

STANDARD METROPOLITAN STATISTICAL AREAS

Although standard metropolitan statistical areas (SMSAs) are neither governmental units or legal entities, they deserve brief mention at this point. As defined by the federal office of Management and Budget, a standard metropolitan statistical area consists of a county or a group of contiguous counties containing at least one city of 50,000 or more. Other adjacent counties are included in the metropolitan area if they are densely populated, contain a large number of non-agricultural workers, and are socially and economically integrated with the central county.[13]

The 264 standard metropolitan statistical areas (SMSAs) range in size from the New York area with a population of over 11.5 million to others with barely 50,000 residents.[14] In number of metropolitan areas, Texas leads with twenty-four and Ohio and California each has sixteen. Only three states—Alaska, Vermont, and Wyoming—have no such urban population concentrations. More than slightly over 70 percent of Americans were living in these 264 SMSAs in 1970 compared to 63.07 percent in 212 such areas in 1960. The areas around the center cities are experiencing a more rapid increase in population than the core city in most SMSAs as the trend toward concentration in large urban communities continues at a rather rapid pace.

Since metropolitan areas are not units of government, they will not be discussed further in this chapter, which is concerned with numbers and types of local governmental units. However, Chapter 18 explores the growth of these areas, their problems, and the governmental patterns evolving or proposed to meet their needs.

THE PARADOX OF NUMBERS

The challenging and illuminating phrase "too many local governments, not enough local government" was advanced by the President's Commission on Intergovernmental Relations about a quarter century ago to describe the basic problem facing state governments in their relationships with local government.[15] While the phrase at first glance may seem to be a better alliteration than a proper diagnosis of local government ills, it is a provocative statement in capsulized form embracing two of the major weaknesses of American local government. Though the phrase is largely self-explanatory, it deserves closer analysis.

The Criterion of Size

Size is not in itself a satisfactory criterion to measure the meaningfulness of the unit. Certainly it must be admitted at the outset that some very small units are well governed while some large ones are poorly governed. The concept of an ideal size for a unit of local government has been a topic of speculation and concern at least since the times of philosophers Plato and Aristotle and it continues to be discussed and researched even today.

According to Plato, the "fairest" standard for the regulation of the size of a city by its guardians was that "the city may go on increasing so long as it can grow without losing its unity, but no further."[16] While the number of citizens in his ideal city-state was limited to 5,040, this seemingly implied a total population of about 25,000 persons, since warriors, slaves, and workers provided protection and other services for the guardian class. Aristotle went beyond this standard of a single ideal size for cities. He believed that the law of size limitation so apparent in nature was equally applicable to cities and that a city might be quite useless if too small or too large. In his words,

> one that is too small has not in itself the power of self-defense, but this
> is essential to a city; one that is too large is capable of self-defense in

what is necessary; but then it is a nation and not a city; for it will be very difficult to accommodate a form of government to it; . . . The first thing therefore necessary is, that a city should consist of such numbers as will be sufficient to enable the inhabitants to live happily in their political community. . . .[17]

The figure of 25,000 as a desirable population standard was advanced by three other writers. In describing their ideal cities, both Italian artist Leonardo da Vinci and Ebenezer Howard, English town planner, envisioned a citizenry of that size.[18] Similarly Arthur Millspaugh selected 25,000 as the necessary population base of a local government if it were to have an adequate staff and perform enough functions to keep those persons meaningfully employed.[19] To Millspaugh this figure represented the minimum population base and he cautioned that the figure for some functions or in some regions of the country might be considerably higher.

In a recent careful assessment of a critical threshold of size below which the opportunities for participation are so great and so fairly distributed that no one would feel left out and everyone would feel that his viewpoint counted, Robert Dahl, political scientist, concluded that the "all-round optimum size for a contemporary American city is probably somewhere between 50,000 and 200,000."[20]

In his *Representative Government,* John Stuart Mill, English philosopher, presented a clear case against the very small municipality. He believed that small villages whose inhabitants or their wants do not differ markedly from those of residents of adjacent rural districts should not be municipalities. His reasoning holds,

> Such small places have rarely a sufficient public to furnish a tolerable municipal council; if they contain any talent or knowledge applicable to public business, it is apt to be all concentrated in some one man, who thereby becomes the dominator of the place. It is better that such places should be merged in a larger circumscription.[21]

A more recent study of the surrender of jurisdiction by a local governing board is vividly described in a case study of "Springdale," a pseudonym for a small community in upstate New York.[22]

Other recent writers searching for the ideal size of local governing units have emphasized the population base needed for the adequate provision of particular public services. Thus, in education the National Commission on School Reorganization has set the minimum school-age population of a district at 1,200 but prefers a base of 10,000 persons between the ages of six and eighteen.[23] Similarly, the American Public Health Association advocates that each public health unit should contain at least 50,000 persons to have an adequate health program featuring a minimum staff of qualified public health personnel.[24]

Other examples of desired population bases could be offered, but these

two illustrations are sufficient to show that the ideal size of a local
government or service area varies according to the values of the criteria
against which size is measured.[25] While such studies are valuable as long as
their limitations are realized, the findings of the British Local Government
Boundary Commission concerning the appropriately-sized unit for specific
functions warrant attention. In its report, the Commission states,

> It is not possible by any process or arithmetic or logic to arrive at an
> optimum size of a local government unit either in relation to local
> government as a whole or to any one function or group of functions.
> At best one can—to use an engineering term—arrive at a reasonable
> tolerance.[26]

The Criterion of Power

Although there is no ideal size for any particular category of local units,
some tests of "reasonableness" which a unit could be expected to meet
might be developed—particularly if it were a community seeking the status
of a municipal corporation. Since the power to create local governmental
units is a state governmental responsibility, state legislatures should enact
minimum standards for incorporation. At least, these requirements should
aim to establish only new units capable of providing essential services and
maintaining frequent and widespread citizen participation in their governmental affairs.

The constitution of Alaska made a significant breakthrough in this regard.
The purpose of the local government article, according to that constitution, is
"to provide for maximum local self-government with a minimum of local
governmental units."[27] While authorizing the creation of boroughs (similar
to counties) in the state, the constitution specifies certain standards to be
considered in establishing such entities including "population, geography,
economy, transportation and other facts. Each borough shall embrace an
area of population with common interests to the maximum degree
possible."[28] These requirements are necessarily somewhat vague and
general, but they present standards other than that of mere legality in
following prescribed procedures for incorporation. Other states have created
county or state agencies to review proposed incorporations to assure that
new municipalities are reasonably viable as local communities. Local
agency formation commissions, for example, exist in each California county
to review and approve proposed incorporations, annexations, and other
proposed boundary changes in existing units.[29]

The reason such standards appear desirable relates to the second part of
the indictment of local government by the President's Commission on
Intergovernmental Relations—the statement that "too little local government" now exists. Without doubt the amount of local self-government that

can be effectively exercised is directly related to the size of the unit practicing it. A unit too small to provide the essential functions of public safety and public health is not really a self-governing unit, since communities too small to finance these two vital services find them passing by default to a higher level of government.

At least a partial explanation for our large number of local governments is the extensive application of the principle that government closest to the scrutiny and control of its citizenry is the best government. While there is much to be admired in this concept, it leaves out any real tests for the creation of a unit of government in terms of size, community served, or reasonable self-reliance as a service-rendering or self-financing unit. It would appear that small units actually thwart rather than abet citizen control since special arrangements that the local citizens can control less directly must be made with state agencies or with other local units to provide these services. Local control of a unit may be effective only if *that* unit is an adequate one to meet the needs of its citizenry. Certainly the theory of local popular control is stretched out of its original intent by small units that make no effort to provide services but contract with larger units to provide such services at negotiated cost. Such communities may be logical communities but illogical governmental units.

In addition to the ineffective local self-government provided by many small units, local self-government also is often thwarted by the nature and number of state controls guiding the affairs of local communities. Home rule is a desirable objective of local government and a benefit to state government because it enables the state legislature to concentrate more on matters of statewide rather than local concern. This point will be discussed in more detail in Chapter 3, which is devoted to state-local relations.

PROPOSALS FOR SIMPLIFICATION

There have been numerous proposals advanced for the reduction in numbers or the elimination of certain classes of units of local government. As Table 1 indicates, the great progress in reduction of numbers has occurred from the consolidation of school districts, although a few mergers of adjacent municipalities and small counties have taken place. Proposals for consolidation of units other than school districts, however, have met but little success and no strong reason exists for optimism concerning further major reduction through the process in the near future.

TABLE 1. LOCAL GOVERNMENTS BY NUMBER AND TYPE, 1942-72

Type of local government	1972	1962	1952	1942
Counties	3,044	3,043	3,052	3,050
Municipalities	18,517	18,000	16,807	16,220
Townships	16,991	17,142	17,202	18,919
School districts	15,781	34,678	67,355	108,579
Special districts	23,885	18,323	12,340	8,299
Total	78,218	91,186	116,756	155,067

Source: Bureau of The Census, *1972 Census of Governments,* Vol I, Governmental Organization, Table 1, Government Printing Office, 1973, p. 23.

Specific proposals for decreasing the number of counties have been made in various states since the 1930s.[30] In contrast to county government in which reduction in numbers is a frequently expressed goal, the complete abolition of townships frequently has been suggested in the non-New England states where they still exist. The Committee for Economic Development recommended in a 1966 study that "Townships not suited to full municipal incorporation should be abolished, and their functions should be assumed by newly consolidated county governments."[31] Since so many thousands of townships operate in these fifteen non-New England states, it would be a highly significant reduction if they were abolished.[32]

Although the number of independent school districts has already declined sharply through consolidations, some recommendations for their abolition have been devised. William Anderson has advocated the elimination of school districts with school administration becoming a function of city and county governments,[33] and the Committee for Economic Development recommends that

> The consolidation of school districts should be continued until every unified school system has at least 15,000 students. Preferably, boundaries would be coterminous with those of restructured counties, which might then be empowered to manage the local school systems on the basis of local option.[34]

William Anderson has constructed the most comprehensive plan for reorganizing American local government. In concluding his study of the units of local government, he proposed what he termed, "A Rationalized Scheme of Local Government Units in the United States," which would reduce the number of such entities to 17,800. This small number would be realized through (1) the elimination of all independent school districts, with school administration taken over by counties, cities, and other incorporated places; (2) the abolition of most special districts through the transfer of their functions to other units; (3) the elimination of townships except for the larger New England towns; (4) the consolidation of small towns in New England; (5) the merger or deorganization of very small municipalities; (6) the consolidation of city and county governments in metropolitan urban centers; and (7) the consolidation of small rural counties.[35]

As a result of the elimination and consolidation recommended by Anderson, only four categories of local governments would continue. The nature and number of these units would be as follows:

Number	Type of Unit
200	City-counties (each having a central city of not less than 50,000)
2,100	Counties for rural and semi-rural areas
15,000	Incorporated places
500	Miscellaneous units
17,800	Total units[36]

The Committee for Economic Development, in its report almost two decades later, reached strikingly similar conclusions to those in the Anderson plan. In a major recommendation, the Committee proposed a decrease in the number of local governments to not more than 16,000.[37]

In addition to the proposals discussed above for reducing the number of local governments, many other suggestions have been made about structural reform, reallocation of functions, functional consolidation, state super-vision, and improved administrative procedures. These proposals are taken up in later chapters that discuss the specific organizations, procedures, or relationships for which these reform proposals have been devised.

Some elimination of counties and townships has occurred in recent years and a number of functional transfers have occurred among local governments. This movement has not reached the flood proportions of school district reorganization, but its potential significance should not be lightly considered.

The reasons for the wide variations in size of local governments are many. One important factor is the reluctance to restructure older units into more viable ones, and the unwillingness of established units to relinquish territorial control over divisions of the original unit which could perform reasonably well as independent units. This condition is magnified by the need for reorganization resulting from the imperative of technology and expertise. As a result we have a paradox between the criterion of largeness for efficiency purposes and the desirability of smallness for effective participatory democracy.[38]

NOTES

1. Roger H. Wells, *American Local Government*, McGraw-Hill, 1939, p. 1.
2. Bureau of the Census, *1972 Census of Governments, Vol. I, Governmental Organization*, Government Printing Office, 1973, p. 13.
3. *Ibid.*
4. According to William S. Carpenter in a study completed over three decades ago, at least thirty-six states have provided for the deorganization of counties, townships, municipalities or special districts through general law. Other states, especially those of New England, provide for such deorganization by special legislative act. See Carpenter, *Problems in Service Levels: The Readjustment of Services and Areas in Local Government*, Princeton University Press, 1940, pp. 96-97.
5. William Anderson, *The Units of Government in the United States*, rev. ed., Public Administration Service, 1949, pp. 8-10.
6. Counties were never organized in Rhode Island, and the eight counties of Connecticut were abolished in 1960 after an existence of over 300 years.
7. Bureau of the Census, *op. cit.*, pp. 1-2.
8. The process of municipal incorporation will be discussed in Chapter 8.
9. The city of Hilo on the island of Hawaii has since incorporated bringing the total to two for the state of Hawaii.
10. Clyde F. Snider, *Local Government in Rural America*, Appleton-Century-Crofts, 1957, p. 238.
11. Bureau of the Census, *op. cit.*, p. 3.
12. *Ibid.*, pp. 3-6.
13. *Ibid.*, pp. 9-11.
14. Bureau of the Census, *Metropolitan Area Statistics*, Government Printing Office, 1972.
15. Commission on Intergovernmental Relations, *A Report to the President for Transmittal to Congress*, Government Printing Office, 1955, p. 47.
16. Plato, *The Republic*, Book IV, p. 108, Everyman's Library Edition, 1948.
17. Aristotle, *A Treatise on Government*, Book VII, Chap. IV, pp. 209-210, Everyman's Library Edition, 1947.
18. Lewis Mumford, *The City in History*, Harcourt, Brace & World, 1961, p. 180.
19. Arthur Millspaugh, *Local Democracy and Crime Control*, Brookings Institution, 1936, p. 86.
20. Robert A. Dahl, "The City in the Future of Democracy," *American Political Science Review*, 61 (December, 1967), 953-970. The quote is from p. 965.
21. John Stuart Mill, *Utilitarianism, Liberty, and Representative Government*, Everyman's Library Edition, 1948, p. 352.
22. See Arthur J. Vidich and Joseph Bensman, *Small Town in Mass Society, Class, Power and Religion in a Rural Community*, Doubleday & Co., Anchor Books, 1960, pp. 114-17.
23. National Commission on School Reorganization, *Your School District*, Washington, 1948, p. 131.
24. American Public Health Association, *Local Health Units for the Nation*, The Commonwealth Fund, 1945, pp. 1-5.

25. Otis D. Duncan, "Optimum Size of Cities" in Paul Hatt and Albert Reiss, Jr., (eds.), *Cities and Society,* rev. ed., The Free Press, 1957, pp. 757-72.
26. Local Government Boundary Commission, *Local Government: Areas and Status of Local Authorities in England and Wales,* (cmd. 9831), H.M.S.O., 1956.
27. Alaska Constitution, 1956, Art. X, Sec. 1.
28. *Ibid.,* Sec. 3.
29. These agencies will be discussed in more detail in the following chapter dealing with state-local relations.
30. Among the many studies are Arthur W. Bromage, *American County Government,* New York, 1933; Committee for Economic Development, *Modernizing Local Government to Secure A Balanced Federalism,* New York, 1966; W. O. Farber, "Improving County Government: Reorganization and Consolidation," *Public Affairs,* Vermillion, (August, 1963); John Stoner, "County Government—Grave Stone or Corner Stone?", *The County Officer,* 21 (December, 1956), 286-89; Weldon Cooper, "Updating Local Government in Virginia: The Post War Period and Beyond," *The University of Virginia Newsletter,* 43 (December, 1966), 13-16; and John C. Bollens, *American County Government,* Sage Publications, Inc., 1969.
31. Committee for Economic Development, *op. cit.,* p. 42.
32. Two other studies recommending township abolition are Clyde F. Snider, "The Twilight of the Township," *National Municipal Review,* 41 (September, 1952), 390-6; and R. C. Spencer, "Iowa Townships Still Here?", *National Municipal Review,* 41 (September, 1952), 397-9.
33. Anderson, *op. cit.,* p. 45.
34. Committee for Economic Development, *op. cit.,* p. 43.
35. Anderson, *op. cit.,* pp. 35-46.
36. *Ibid.*
37. Committee for Economic Development, *op. cit.,* p. 17.
38. For a careful study of this problem and its potential, see Robert A. Dahl, "The City in the Future of Democracy," *op. cit.*

Chapter 3
State-Local Relations

The American Revolution freed the thirteen colonies and resulted in their creation as states. It had an opposite effect on colonial local governments. Instead of gaining more freedom, the cities actually had less as they passed from the control of the colonial governors to that of the early state legislatures.

Fear of strong executives resulted in the establishment of strong legislatures as the dominant organ of state government. Thus the power of colonial governors to grant charters passed to the state legislative assemblies. The legislative article of the new state constitutions clearly recognized this new power of making and amending city charters. Illustrative was the provision of the New York Constitution of 1777 which stipulated that borough charters would remain in force "until otherwise directed by the legislature."[1] With this development, a municipal charter became similar to a statute and might be replaced or amended at the whim of the legislature.

Although extensive state control over local government was possible, legislatures generally did not intervene in local affairs except upon request by the municipality. As cities grew in importance, however, the attitude of state legislators underwent a decided change. Local offices provided a source for patronage and city franchises and contracts provided a tempting source of income in return for favors granted. Accordingly about 1850 the state legislatures began to exercise more extensive controls over local governments not only for pecuniary and selfish benefits but also to correct certain local defects called to their attention by alarmed citizens and reformers.

Local government opposition to this exercise of state control was soon aroused and became more vocal. However, no serious question was raised about the legal power of the state legislature to control the sub-units it created in whatever ways and to what degree it desired. This legal relationship was well defined by Judge John F. Dillon of the Iowa Supreme Court in 1868 in these words:

> Municipal corporations owe their origin to, and derive their powers from, the legislature. It breathes into them the breath of life, without which they cannot exist. As it created, so it may destroy. If it may destroy, it may abridge the control. Unless there is some constitutional limitation on the right, the legislature might, by a single act, if we can suppose it capable of so great a folly and so great a wrong, sweep from existence all of the municipal corporations of the state, and the corporations could not prevent it. We know of no limitation on this right so far as the corporations themselves are concerned. They are, so to phrase it, the mere tenants at will of the legislature.[2]

Judge Dillon definitely recognizes that a significant difference may exist between acts that are legal and those that are politically practicable. Thus while the state could "destroy, abridge, and control," he warned that this would be a great folly and wrong if carried to excess.

A counter-doctrine developed as a reaction to the acts of excessive legislative interference in local affairs. Known as the "inherent right of local self-government" theory, this doctrine held that as corporations local governments possessed the common-law rights and powers of other corporations. Similarly, since local governments existed before the states had been established, the right of local self-government was an inherent right that the state could not take away. This point of view received its highest form of expression in an opinion of Judge Charles Cooley in 1871.[3]

The statement of Judge Dillon quoted above still remains the classic expression of the legal relationships between a state legislature and the sub-units of government it creates. While the state could legally control and even deorganize its local governments, it would be politically impracticable—if not impossible—to do so. The result then is a finely balanced relationship between the state and its local government in which state aid and assistance exists alongside state direction and supervision in an intricate pattern of cooperative relations.[4] In the last century, however, many restrictive provisions have been placed in state constitutions to protect local governments from the whims of state legislatures which might be directed against particular local units.

CREATION OF LOCAL GOVERNMENTS

Since units of local government are legally established by the state government, the right of the state to provide a general framework for its subdivisions is unquestioned. The nature of and the specific provisions in the state-prescribed framework, however, are subjects on which complete agreement does not exist.

In the local government article of the Model State Constitution, prepared by the National Municipal League, which is a citizen-reform organization, the legislature is assigned a six-fold task in shaping its local governments. Specifically, it stipulates that the legislature will (1) provide for the incorporation of local units; (2) determine the powers of local governments; (3) provide alternative forms for local governments through general law and home-rule charters; (4) prescribe methods for the alteration of boundaries; (5) permit the consolidation of neighboring local units; and (6) enact provisions for the dissolution or deorganization of such civil divisions.[5] Each of these proposed state powers over local governments now will be discussed in turn.

Types of Municipal Corporations

Local governmental units are usually accorded the status of municipal or public corporations or that of bodies corporate and politic in terms of the laws of the creating state. Following a practice that existed in England and was transplanted to the American colonies, American courts have distinguished between two types of such public corporations, designating them as municipal or quasi-municipal agencies. While the distinction between the two classes is blurring in a number of states, the distinction is still firmly embedded in law and will continue to have practical significance in the years ahead.

The basis for the distinction between these two types of corporations lies in the nature of the created units. Concerning municipal corporations, it has generally been held that they are created upon the request of, or with the consent of, the inhabitants and primarily for local benefit and advantage since such units provide services of a local nature. Quasi-municipal corporations, on the other hand, are created without reference to local wishes, primarily as administrative subdivisions of the state for carrying out activities of statewide interest. As such, units of the latter type have a more limited corporate existence.

Other differences are present between the two types of corporations. Quasi-municipal corporations usually have a greater immunity from suit than do municipal corporations since the former are agencies of the state as well as for local services. In many states municipal corporations have a more extensive liability for torts (a wrongful act for which civil action may be brought) and have a broader power of eminent domain (right to take private property for public use) than do quasi-municipal corporations. Municipal corporations have broader law-making powers, and have greater freedom from state control and regulation than do quasi-municipal corporations in acquiring, holding, and disposing of property.[6]

Although allowance must be made for the frequent variations from the general rules existing among the states, local governments may be classified in terms of their corporate status as follows:

Municipal Corporations

1. Cities.
2. Villages.
3. Boroughs.
4. Towns (other than in New England states).

Quasi-Municipal Corporations

1. Counties.
2. Townships.
3. Towns (in New England states).
4. Special districts.

In recent years a number of states have turned to the use of administrative controls to regulate the incorporation of municipalities. Minnesota has established a state-level municipal commission to review incorporation and annexation proposals. The Minnesota Municipal Commission must make findings as to nine factors: (1) the population of the area within the proposed incorporation; (2) the area of the proposed incorporation; (3) the area of platted (mapped and planned) land relative to unplatted land; (4) the character of the buildings on both the platted and unplatted lands; (5) past expansion in terms of both population and construction; (6) prospective future expansion; (7) assessed value of platted land relative to that of unplatted land; (8) the present and expected necessity and feasibility of providing governmental services such as sewage disposal, water, zoning, street planning, and police and fire protection; and (9) the adequacy of the township form of government to cope with the problems of urban and suburban growth in the area wishing to incorporate.[7]

In 1963 the California legislature passed an act requiring the organization of local agency formation commissions in each county. Composed of four city and county officials and one citizen member, these commissions are empowered to review and approve or disapprove with or without amendment, wholly, partially, or conditionally proposals for the incorporation of cities and the creation of special districts and to adopt standards and procedures for evaluating such proposals.[8]

In assessing such administrative controls, two writers concluded,

Administrative control over municipal incorporation appears to be a promising device for bringing some order into the process of establishing municipal governmental organization in urbanizing areas. The fact that such control by either a local or state agency is being tried in different states will in time provide an opportunity to evaluate the relative merits of these two approaches.[9]

Prescription of Powers

Since local governments are created by the state, it follows that such units derive all their powers from their creator. It is also clear that local laws and administrative actions must not be in conflict with higher forms of law at either the state or national level. Beyond this definite limitation, however, are the restrictions inherent in the classic statement of municipal powers by Judge Dillon. Often referred to as "Dillon's Rule," the statement holds that,

> It is a general and undisputed proposition of law that a municipal corporation possesses and can exercise the following powers, and no others: First, those granted in express words; second, those necessarily or fairly implied in or incident to the powers expressly granted; third, those essential to the accomplishment of the declared objects and purposes of the corporation—not simply convenient, but indispensable. Any fair, reasonable, substantial doubt concerning the existence of power is resolved by the courts against the corporation, and the power is denied.[10]

Inevitably a large number of cases have arisen concerning the meaning of the "implied powers" recognized by both John Dillon and Eugene McQuillen, another legal scholar, and the intent of the "powers essential to the declared objects and purposes of the corporation." This relatively narrow grant of implied powers for local governments contrasts sharply with the broad interpretation and effect of the "necessary and proper" clause regarding powers of the national government.

Although judicial interpretations vary in strictness or liberality from state to state, some courts tend generally to adopt a more liberal interpretation of these restrictions when dealing with matters arising from the exercise of proprietary powers than they do in matters arising from powers strictly in the governmental field. Basically the distinction between these two kinds of powers is that governmental functions are exercised by the local unit as an agent of the state, while proprietary functions are exercised by the unit as a municipal corporation and are more private or corporate in nature. Some of the commonly recognized governmental functions are public safety, public health, education, and welfare, whereas such functions as water supply, power production, gas supply, and mass transit facilities are classified as proprietary. Many of the newer functions exercised by local governments exist in a so-called "twilight zone" or "no man's land" and are recognized as governmental powers in some states and as proprietary functions in others.[11]

Provision of Alternative Forms

Two movements to decrease the burden on state legislatures while allowing maximum freedom for local discretion within a general range of state policy have resulted in the adoption of home-rule and optional charter legislation or constitutional amendments in various states. In general harmony with this objective is a reviving effort to prohibit special legislation by state legislatures by requiring local approval of such legislative acts before they become operative in the community singled out for such prescription.

The home-rule movement often has been heralded as the most satisfactory alternative to state controls over local affairs. While the term "home rule" has no precise meaning, it is customarily used to denote the power of a local government to draft and control its own charter and to control its own "local" affairs. The end result of such action confers more power of local self-government and self-determination on local governments, freeing them from legislative control and domination. The major objectives of home rule are to prevent state legislative interference with local governments, enable local governments to adopt the kind of government they desire, and provide local governments with sufficient powers to meet the increasing needs for local services.[12]

Heralded as a means for providing charters to meet the specific needs of particular local governments, the optional charter plan adopted in New Jersey in 1950 provides the best example of the full possibilities of this device. Municipalities in that state may select one of three general alternative plans—mayor-council, council-manager, or small municipalities plan. But within each of the three basic plans are a number of options so that the choice can be further refined to one of six kinds of mayor-council city, one of five council-manager options, and one of four varieties in the small municipalities plan. Among the possible sub-options available are those relating to size of council, partisan or non-partisan election of council members, and election of councilmen at large or by wards. The citizens of a community may vote for one of the possible optional plans either after a report of an elected charter commission or by direct citizen petition and referendum. New Jersey's liberal optional charter plan appears to be a satisfactory method of granting a local charter while retaining some state supervision over its chartered cities.

Alteration of Boundaries

Legal boundaries of cities in particular have tended to lag behind the actual boundaries that result from the growth of the urbanized areas. This problem is most acute in metropolitan areas and will be discussed in detail in Chapter 18. The most common method for extending boundaries is through annexation of territory by a city. Most states permit annexation to occur only after an election called for that purpose in which a majority of the voters both in the city and in the area to be annexed voice their approval. Some states, however, allow the courts to determine the desirability of an annexation proposal, and others prescribe that simply unilateral approval by the annexing city without the consent of the residents in the area to be annexed is necessary. Missouri and Texas both allow the latter procedure, while the Virginia system permits court determination in such cases.[13]

Another method of altering local boundaries is to permit the consolidation of neighboring or contiguous local governments. Since the use of this method is most frequently discussed in terms of units of government within metropolitan areas, the details of this method will also be discussed in Chapter 18.

Before a municipal corporation may be dissolved, it is usually necessary for a judicial decree or a legislative act to acknowledge the unit's deorganization, although some states apparently provide for automatic dissolution. The three most common means for dissolution of local units provide for (1) presentation of a petition by a designated number of citizens of the community to a named court which orders an election to be held on the question; (2) presentation of a similar petition to the legislative body of the community in question with an election to be called on the matter; and (3) direct judicial or legislative action for dissolution after presentation of the petition without the need of a popular vote on the question.[14]

FORMS OF STATE CONTROL

State constitutions contain varying specific directions and prohibitions for their local governments. Local debt and tax limitations are common and further provisions relating to the control of local financial abuses or transactions may be present. Other constitutions enumerate county or township officers and thus present a common mold for their governmental organization. Generally speaking, cities are freer than other local units of such elaborate controls regulating officers. Some of the more specific constitutional controls are discussed in later chapters relating to particular types of local units, their finances, and their governmental processes.

Legislative Control

The more traditional and inclusive manner for the state to exercise control and direction over its local governments is through legislative prescription and supervision. Such legislative control is exercised largely through the enactment of statutes, appropriations for subsidies or grants-in-aid, and legislative investigations. Typically committees on cities, counties, or local government exist and frequently special committees or legislative commissions on the problems of local governments are formed.

Initially legislative supervision over local governments was exercised mainly through the device of special legislation pertaining to a single local community named in the act. Special legislation is still an important feature in state-local relations but it encourages logrolling (mutual exchange of favors among legislators).[15]

As previously noted, legislative supervision has declined since the turn of the present century, but this does not mean that supervision by state government has decreased. Instead, much of the direction and control formerly exercised by the legislature has now been entrusted to agencies of the administrative branch of the state government. For instance, the California Council on Intergovernmental Relations has compiled a handbook of more than 300 pages entitled *State Services for Local Governments* to serve as a quick, handy reference to the services and the persons available in state government to help city, county, school, and other local officials.[16] Other forms of supervision are exercised through independent bodies such as the previously mentioned local agency formation commissions in California counties.

Administrative Control

Supervision of local activities by state administrative agencies has principally developed in the twentieth century in the United States. European countries, however, have provided for such control for a much longer time. Such agencies as the Ministry of Local Government in England and the Ministry of the Interior of France have concentrated supervisory controls over their local governments. Not only did this develop later in the United States, but the tendency in this country has been to entrust such controls on a functional rather than on an agency basis. Thus, instead of a single agency of local government exercising general controls, local health activities are supervised by the state health department, local welfare programs and standards by the state welfare agency, local education by a state department of education, and so on.

As the functions of local governments have expanded, a parallel growth in administrative regulation by state agencies has occurred.[17] The general purposes of such regulation are to raise public services to higher levels of performance, lessen the inequities of service levels among local governments, improve the efficiency of administering such services, and distribute their costs more equitably among the governmental units.

Administrative supervision is believed to be superior to legislative control because it offers more certain means for achieving efficiency in the administration of programs of statewide concern while granting local governments a larger measure of freedom in meeting their own day-to-day problems. Two specific advantages of administrative supervision include greater flexibility in application and more expedient exercise of supervision without the delay of time-consuming litigation. Administrative control is also more effective because it can be remedial rather than punitive in effect as legislative control must be.[18]

The methods of state administrative control are several in number and range from techniques of persuasion to those of coercion. In a pioneering and still widely noted study of state administrative supervision of cities, eleven devices in an "ascending order of their individual effectiveness" are listed. They are reports, inspection, advice, grants-in-aid, approval, review, orders, ordinances, removal, appointment, and substitute administration.[19] While the right of state agencies to utilize the more coercive devices, if they are authorized to do so, cannot be challenged, the long-term effectiveness of heavy-handed methods as against more persuasive techniques has been questioned. As a result, the Council of State Governments has recommended that state administrative programs should be based on six principles. First, control devices should be utilized only to established minimum standards of performance, and to meet energy situations, while persuasion, consultation and education should be employed in most situations. Second, certification of employees by state agencies should be limited to certifying the qualifications of teachers, while the prescription of minimum standards should be used for other local employees. Third, states should increase their facilities for aiding and improving local personnel administration. Fourth, states should expand their facilities to assist in training local officials and employees. Fifth, states should increase and improve programs of technical assistance and initiate more cooperative undertakings with local governments. And sixth, state grant-in-aid programs should be administered and supervised to insure adequate standards of service performance by the receiving local governments.[20]

State administrative supervision over local governments and state programs to aid local governments are growing numerically and financial aid is increasing to assist them in meeting their service needs and revenue problems. However, two recent studies both conclude that the states are not doing enough and the aid is still insufficient.[21]

Judicial Control

Because of the subordinate legal position of local governments, such units are continuously called upon to prove or defend their rights to exercise powers or to employ them to accomplish specific purposes. Although judicial review is an important principle in our system of American government, it has particular pertinence to local governments. This point is aptly emphasized by Jefferson Fordham, law professor, who states that while judicial review of legislative, executive, and administrative action is extensive and crucial at all levels of government, it is most detailed and most persuasive at the local level.[22]

Since local law is subordinate to both national and state enactments, local governments must act within the recognized limits of these higher levels as they relate to both substantive powers to be exercised and the procedures to be followed. Through the issuance of a writ of *mandamus,* local governments or their officers may be compelled to act, while a writ of *prohibition* may be issued to stop their actions. Other judicial writs of *quo warranto* (asking by what power or right an action is being promulgated) or of *certiorari* (calling a lower court judgment up for full review by a higher level) may also be issued. In addition, courts may issue judgments relating to civil liability for damages, criminal liability for action or inaction, and equitable relief by injunction, all of which are binding on local governments. One writer thus has drawn a simile between the relationships of a baseball umpire looking over the shoulder of the catcher and the role of the judge overseeing the actions of local officials.[23]

In summary, judicial control over local government is basically no different from judicial review over the state itself. State administrative supervision, though increasing, should not be construed as meaning that the ordinary activities of local governments are under continuous state inspection. While quite extensive state supervision exists in some service areas, such as education and health, in other service fields, such as police and fire, the state often intervenes only upon request of a local government unit.

A STATE DEPARTMENT OF LOCAL GOVERNMENT

As indicated in the preceding discussion, administrative relations between states and their local governments have stressed aid and service rather than supervision and control. The increased number and growing complexity of these relationships, however, have caused some concern among some observers who believe that further fragmentation of state supervisory activities along functional lines may result in undesired problems of coordination for both state and local governments. Sentiment thus is growing for the creation in each state of a department or agency of local government where general responsibility for supervision of local activities could be centered.

The functions of such a local government agency usually include certain major programs and services. First, the organization assists the governor in coordinating information and action regarding local government problems and in developing appropriate legislative programs and administrative policies. Second, it serves as the central point in state government for information, study, and evaluation of proposals relating to local governments and their affairs. Third, the agency serves as a collection point and clearing house for studies of local governments conducted by private and other public agencies. Fourth, it acts as a coordinating unit for local governments seeking assistance from other local, state, or federal agencies. Fifth, it carries out legislative requirements relating to local standards of performance or service. And sixth, the agency initiates and recommends to local government useful state services not currently existing.[24]

The Council of State Governments recommended the creation of an office of local affairs in its *Suggested State Legislation, Program for 1957* and again in its 1963 edition of this annual publication. By 1969, such departments had been established in a majority of the states as agencies within the office of the governor or the lieutenant governor, as an executive department, or as an independent commission or council. Typical functions of such an agency included fiscal advice, municipal management, economic development, personnel training, interlocal cooperation, and research and information. Program responsibilities typically include regional planning, local planning, housing, Model Cities, manpower, law enforcement, and highway safety.[25]

The actual functioning of such an agency is revealed in a recent annual report of the New Jersey Department of Community Affairs. The letter of transmittal from the Department's Commissioner to the Governor of New Jersey reads, in part:

> This year was one of achievement as well as innovation for the Department. It began the administration of such new and important programs as the $12 million Safe and Clean Neighborhoods Program, designed to reduce crime and clean up neighborhoods in urban cities and restore a sense of security in these communities, and the Champion Games Program, which for the first time enabled physically handicapped children to participate in statewide athletic competition. ... We helped New Jersey's 588 local governments by initiating a revenue sharing unit to provide up-to-date information on federal revenue sharing legislation.... In the area of planning, the Department organized a Government Studies section to study and recommend a state policy for the development of new communities

and to assist municipalities considering such a development approach.[26]

However, not all agencies operate with the apparent effectiveness of the New Jersey Department. Most such little HUD's (named after the Department of Housing and Urban Development of the national government) appear to serve the needs of small municipalities much better than those of large cities. In terms of what such departments have to offer, large cities often provide better services for themselves and do not need or utilize the programs of the state agency.

INTERLOCAL RELATIONS

Cooperative arrangements among local governments have long been utilized to meet common problems. The earliest recorded examples were mutual aid arrangements to defend towns against surprise Indian attacks in the New England colonies; ever since those early times such agreements have grown in number. Because state courts have generally approved the principle of limited local powers as set forth in "Dillon's Rule," the power to enter into formal cooperative arrangements must be conferred upon local governments through either direct legislative grant or reasonable indirect or implied legislative grant. Although these arrangements are known by various names, they might properly be identified as interjurisdictional agreements. This term then could be defined to include both formal or written compacts and informal or clearly understood unwritten agreements by which two or more local units voluntarily attempt to solve or ameliorate a mutual problem. A study completed in 1960 counted a total of 693 such agreements among the local governments in a five-county area in southeastern Pennsylvania centering around Philadelphia. The four suburban counties, their 237 municipalities and 238 school districts, and the City-County of Philadelphia had a network of interlocking agreements that were almost areawide in such fields as police radio and fugitive search plans, but which were much more limited in such important services as health, zoning, water supply, and refuse disposal.[27]

Interjurisdictional agreements represent merely one of several methods by which local governments may cooperate for mutual advantage. A statement prepared by the International City Managers' (now Management) Association lists conferences, exchange of services, temporary loans, and joint use of equipment or personnel, performance of service by one governmental unit for another, joint performance of a service, and cooperative administration through state leagues as six common methods for cooperative undertakings.[28] Thus the term interlocal cooperation embraces cooperative arrangements between like units (e.g., two neighboring cities for sewage disposal), and between different types of units (e.g., a city and a township for fire protection), as well as those activities that a county performs for some or all of the other local units within it.

While interlocal cooperative arrangements cannot solve all the problems arising from the interrelationships between local governments, they are useful in achieving some degree of coordination of the efforts of local units to provide common services. Such arrangements allow joint action on problems of mutual concern without any loss of corporate identity by any of the cooperating units. Thus, as an acceptable device to meet common problems, the interjurisdictional agreement and the other means of interlocal cooperation probably will be increasingly called upon in the near future to meet the problems of small governments in metropolitan areas as well as those of governmental units across the nation.

SUB-STATE DISTRICT SYSTEMS

In the last decade, interlocal cooperation has become more mandatory and less voluntary through the establishment of statewide sub-state district systems. These are structures through which local elected officials can coordinate the use of federal, state, and local resources in solving areawide problems. While these entities are essentially aggregates of local jurisdictions, state governments play a pivotal role in their creation and maintenance by the enactment of necessary enabling legislation, designation of sub-state district boundaries, and provisions of financial and technical support.

The Intergovernmental Cooperation Act of 1968 emphasized the importance of local government coordination and the creation of sub-state districts was encouraged further by provisions of circular A-80, issued in January, 1967, and Circular A-95, released in February, 1971, by the federal Office of Management and Budget. Part IV of the latter circular added the objective

> To encourage the states to exercise leadership in delineating and establishing a system of planning and development districts or regions in each state, which can provide a consistent geographic base for the coordination of federal, state, and local development programs.[29]

The Council of State Governments in an informative and useful report says a fully-developed sub-state district system

> (1) provides a structure which enables state and local elected officials to coordinate an intergovernmental approach to areawide problems without creating a new layer of government; (2) meshes with the thrust of the federal government approach to areawide problems and offers intergovernmental consistency; (3) is politically acceptable and

responsive to elected officials; and (4) does not preclude use of other mechanisms nor create barriers to innovative variation.[30]

Coordination of local planning, uniform alignment of federally-initiated areawide programs, and uniform districts for planning and/or delivery of state government programs were identified as primary functions to be exercised by sub-state districts. This study concludes,

> In broadest terms, objectively defined systems of districts have offered a manageable framework for planning, coordination, and delivery of governmental services. Because they provide a structure for comprehensive planning on an areawide basis, district systems have facilitated the acquisition and programming of federal assistance funds.[31]

While the number and functions of sub-state districts vary from state to state, the organization and operation of the districts in Kentucky generally illustrate them. The governor established fifteen multipurpose Area Development Districts for Kentucky by executive order. State assistance is provided by state matching of federal planning assistance funds and provision of planning and programming assistance on request. All the districts serve as "701" (national grants for planning) agencies, some as Economic Development Districts, and the others as Local Development Districts. In addition, all have been utilized as Comprehensive Health Planning Areas, and all state agencies have been instructed to recognize the district delineation as the basis for the administration of state programs.[32]

The Advisory Commission on Intergovernmental Relations recently completed a six-volume study of the problems and future of sub-state regions. Identified by the Commission as "umbrella multi-jurisdictional organizations" (UMJOs), such entities would be responsible for many of the functions now performed by councils of governments and regional planning commissions, such as areawide planning, communications, research and technical assistance. This study and its major recommendations will be discussed in more detail in Chapter 4, which considers national-local relations.

SUMMARY

State-local relations have undergone a continuing transition from the constitutional precepts noted at the start of this chapter to patterns of administrative relationships. In part, the change has resulted from a growing recognition of the interdependence between local governments and the state. The future development of this pattern of interdependence, however, is difficult to project. The lack of integration among governmental units in metropolitan areas prompts the state to enact policies to aid the center cities, but such actions are resisted vigorously by more wealthy suburban communities. Redistricting has tended to enhance the suburban voice in state legislatures and state policies may tend to follow this strength and result in fiscal neglect of big cities. The question of whether local governments fare better under present administrative relationships than they did under older forms of state direction and control is not easily answered but is significant enough to merit careful and continung study and consideration.

NOTES

1. Raymond G. Gittell, *History of American Political Thought*, Appleton-Century, 1928, p. 596.
2. *City of Clinton v. Cedar Rapids and Missouri Railroad Company*, 24 Iowa 455 (1868).
3. *People ex rel, Le Roy v. Hurlbut*, 24 Michigan 44 (1871).
4. For current discussions of developments in state-local relations, see the article on "State-Local Relations" in the biennial editions of *The Book of the States*, published by The Council of State Governments.
5. National Municipal League, *Model State Constitution*, 6th ed., 1963, Art. VIII, Secs. 8.01, 8.02, and 8.03.
6. The widely accepted authorities on this subject are John F. Dillon, *Commentaries on the Law of Municipal Corporations*, 5th ed., Vol. I, Little, Brown, 1911; and Eugene McQuillen, *The Laws of Municipal Corporations*, 3rd ed., Vol I, Callaghan, 1949. See also Jefferson B. Fordham, *Local Government Law*, Foundation Press, 1949; and Roger W. Colley, *Handbook of the Law of Municipal Corporations*, West, 1914.
7. *Minnesota Statutes Annotated*, 414.02.
8. *California Government Code*, sec. 54780.
9. Clarence J. Hein and Thomas F. Hady, "Administrative Control of Municipal Incorporation: The Search for Criteria," *Western Political Quarterly*, 19 (December, 1966), 704. For an evaluation of the California experience, see Richard T. Legates, *California Local Agency Formation Commissions*, Institute of Governmental Studies, University of California, Berkeley, 1970.
10. Dillon, *op. cit.*, sec. 237. The same conclusions were reached by McQuillen in a slight modification of the Dillon Rule. See McQuillen, *op. cit.*, Vol. II, sec. 10:09.
11. J. C. Phillips, " 'Active Wrongdoing' and the Sovereign-Immunity Principle in Municipal Tort Liability," *Oregon Law Review*, 38 (February, 1959), 122-57.
12. Rodney L. Mott, *Home Rule for American Cities*, American Municipal Association, 1949, pp. 11-12.
13. For interesting descriptions of annexation procedures in these states, see J. M. Claunch, "Land Grabbing—Texas Style," *National Municipal Review*, 42 (November, 1953), 494-6; and Chester W. Bain, "Annexation: Virginia's Not-so-Judicial System," *Public Administration Review*, 15 (Autumn, 1955), 251-62.

14. Charles M. Kneier, *City Government in the United States,* 3rd ed., Harper, 1957, p. 47.
15. The reaction against legislative control by special act resulted in prohibition of this practice in state constitutions adopted after the middle of the nineteenth century. By this device local units could be divided into groups on the basis of population, providing a compromise between special and general legislation. While early classifications were often artificial and overlapping, order and common sense gradually prevailed and the concept of classification became an important feature of state legislation pertaining to local government.
16. California Council on Intergovernmental Relations, *State Services for Local Governments,* Sacramento, 1970.
17. Council of State Governments, *State-Local Relations,* Council of State Governments, 1946, pp. 11-12.
18. *Ibid.,* pp. 12-13.
19. Schuyler Wallace, *State Administrative Supervision Over Cities in the United States,* Columbia University Press, 1928, p. 39.
20. Council of State Governments, *op. cit.,* pp. 41-46.
21. See Ira Sharkansky, *The Maligned States,* McGraw-Hill Book Co., 1972, chap. 6, and Harold Herman, *New York State and the Metropolitan Problem,* University of Pennsylvania Press, 1963, pp. 178-88.
22. Fordham, *op. cit.,* p. 36.
23. Charles R. Adrian, *State and Local Governments, A Study in the Political Process,* McGraw-Hill, 1960, p. 96.
24. For a fuller discussion of the functions or powers of such a state agency of local government, see James R. Bell, "The Desirability of a Special Unit for Local Government in State Administration," *Metropolitan California,* Report of Governor's Commission on Metropolitan Area Problems, 1961, pp. 149-51; Harold Alderfer, *American Local Government and Administration,* Macmillan, 1956, pp. 169-70; and John G. Grumm, "A State Agency for Local Affairs?" *Public Affairs Report,* 2 (October, 1961), pp. 3-4, Bureau of Public Administration, University of California, Berkeley.
25. Council of State Governments, *State Offices of Community Affairs: Their Functions, Organization and Enabling Legislation,* Washington, September, 1969.
26. *Sixth Annual Report, Fiscal Year 1973, New Jersey Department of Community Affairs,* Trenton, 1974, p. 2.
27. George S. Blair, *Interjurisdictional Agreements in Southeastern Pennsylvania,* Fels Institute, University of Pennsylvania, 1960.
28. International City Managers' Association, "Relations with Other Local Governments," *Public Management,* 24 (March, 1942), 73-79.
29. Office of Management and Budget, *OMB Circular A-95,* Part IV, Washington, February, 1971.
30. Council of State Governments, *Sub-State District Systems,* Lexington, Kentucky, September, 1971, p. 10.
31. *Ibid.,* pp. 11-12.
32. *Ibid.,* p. 21.

Chapter 4

National-Local Relations

Although the national (or federal) government has never been isolated from certain types of contacts with units of local government, they were largely of a negative character until the early 1930s. Up to 1850, there were only 11 national services affecting urban communities; between 1851 and 1875 four new services were added, and 16 further ones were initiated in the next quarter century. The total federal services affecting cities thus stood at only 31 by 1900. In the next four decades, however, the number increased substantially—12 by 1910, 19 more by 1920, 17 more by 1930, and 41 new services from 1930 to 1937.[1]

Though national-local relations existed before 1932, the traditional theory of American federalism asserted that the national government had no direct concern with local governments. Thus, it was not unexpected, for President Calvin Coolidge to state in his message to Congress in December, 1925,

> The functions which the Congress are to discharge are not those of local government but of national government. The greatest solicitude should be exercised to prevent encroachment upon the rights of the states or their various political subdivisions. Local self-government is one of our most precious possessions. It is the greatest contributing factor to the stability, strength, liberty, and progress of the nation. It ought not to abdicate power through weakness or resign its authority through favor. It does not at all follow that because abuses exist it is the concern of the Federal Government to attempt their reform.[2]

A TURNING POINT: 1932

While it is usually difficult to pick a single point in time to signify a change in a continuing policy development, the year 1932 can serve as such a major point in tracing the pattern of direct relationships of the national government with units of local government. In initiating a broad program for combatting the economic depression, wide-ranging programs were adopted that matured into an entirely new role for the national government vis-a-vis the people, the states, and local governments.

A delegation from the United States at the International Congress of Cities held in London in 1932 reported that no direct administrative relationships then existed between the local and national governments. Also in that year the word "municipalities" appeared for the first time in an act of Congress authorizing the Reconstruction Finance Corporation to make loans to cities for self-liquidating public works projects.[3] This specific act may be singled out as the beginning of a more positive approach by the national government, since many of these newer problems had technological and economic causes beyond the control of local government. The development of a national system of transportation and communication and the welfare needs arising from the great depression prompted federal actions that affected local governments more directly.

The start of a basic change in our interpretation of the American federal system thus was initiated in 1932. Local governments now began to emerge as partners in a system of cooperative federalism instead of being viewed as the bottom layer of governments in a three-tier federal system. One writer has described this change as discarding a layer-cake for a marble-cake theory of federalism. In his words,

> The American form of government is often, but erroneously, symbolized by a three-layer cake. A far more accurate image is the rainbow or marble cake, characterized by an inseparable mingling of differently colored ingredients, the colors appearing in vertical and diagonal strands and unexpected whirls. As colors are mixed in the marble cake, so functions are mixed in the American federal system.[4]

Political scientist Daniel Elazar presents a rather convincing case that the change in the city-national relations since 1933 is not as abrupt as it is often believed. In a carefully researched article, he concludes that

> . . . failure to understand the federal-city relationship before 1933 may lead to erroneous conclusions regarding the impact—or the proper management—of the federal-city relationship today. Such conclusions could, in turn, drastically affect the future of the American system as we know it.[5]

The absence of numerous federal-city relationships in the nineteenth century was due to several factors: (1) the lack of many large cities; (2) the development of specialized public needs that could not be handled by local governments had not yet occurred; (3) the absence of a "city" outlook in the political arena; (4) the relatively few conflicts between states and their big cities; and (5) the more frequent use of annexation to permit physical growth of cities.[6] Specialized demands of cities began to be expressed at about the turn of the present century, but the national government delayed its response to them until the 1930s.

We have come a long way from the view expressed by President Coolidge about a half century ago, but the change has been gradual and accumulative rather than sudden and dramatic. For example, social work organizations vigorously opposed federal programs and funding and still object to revenue sharing. A major factor in this changed relationship has been the expansion of the intent of the Fourteenth Amendment and a series of Supreme Court improvisations through decisions in such areas as civil rights, reapportionment, and right of the accused in police actions.

The degree of this change is vividly shown in messages to Congress by three recent presidents. In his special message on housing and community development submitted March 9, 1961, President John F. Kennedy said,

> Our communities are what we make them. We as a nation have before us the opportunity—and the responsibility—to remold our cities, to improve our patterns of community development, and to provide for the housing needs of all segments of our population. . . . An equal challenge is the tremendous urban growth that lies ahead. . . . We must begin now to lay the foundation for livable, efficient and attractive communities of the future. . . . We must do more than concern ourselves with bad housing—we must reshape our cities into effective nerve centers for expanding metropolitan areas.[7]

Five years later, President Lyndon B. Johnson's message to Congress included these statements:

> Nineteen hundred and sixty-six can be the year of rebirth for American cities. This Congress, and this people, can set in motion forces of change in great urban areas that will make them the masterpieces of our civilization. . . . We know that cities can stimulate the best in man, and aggravate the worse. We know the convenience of city life, and its paralysis. We know its promise, and its dark foreboding. . . . I recommend that both the public and private sectors of our economy join to build in our cities and towns an environment for man equal to the dignity of his aspirations.[8]

In 1971 President Richard M. Nixon, in a message encouraging support for his revenue-sharing proposal, reported to Congress that "State and local governments need Federal help, but what they need most is not more help of the sort they have often been receiving. They need more money to spend, but they also need greater freedom in spending it." [9]

In large measure the growth of direct national-local relations has resulted from economic needs of local governments to meet the demands of their rapidly growing, dwindling, or changing populations. Since state governments are constantly called upon to provide new statewide services, the needs of local governments cannot be fully met by sympathetic lawmakers in state capitols because of state financial problems. Limitations on taxing powers and indebtedness plus the fear that increasing tax burdens may have an undesirable impact on business within the state create difficult financial hurdles in most states. Thus, both urban and rural communities have turned to Washington for financial aid and programmatic grants to enable them to meet their seemingly ever-growing wants and demands.

While some loss of local autonomy results from programs that have matching money requirements or other conditions, the same is true for both federal or state grants. To harassed local officials, it probably matters little whether the loss of autonomy depends on the purse strings of one level or the other until a more equitable reapportionment of tax resources may be realized. In 1929 local governments received 6.8 percent of their total revenues from state government payments and only 0.3 percent from federal funds. By the mid-1970s state payments had increased more than five times and federal grants had grown nearly fifteen times.[10] State sharing is typically for such costly local programs as schools, health, and roads, while federal-aid programs have often been more in the nature of suburban subsidies such as housing and highway acts or for more restricted clientele as in the case of veterans, welfare, and social security legislation.

ADVISORY COMMISSION ON INTERGOVERNMENTAL RELATIONS

Recognizing the increasing national activities in interlevel relationships, a temporary Commission on Intergovernmental Relations was appointed by President Eisenhower in 1954. Five years later, the Advisory Commission on Intergovernmental Relations (ACIR) was established by action of Congress as a permanent bi-partisan board of twenty-six members. The composition of the Commission includes three United States senators appointed by the president of the Senate, three United States representatives appointed by the speaker of the House, three officers of the executive branch appointed by the President, and three private citizens also appointed by the President. In addition, the President appoints four governors as members from a panel of at least eight names submitted by the Governors' Conference, three state legislators from a panel of at least six submitted by the Council of State Governments, four mayors from a panel of at least eight submitted jointly by the American Municipal Association and the United States Conference of Mayors, and three elected county officials from a panel of at least six submitted by the National Association of Counties.[11]

The primary purpose of the Commission is to serve as a forum for discussing the administration and coordination of federal grants and other programs requiring intergovernmental cooperation. In performing its duties, the Commission provides a forum for the consideration of problems common to all three levels, gives sustained attention to the conditions and controls in administering federal grants, provides technical assistance to the President and Congress in the review of proposed legislation, and recommends new policies or changes in existing policies.[12]

A valuable and informative publication of the ACIR is its annual report which must be submitted to the President, the Vice President, and the Speaker of the House of Representatives by January 31 of each year. These excerpts from the "Prologue" of its sixteenth annual report issued in January, 1975, show the general nature of these reports:

> The work of the Advisory Commission on Intergovernmental Relations in 1974 centered on efforts to identify and suggest remedies for the revenue problems of state and local governments, the structural problems of those units, and the problems of providing services at the state, regional, and local levels. These three goals were purused through a series of related research efforts and through an expanded effort at publicizing Commission recommendations and providing technical assistance to governments interested in adopting them.
>
> Focusing on state and local revenue, the Commission concluded the first phase of its revenue sharing monitoring project; conducted additional research and surveys and published new studies on the local property tax; encouraged local revenue diversification by reversing an earler position and calling for adoption of local sales and income taxes; and, at year's end, began a major study of Federal grant programs.[13]

FEDERAL ADMINISTRATIVE DEPARTMENTS

No attempt will be made to catalog all the agencies of the national government that provide grants, services, or assistance to local governments. However, two agencies will be singled out for brief discussion because of their direct relationships with citizens and local governments. They are the Departments of Housing and Urban Development and Health, Education and Welfare.

Department of Housing and Urban Development

The department came into existence on November 9, 1965. It absorbed all the programs formerly administered by the Housing and Home Finance Agency and assumed responsibility for a wide range of federally-aided programs for urban renewal, public housing, urban planning, open space lands, and community facilities. In addition, the 1965 Act entrusted the department to administer rent-supplement programs, which permit private builders to construct housing for low-income persons, and a new grants program for cities to finance water and sewer systems and neighborhood facilities.

Urban renewal, one of the most widely heralded and utilized departmental programs, shows the nature and extent of direct national-local relationships in this programmatic area. Urban renewal is conceived as a long-range effort to achieve better communities through planned redevelopment of deteriorated and deteriorating areas by means of a partnership among local governments, private enterprise, citizens, and the national government.

More specifically, urban renewal assists cities undertaking local programs for the elimination and prevention of slums and blight, whether residential or nonresidential, and the elimination of the factors that create slums and blight. Examples of urban renewal programs are (1) communitywide renewal programs that identify needs and resources and establish schedules and priorities for accomplishing the work to be done, (2) those that plan and carry out urban renewal projects for the rehabilitation and redevelopment of blighted areas, and (3) programs of concentrated code enforcement and demolition of buildings that are substandard and constitute a hazard to public health and welfare.

Urban renewal activities and projects are financed with federal advances and loans, federal grants, and local contributions. Federal grants generally pay up to two-thirds of the net project cost, but sometimes they are for as much as three-fourths of the total. Local contributions may be in cash or in noncash grants-in-aid. Special loans and grants are available for rehabilitation and for housing assistance programs for the low income, the elderly, and the handicapped who reside in renewal project areas.

To secure federal assistance, the participating community has to certify its inability to carry out its needed renewal plans with local resources alone. Second, it has to adapt a workable program for community improvement and have it certified by HUD. Third, the community has to develop a feasible plan for the relocation of families and individuals displaced by the project into decent, safe, and sanitary housing at prices or rentals within their means.[14]

In 1973 the Secretary of Housing and Urban Development was assigned the disaster program responsibilities previously administered by the Office of Emergency Preparedness. Federal disaster assistance is a comprehensive program of emergency relief and recovery assistance to individuals, businesses, and local and state governments suffering from major disaster situations, for predisaster assistance to avert or lessen the effects of a threatening disaster, and for help in developing local and state government capabilities to cope with disasters.

In a recent three-year period, there were 222 major disaster declarations involving fifty-one states and territories. A total of $1.2 billion dollars was allocated from the President's Disaster Relief Fund to aid these areas. In the period 1961-1970, damages from severe storms accounted for 45 percent of major disaster declarations with floods constituting 22 percent, tornadoes 12 percent, hurricanes and typhoons 12 percent, forest fires and earthquakes each 2 percent, and all others 5 percent. For the same decade, allocations of disaster fund relief were distributed as follows: severe storms 44 percent, hurricanes and typhoons 31 percent, earthquakes 8 percent, floods and tornadoes each 7 percent, forest fires 2 percent, and all other 1 percent.[15]

Department of Health, Education and Welfare

The Department of Health, Education and Welfare was established in 1953 to improve the administration of programs to promote the general welfare in health, education, and social security. By 1969, the Department had more than 250 widely varied programs to help people and communities.[16] The Consumer Protection and Environmental Health Service offers assistance to local governments for air pollution control, environmental control of public wastes, communicable disease control, and comprehensive health planning and services. The Health Services and Mental Health Administration provides assistance for the construction of hospital and public health centers, the building and staffing of community mental health centers, and the erection and staffing of alcoholic and narcotic rehabilitation facilities.

The Program, Instruction and Administration Division of the U. S. Office of Education supplies varied types of assistance to local education agencies. These range from grants for school maintenance and operation, to those for instruction in critical subjects in both public and private schools, to grants for education of children from low-income families, to grants for desegregation assistance.

The programs of the Rehabilitation Services Administration illustrates the wide-ranging types of assistance available from the Social and Rehabilitation Service. These include grants for the construction, innovation, or expansion of vocational rehabilitation services; grants for research in mental retardation; grants for hospital improvement; and grants for communities service facilities for the mentally retarded and social security beneficiaries.

Other Major Programs

Many other federal programs and policies deal directly with local governments and their problems. The federal impetus for sub-state district systems and UMJOs (umbrella multi-jurisdictional organizations) or councils of government was discussed in Chapter 3. The programs and activities of the Law Enforcement Assistance Administration and War on Poverty programs will be discussed in later chapters. The specific programs mentioned here are intended to be illustrative of existing federal programs rather than a comprehensive discussion of such services, aids, and policies.

ADVISORY COMMISSION REPORTS

Another form of direct national-local relations derives from informational reports of special commissions appointed by the President. Three such recent reports are those of the National Advisory Commission on Civil Disorders, the National Commission on Urban Problems, and the Commission on Population Growth and the American Future.

National Advisory Commission on Civil Disorders

This Commission was established in July, 1967, as a result of the racial disorders occurring that summer. It was directed by President Johnson to answer three basic questions: What happened? Why did it happen? What can be done to prevent it from happening again? The President's charge to the Commission was "Let your search be free. . . . As best you can, find the truth and express it in your report." The eleven-member group was chaired by Otto Kerner, Governor of Illinois, with John V. Lindsay, Mayor of New York City, serving as vice chairman.

After seven months of investigation and study, the Commission submitted its report which began

> This is our basic conclusion: Our nation is moving toward two societies, one black, one white—separate and unequal. . . . What white Americans have never fully understood—but the Negro can never forget—is that white society is deeply implicated in the ghetto. White institutions created it, white institutions maintain it, and white society condones it.[17]

The Commission identified and ranked twelve deeply-held grievances at three levels of relative intensity. First level of intensity grievances (those both most serious and frequent), in order, related to police practices, unemployment and underemployment, and inadequate housing. These were followed by inadequate education, poor recreation facilities and programs, and ineffectiveness of the political structure and grievance mechanisms. The six grievances of the third level of intensity were disrespectful white attitudes, discriminatory administration of justice, inadequacy of federal programs, inadequacy of municipal services, discriminatory consumer and credit practices, and inadequate welfare programs.[18]

Based on the information collected, the Commission concluded that "The urban disorders of the summer of 1967 were not caused by, nor were they the consequence of, any organized plan or conspiracy." In Part III of its report, the Commission offered specific recommendations concerning community response, police and the community, control of disorder, administration of justice, news media, and the future of cities. Recommendations for national action included needed reforms in such areas as education, welfare, and housing.[19]

National Commission on Urban Problems

This sixteen-member commission was established by President Johnson in January, 1967, with Paul H. Douglas, former United States Senator from Illinois, selected as chairman. The Commission's charter was two-fold:

> First: to work with the Department of Housing and Urban Development to conduct a penetrating review of zoning, housing and building codes, taxation, and development standards. These processes have not kept pace with the times. Stunting growth and opportunity, they are the springboards from which many of the ills of urban life flow.
> Second: to recommend the solutions, particularly those ways in which the efforts of the Federal Government, private industry, and local communities can be marshaled to increase the support of low-cost decent housing.[20]

After nearly two years of research, public hearings, and study, the Commission issued its 500-page report entitled *Building the American City*. Its basic theme was to encourage local units to stimulate consolidation among them, thus reducing the proliferation of small governments. Achievement of these goals was to result from the "carrot and stick" approach—that is, financial and other inducements to encourage such actions along with financial and other penalties for not doing so. The Report states,

> Action along these lines is most urgently needed. Unless widespread vigorous, and effective steps are taken to civilize the existing jungle of local government jurisdictions, the Nation faces the prospect of a further and drastic centralization of governmental powers and a possible smothering of the grassroots of American democracy.[21]

The "carrot and stick" philosophy is especially apparent in the Commission's recommendations relating to revenue sharing. Such funds would be limited to "municipalities of 50,000 or more and those county governments above the same minimum size in which at least half the population is urban."[22]

The report presented 150 specific recommendations dealing with housing programs, urban development, building codes, housing codes, development standards, urban government structure, neighborhood regeneration, state-local actions toward better urban financing, revenue sharing, reducing housing costs, and urban design. The Commission recognized that its proposed solutions were a "tall order," but it believed they were in proportion to the enormity of the problems of urban areas. In the Commission's words,

> We must ease the tension between central city and suburb, between rich and poor, and especially between black and white. Too few have recognized how these basic democratic issues are related to local government structure and financing, to zoning policies, land and housing costs, or to national housing policies. The recommendations we make in these areas are a test of our most fundamental belief.[23]

Commission on Population Growth

The Commission on Population Growth and the American Future was established by a congressional act in 1969 to examine the probable extent of population growth and internal migration in the United States up to the end of the present century and to assess the impact of population change upon government services, the economy, and resources and environment. Under the chairmanship of John D. Rockefeller III, the Commission conducted studies and hearings and sponsored research for more than two and a half years. It submitted its report in March, 1972.[24]

Among its many recommendations, the following six are fairly representative of the tone of the report. First, the nation should give the highest priority to research in reproductive biology and to the search for improved methods by which individuals may control their own fertility. Second, a national policy and voluntary program should be developed to reduce unwanted fertility, improve the outcome of pregnancy, and improve the health of children. Third, the nation should welcome and plan for a stabilized population. Fourth, immigration levels should not be increased and immigration policy should be reviewed periodically to reflect demographic conditions and considerations. Fifth, action should be taken to increase freedom in choice of residential location through eliminating current patterns of racial and economic segregation and their attendant injustices. And sixth, vigorous and concerted steps should be taken to promote free choice of housing within metropolitan areas.[25]

Although many specific recommendations of these three special commissions have not been fully implemented and others probably never will be, each Commission report had some impact on public policies and programs. For example, policy-community relations programs have been set up in many communities, and the Intergovernmental Personnel Act uses the population of 50,000 as a minimum for local agencies for contracting purposes.

FEDERAL REVENUE SHARING

After a decade of political debate, a turning point in intergovernmental relations was achieved in October, 1972, with the enactment into national law of the State and Local Fiscal Assistance Act of 1972.[26] More commonly referred to as the Revenue-Sharing Act, its major purposes are to reduce the fiscal imbalance in the American federal system and to enhance state and local control over public expenditures. An alliterative, if exaggerated, caricature of existing conditions was that local governments had the problems needing solution or amelioration, state governments had the power to do something about them, and the national government had the purse that made financing corrective action possible.

Revenue sharing had been advocated by some scholars and government practitioners for about fifteen years and had been considered in Congress in each session since the late 1950s. It received a major boost in 1964 when the "Heller-Pechman" plan was developed and supported by Walter W. Heller, chairman of the Council of Economic Advisers and Dr. Joseph A. Pechman of the Brookings Institution.[27] Both major political parties adopted revenue-sharing planks in their 1968 platforms. Shortly after his electoral victory in November of that year President-elect Richard M. Nixon appointed Dr. Richard P. Nathan of the Brookings Institution to head an Intergovernmental Fiscal Relations Task Force to study and recommend means for restructuring federal assistance programs to state and local governments. Predictably the Task Force recommended a program of revenue sharing.[28]

In a special message to Congress in August, 1969, President Nixon endorsed revenue sharing and a bill on behalf of the administration was introduced, but it did not receive favorable action. In his 1971 budget message to Congress, the President again gave top priority to revenue sharing, but Congressional action did not proceed until early in the next year. The House of Representatives approved the bill in June and the Senate gave its approval two months later. The bill finally enacted was a compromise plan that included two formulas—the House version seeming to favor the large, populous urban states and the Senate plan favoring less populated, more rural states.

The Revenue Sharing Act has a number of major features. First, it provided an automatic payout guaranteeing payments of $30.2 billion from January 1, 1972, through December 31, 1976. Distributions for 1972 totaled $5.3 billion with the annual figures progressing to $6.5 billion in 1976. (This legislation was renewed in 1976 at its most recent distribution level.)

Second, the distribution of funds to the fifty states and 38,000 general-purpose local governments (school districts and special districts being excluded) occurs quarterly, except in 1972. States retain one-third of the state share, with the other two-thirds passing directly to its eligible local governments.

Third, the Act contains two formulas as mentioned above. The House of Representatives approved a five-factor formula consisting of (1) total population, (2) urbanized population, (3) per capita income weighted inversely, (4) state income taxes, and (5) general tax effort. The three-factor formula developed by the Senate recognized these criteria: (1) total population, (2) general tax effort, and (3) per capita income weighted inversely. The choice of formula to be utilized is left to each state, and each predictably has opted for the plan most favorable to it. For example, the three-factor formula for any state would be computed by the following method:

$$\frac{\text{State share}}{\text{of \$5.4 billion}} = \frac{\text{State population}}{\text{50-state population}} \times \frac{\text{State GTE}}{\text{All states' GTE}} \times \frac{\text{U.S. per capita income}}{\text{State per capita income}}$$

Fourth, the Act provides that per capita amounts to local governments may not exceed 145 percent or be less than 20 percent of the per capita local share for the state in any given year. It is further provided that no local government may receive an allotment that exceeds 50 percent of its adjusted taxes plus intergovernmental transfers during the preceding year.

Fifth, funds from revenue sharing sources must be utilized for "priority expenditures." These expenditures are defined to include (1) ordinary and necessary maintenance and operating expenses for (a) public safety, (b) environmental protection, (c) public transportation, (d) health, (e) recreation, (f) libraries, (g) social services for the poor or aged, and (h) financial administration; and (2) ordinary and necessary capital expenditures authorized by law.

Sixth, the Act includes an anti-discrimination provision stipulating that no person should be excluded from participation, be denied the benefits of, or be subjected to discrimination on the basis of race, color, national origin, or sex. Prohibitions against unfair labor practices are also prescribed including the requirement to pay not less than the prevailing wage rates to all laborers and mechanics working on facilities financed by revenue-sharing funds.

And, seventh, state and local governments are required to submit reports to the Office of Revenue Sharing in the Treasury Department on both their planned actual uses of revenue-sharing funds. Failure to comply can result in the forfeiture of funds or in their delay until the required reports have been filed.

While the actual expenditure of revenue-sharing funds has varied slightly from quarter to quarter, the reported uses for the fourth entitlement period ending June 30, 1974, are illustrative. County governments utilized a little over two-fifths of their funds for operating and maintenance programs and nearly three-fifths for capital items. Cities reversed these ratios, and townships split their funds nearly equally between operations and maintenance and capital projects.[29]

Categories of expenditures by counties for this period, in declining rank, were public safety, public transportation, general government, health, and environmental protection. The order for city expenditures was public safety, public transportation, environmental protection, recreation, and general government. For townships the five largest items of expenditures were public safety, public transportation, general government, environmental protection, and recreation. Social services for the poor or aged stood relatively low for each of the three major types of local governments.[30]

A study of the first year's experience with revenue sharing by local governments in the greater Birmingham, Alabama, area concluded,

> Although the initial year did not provide a genuinely valid test, budget officials in the local governmental units studied did not seem inclined to treat revenue sharing funds much differently from the way in which they had become accustomed to handling ordinary budgetary resources. In other words, it was "business as usual" at a time, when given the crucial and historic role that revenue sharing was expected to play, more sophistication about public planning was required.[31]

In another analysis, which measured the views of state and local officials toward revenue sharing in Indiana, Kentucky, and Ohio, Keon Chi, a political scientist, found that nearly 90 percent of his sample endorsed the revenue-sharing plan as a better approach than the more highly proliferated categorical grant-in-aid programs. A majority believed that the old categorical grants should be replaced by general revenue sharing, while two fifths felt that revenue sharing should be supplementary to categorical grants. The decentralization feature of revenue sharing was confirmed in Chi's study when 96 percent of his sample agreed that revenue sharing had returned decisionmaking to the state and local levels. Chi's statement "Direct Federal-local relationship would undermine the position of the states for a balanced federal system" was disapproved by mayors of big cities but strongly supported by state officials.[32]

THE FUTURE OF NATIONAL-LOCAL RELATIONS

The recent expansion of direct national-local relationships has not gone without challenge nor has it been free of difficult problems many of which have not yet been answered satisfactorily. According to one writer,

> Let us admit that a freely granted power is not "usurpation." But a power "freely" granted under financial pressure or under an increasing political and economic lassitude on the part of individuals

may very well result in a concentration which is dangerous to individual liberty of thought and action. Contrarily a mechanism which forces back onto individuals and onto state and local officials a sense of dignified responsibility seems to have inherent value.[33]

The crucial questions in the future of national-local relations, however, are not likely to be closely tied in with past concepts of our federal structure. Rather these questions will seek to determine whether or not certain governmental functions may be performed better or governmental problems solved more effectively by cooperative national-local relations than by state-local actions or by local actions alone.[34] Apparently our large cities have accepted an affirmative answer to these queries and are working toward more effective national-local relationships. This acceptance is evident by making Washington, D. C., the headquarters of the National League of Cities, and the site of an office of the American Municipal Association, an organization of state municipal leagues with headquarters in Chicago. In addition, the National Association of Counties has its headquarters in the nation's capital. These three large organizations comprise an effective lobby in Washington to advance and protect local government interests.[35]

The desire for continuous and strengthened national-local ties and relationships comes through clearly in the National Municipal Policy statement adopted by the National League of Cities in 1970. The statement resulted from a year-long policy updating process that involved 1,100 municipal officials throughout the nation and contains six major policy planks. First, the national government is urged to re-channel the nation's wealth to assist municipal governments. Second, social problems that ignore state and local political boundaries require national solutions. Third, if city decay is to be arrested, federal programs for community improvement must be expanded. Fourth, effective local pollution control and standards must have both federal legal and fiscal support. Fifth, federal efforts must be expanded if the rapid growth of crime in cities is to be stemmed. And sixth, the national government must expand its programs to improve urban transportation systems.[36]

The developments in national-local relations in the last four decades represent a sharp departure from the traditional concept of the relationships of these two levels of government. The "Great Society" programs of President Johnson's administration went far beyond those of his predecessors. These programs aimed at the root causes of the major problems so evident in local communities—racism, bad housing, poor education, lack of transportation, and the feeling of political powerlessness—were all fairly well under way by late 1968. Such programs were the hallmarks of Johnson's "Creative Federalism" policies.[37]

The basic framework of President Nixon's "New Federalism," which was continued by President Gerald Ford, reflects the degree and extent of these changes in its four "D's"—dollars, discretion, decentralization, and delivery. The program's philosophy was aptly summarized in these words:

> Federal, state, and local participants in the New Federalism should recognize the new change in policy that has occurred. If all levels develop a healthy attitude toward the system, there are few limits to the achievements that can be made. But, it is only through a recognition that each level has new responsibilities, some expanded, and some diminished, that real progress will be achieved.[38]

Thus, it seems reasonable to conclude that recent concepts of cooperative fiscal federalism will not only remain but will continue to expand in the immediate years ahead.

NOTES

1. National Resources Committee, *Urban Government*, Vol. 1, Supplementary Report of the Urbanism Committee, Washington, 1939.
2. As quoted in Roger H. Wells, *American Local Government*, McGraw-Hill, 1939, p. 137.
3. Raymond S. Short, "Municipalities and the Federal Government," *The Annals of the American Academy of Political and Social Science*, 207 (January, 1940), 44-53.
4. Morton Grodzins, "The Federal System" in *Goals for Americans*, Report of the President's Commission on National Goals, Prentice-Hall, 1960, p. 265.
5. Daniel Elazar, "Urban Problems and the Federal Government: A Historical Inquiry," *Political Science Quarterly*, 82 (December, 1967), 505-525.
6. *Ibid.*, pp. 507-11.
7. *Congressional Quarterly Weekly Report*, XIX (March 10, 1961), 402-4.
8. Message from President Lyndon Johnson to the Congress, January 26, 1966, H. R. doc. 368, 89th Congress, 2nd Session.
9. Message from President Nixon to the Congress, February 4, 1971, 92nd Congress, 1st Session.
10. Bureau of the Census, "Governmental Finances and Employment at a Glance," Government Printing Office, January, 1976, pp. 1-3.
11. P. L. 380, 86th Congress, 1st Session, September, 1959.
12. The program of studies and reports prepared by the Advisory Commission on Intergovernmental Relations has been particularly valuable. They include: *Federal-State-Local Finances: Significant Features of Fiscal Federalism*, 1974; *Multistate Regionalism*, 1972; *Regional Decision Making: New Strategies for Substate Districts*, 1973; *Regional Government: Promise and Performance*, 1973; *State-Local Relations in the Criminal Justice System*, 1971; *Labor-Management Policies for State and Local Government*, 1969; *Urban and Rural America: Policies for Future Growth*, 1968; *Building Codes: A Program for Intergovernmental Reform*, 1966; *Apportionment of State Legislatures*, 1962; *Unshackling Local Government*, 1968; and *Performance of Urban Functions: Local and Areawide*, 1963.

13. Advisory Commission on Intergovernmental Relations, *ACIR: The Year in Review,* 16th annual report, Washington, 1975, p. 1.
14. Department of Housing and Urban Development, *Programs of the Department of Housing and Urban Development,* Washington, May, 1966, pp. 4-5.
15. "Is Your City Prepared for a Major Disaster?", *Nation's Cities,* 11 (May, 1973), 25-32.
16. Department of Health, Education and Welfare, *HEW-Cities Handbook,* Washington, June, 1969.
17. *Report of the National Advisory Commission on Civil Disorders,* Bantam Books, March, 1968, pp. 1-2.
18. *Ibid.,* pp. 7-8.
19. *Ibid.,* pp. 283-482.
20. National Commission on Urban Problems, *Building the American City,* 91st Congress, 1st Session, H.D. 91-34, Washington, 1968, p. vii.
21. *Ibid.,* p. 324.
22. *Ibid.,* p. 380.
23. *Ibid.,* p. 31.
24. Commission on Population Growth and the American Future, *Population and the American Future,* New American Library, March, 1972.
25. *Ibid.,* pp. 182-218 *passim.*
26. P. L. 92-512, 92nd Congress, 1st Session.
27. Walter W. Heller, *New Dimensions of Political Economy,* W. W. Norton & Co., 1967.
28. Domestic Council of the President, *The History of Revenue Sharing,* Washington, 1971, p. 4.
29. Office of Revenue Sharing, *General Revenue Sharing: Reported Uses 1973-1974,* Government Printing Office, February, 1975, pp. 38-40.
30. *Ibid.*
31. William M. Kimmelman, *Revenue Sharing and Local Government: The Case of the Birmingham Planning District,* Citizen Information Report No. 10, Bureau of Public Administration, University of Alabama, 1974, p. 60.
32. Keon S. Chi, "Revenue Sharing and Decentralization: The Views of State and Local Officials", unpublished paper draft, May, 1974.
33. George C. S. Benson *et. al., Essays in Federalism,* Institute for Studies in Federalism, Claremont Men's College, 1961, p. 7.
34. For instance, see Michael D. Reagan, *The New Federalism,* Oxford University Press, 1972, for a logical and forceful presentation of this view.
35. For an excellent study of the lobbying activities of such organizations, see Suzanne Farkas, *Urban Lobbying, Mayors in the Federal Arena,* New York University Press, 1971.
36. National League of Cities, *National Municipal Policy,* Washington, 1971.
37. Robert C. Wood, *The Necessary Majority: Mid·lle America and the Urban Crisis,* Columbia University Press, 1972, p. 7.
38. James S. Dwight, Jr., "The Four 'D's' of the New Federalism" in Leigh E. Grosenick (ed.), *The Administration of the New Federalism: Objectives and Issues.* American Society for Public Administration, 1973, p. 19.

Chapter 5

Local Politics and Elections

In Chapter 2 a local government was defined as a subordinate territorial unit of an American state enjoying a reasonable degree of independence from external control and accountable to its citizenry. The degree of outside control exercised by the state and national governments in their relations with local units has been examined, and we are now ready to look at the role of the citizen in determining, conducting, and controlling the public affairs of his own community. In this chapter the role of the citizen is considered in both theoretical and practical terms, and local political organizations and processes are discussed.

DEMOCRACY IN LOCAL GOVERNMENT

Since the essence of democracy is respect for the individual, a democratic community is devoted to the principle that everybody counts and its government is controlled by its whole citizenry rather than by a particular group or fraction of the whole. The decline of faith in at least some of the basic tenets of liberalism has prompted a more detailed study of local communities in recent years and the focus of many of these studies has been political power—its bases, distribution, use, and consequences. While the researchers and their studies could be ranged along a continuum in terms of their findings, these analysts of community power are divided for better understanding into three broad groups—the elitists, the pluralists, and the anti-pluralists.

Elitism

In the *Republic,* Plato argues persuasively that the ideal and best form of government would be rule by a highly trained and selected elite—the philosopher-king. In recent studies of community power, the question has shifted from the philosophical question of should there be an elite to the empirical question of does an elite exist.

Although there had been earlier analyses of power in American local communities,[1] the current serious study may be dated from the appearance of sociologist Floyd Hunter's *Community Power Structure* in 1953.[2] Hunter describes Regional City (really Atlanta, Georgia) as being run by a small group of powerful men who interacted socially and determined city policies informally and behind the scenes. To find out who held power in Atlanta, Hunter employed a reputational approach to determine leaders in business, government, civic associations, and society. Then relying on a panel of judges and a system of self-selection, Hunter arrived at a list of forty persons in the top levels of power in that city. He described these leaders as persons of "dominance, prestige, and influence" who could enforce their decisions by "persuasion, intimidation, coercion, and, if necessary, force." Hunter warned that the leaders were not a "true pyramid of political power." Some political issues did not interest them and they therefore did not figure in policy outcomes in these areas.

Non-empirical support for the Hunter thesis of elitism in community leadership is evident in this quote from sociologist C. Wright Mills:

> In every town and small city of America, an upper set of families stands above the middle classes and towers over the underlying population of clerks and wage workers. The members of this set possess more than do others of whatever there is locally to possess; they hold the keys to local decisions;. . .[3]

Further support for the elitist concept comes from the persuasive writings of another sociologist—G. William Domhoff.[4] His thesis is that the American upper class is a governing class consisting of less than one percent of the total population. In his words, a governing class is "a social upper class which owns a disproportionate amount of the country's wealth, receives a disproportionate amount of the country's yearly income, and contributes a disproportionate number of its members to positions of leadership." He does not deal specifically with power in local communities, but clearly he would extend his "governing class" concept to that level.

Describing such studies as "stratification studies," Nelson Polsby, a political scientist, believes they share five assertions about power in American communities. These are: (1) the upper class rules in local community life; (2) political and civic leaders are subordinate to the upper class; (3) a single power elite rules in the community; (4) the upper-class power elite rules in its own interests; and (5) social conflict takes place between the upper and lower classes.[5]

Pluralism

A challenge to the elitist methodology and concept to the proper approach to the study of community power emerged in 1961 when *Who Governs?*, a study of New Haven, was published.[6] Robert Dahl believes the proper methodology for finding out who has power in a community is to study decision-making. He selects three issue-areas—urban redevelopment, public education, and political nominations—for analysis. After studying the leaders in these three areas, Dahl found that only a small number of people has direct influence in the sense that they can successfully initiate or veto proposals for policies, but he found little overlap among leaders in the three issue-areas. He thus concludes that power was not located in a single group but in several groups, depending on the issue, resulting in "pluralistic democracy" in New Haven.

Polsby carries the pluralistic torch even further. Offering the "pluralist" alternative for studying community power, he posits several basic propositions. First, the pluralistic approach is that nothing categorical may be assumed about power in any community. Second, pluralists believe power may be tied to issues, fleeting or persistent, around which momentary or semi-permanent coalitions form. Third, pluralists emphasize the interest group and the public as the most relevant social collectives to be studied. And, fourth, pluralists concentrate on the exercise of power itself rather than on the holders of power—real or potential. Accordingly Polsby recommends that the researcher studying community power pick issue-areas as the focus of his study, make sure that the issue-areas are important, that he study actual behavior, and that he study the outcomes of the decisions in the community. In Polsby's words, "It is important, but insufficient, to know what leaders want to do, intend to do, and think they can do."[7]

A third major voice in the pluralist school is that of sociologist Arnold Rose. He concludes that the power structure of the United States is highly complex and diversified and that the political system is more or less democratic with the glaring exception of the black's position in the 1960's. He further states that in

> political processes the political elite is ascendant over and not subordinate to the economic elite, and that the political elite influences or controls the economic elite at least as much as the economic elite controls the political elite.[8]

The Anti-Pluralist Position

Just as the supporters of pluralism faulted the methods and findings of studies that found elitism in local communities, the pluralists have been similarly criticized by a group of writers who may be identified as the anti-pluralists. To this group, the four tenets of pluralism which the anti-pluralists attack, hold that (a) power is shared among representative sectors of the population, (b) public policy is shaped by inputs from a wide range of competing groups, (c) no one group enjoys permanent dominance or suffers permanent defeat, and (d) the distribution of benefits is roughly equitable or at least not consistently exploitative.[9]

The anti-pluralists challenge these tenets vigorously. They believe that public policies fairly consistently favor the large corporate interests at the expense of workers, small farmers, consumers, low-income people, slum dwellers, and taxpayers among others. Second, our political system gives symbolic allocations to public sentiment but substantive allocations to powerful private interests. Third, the political efficacy of individuals and groups is largely determined by their available resources of which wealth is the most important. Fourth, the interplay that occurs between and among groups is largely limited to organized groups rather than between groups and the unorganized public. And, fifth, ample evidence is present of continual collusion between elites—even if there is not one cohesive, conspiratorial elite.

In a careful assessment of the present status of studies relating to community power, political scientist David Ricci concludes that we have a "scholarly impasse." Scholarship continues but it proceeds along theoretical lines already laid down by the earlier research of the elitists, pluralists, and anti-pluralists. He suggests that possibly the impasse can be circumvented by replacing the question "What shall we study in relation to democracy?" with the question "Where do we enjoy democracy and where do we lack it?" and by applying democratic process theory directly to specific issues and problems in communities rather than to the pattern of governance in communities.[10]

Fairly general agreement exists among all three schools, however, that the ideal of an elite trained for civic purposes advanced by Plato has been replaced by the actuality of a community elite trained for and successful in money-gathering activities.

THE RIGHT TO VOTE

A commonly accepted definition of a citizen is a person owing allegiance to a government and entitled to protection by it. However, this definition is so broad as to embrace a number of persons unable or unfit to participate in community affairs. Obviously very young children, the mentally incompetent, and certain other groups should not share in community decision-making. Thus, specific standards are prescribed, and only those who meet them are entitled to take part in running the affairs of their community. The common term for this portion of the total citizenry is the electorate, which is the group that selects the public officials and guides their actions in determining the nature, character, and services of their government.

Voter Qualifications

The power to establish suffrage qualifications for voters is a power reserved to the states in our federal system. Restrictions of this general power of the states, however, have resulted with the adoptions of the fifteenth, nineteenth, twenty-fourth, and twenty-sixth amendments to the national Constitution. The fifteenth prohibits states from discriminating against persons because of their "race, color, or previous condition of servitude" and guarantees equal protection of the laws in relation hereto. The nineteenth prohibits such discrimination on "account of sex." The requirement of a poll tax for voting for national officers was banned by the twenty-fourth amendment, while the twenty-sixth lowered the voting age to eighteen years. In addition, the Federal Voting Rights Act of 1970 suspended all literacy tests as a requirement for voting. Subject to these limitations, the states retain the power to determine voter qualifications.[11]

Since Americans generally subscribe to the ideal of universal suffrage, the specific qualifications that are prescribed are basically not intended to disfranchise groups of potential voters but to assure that the enfranchised electors will have the capacity to participate meaningfully in the selection of local officials and in shaping local public policies. The three general requirements relate to age, residence, and citizenship, while further qualifications pertain to registration, property ownership, literary requirements and other miscellaneous qualifications.

The ratification of the twenty-sixth amendment to the U.S. Constitution in 1971 reduced the voting age to eighteen and ended a long, often bitter debate on this subject. The period of necessary residence for voting in local elections varies widely, ranging from a low of ten days to a maximum of one year. A definite trend is underway to lower the length of residency since its former use as a restraint upon voting has been largely negated by court decisions. Judicial decisions have definitely attempted to open the local political process to those previously disfranchised, even to the extent of requiring ballots in local elections to be printed in several languages including Chinese and Tagolog in San Francisco.

Property as a Special Restraint

In the early history of our nation, property ownership was a uniform requirement for voting in state and local elections. Particularly with the rise of Jacksonian democracy, the property qualification was attacked as an aristocratic concept. By the end of the Civil War it had disappeared as a requirement in all states.

A new interest in property ownership as a qualification for voting arose during the depression of the 1930s and took two forms. The first was the reinstitution of a property ownership requirement for voting in a number of states and the second was a denial to paupers of the right to vote. More generally property ownership as a qualification is limited to questions concerning the expenditure of public money or the issuance of bonds.

Voting Problems Today

The mobility of Americans presents a special problem to many voters who find that they will be away from home on election day. While the details of the absentee voting provisions vary among the states, there are two principal types. The more widely used plan requires the securing of an absentee ballot from the voter's local voting district before election day. Application for the ballot must be made a specified number of days preceding the election; the ballot must be marked in the presence of a notary and returned in a sealed envelope along with the notary's affidavit that the ballot was cast in secret and by the voter intended. The other major type of absentee voting law pertains only to voters who are in their home states but away from their home districts. Such a voter secures a ballot from the local election board in the community where he or she is on election day, marks and returns it to his home county which in turn delivers it to the proper election district for counting.

Although no general studies of non-voting in local governments exist, a growing number of case studies of particular communities confirm the point that large numbers of citizens do not participate directly in the electoral process. Without question continued small turnout of voters may have undesirable results to the voters, public officials, and community alike. However, the most common reason given for not voting is apathy or lack of interest. Too large a number of voters apparently have a sense of futility. They believe that even casting their vote will have no effect on the outcome of the election and that city affairs will be handled in the same way regardless of which candidate or party wins.

As indicated earlier, it is highly significant that the voter has the privilege of exercising his voting right if he chooses to do so. It is less important that he exercise this privilege with any high degree of consistency. Probably more responsive local government will result when a larger number of citizens become interested and participate in choosing their elected representatives and in deciding questions of public policy. But the means to the end must be largely through education rather than compulsion or regulatory legislation.

LOCAL VOTER PROFILE

While generalization is often risky, probabilities may be advanced concerning groups within the community electorate. On the basis of completed studies, it is possible to predict that men will vote more than women, older persons more than young, property owners more than non-owners, conservatives more than liberals, and white voters more than black voters. In an interesting study of voting patterns in New Haven, Connecticut, Robert Dahl discovered that participation in local political affairs was greater among citizens with (1) high income than among those with lower income, (2) high social standing than among those with lower standing, (3) more formal education than among citizens with little, (4) occupations in the professional, business, and white-collar classes than among those with working-class occupations, and (5) homes in better residential areas than among citizens living in poorer neighborhoods.[12]

The correlations indicated above seem to bear out the general theory that people will vote more often if they feel they have a stake in or can influence the outcome of elections. This is not meant to imply that such voters are not also responding to the civic impulse of exercising their privilege of voting. This is undoubtedly an important factor, but its reinforcement by a feeling that the outcome of the election is important to themselves is particularly significant. Apathy among some groups of the electorate enhances the political importance of other groups, and in a democracy we must have an increasingly alert public. This will result also in a citizenry increasingly active in the community's electoral and governmental processes.

Periodically voters in communities across the nation face the task of selecting in excess of 500,000 men and women to fill policymaking and executive positions in our local governments. For the citizen whose participation in local politics is limited to casting a ballot on election day, the electoral process seems to operate smoothly, and he may be a bit chagrined about a few friends and neighbors who become deeply involved in such a simple process. While performing his occasional act of civic responsibility, the voter also may wish that he were choosing among better known and more qualified candidates for fewer offices. This description of the local voter is inadequate and even unfair to many citizens; however, unfortunately for many citizens the local political process begins with the opening of the polls on election day and ends when the ballots have been tallied.

By its very nature, the electoral process in local government is a political process. Some form of organization must exist to recruit candidates for less popular offices, screen those willing to run for the top posts, advance positions on matters of public policy, and work for the election of candidates to implement those policies when in office. Anyone legally eligible to do so can seek local office, but some minor offices go uncontested and candidates for other positions are recruited only with urging and persuasion. As a consequence, without local political organizations to set the wheels of the political process in motion, local representative government would be both less representative of and responsive to the community of voters.

The local political process will be examined by identifying local political parties and organizations, examining their functions and operation, and reviewing the major proposals for improving their performance. While many definitions of the political process exist, the one most relevant at the local level is that it "changes citizens into public officials and individual wishes into public policy."[13] So defined, the political process is essential to local democratic government and is deserving of more sympathetic and unprejudicial acceptance and involvement.

LOCAL POLITICAL ORGANIZATIONS

The opening sentences of Frank Kent's interesting and rewarding *The Great Game of Politics* dramatically underscores the importance of local party organization. In his words,

> No clear idea of a party organization can be had unless you start from the bottom. To discuss Presidential politics without understanding precinct politics is an absurdity. It is like trying to solve a problem in trigonometry without having studied arithmetic.[14]

Party organization charts typically take the form of a hierarchy of committees arranged in descending order from the national party committee to the precinct committee. Each committee layer has jurisdiction over specified geographical areas ranging from the nation as a whole to an area of a few city blocks. Interrelationships between local communities and state and national committees are increasing, but our concern is with organization at the precinct, ward, and city or county levels, in that order.

Precincts and Wards

The precinct is the unit cell in the organization of a political party; the term is used throughout the nation to connote a voting district of from 200 to 2,000 voters with an average voting strength of 600. About 130,000 precincts are present in the United States with as many as 3,000 existing in several of the largest cities. Although precinct organization varies among the states, two common patterns emerge. One is to have two coequal officers—a committeeman and a committeewoman—to guide the affairs of the party in that area. The second is to place party matters in the hands of a committee of three or more members with one of them serving in a dominant capacity.

In most states precinct committeemen or committee members are elected at the primary election, usually for a term of two years. However, in various large cities these local officials are appointed by the ward leaders, and in other cities precinct officers are selected at party caucuses. Precinct workers are in charge of the affairs of their party in their area.[15] Their major function is to get out a big vote and carry their precincts by as large a margin as possible. Usually all precinct workers have one thing in common. They recognize that a job well done in the precinct can serve as a springboard to a higher party post or even an elective public position.

A message of hope and reward is held out to precinct workers in a typical party publication that assured these persons that

> Being a Precinct Worker is a hard job but it has its own rewards. You're helping people to understand the issues that affect us all. You're making the machinery of government work. You're doing your job as a citizen in a working democracy. You're working to keep America free through the ballot box. You're proud to be a Precinct Worker. You're stepping up as a Party Leader.[16]

The next rung in the ladder of party hierarchy is the organization at the ward level which typically embraces several precincts. Two patterns are found at this level—the ward committee and the ward president or executive systems. The ward committee, which is the more common of the two, is normally composed of the committeeman and committeewoman from the constituent precincts. The committee selects a chairperson to manage its affairs, but it remains an approval body and directs actions and policies. Under the ward president or executive system, this individual typically appoints the precinct officers in his area.

The party organization at the ward level is becoming more important because this election unit is often the point at which the party begins to nominate candidates such as council members for local public office. Because of its strategic position in the party organization, the ward committee or executive has real importance in determining the fortune of his party. Through this committee the patronage and campaign funds are funneled to the precincts and the money from the precincts is channeled through the ward organization on its way to party coffers at higher levels. Increasingly strong party organization at the ward level thus seems to be necessary, particularly in large cities.

City or County Organizations

The city and county are important political units throughout the nation; both serve as the election area for a number of local officers and for state legislative districts as one house typically follows county lines to the extent possible. The party organizations at this level reflect the significance of these units for the fortunes of the party at both the local and higher levels. Since the merit system has made little headway in county government and both national and state patronage are dispensed at the county level, county committees—or their chairpersons—are usually influential links in the chain of the party command.[17]

In cities the ward committeemen usually serve as the city committee, but in some states the city committee members are elected at the primary election. The organization of county committees takes one of three forms in various parts of the nation. Often the county committee is made up of all the precinct committeemen in the county; sometimes its members are elected in party primaries; and in some areas committee members are chosen in county party conventions. The chairpersons of both city and county committees are usually chosen by the committee they serve and normally are the most powerful member of that committee. In counties with large cities, the county committee, though important, does not tend to dominate the political affairs of the city. This is sometimes the case because the party alignment in the city differs from that in the outlying area of the county.

The responsibilities and functions of the city and county committees are the same for their larger jurisdictions as are those of the precinct leaders in their much smaller areas. It is at this level of party machinery that "bossism" once ran rampant and may still be important. However, most of the new city and county chairpersons are leaders rather than bosses and they head organizations instead of machines. The difference between the two is much more than a semantic one; this becomes evident in contrasting present techniques of leadership with those of the old-style boss.[18]

In an interesting study of social characteristics, political activity, political careers and personal perceptions of county chairpersons in New Jersey, Gerald Pomper, political scientist, found that Republican and Democratic chairpersons are of approximately equal experience, but Democrats tend to be of longer tenure and face opposition more frequently. Democrats also tended to be a more professional group, devoting themselves more strictly to partisan activities and less to "civic" enterprises. The Democrats are also more active in such organized activity as national conventions, statewide election campaigns, and charity and health drives, while Republicans lean toward individualistic and nonpartisan actions such as public testimony, speeches, and newspaper letters.[19]

PARTIES AT THE LOCAL LEVEL

The question of the desirability of partisanship in local government has been a continuing controversy during all the present century. Students and practitioners of local government align themselves on both sides of the question with about equal fervor and intensity. However, partisan elections remain the most common basis for selecting local officials at the county, city, and township levels. Partisanship is much less a factor in school district and other special district elections.

Much of the controversy has stemmed from a bad choice of words by those opposed to deciding local issues on the basis of national and state party labels. In choosing ''nonpartisan'' as the adjective for elections decided locally without Republican or Democratic labels, the reformers were placed in a paradoxical position. ''Nonpartisan'' elections imply the absence of party or group activity to advance particular candidates and policies, and this is antithetical to the political process. While many people might agree that there is no ''Republican or Democratic way to pave a street or lay a sewer,'' there might well be policy differences over the needs for such public works programs as against the needs for expanded health, welfare, and housing activities.

The proponents of nonpartisan elections in local government still may be fighting the city bosses, machines, and corruption of the late nineteenth and early twentieth century and still may be blaming the political party almost entirely for those conditions. As described by Lincoln Steffens, Harold Zink, and others, these conditions were deplorable and shameful, but it is unfair to continue to project this image of the American city and of its political parties.[29] In 1946 political scientist Luther Gulick wrote that

> Graft and corruption and the dominance of bosses are not the shame of the cities today as they were 40 years ago. The shame of the American city today is found in three things: first, lazy citizenship with low standards; second, lack of city pride; and third, failure to look ahead and make great plans for the future.[21]

A fascinating study of Chicago concluded that political power there was decentralized formally but highly centralized informally. While the city had a ''weak-mayor'' form of government, it also had a powerful mayor. The Democratic machine, an organization parallel to but outside the city government, had sufficient power to run the city and the weakness of the city government was offset by the strength of the party. The authors concluded that

> If overnight the bosses became model administrators—if they put all of the city jobs on the merit system, destroyed the syndicate and put an end to petty grafting, then the city government would really be . . . weak and ineffective. . . . ''[22]

Three methods for possible change in local party organization and operation have been suggested. One would create a separate system of local parties as a means to keep national politics out of local elections. The second would integrate the actions and policies of local party committees more closely with principles and policies of parties at the state and national levels. A third method would be to establish nonpartisanship by eliminating local parties.

NONPARTISANSHIP AS A LOCAL PRINCIPLE

An innovation in local government originating in the efficiency and economy movement in the early years of the current century was the concept of nonpartisan elections or election of local officials without party designation. Grounded in the theory that local governments were corporations rather than political bodies and questions in local government were administrative and not political in nature, it followed that local officials should be more like businessmen than politicians. To recruit such candidates, party labels would have to be abolished and local contests waged around the qualifications of candidates for the positions being sought.

Nonpartisan elections depend on the use of the nonpartisan primary or nomination by petition as the means for nominating candidates. While the features of this type of primary vary in some details among the states using it, names of candidates in the primary election are placed on the ballot by petition and appear with no party label after their names. Often the occupation of the candidate is placed on the ballot to give the voter an indication of his experience and qualification for the post. Typically the two persons gaining the highest vote totals in the primary are nominated for that office and their names appear on the general election ballot—again without party designation. If a candidate receives a majority of votes cast for the office in the primary, he or she is usually declared elected and the runoff feature of the general election is eliminated.

Until recently nonpartisan elections were generally accepted on faith. Supporters argued that such elections would weaken national political parties at the local level, better candidates would be willing to seek local office if party labels were abandoned, and local elections would be decided strictly on local issues. Recent studies, however, have cast doubt as to the nonpartisan nature of nonpartisan elections.[23] In a study of nonpartisan elections, Charles Adrian concluded that such elections serve to weaken political parties because the number of offices to be filled is reduced and the incentive to recruit new members is lessened. He also found that fewer new channels for the recruitment of candidates to fill local offices are opened by nonpartisanship. He cautioned, however, that nonpartisanship did not insure that local offices would be filled by successful persons since the perennial officeseeker was a familiar figure in many communities utilizing nonpartisan contests.[24]

Adrian advanced several other propositions concerning nonpartisan elections, however, that are less commendable in their effects. First, nonpartisan elections tend to segregate political leaders into strictly partisan or nonpartisan paths as a general rule. As a result, a successful mayor in a nonpartisan city may make an unsuccessful candidate for higher partisan office. Second, nonpartisanship encourages the avoidance of issues of policy in local campaigns. Candidates prefer to take an ambiguous stand or none at all on issues to avoid the possible loss of potential electoral support. Third, nonpartisanship tends to frustrate protest voting since "in" and "out" groups are not identifiable. Fourth, nonpartisanship tends to advance conservatism by the re-election of officeholders. And, fifth, no collective responsibility is present in a nonpartisan body because the members are elected as individuals rather than as members of a slate of nominees.[25]

In a study of nonpartisan elections in four cities with populations between 50,000 and 75,000, Adrian and Williams discovered that there was a similarity of voting patterns between local support for slates of nonpartisan candidates and political support for partisan candidates for higher office. This finding mitigates somewhat the assumption that local voting will be based on local issues. A second finding showed that a nonpartisan election or an election-at-large in these cities tended to increase the relative voice of persons who normally vote Republican. The authors warn, however, that the nonpartisan ballot is not a device favoring Republicans since the system does permit the recruitment of Democrats for elective posts in cities with strong Republican majorities.[26]

A study of voting data from forty-nine cities released by the International City Managers' Association in the early 1970s reported that despite the lack of party labels, voting in nonpartisan elections often closely parallels voting in partisan state and national contests. This study found that northwestern cities exhibited the lowest partisanship while voters in southern cities showed marked partisanship based on racial divisions. Another finding showed that partisanship is higher in council-manager cities than in mayor-council cities. The study also reported that middle-class cities with citizens displaying high education level, mobility, and high income showed the highest partisanship in voting.[27]

The ICMA-conducted survey echoed the findings of an earlier study of nonpartisan elections in California cities. On the basis of a detailed study of elections in six cities, political scientist Eugene Lee concluded, "Political parties and partisanship are not irrelevant in nonpartisan politics. In California party influence varies widely from city to city, from unimportance to a major force in shaping local political life."[28]

A recent analysis of attitudes of party chairpersons and mayors in North Dakota toward nonpartisan elections found broad support for such elections. Respondents felt that almost as many people would be excluded from voting in partisan elections as would be included, political parties would be more active in city politics, more controversial issues would be interjected in city elections, and the administration of local projects would not be as smooth or as efficient with partisan elections.[29]

A serious questioning of the nature and desirability of nonpartisanship as operating in suburban communities has been raised by political scientist Robert Wood. In his words,

> ... the importance of the professional public servant—the expert and the bureaucrat—obviously increases. The new positive role of local government makes his existence necessary. The non-partisan vacuum places him in a strategic position to assume a role as community leader, especially since political leaders are suspect. ... Under modern conditions, the power of the expert is the price the suburbanite pays for maintaining order in his home town.[30]

Political scientist Willis Hawley believes nonpartisanship goes far beyond the form of ballot used in elections and may become a way of political life that shapes the character and direction of public decision-making. His study demonstrates that the use of nonpartisan ballots increases the probability of Republicans winning elective office in middle-sized and large cities and of the policies in communities with nonpartisan elections being more conservative. He also believes that the voter, particularly if a Democrat, casts more rational ballots in partisan than in nonpartisan elections.[31]

SELECTING THE CANDIDATE

Whether a unit of local government uses a system of partisan or nonpartisan elections, some means must be present for determining the names of candidates to appear on the primary and general election ballots. Since selecting candidates and then supporting them for office are the major political activities at the local level, it is important to understand the process by which citizens are converted into public officials. Most nominees for local office are selected by either partisan or nonpartisan primaries, but several other methods also may be utilized in many states.

The first and oldest method may be called simply an act of self-announcement. Under this procedure a person aspiring to local office merely indicates his intention to seek the post by an announcement that may take the form of a public address, newspaper story, or extensive mailing of a letter. A second method of nomination is the caucus, or meeting of political leaders. Nomination by party convention is a third method of selecting candidates.

Nomination by petition is a further means by which a candidate can get his name on either the primary or general election ballot. The petition for a place on the primary ballot is the means that must be used in nonpartisan primaries. For the general election ballot, the petition provides a means by which independent candidates can have their names put on the ballot alongside those nominated by other methods.

A fifth procedure that in effect combines the primary and general election process is the system of preferential voting. Under this arrangement the voter is asked to indicate the order of his choices rather than merely his first choice. Such an election assures that a majority candidate will be elected since second-choice votes (and if needed third-and fourth-choice votes and so on) are counted until one candidate has a clear majority.

THE IMPORTANCE OF PRIMARIES

The direct primary is the most common means for selecting candidates. The partisan primary is an intraparty affair in which party members select their candidates from among their aspirants to public office. The winning candidates in the partisan primary then face the winners of the primary election of the other party or parties in the general election.

A further refinement of the partisan or closed primary is the "runoff" primary which is most commonly utilized in southern states. Under this adaptation if no candidate receives a majority of the primary votes cast, then the two highest candidates face each other in the special or "runoff" primary. This system is used in those states where nomination in the Democratic primary almost assures election to office in the general election. The runoff feature makes sure that the eventual winner secures a majority of the votes in his own partisan primary.

The final common means of nomination occurs through the use of the nonpartisan primary. This device has already been described in the section on nonpartisanship above. As is true of the other nomination procedures, this means an elimination process so that the choice of the general-election voters is usually limited to one of two candidates, unless other names appear on the ballot through nomination by petition or as write-in candidates.

While the direct primary is the most common and probably the best of the alternative systems of nomination, it has disadvantages. It is an expensive system for both the public and the candidates, and it increases the burden on the voter by requiring two separate elections. The system results in a long ballot since most positions—particularly in county and townships—are elective. In states not using the runoff election, candidates may be nominated by a plurality rather than by a majority of voters. Primary elections are often held too far in advance of general elections, thereby producing unnecessarily long and expensive campaigns. Primary elections discourage independent candidates and independent voters who choose not to align themselves with either major party, and tend to weaken party responsibility by making the appeal of the candidates voter-oriented rather than party-oriented.

And, finally, despite the ease of getting one's name on the primary ballot, voters are often given little if any choice of candidates for a number of elective offices.

Despite the shortcomings of the direct primary, it has worked reasonably well and certainly better than its opponents predicted. It is doubtful that better candidates are nominated by this system, but it does provide the citizenry of a community with a potential weapon of real importance. One writer concludes that

> The direct primary is in a sense a shotgun over the door of the municipal electorate. Such a weapon need seldom be used. As long as the party organization presents satisfactory candidates, there is no serious objection to the fact that they are "organization candidates." If the organization falls to the level that it did in some cases under the convention, then the voters have an effective weapon in the direct primary.[32]

The political process in local government does not end with the nomination of candidates for public office or is it without activity by pressure or interest groups. The methods of citizen control over their local governments are discussed in Chapter 6, which begins with an examination of the election process, because this vehicle gives the citizen his greatest control over his government and with the devices of direct democracy—the initiative, referendum, and recall. That is followed by a discussion of pressure groups which provide another important means whereby the citizen may give direction to and exercise some control over his local government.

NOTES

1. Among the best early studies are: Robert S. and Helen M. Lynd, *Middletown* (Harcourt Brace, 1929), and *Middletown in Transition* (Harcourt, Brace, 1937); W. Lloyd Warner and associates, *The Social Life of a Modern Community* (Yale University Press, 1941), *The Status System of a Modern Community* (Yale University Press, 1942), and *Democracy in Jonesville* (Harper, 1949); and August B. Hollingshead, *Elmtown's Youth* (Wiley, 1949).
2. Floyd Hunter, *Community Power Structure*, University of North Carolina Press, 1953.
3. C. Wright Mills, *The Power Elite*, Oxford University Press, 1956, p. 30.
4. G. William Domhoff, *Who Rules America?*, Prentice-Hall, 1967.
5. Nelson W. Polsby, *Community Power and Political Theory*, Yale University Press, 1963, pp. 8-10.
6. Robert Dahl, *Who Governs?*, Yale University Press, 1961.
7. Polsby, *op. cit.*, p. 121.
8. Arnold Rose, *The Power Structure*, Oxford University Press, 1967, p. 492.
9. Michael Parenti, *Democracy for the Few*, St. Martin's Press, 1974, pp. 271-2. For other statements of the anti-pluralist position, see Thomas R. Dye and L.

Harmon Zeigler, *The Irony of Democracy*, Duxbury Press, 1971; David Ricci, *Community Power and Democratic Theory: The Logic of Political Analysis*, Random House, 1971; Charles A. McCoy and John Playford (eds.), *Apolitical Politics*, Crowell, 1967; and Marvin Surkin and Alan Wolfe (eds.), *An End to Political Science: The Caucus Papers*, Basic Books, 1970.

10. Ricci, *op. cit.*, 217-22.

11. For the range in qualifications, see table "Qualifications for Voting" in Council of State Governments, *The Book of the States*, 1972-73, Lexington, 1972, pp. 36-37.

12. Dahl, *op. cit.*, pp. 282-3.

13. Charles Adrian, *State and Local Governments, A Study in the Political Process*, McGraw-Hill, 1960, p. 158.

14. Frank R. Kent, *The Great Game of Politics*, Doubleday, 1923, p. 1.

15. For more information on precinct organization and politics, see Don P. Cass, *How to Win Votes and Influence Elections*, Public Administration Service, 1962; Grenville T. Emmet III and Patricia B. Emmet, *What the Pros Know, The Anatomy of Winning Politics*, Information Incorporated, 1968; and Edward Schneier and William T. Murphy, *Vote Power: How to Work for the Person You Want Elected*, Doubleday, 1974.

16. Democratic National Committee, Women's Division, *The Key to Democratic Victory, A Guidebook for County and Precinct Workers*, Washington, 1952.

17. For an entertaining and enlightening discussion of national and local politics at the county level in a presidential year, see James A. Michener, *Report of the County Chairman*, Random House, 1961.

18. For an in-depth study of county chairmen in California, see David K. Hart, "The Office of the Party County Chairman in California," unpublished doctoral dissertation, Claremont Graduate School, 1966.

19. Gerald Pomper, "New Jersey County Chairmen," *Western Political Quarterly*, 18 (March, 1965), 191.

20. Lincoln Steffens, *The Shame of the Cities*, McClure, Phillips and Co., 1904; Harold Zink, *City Bosses in the United States*, Duke University Press, 1930; J. T. Salter, *Boss Rule: Portraits in City Politics*, McGraw-Hill, 1935; and W. B. Munro, *The Invisible Government*, Macmillan, 1925.

21. Luther Gulick, "The Shame of the Cities—1946," *National Municipal Review*, 36 (January, 1947), 18-25.

22. Martin Meyerson and Edward C. Banfield, *Politics, Planning and the Public Interest*, The Free Press, 1955, pp. 286-7.

23. Some of this "surprise" over finding that nonpartisan elections are not totally nonpartisan is unwarranted since we have known for a long time that partisan elections are not totally partisan. It is uncommon when one of the two candidates in an election does not catch the public eye and win considerable support from members of the opposite party.

24. Charles R. Adrian, "Some General Characteristics of Non-Partisan Elections," *American Political Science Review*, 46 (September, 1952), 766-76.

25. *Ibid.*

26. Oliver P. Williams and Charles R. Adrian, "The Insulation of Local Politics Under the Nonpartisan Ballot," *American Political Science Review* 53 (December, 1959), 1052-63.

27. International City Managers' Association, *Local Elections and City Politics: Partisanship in Non-Partisan City Elections,* Urban Data Service Reports, Vol. 3, No. 1, January, 1971.

28. Eugene C. Lee, *The Politics of Non-Partisanship, A Study of California City Elections,* University of California Press, 1960, p. 117.

29. Philip Gust (ed.), "Survey of Attitudes of Party Chairmen and Mayors on Partisan Election of Municipal Officials," Bureau of Governmental Affairs, University of North Dakota, Special Report No. 16, April, 1970.

30. Robert C. Wood, *Suburbia, Its People and Their Politics,* Houghton Mifflin, 1958, pp. 195-6.

31. Willis D. Hawley, *Nonpartisan Elections and the Case for Party Politics,* John Wiley & Sons, 1973, pp. 143-46.

32. Charles M. Kneier, *City Government in the United States,* 3rd edition, Harper; 1957, p. 363.

Chapter 6

Citizen Action and Control

The foundation of the democratic process in local government lies in open and free elections at reasonably frequent intervals. At such periods of public accounting by the "ins" and their challenge by other contestants, the individual voters must act as independent citizens rather than as ciphers of election statistics. When the voter enters the voting booth on election day, he holds its eventual outcome in his hands. Regardless of how thorough the work of the local party, group, or organization has been, the individual voter in the secrecy of the private booth is free to re-examine his predilections and capable of doing unexpected things. The importance of the voter to the cause of good government in his community is well indicated in this quotation,

> The word idiot is derived from the classical Greek idiōtēs, which meant "those citizens who did not take part in public voting." In ancient Greece it was because they could not; in the United States today it is because they do not—and the word idiot is still appropriate.[1]

LOCAL ELECTION ADMINISTRATION

The conduct of both primary and general elections is governed by state law, but most local electoral functions are performed by citizens of the local community. At the state level, the office of secretary of state usually oversees elections to the extent of checking compliance with state laws, and a state election board canvasses and certifies the results. However, the responsibility for local election administration is entrusted to the election board of the local community. At the county level, this board is normally the board of county commissioners, while the city council sitting as an *ex officio* board or a special election board acts in this capacity in cities. This local election board has ballots printed as prescribed by state law, designates and makes provisions for polling places, sets up the election machinery, and reports the results to the state election board. The executive officer for local elections is usually the county clerk and city clerk for county and city elections, respectively, but many large counties have established a special office or department to operate and supervise elections.

In the actual conduct of elections, the local governmental unit, except when very small, is divided into precincts or election districts ranging from 200 to 2,000 voters. A polling place is established in each precinct or district with public buildings such as schools, fire stations, or police stations usually so designated. Private residences, rented buildings, or portable structures also are sometimes used, but this practice is less frequent than earlier when more partisan favors were passed out to party workers on election day. A board consisting of judges or inspectors to conduct the election is set up in each precinct. It normally consists of two or more judges or inspectors from each major political party and a few clerks to assist. The bipartisan nature of the board is to promote honest elections by having workers of one party checking those of the other. In nonpartisan elections, of course, the board may also be nonpartisan in its composition. Normally these local election officials are appointed by the election boards of the governmental unit, but sometimes they are elected or selected by a merit system procedure.

Typically the polls are open for a ten- or twelve-hour period beginning at seven or eight o'clock in the morning. The precinct or district election board must see that the voter is properly identified and given a ballot, and that the ballot is deposited in the ballot box after it has been marked. If the district has voting machines, workers must keep them in proper working condition and see that the elector gets his vote duly recorded on the machine. Then when the polls close, the election board tabulates the votes and certifies the results to the city or county election board. To relieve the burden of the long day on the election board, several states now authorize two election boards. One board performs the functions outlined above except for counting ballots and certifying the results. These two functions are performed by a second election board which comes on duty a few hours before the polls close to begin the tally of the ballots in a room adjacent to the election room itself. In an effort to prevent fraud in counting ballots in the election districts, some cities and counties require the tabulation of all votes at a central headquarters. Central counting also occurs in jurisdictions that utilize certain electronic methods of voting.

Ballot Forms

The ballot form in common use in all fifty states is known as the

"Australian ballot," named for the country of its origin. As defined by one
writer, this ballot is "an official ballot, printed at public expense, by public
officers, containing the names of all candidates duly nominated, and
distributed at the polls by the election officers."[2]

The original form of the Australian ballot carried no party designation to
identify the candidates, but today two basic forms of ballots are employed.
The office-block type originated in Massachusetts in 1888 and groups
candidates by office. Under the heading of "treasurer," for example, the
names of the several candidates with their party affiliations are listed in a
block on the ballot. This block is followed by similar groupings of
candidates for the other offices to be filled. The other common form, the
party-column ballot, originated in Indiana in 1889. Under this form, all
candidates of one party are placed in a single column headed by the name of
the party. It is possible under this form to vote a straight party ticket by
placing a single mark in the spot provided by the name of the party. Party
leaders favor this form because it makes voting a straight party ticket
simpler.

Voting machines make the use of paper ballots unnecessary, because the
decisions of the individual voter in no way deface the ballot form set up on
the machine. The machine enables the office titles, names of candidates, and
party affiliations to be arranged in either the party-column or office-block
type of ballot, and space is provided for write-in candidates. When the
party-column ballot is utilized, a party lever makes possible the voting of a
straight ticket. In addition, another lever is above the name of each
candidate which the voter pulls down to indicate his choice if he does not
move the party lever or when the machine is organized for the office-block
ballot. It is impossible to vote for more than one candidate for each office
on the machine or to spoil the ballot in any other manner. Before the voter
leaves the booth, he may change any part of his vote since the votes are
recorded only when he opens the curtains to leave the booth.

The voting machine offers various advantages over the printed paper
ballot. First, the voter may select his choices on the machine and have his
vote recorded in less time than it takes to mark and deposit a paper ballot.
Second, it is impossible to spoil a machine vote. Third, the votes are
automatically tallied by the machine as the individual votes are recorded.
Fourth, the results are tallied more accurately because it is almost impossible
to tamper with the voting machine. And fifth, machines result in more
economical elections since precincts may be larger, fewer election officials
are needed, and much less time is required to count the votes. Continuing
wider use of voting machines probably will occur in the future. However,
two aspects of machine use present serious problems to local governments.
The first is the necessary large outlay of funds to purchase the machines and
the second relates to the size of the face of the machine. A machine

adequate for general election purposes may be too small to provide the space necessary for listing the names of all the contestants in the primary election.

These two problems have been largely overcome by the development of the votomatic type of voting machine, a major breakthrough in such equipment. This is a small, lightweight, easily portable machine into which a computer card is inserted. The ballot is reconstructed on pages that can be turned, and the voter's preference among the office candidates and his stands on propositions or amendments presented on each page is recorded in a separate column on the computer card. When the voter has completed his total ballot, he removes the card and deposits it in a locked container. The cards then may be collected at the close of the polls and machine counted centrally.

Whether the voter is asked to mark a paper ballot, pull the levers of a voting machine, or punch his preferences with a stylus on a computer card, the form of the means by which he indicates his choice gives him an essential control over his local government and its officers. By recording his will secretly, the voter is free to express his convictions by splitting his ballot, voting for a change, or electing to maintain the present officers or their party in control of the affairs of his community.

The Short Ballot

The control the voter has through the secret ballot is considerably strengthened if the job facing him on election day is to choose a limited number of officers to fill important decision-making positions rather than to select a large number of officers, many for minor posts with only non-discretionary duties. A long ballot listing many minor offices may be more than a little frustrating when the voter is asked to choose between candidates he does not know to fulfill the duties of an office with which the voter is unfamiliar. In such cases, the voter's control passes from his hands by the process vividly described by reformer Richard S. Childs, since the voter begins to

> accept ready-made tickets of candidates tied up in bunches like asparagus, and power thereby leaves the hands of the voter and gravitates to the politicians and ticket makers. The persons who get elected on long ballots are frequently under more obligation to the ticket makers than to the rank and file of voters.[3]

A position contrary to that of Childs' also may be advanced. To believe that "ticket makers" have disappeared because of the short ballot is naive. In fact, their power may have been enhanced because of the big sums of money needed to run successfully for office in large jurisdictions. Candidates must often be bankrolled by community elites or interest groups, and may prove to be less representative, and even less accountable, to the general citizenry than candidates elected via the long ballot. In general, short ballots also have tended to favor incumbents over challengers because of the name identity and free publicity normally awarded officeholders seeking to succeed themselves.

METHODS OF DIRECT POPULAR CONTROL

The devices of initiative, referendum, and recall found fertile soil in the minds of American reformers who heralded them as the means to end boss rule and to restore government to the people. The initiative and referendum—as the two methods of direct legislative action—were intended to give the voter ''more democracy'' by letting him take remedial actions when his elected representatives failed to act or made a decision with which he did not agree.

A similar logic was advanced for placing the device of recall in the voter's hands. While not directly concerned with the determination of policies as is true of the initiative and referendum, it seeks to insure honesty and good behavior by public officers. The case for the use of the recall was aptly phrased by political scientist W. B. Munro who stated,

> Just when the people have elected a man burning with patriotic zeal, he suffers some sort of intercerebral accident. He is no longer able to interpret *vox populi*. His memory fails him. His formerly clear-cut views upon public questions become confused and incoherent. . . . The recall proposes to aid the officeholder in retaining a candidate's state of mind.[4]

The recall originated in the city of Los Angeles in 1903 and was first applied to elective state officers in Oregon by a constitutional amendment approved by the voters five years later. The recall now pertains to elective state officials in thirteen states and has spread even more widely on the local level.

Direct legislation provisions are more common in local governments with strong legislative councils than in those with weaker lawmaking bodies. Thus they are found more often in cities with newer, stronger forms of government such as the council-manager, commission, or strong mayor-chief administrative officer forms and in counties with executives serving at the pleasure of an elected board. Citizens have seemed to be willing to accept the stronger governing councils inherent in these plans if the public is provided the safeguards of the initiative, referendum, and recall.

The Initiative

Simply defined, the initiative is a device whereby a prescribed number or percentage of qualified voters, through the use of a petition, may have a charter amendment or local ordinance placed on the ballot for adoption or rejection by the electorate. Such petitions for ordinances are normally submitted to the local legislative body. If that group adopts the proposed ordinance, the matter is not placed before the electorate since the objective sought by the petitioners has been gained. If the legislative body fails to approve the proposal, it is put on the ballot at the next general election or at a special election. If approved by a majority of the voters it becomes a statement of local policy with the same force as an ordinance approved by the council or commission.

The direct initiative process involves various steps. The first consists of drafting the proposal. This may be done by any group of interested citizens but commonly they request legal assistance to assure acceptable wording. In the second phase, the proposal is given a preliminary filing with the proper local official who prescribes the form and outlines the procedures to be followed in its circulation for signatures, which is the third step. The actual percentage or number of signatures required varies among governmental units but generally is prescribed as either a fixed percent of qualified voters or of votes cast in the last preceding election. At the fourth stage, the petitions are filed with the proper official and the signatures are checked for irregularities and unqualified signers. The fifth step is a continuing one that began simultaneously with the first phase. This concerns the education of the electorate about the nature and purpose of the proposal. However, the educational campaign becomes intensified at this stage and deserves listing as a separate step. The sixth step is the election at which the proposal is submitted to the voters. If rejected by them, the matter ends, at least temporarily; but if approved by a majority, then the seventh step—the promulgation of the proposal in ordinance form—is made and becomes a part of the law of the community.

Under indirect initiative proceedings, the same first four steps are followed, except that a different number or percentage of signatures may be required. At this point, however, the proposal goes to the local lawmaking body for consideration. If this group approves the proposal without amendment, the fifth and sixth steps outlined above are eliminated and the proposal becomes law upon passage of the implementing ordinance by the legislative body.

The Referendum

The referendum is a means by which decisions of local lawmaking bodies do not become public policies until the community's electorate votes its concurrence with the policies by accepting them by majority vote. The concept of the referendum as a method of securing public approval of proposals is not a recent development. It was used as early as 1641 in Massachusetts, and the 1780 constitution of that state was ratified by a popular vote of its citizens.

The referendum vote may take three distinct forms. The oldest is usually identified as the compulsory referendum; it pertains to the mandatory referral to the electorate of such issues as charter amendments, bond issues, special tax levies, and boundary changes. Referenda on such issues are stipulated in local charters, state constitutions, or state laws; being required they are examples of the compulsory referendum. Some measures thus must always be submitted to voters for approval, even in states where the initiative and referendum systems herein described do not prevail.

A second form is known as the optional referendum because the decision to put the proposal to a popular vote lies with the local legislative body. This method of measuring public sentiment is sometimes used on controversial matters on which local lawmakers may be hesitant to take a stand. Examples might be approval of certain types of activities such as horseracing or the prohibition of beer parlors or key policy questions such as a master plan for the community's development. A difference of opinion exists as to the nature of the electorate's decision on optional referendum questions. In most communities the vote is considered binding on the lawmaking body, but in some areas the vote is considered to be advisory only and members of the local legislative body may either implement or ignore the results as they see fit. In a few states action by a local governing body referring a measure, in the absence of state permission, is deemed an act of improper delegation.

The third type of referendum is known as the protest or petition form. This procedure enables the voters to pass upon measures already approved by their lawmaking body. In communities authorizing this form of popular referendum, the charter stipulates (or state law may prescribe) that ordinances will not become effective for a period of 30, 60, or 90 days after their passage. During this interim, citizens may file a protest petition by acquiring a certain number of signatures asking for submission of the ordinance to the electorate. If the petitions are in order and a sufficient number of signatures are obtained, the legislative body must submit the ordinance to the voters at either a special election or at the next general election. If the vote by the electorate is unfavorable, then it has been popularly vetoed and does not go into effect. Some types of actions by the lawmaking body are exempt from this kind of protest referendum because of their importance and controversial nature. Such matters normally include tax rates and appropriations, location of public buildings, major public works program, and emergency measures.

The procedural steps in the referendum process, if petitions are required, are very similar to those in the initiative. The basic difference between the two devices is clear, however: the referendum is negative in character because it seeks to check actions that have been or might be taken while the initiative is used to originate policies when the lawmakers refuse or fail to act. The referendum then is a tool to combat errors of commission while the initiative is employed to correct errors of omission.

The Recall

Methods have always existed for removing public officials from their positions by the judicial process, impeachment, or legislative or executive action. Recall provides a procedure for voters to remove an unsatisfactory local official before the expiration of his elective term. The recall is similar, to the initiative and referendum in that it is set in motion and executed by citizen action and is another weapon in their hands to make more effective control of their government.

The procedural steps in starting recall proceedings are comparable to those in other direct legislation actions, but several significant differences are present. While the process is begun by petitions, they must state the precise grounds for the removal of the official and the percentage of signatures required is usually from two to three times higher than that for initiative proceedings. The petitions must be filed, and if found valid upon checking by the appropriate official, the election must be called within a definite time limit.

The recall ballot may take one of three general forms. Under the first, the name of the official in question is put on the ballot and the voters are asked to decide whether he should or should not be removed from office. If a majority vote for his removal occurs, then a second election must be held to select his successor. This method has the disadvantage of two elections, but it usually assures that the successor will be a majority rather than a plurality choice of the voters. More important is the fair consideration it gives the incumbent, because he runs against his record in office rather than engaging in a popularity contest with the other candidates.

A second ballot form combines the questions of removal of an officer and the selection of a successor. The question of removal is at the top of the ballot and those who vote "yes" are asked to vote for their choice of successors listed below. The successor is almost certain to be a plurality choice because usually several candidates seek the office.

The third type of recall ballot requires the official in question to run against other candidates to determine whether the incumbent or someone else shall complete the balance of the term. This is the least desirable form because the voters favoring recall may split their votes among several candidates to succeed the incumbent, while his supporters will vote solidly for his retention. As a consequence the officer may be retained in office although a majority of the voters favor his removal. This type of election also amounts to a new popularity contest rather than an evaluation of whether the incumbent's performance violates his original mandate.

Evaluation of Initiative, Referendum, and Recall

The democratic devices of initiative, referendum, and recall were extensively adopted at a time when reformers were demanding the return of government to the control of the people from whom it had been wrested by bosses and political machines. However, a word of caution was sounded even when these reforms were being widely championed. Writing in 1909, historian Charles Beard stated that,

> We have apparently assumed that it (the electorate) can do everything from deciding who among ten thousand should be the clerk of a municipal court to prescribing what should be done with the surface dirt removed from a street by a public contractor.[5]

As with reforms in general, the results have not lived up to the expectations of their proponents or caused the dire consequences predicted by their opponents. And, as with all reforms, there are both merits and shortcomings to the direct legislation devices.

Concerning the initiative and referendum, the case for their use may be built on the following merits: (1) popular sovereignty is strengthened because these devices may be used by the people to enact desired proposals and to defeat objectionable legislation; (2) the devices may be employed by the people as a counterbalancing force to the efforts of special interest groups to secure favorable legislation; (3) their use stimulates the interest of many persons in issues of public policy and helps to educate voters; (4) their availability lessens citizen fear in authorizing strong local legislatures, and results in fewer charter restrictions on legislative action; (5) their possible use has a salutary effect on lawmaking bodies, stimulating them to take action in cases where they might otherwise take no action if such direct citizen controls did not exist; and (6) the devices function as an essential check on legislative action (except for emergency and other excepted measures) thus giving the voters the opportunity to participate in the enactment of much important legislation—if they desire to do so.

The major counter arguments are largely reverse statements of the merits of direct legislative devices, which may become shortcomings through excessive use. Briefly outlined, they are as follows: (1) while popular sovereignty may be strengthened, representative government is impaired because popular distrust of elected representatives is encouraged and some lawmakers may refuse to take stands, leaving too many decisions to the voters; (2) use of these devices assumes that the voters are informed on the many issues they are called upon to support or defeat, but in practice they operate to further the interests of special groups; (3) their utilization runs counter to the principle of the short-ballot movement since the ballot is lengthened by these proposals; (4) many important decisions of public policy are decided by a mere plurality because many voters will not participate in special elections on such issues, or on all the issues at any single election; (5) their use adds significantly to the costs of elections and campaigns and often results in special elections; (6) their employment ignores the fact that government is becoming so technical and complex as to make it politically unfeasible to frame many issues of policy so that a simple ''yes'' or ''no'' vote by the electors results in a satisfactory decision; (7) the availability of the devices enables elected representatives to ''cop out'' on making controversial policy decisions by shunting them off to the voters; and (8) funding for their use—from signature-gathering to billboards, newspaper advertisements and mailers—is costly, thereby making these devices a special tool of big interests.

Similarly a case both for and against the use of the recall may be made by considering its advantages and disadvantages. And its practice has revealed that it may be used either in behalf of the public interest or to serve the selfish or partisan interests of a strong and vocal minority. On the positive side, the availability of the recall may (1) produce a salutary effect on the conduct of public officials who recognize the possible force of this ''gun'' behind the door; (2) encourage citizens to grant their officers a longer term in office because this device for their removal, if deemed desirable, exists; and (3) increase voter confidence in his government because the unfaithful officeholder may be removed before the end of his scheduled term. Certainly this device has been used to remove some local officials who betrayed the trust placed in them or who lost the confidence of the voters. However, other officials have been recalled because they voted for unpopular policies or performed the duties of their offices too vigorously to please certain groups or interests in the community.

As in the case of the initiative and referendum, the use of the recall may result in a longer ballot, increase the public costs when special elections are called, and impose a greater burden on the voter by asking him to make a further public decision. In addition, the threat of recall may serve as a restraining influence on public officers to tread softly and take no controversial stands. Also, a case may be made that the recall is not necessary as other means for the removal of unfaithful officials exist, and the device is sometimes activated more for political recrimination than for the purposes intended.

As a summary evaluation, citizen use of the initiative, referendum, and recall should not be condemned because of occasional misuse. Certainly some poor choices for elective offices have won the support of the people and yet we would not seriously consider doing away with elections even though some demagogues have been chosen over more public-spirited candidates. The three devices are a useful and effective means of citizen control and should be recognized as such rather than as cure-alls for the ills of local government. When the devices are so conceived, they may be employed to achieve their purposes and citizen control is appreciably enhanced.

OPEN MEETINGS OPENLY ARRIVED AT

In an effort to achieve the goal of "open decisions arrived at openly," public hearings have long been widely used in local government. Meetings of local governing bodies are open to the public, and the meeting chambers of city councils, county commissions, and township officials are designed to accommodate interested citizens and to enable them to participate in the proceedings. When controversial matters are under consideration, the governing body commonly holds public hearings. Normally these proceedings are run fairly informally and interested citizens who desire to do so may speak for or against the pending matter. Such hearings serve the double purpose of letting citizens air their grievances and informing the public body of citizen opinion.

While general agreement exists that public business should be open to the public, this has not always occurred in practice. Some public meetings of public bodies have been held after private sessions before the open meeting. Decisions have been actually arrived at in discussion behind closed doors, and the formal meeting became a "rubber stamp" session to legalize the decisions reached in the closed session. In such cases, the public has been denied the opportunity to listen to the discussion of the matter or to participate effectively in decisions affecting local public policy. Even the architecture of many council chambers or hearing rooms is intimidating to the citizen. The council or board often sits on a raised platform and looks down on the speakers and the audience. The massive size of some chambers and the marbled columns are other intimidating features. The scheduling of such meetings often makes it impractical for some interested citizens to attend because of commitments to work and other activities.[6]

In several states legislation has been recently enacted forbidding closed meetings by local governing bodies. Such a law passed in California in 1953 is typical of similar laws in other states. The key words of the California legislation state that "All meetings of the legislative body of a local agency shall be open and public, and all persons shall be permitted to attend any meeting of the legislative body of a local agency, except as provided in this chapter."[7] The exception refers to personnel matters and consideration of contracts, but all other deliberations of such agencies as city councils, school boards, planning commissions, library boards, or recreation commissions must be held in open sessions. The California act even extends this requirement to the meetings of private agencies if they are supported in part by public funds and have a public official as an *ex officio* board member. Violation of the act is a misdemeanor, and a citizen may obtain a court order to prevent secret or closed sessions.

PRESSURE OR INTEREST GROUPS

An acceptable working concept of a pressure group is any organized group that attempts to influence some phase of public policy. This definition points out the two principal differences between political parties and pressure groups.[8] The latter are more interested in controlling or affecting specific policies of governmental agencies than in controlling their principal officers and are more homogeneous groups than political parties. Pressure groups consist of persons who share the same basic interests and point of view while a political party has to be considerably broader in interests and policy viewpoints to gain sufficient support to fulfill its basic purpose of winning public office.[9]

Political parties and pressure groups have much in common, however, in the arena of the local political process because both seek the implementation of policies. Only in recent years have pressure groups been accorded the dignity of being recognized as "necessary evils" rather than merely as evils, and local public policies sometimes may be identified as the result of the interaction of the various interested pressure groups upon one another. In rural areas the agricultural interests usually predominate, while labor groups normally wield considerable influence in industrial cities. The business community is always an active interest group and so are many citizen organizations such as taxpayers' associations, homeowners' leagues, roadside councils, and other groups. In fact, it is difficult to think of any organized group that does not attempt to influence policy at some time or another; in this sense all of them function as interest groups. Churches, women's clubs, Kiwanis, Rotary, Boy Scouts, Parent-Teacher Associations, and so on take formal stands in support of or in opposition to particular policies, and when they do they become pressure groups the same as chambers of commerce, labor leagues, farm groups, and other organizations more generally identified with special interests.

Because the basic objective of all pressure groups is to influence action favorable to their own interests, they engage in various common techniques or methods of action. Included are: (1) appearing at public meetings of local legislative bodies or at other public hearings to present the views of their members; (2) initiating legislation favorable to them and working to defeat proposed laws deemed harmful to their interests; (3) exerting influence on lawmakers by direct or indirect means or both; (4) issuing news stories, reports, or other forms of publicity; (5) spearheading letter-writing or telephone campaigns to disseminate their views; (6) engaging in research to prepare reports and uncover evidence in support of their views; and (7) attempting to influence the selection of candidates within local political parties and then working to secure their nomination and election. Many other methods may be used by particular groups at specific times, but this list represents the general activities common to most pressure groups.

Recognition of these groups as vital to the democratic process, or at least as evils necessary for its proper functioning, means they fulfill some useful functions. First, pressure groups help inform the citizenry on policy issues and stimulate open discussion. Second, they may supply public officials with useful information that enables the persons in office to make more informed decisions. Third, they gather, organize, and present individual opinions on specific issues in a more effective way than if the voices remained unmarshaled. Fourth, they provide a form of functional representation for their members since it is extremely difficult for a city councilman or county commissioner to know and reflect the views of all the different groups within his constituency. And, fifth, they serve in large part to fill the political vacuum caused by weak political parties at the local level.

The activities of pressure groups, however, are not always commendable and a number of criticisms are directed at them and their actions. Chief among them are (1) the use of certain methods or techniques inimical to the proper functioning of local democratic government—such as inordinate pressure or the offer of bribes; (2) the inequality of groups because of their wide differences in membership, financial resources, and cohesion; (3) the fact that social-oriented or consumer groups often fare badly in contests with other groups; (4) the inability to determine the real purpose of some organized groups with impressive but unrepresentative names; and (5) the absence of internal checks within the machinery of local government to counterbalance the influence of interest groups.

Although such internal checks may be missing, some external checks operate to hold pressure groups in line. First is the rise of new interest groups to espouse other points of view than those championed by existing organizations. Second, local lawmakers usually must rely on the support of various interest groups instead of on a single organized interest, thus helping the groups to keep each other in balance. Third, there are standards of conduct that no pressure group may flaunt too often or too deliberately. Fourth, the quality of leadership in local government is improving so that the public interest is more effectively represented as a countervailing force to special interests. The system of checks and balances in local government operates somewhat imperfectly to limit the effectiveness of such groups, but their influence does not normally embrace all three branches of government, which act as brakes or checks on the actions of each other.

Political scientist Betty Zisk has conducted an interesting study of council members and interest groups in eighty-two cities of the San Francisco Bay Area.[10] She distinguishes three types of council members: (1) pluralists, those who esteem groups and perceive many of them; (2) tolerants, those who are neutral towards groups; and (3) antagonists, those who reject groups. When asked what makes a group influential, the most frequent responses in order were that they (a) represent important people other than business, (b) are active and interested and attend council meetings, (c) represent the business community, (d) have council and community interests at heart, (e) possess issue expertise, (f) are concerned with important problems and projects, (g) are large in size, and (h) represent voting power, such as activity in or expenditures on elections.[11]

Zisk's study was guided by the general hypothesis that the behavior of elected officials toward those attempting to influence policy outcomes is related to their previous view toward lobbying. She found that the political activities of interest groups make a difference—not only for the attitude and work of local policymakers but also for the content of public policy decisions. She concludes that the local group is perhaps the major functional equivalent in the local nonpartisan setting to the political party or to less obvious power elites.[12]

The effectiveness of interest groups on local governments possibly may be overemphasized, as the presence of veto groups at higher levels of government tends to depress the importance of any single group to exert unusual influence. Most local communities, however, do not have the intermixture of competitive and opposing interests that operate in political arenas at higher governmental levels. As a result, certain interest groups may be considerably more effective at the local level.

INFORMATION FOR CITIZENS

If the citizen is to carry out his responsibilities to his local government, he needs to give considerable time to the study of politics in his community or have various resources that may assist him in assembling the necessary information. The important relationship of available knowledge to the exercise of responsible citizenship by a voter is drawn by one writer in these words, "a lack of information about city government usually results in a paucity of interest in government." [13] This section is devoted to a discussion of several important sources of information helpful in aiding the citizen to be informed about his community and its government.

Among community resources for informing citizens and shaping their opinions, special mention must be made of the local newspaper, or the local section of a larger newspaper serving that community. Although few people would go so far as to agree with columnist Walter Lippman that the newspaper is the "Bible of democracy," its influence as a constructive—or obstructive—force in the community is undeniable. The influence of the local press extends to both the voter and the public officials. The fear of adverse newspaper publicity in the local press helps keep public officers toeing the mark in the performance of their duties. The power of the press may be misused, but this suspicion is rightly or wrongly largely reserved for newspapers of large circulations and big advertising accounts such as metropolitan dailies. While recent studies report a declining role for the newspaper in the shaping of public policies and in the success of press-supported candidates in elections, the newspaper remains an important source of information regardless of whether its recommendations win public acceptance at the polls.

Television and radio are other media of expanding importance in numerous communities. Many candidates and proponents of policies rely more on spot announcements on radio and TV than on newspaper support and on radio and TV editorials than on newspaper endorsements. The point is that the means of mass media have an important role in informing the citizenry, but their influence may be difficult to counter by candidates or policies not endorsed or opposed by these media.

Local election campaigns are another important way of informing citizens about their government and local officials. Too many local campaigns are still devoted to "mud-slinging" tactics, and the outcome of local elections is still too frequently determined by inconsequential factors. However, most campaigns are filled with public appearances by the candidates, and citizens have many opportunities to direct questions to such aspirants for public office. Although the primary purpose of campaigns is to win votes rather than to inform the voters, there is reason to hope that local campaigns can be and are being conducted on a higher plane than earlier. This is the responsibility of the citizen himself, since candidates, as their political parties, will conduct the type of campaign necessary to win voter support. If buffoonery, appeal to prejudices, and mud-slinging prove successful, then these methods will persist. As a long time politician has commented,

> The Madison Avenue experts in public taste and public demand demonstrated that logic and pertinent facts were second in effectiveness to oft-repeated emotional stimuli. Campaign managers discovered that portraits of a good-looking candidate, accompanied by a catchy slogan, influenced more votes than did treatment of the real issue.[14]

On the other hand, if voters support candidates because of their personal qualifications, stand on public issues, and promises of performance in office, these factors will become increasingly important campaign issues. In general, room for optimism exists in view of the belief that "good government is good politics'' seems to be gaining greater acceptance at the local level.

Citizen organizations constitute a third important source of information. As used here, the term "citizen organization" is limited to citizen research and fact-finding agencies with a broad interest in local government and to community councils. These agencies bear such labels as bureaus of municipal or governmental research, voter leagues, leagues of women voters, citizen unions or leagues, civic councils or leagues, and citizen committees. Regardless of their specific names, such agencies share the common features of being nonpartisan in composition and of working to improve the government of their community. These organizations can be quite effective in arousing and sustaining citizen interest in government and in focusing voter attention on community problems.

Agencies or avenues to provide information also are present within the government structure itself. Within the local governmental level, extensive use is made of citizen advisory commissions or councils to work with government agencies and programs. Park commissions, library boards, planning commissions, recreation commissions, welfare boards, and health boards, to name only a few, are adjunct agencies of local governments in communities all across the nation. Besides such standing boards and commissions, special or *ad hoc* citizen committees are appointed as the need for their services arise.

The annual local government report to its citizens is becoming increasingly common in communities across the nation. By giving the citizen the facts about his government, the purpose such reports are aimed to serve, it is hoped that the citizens can reach a more informed judgment in selecting the officers to serve them and in shaping the policies of their government. In earlier years, annual reports were too often tabulations of uninterpreted statistics and columns of figures or "publicity statements" in praise of current officials. Modern reports, however, are often attractive and readable accounts of the progress, projects, and problems of the community prepared in pamphlet form or as supplements to the local newspaper.

In addition to the public hearings discussed earlier, budget hearings provide another means for the citizen to inform himself about the operations and programs of his local government. Such hearings open to the public are required by law in most states, but few citizens normally attend. Too often those attending do so in protest against a proposed tax increase or expenditure rather than to gain information about their government. Such hearings, however, may be a valuable source of information to citizens and furnish the local legislative body with insight into the sentiments of the community.

STRUCTURED CITIZEN PARTICIPATION

Citizen participation became a key element in several recent federally-sponsored programs including urban renewal, community action, and model cities. In urban renewal programs, the concept of citizen participation originally involved civic leaders in an advisory capacity to the local planning agency but it later was expanded to include citizens in the area affected by the renewal plan.

The key phrase for citizen input in war on poverty programs was "maximum feasible participation," and the hope was to achieve a role for the poor as citizen advisers because the goal was to rehabilitate people rather than buildings. The emphasis was placed on organizing and directing the demands of the poor toward the institutions serving them to make those agencies more responsive. Known as Community Action Programs, the poverty programs became embroiled in political questions and the expected role for the poor became less acceptable to established political and economic elites.

While the model cities program also called for widespread citizen participation, the role was less ambitious than in the war on poverty programs. The act provided channels to enable the poor to express "desires and identity" with the projects being planned, but the actual planning and decision-making rested with the official city agencies.

General evaluations of these attempts to "build-in" citizen participation are fairly pessimistic, but a primary legacy of the efforts was the development of new political elites from the ranks of minorities formerly unrepresented in the pluralism of city politics. A recommendation made by many commentators has been for the further development of new institutional forms to represent the interests of the poor and elevate them to the larger political and social structure of the communities across the nation. The problem appears to be one of developing means so that the interest of the poor may be accommodated without arousing the countervailing power of the non-poor so that the anticipated change does not become stalemated.[15]

A result of these efforts to bring new activists into local politics has been the success of some of them in the local electoral arena. University and college cities are particularly fertile sites because of the large student vote. Such candidates have been elected in such places as Berkeley and Santa Barbara, California; Boulder, Colorado; Champaign-Urbana, Illinois; Lincoln, Nebraska; Austin, Texas; and Madison, Wisconsin. In his survey of these success stories, columnist Neil Peirce states,

> Whether one agrees or disagrees with the politics of the new radical politicans, the vitality of American democracy is reaffirmed by their decision to work through elective politics, rather than fulminating in vain against "the system" from without.[16]

SUMMARY

Democratic local government is based on the premise of informed citizen interest and participation in community affairs. Educational programs to interest citizens and to inform them about their government thus are to be encouraged. Although local governments are now faced with a number of serious problems in finding adequate sources of financial support, improving levels of particular services, providing new services, and so on, the greatest problem lies in arousing their citizens to take an active interest in and to participate in the affairs of their community. Democracy functions most adequately when each citizen contributes his best to the community, and this may be achieved only if citizens are informed. Citizens who are informed are active citizens, and these are two of the surest safeguards against corrupt and unresponsive local government.

A possible unfortunate result of citizen abdication of their responsibilities and obligations has been pointed out in a study of suburban politics. [17] According to Robert Wood, the suburbanite, an escapee from the divisive conflicts and hostilities of big cities, may become apolitical altogether and indifferent in his new "peaceful" setting. Trusting problems of the community to the experts—the trained and educated local administrators— the suburban citizen seeks and receives local government by automation. In such a community, the individual abdicates his responsibility and no action is required in this democratic haven of right-thinking citizens.

NOTES

1. From *The Ladies' Home Journal* as cited in Joseph E. McLean, "Politics is What You Make It," Public Affairs Pamphlet No. 181, New York, 1954, p. 1.
2. Joseph P. Harris, *Election Administration in the United States,* Brookings Institution, 1934, p. 154.
3. Richard S. Childs, "Theories of Responsive Government Prove Practical," *Public Management,* 29 (December, 1947), 353-5.
4. W. B. Munro (ed.), *The Initiative, Referendum and Recall,* D. Appleton & Co., 1912, pp. 299-300.
5. Charles A. Beard, "The Ballot's Burden," *Political Science Quarterly,* 24 (December, 1909), 589-614.
6. For a devastating description of how a county supervisor used his official prerogatives to intimidate speakers, see Bill Boyarsky, *Back Room Politics, How Your Local Politicians Work, Why Your Government Doesn't, and What You Can Do About It,* J. P. Tarcher, 1974.
7. *California Code,* Sections 54950-54958.
8. For an excellent distinction between political parties and pressure groups, see Lewis Froman, *People and Politics,* Prentice-Hall, 1962, p. 101.
9. The increasing literature on interest groups may be classified into four broad categories. The group theory approach is well represented by David Truman,

The Governmental Process, Alfred A. Knopf, 1951. Lester Milbrath's *The Washington Lobbyists,* Rand McNally, 1963, illustrates the communications model. The interaction model is shown in Harmon Zeigler and Michael Baer, *Lobbying: Interaction and Influence in American State Legislatures,* Wadsworth, 1969. The fourth model, which is the role analysis approach, is utilized by John Wahlke *et. al., The Legislative System: Explorations in Legislative Behavior,* John Wiley and Sons, 1962.

10. Betty H. Zisk, *Local Interest Politics: A One-Way Street,* Bobbs-Merrill, 1973.
11. *Ibid.,* p. 26.
12. *Ibid.,* pp. 140-41.
13. Murdock Martin, *The Annual City Report: Why and How,* Bureau of Governmental Research and Service, Florida State University, 1955, p. 1.
14. John A. Ford, *Thirty Explosive Years in Los Angeles County,* Huntington Library, 1961, p. 209.
15. See Daniel P. Moynihan, *Maximum Feasible Misunderstanding, Community Action in the War on Poverty,* The Free Press, 1969; Jon Van Til and Sally Bould Van Til, "Citizen Participation and Social Policy: The End of the Cycle," *Social Problems,* 17, No. 3 (Winter, 1970), 313-23; James Q. Wilson, "Citizen Participation in Urban Renewal," in Wilson (ed.), *Urban Renewal: The Record and Controversy,* M. I. T. Press, 1966; John C. Donovan, *The Politics of Poverty,* Pegasus, 1967; and Hans B. Speigel (ed.), *Citizen Participation in Urban Development,* NTL Institute for Applied Behavioral Sciences, 1968.
16. Neil R. Peirce, "Some Activists Join City Hall," in *Los Angeles Times,* February 22, 1976, Part IX.
17. Robert C. Wood, *Suburbia, Its People and Their Politics,* Houghton Mifflin, 1958, p. 197.

Chapter 7
County Government

Counties range greatly in population throughout the United States and even often in one state. In a section of a state, for instance, counties typically will be rural governments, while in another part of the same state they may be primarily urban in character. As a reflection of such differences, counties have been the object of classification in a number of states. Its purpose is to provide greater freedom and variation of treatment than would be possible under uniform legislation, with less state interference and direction than is customary under special legislation.

TABLE 2
NUMBER OF COUNTIES BY POPULATION CATEGORIES

Population category	Number of counties
1,000,001 and over	23
500,001-1,000,000	53
250,001-500,000	51
100,001-250,000	185
75,001-100,000	118
50,001-75,000	208
25,001-50,000	566
5,001-25,000	1,535
1,001-5,000	280
1,000 and fewer	25

Source: Bureau of the Census, *County and City Data Book, 1972,* Government Printing Office, 1973.

Classification by population alone, however, is somewhat inadequate because various factors may tend to distort the basic plan. An unusually large rural county may be grouped with counties essentially urban if total population is the only base, or a more densely populated county may be so small in area that its total population is low enough to classify it with more rural counties. Although not now used, a population density classification seems more realistic for differentiating among the several classes of counties. Under this plan, the area of the county becomes an important adjunct of its population since the two are combined for determining average population density. The population density of the more than 3,000 American counties ranges from a high of 66,923 persons per square mile in New York County, New York to a low of less than one-half person a square mile in fifteen counties scattered across the United States.[1]

FOUR-FOLD DIVISION OF COUNTIES

The classification of *rural* would be reserved for counties with a population density of 100 or fewer persons per square mile. Citizens in such areas receive only minimum governmental services and usually are not very vocal in demanding the newer, so-called "urban-type" services. The second classification, *semi-rural,* would embrace counties with densities ranging from 101 to 250 persons a square mile. The third classification is *semi-urban* or *rurban,* a grouping to include counties with densities ranging from 251 persons per square mile to a maximum of 1,000 persons. Counties in this group discharge a number of services and functions not provided by their more rural counterparts. The fourth classification, *urban,* is reserved for counties with population densities of 1,001 or more persons a square mile. These counties are truly units of urban government and are called upon to perform all the urban type services.[2]

Table 3 illustrates the application of this proposed classification plan in selected states. The states were chosen to represent geographic sections of the nation as well as to include states that are primarily urban or rural in character. A meaningful classification system, however, is only the first part of a two-phase program for making counties more effective governmental units. The other part relates to a system of optional charters, under which the citizens of any county may select, by popular vote, one of several alternative plans of organization. General legislation by class is more beneficial if the substance of the laws may be implemented through a governmental organization selected by the citizens in any specific county. Laws providing optional forms of county government are still the exception rather than the rule, but progress in this area has been realized in the past few years. The typical alternatives open to counties in those few states that grant county home-rule privileges are discussed later in this chapter.

TABLE 3
PROPOSED CLASSIFICATION OF COUNTIES IN SELECTED STATES

State	Number of counties	Average density	No. of counties by classification			
			Rural	Semi-rural	Semi-urban	Urban
New Jersey	21	953	0	6	7	8
Massachusetts	14	727	3	3	4	4
Pennsylvania	67	262	32	13	18	4
California	58	128	41	6	6	5
Florida	67	126	48	12	6	1
Missouri [a]	114	68	102	8	1	3
Mississippi	82	47	77	5	0	0
Kansas	105	28	99	2	3	1
Oregon	36	22	33	2	0	1
Nevada	17	4	16	1	0	0

[a]St. Louis City is separated from St. Louis County and is not shown in this table.

Although the classification system based on population density outlined above does not yet exist in any state, the four-fold classification of counties as rural, semi-rural, semi-urban, and urban are employed for discussion purposes in this chapter. This avoids a stereotyped approach to counties, their organization, problems and prospects. The four-fold classification system also enables us to differentiate more meaningfully among the three major roles that counties undertake. In its first role as an administrative district of the state, the county performs various functions including those of an elections and judicial district. In its second role, as a unit of local government, the county is recognized increasingly as a municipal rather than a quasi-municipal entity and performs both governmental and proprietary functions. In its third role, the county is becoming a coordinating agency for certain programs and functions of the local governments within its boundaries in such fields, as planning, zoning, centralized purchasing, personnel administration, library services, air pollution control. While the first role is common to all counties, the second and third roles are limited to the more urban counties.

The Rural County

Rural counties in America largely assume only the first of the three suggested roles of county government—that as an administrative district of the state. As such, a number of traditional functions are performed, but direct services to citizens are limited. Typically the county renders such required functions as law enforcement and judicial administration, elections administration, road construction and maintenance, public welfare, and recording of legal documents. Health is another function normally assigned to counties, but in rural counties this means the part-time services of one doctor. While this limited activity might meet the legal requirement for filling this county office, it fails to provide even the minimum health services expected of such an office.

A further important function of rural counties is agricultural extension work through the office of the county agent. The program is financed jointly by national, state, and county governments, but actual administration of the program rests with the county agent working in close cooperation with the state agricultural college. In many counties services to farm wives are provided by a home demonstration agent, and a 4-H Club agent works with the boys and girls in Club activities.

The structure of government in rural counties usually is as simple as the constitution of the state and its statutes permit. Normally none of the optional offices is created, but the required elective offices are filled. The incumbents provide minimum services required by law but the positions are not full-time and the officers usually pursue other means of livelihood. Such counties provide the intimate and personal government of friends and neighbors often stoutly defended as a bastion of local democracy in action—or sharply criticized as inadequate and unresponsive.

The Semi-Rural County

The semi-rural county differs from the rural county in degree rather than in kind. It probably has a few more and slightly larger cities and towns that combine to pull the average density of its population above 100 per square mile. Usually the largest of these towns is the county seat and its citizens receive urban-type services from their own city government. As counties approach the upper limit of the suggested density range of this classification (250), their governmental problems change in both degree and kind from those in counties at the lower end of the density scale, and citizen demands begin to mount for expanded county services in health, welfare, libraries, and law enforcement.

Such counties present really two patterns of living—rural and small town. However, the county has a uniform pattern of limited services except within the town that is the county seat. Here often a rivalry may develop between city law enforcement officers and those of the county, between the city health officer and his county counterpart, and so forth. What county parks exist are usually found in or near the county seat, but these are provided for the use of all its citizens.

Again the pattern of government is fairly simple and provides few of the optional offices permitted by state law. Normally the elective offices are full-time positions and the county courthouse serves as the center of county government. The county governing board continues to perform most of the functions that might be lodged in more densely settled counties in special-function boards for such purposes as welfare, assessment, and elections.

The Semi-Urban or Rurban County

The semi-urban county still has sections of an agricultural character, but the number and size of its urban centers are greater than are those in the semi-rural counties. A portion of the county's area is quite urban in nature as a number of cities and towns probably cluster around each other. Often the clustering of people extends beyond the incorporated limits of the cities and towns into surrounding county areas. In such unincorporated but urban sectors the citizens require more intensifed police and fire protection services, garbage and refuse collection, and sewer services. If they are not furnished by the county, then special districts are established, because the citizens need these services and will secure them by one means or another.

In counties of this class, an increasingly common practice is for the county to establish service districts (tax areas) in which only the citizens who benefit from the special services provided are taxed to support them. Such services include street lighting and paving, garbage and refuse collection, sewers, and recreational facilities. Also the county provides expanded and more adequate services in such fields as health, welfare, and libraries for all its citizens without forming service districts. Here the county begins to assume the second and third roles—as a unit of local government supplying direct services and as a unit to coordinate certain activities of cities and towns, especially in planning, zoning, and subdivision control.

The governmental structure in rurban counties becomes more complex. Deputies or assistants are needed for some offices, and citizen advisory boards are established to work with the government agencies. In addition, several special-function boards are organized to lighten the work load of the county governing body.

The Urban County

Counties with population densities of 1,001 or more persons per square mile are likely to be truly urban in character and render urban-type services for their citizens in unincorporated areas. Such counties contain at least one large city and are recognized as a metropolitan area or as a constituent part of such an area. Among the services such counties probably provide, in addition to those offered by the other classes of counties, are one or more public utilities, public housing, airports, and expanded recreational and cultural programs.

The urban county is discussed at some length in Chapter 18 and will not be further considered at this point. The number of urban counties across the nation is still relatively small, but they fulfill all three of the important roles of counties identified previously and are major units of local government.

FORMS OF COUNTY GOVERNMENT

Three general patterns of county government developed to meet the local values and needs of people in different sections of the United States. However, with the admission of new states and the rapidity of population growth, counties began to develop a great organizational variety across the country and sometimes even within a single state because of classification and home-rule charters. This variety is very apparent in county governing bodies, which are known by fourteen different titles.[3]

The Commissioner Form

From its beginning in Pennsylvania in 1724, the commission form of county government spread rapidly and is now the basic pattern in nearly two-thirds of the counties. Its distinguishing feature is that the county governing board members fulfill both legislative and executive functions. Governing bodies under this form are usually small in number, with three or five members chosen by district or at large. In some counties with election at large, candidates stand for election as representatives from the districts laid out within the county.

In addition to legislative and executive functions, county commissioners (called supervisors in some states including Iowa and California) still exercise judicial powers in some states. This is not common practice, however, because the county courts are usually separate. Normally the members of the county board hold no other county office, but as board members they may be called upon to wear a number of different "hats." They may serve, for instance, as the elections board, the assessment board, the tax appeals board, the planning board, and so on in addition to their basic roles as members of the county governing board.

An adaptation of the commission form exists in about 350 counties in which the chairperson of the board is a judicial officer, usually a judge of probate. The other board members, however, are commissioners and function solely in this role. The common size of these boards is again small, with three or five members as a rule.

The Supervisor Form

The second most frequent pattern of county government, which evolved in New York in 1703, is known as the supervisor form. The distinguishing feature of this plan is that the composition of its governing body is made up of persons who were first elected as township supervisors and who sit on the county board in an *ex officio* capacity. This plan is now used in nearly one-third of the counties. The size of the governing body in such counties differs widely, depending on the number of townships and cities (which are usually given representation based on population) lying within the specific county. While the more typical size of such boards is about 20 supervisors, 49 counties have boards of over 50 members, and 2 counties have more than 100 on their governing bodies.[4]

The nature and size of the governing board in these counties make it necessary for much of its actual work to be done through committees. This practice tends to make county government more obscure to the citizens because they often will know few of the committee members by name and even fewer of the members of the whole board. ''Buck-passing'' also is made easier since there is safety in large numbers if inaction becomes the board's general policy.

An adaptation of the supervisor form operates in most Kentucky and Tennessee counties. In these states the members of the county board are justices of the peace within the county and the chairperson is a county judge, usually the judge of probate. The members of these county governing boards thus serve judicial as well as administrative and legislative functions.

County Executive Forms

Since 1930 when Durham County, North Carolina, adopted a county manager form of government, a slow but continuing trend has been under way to correct a major weakness of county government in general—the absence of a single executive officer as a counterpart of the mayor or manager in American cities. Elected county executives have existed in counties since 1893 when Cook County, Illinois, established the position of President of the Board.[5] Plans calling for an elective chief executive officer have been adopted in recent years in several large counties.

The council-elected executive plan of county government is patterned after the council-manager plan of city government and has the same two essential features. The first is a relatively small elective governing board that serves as the policymaking body. The second is an appointive manager selected by and serving at the pleasure of the county board. Thus, the plan separates the determination of policy from its administration, with the latter the responsibility of the manager within the limits prescribed by the board. The principal board functions are to adopt ordinances expressing policy decisions, approve appropriations and tax levies, and appoint the manager. The manager's major duties, in turn, are to enforce the ordinances established by the board, appoint and supervise his principal subordinates, prepare the budget for board review, and give recommendations to the board on policy and administrative matters.

At present, forty-six counties in eighteen states have adopted the council-elected executive form of government. The counties with this form range from a low of about 1,000 in Haines Borough, Alaska, to a high of about 1.3 million in Dade County, Florida. County manager plans are most common in the states of New York, Alaska, and Maryland, which have nine, eight, and six counties, respectively. Of the 46 counties with this plan, 15 have populations of over 600,000; 13 are in the 250,000-600,000 range; 7 are in the 100,000-250,000 population range; and 11 have populations of under 100,000.[6] This form is suitable to urban or large-density counties as the need for executive controls becomes more recognized. This form of county government has been growing particularly rapidly in recent years.

County commission-administrator plans are more common than the council-elected executive plans. The former is similar to the latter in that the chief administrative officer (hereafter referred to as CAO) is appointed by and is responsible to the county governing board. The major differences pertain to the lesser powers of this officer in budget and personnel matters and his fewer "functional" powers, because more elective officers are likely to exist than under the county executive plan. While the executive is expected to "prepare" the annual budget for submission to the board, the CAO "collects" annual departmental requests and "transmits" them with recommendations to the board. In personnel matters, the executive's power is broader; he appoints his subordinates while the CAO "makes recommendations" on which the board takes action.

The office of CAO was first created in Iredell County, North Carolina, in 1927. The number has increased to 325 counties in thirty-eight states. Virginia with 62 counties has the largest number followed by 49 counties in North Carolina and 43 in California.[7] The plan seems to have worked with considerable success where adopted, and there have been but few abandonments. It seems to provide a reasonable compromise for counties desiring to achieve substantial administrative integration but not wishing to adopt the executive plan. The commission-administrator plan is the fastest growing form of county government in the United States, with 250 of the 325 adoptions occurring since 1960.

A form of quasi-executive leadership is present in numerous small counties through assigning administrative functions to an existing elective official. And the form has existed for quite awhile in some of them. A study of Wisconsin counties, for example, reveals that as long ago as 1942 the county clerk in seven counties "performed all the functions of a full county executive" and clerks in twenty-three additional counties were "the key general administrators of their counties."[8] Other studies have shown that such roles are assigned to or assumed by, for instance, the county judge in Arkansas; the "ordinary" or commissioner of roads and revenues in Georgia; the probate judge in Tennessee, Alabama, and Kentucky; the chairman of the county board in Wisconsin and North Carolina; the auditor in Indiana; and the chancery clerk in Mississippi. In many of these counties, however, the leadership exercised depended mainly on the ability of the incumbent of the office to get along with other county officials. While almost any arrangement to provide executive leadership in county government is worthwhile, the informal strengthening of an existing office seems hardly sufficient to meet a continuing need adequately.

THE STRUCTURE OF COUNTY GOVERNMENT

Since the substantial variety among American counties has been pointed out, to describe the structure of a "typical" county government may seem unrealistic. However, except for the nature of the composition of the governing board under the so-called commissioner and supervisor forms, the remaining structure of government in these counties is strikingly parallel. Since these plans are used in over four-fifths of all American counties, the structure of county government may be reasonably discussed in rather general terms.

The County Board

Except in a few instances when a single judge or nonjudicial officer serves as the central governing agency, county government is organized around a plural-member governing body. Although known by many names and consisting of a varied number of members serving differing terms of office, the administrative and legislative functions of county boards are quite uniform. As a quasi-municipal corporation serving primarily as an agent of state government, the primary legislative powers of the county board are fiscal and regulatory. In exercising its fiscal powers, the board levies county taxes, appropriates funds for public purposes, and incurs indebtedness. County regulatory powers embrace such actions as local health ordinances, zoning ordinances, licensing businesses and amusements, regulating the sale of fireworks. Among the administrative powers of county boards are responsibility for such county activities as the courthouse, jail, poor farm, and other county property; appointment of some officials; negotiation of contracts on behalf of the settlement of claims against the county; and administration of elections.

TABLE 4
TITLES OF COUNTY GOVERNING BODIES

Title of Governing body	States	No. of counties
Board of County Commissioners	14	743
Board of Commissioners	6	438
Board of Supervisors	6	424
County Board of Commissioners	6	342
County Court	4	299
Commissioner Court	1	254
County Board of Supervisors	2	181
Fiscal Court	1	120
Levy Court	2	78
Parish Council	1	62
Board of County Legislators	1	57
Board of Chosen Freeholders	1	21
County Judge	1	14
Borough Assembly	2	11
Totals	48	3,044

Source: Bureau of Census, "Governing boards of County Governments, 1965," Government Printing Office, 1965, and *County and City Book*, 1972, *op. cit.*

Except in a very small number of counties, members of county governing boards are popularly elected. Within the general framework of popular choice, however, there are five general methods for forming county boards. They are (1) election of all members at large; (2) election of all members at large with district residence required; (3) election of some members at large and some by district; (4) election of all members by district; and (5) election of all members by township or city or both. Election of members at large and by district both have some advantages. If the board is small and terms are staggered, election at large assures that the members feel a loyalty to the whole county and gives the voters a greater voice in choosing members of this board. Election by district is defended as assuring the spread of board membership geographically throughout the county and more adequate representation of local interests. In counties with larger boards, the plan combining election of some at large and district election of others has considerable merit.

Terms of county board members also show considerable diversity from state to state. Township supervisors serving on county boards in some states have only one-year terms, while county judges who function as board chairpersons in Tennessee have eight-year terms. Two and four-year terms are by far the most prevalent, although other boards serve terms of three and six years. In slightly over half the counties, terms of board members are staggered so that those of only a part of the membership expire in any election year. Four-year terms are most common, followed by two-year terms, three-year terms, and six-year terms in that order. Most commonly all members have terms of the same length, but this is not true in about 175 counties where the chairperson has a longer term than other members and in another 240 counties in which the terms of some members exceeds those of others.

Elective Officers

Elective county officers in American county government may be divided into two groups—general administrative officers and law enforcement or court officials. In the first group are the officers of treasurer, surveyor or engineer, assessor, superintendent of school, recorder or register of deeds, and county clerk. In the "judicial group" are the positions of sheriff, attorney or solicitor, court clerk, and coroner. While other elective county officers operate in a number of states, the ten listed above are the only ones found in over half of the states. These ten qualify as fitting into the structure of the "typical" county government. The duties of each of the ten are now presented in concise form.

Where existing, the office of *treasurer* usually has both tax collection and funds custody powers. This officer receives all moneys paid to the county and holds them in safekeeping until ordered to pay them out by warrants. In some counties the office has been abolished or consolidated with another such as tax collector.

Although a county post of long standing, the office of *surveyor or engineer* is of declining importance and sometimes goes unfilled. Principal duties include location, design, and construction of roads and bridges; making land surveys; and determining boundary lines.

As the title of the office of *assessor* implies, its principal responsibilities are to locate, identify, and appraise the value of all property—both real and personal—subject to county taxation. Since county revenues are deprived principally from the property tax, impartial and qualified administration of this office is basic.

While the duties of the office of *county superintendent of schools* vary considerably among the states, in general they include assisting in curricula development, checking the physical condition of schools, preparing reports for the state department of education, and advising local school district boards. Sometimes the superintendent actually manages the affairs of local districts that have defaulted on their responsibilities.

The duties of the office of *recorder or register of deeds* relate almost exclusively to the recording of documents. Among the recorded items are real-estate title deeds, mortgages, leases, articles of incorporation, real estate subdivisions, livestock marks and brands, wills, and decrees of bankruptcy.

The *county clerk* is the chief recordkeeper for the county governing board and usually operates as the registrar of voters and performs other functions regarding election administration. Such records as births and deaths, marriages and divorces, and election returns are normally kept by this officer. The clerk often performs as the county's chief financial officer and issues licenses for hunting and fishing, amusement permits, and marriages.

The *sheriff* is the most common of all county offices and historically has served as both a law enforcement and court official. Major functions include keeping the peace, operating the county jail, and regulating traffic. As a court official, the sheriff issues writs and subpoenas, conducts foreclosures, and confiscates abandoned property.

The *attorney or solicitor* prosecutes all persons accused of crime, advises the county on legal matters, and represents the county in court cases. Although variously known as the prosecuting attorney, district attorney, state's attorney, or solicitor, the duties of the office are fairly uniform throughout the states.

The *clerk of court* is attached to the general trial court of the county to issue the processes of the court and to keep its records. Typically this officer records all actions and writs of the court and keeps records of all court proceedings.

The principal remaining function of the *coroner* is to make inquests on the bodies of persons who have died by violence or under suspicious circumstances. Although the duties of the office call for a knowledge of both law and medicine, incumbents are usually trained in neither and the office has given way to a *medical examiner* in a number of counties. In many states, the coroner succeeds to the office of the sheriff if the latter is removed or is unable to perform his duties for any reason.

Among the other elective county offices existing in some but not majority of states are the auditor or controller, county judge, probate judge, register of wills, prothonotary, revenue commissioner, welfare commissioner, bailiff, public weigher, and public administrator.

Appointed Officials

While considerably less standardized among American counties than the elective offices, a few county officials usually obtain their offices through appointment by the county board. Principal among them are the health director, public welfare commissioner, and road commissioners. County offices that are elective in some states are appointive in others, with each of the ten officers listed above being appointive in one or more states. Other county officers usually appointive when they exist are the county veterinarian, inspector of weights and measures, horticultural inspector, public defender, and probation officer.

The county agent and home demonstration agent also are appointed by the county board, but they are not strictly local officials because they also are representatives of and approved by the state agricultural extension service. In some states certain county officers are appointed by the governor, but these again would not qualify as strictly local officials.

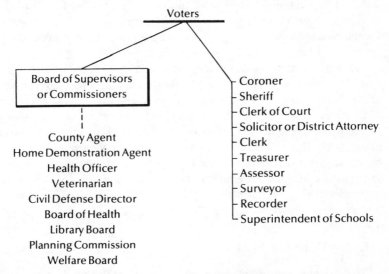

Voters

Board of Supervisors or Commissioners

County Agent
Home Demonstration Agent
Health Officer
Veterinarian
Civil Defense Director
Board of Health
Library Board
Planning Commission
Welfare Board

Coroner
Sheriff
Clerk of Court
Solicitor or District Attorney
Clerk
Treasurer
Assessor
Surveyor
Recorder
Superintendent of Schools

Figure 1. Organization of a Typical County Government

In some states one or more county offices may be consolidated. For example, twenty possible combinations of county offices are allowed in general-law counties in California. California has two classes of counties, charter and general law; other states may classify these as home rule and non-home rule counties. Each of the forty-seven general-law counties in California has completed at least one of the permitted combinations of county offices.

Special-Function Boards and Commissions

A long time practice in county governments is to superimpose upon the general structure of government a number of special boards and commissions with prescribed administrative functions. Counties vary widely in their implementation of optional legislation for establishing such boards and commissions. In general, New England counties and small rural counties have the fewest and heavily populated urban counties have the largest number. No count of such agencies has ever been undertaken, but Clyde Snider reasons that the total number would run "far into the thousands."[10]

Among the common activities of such boards and commissions are welfare, health, libraries, elections, hospitals, property assessment, planning, zoning, personnel, recreation, airports, school finance, penal institutions and agriculture. This part of county government structure is further complicated by the presence of two or more boards responsible for different aspects of the same basic function, e.g., two welfare boards, one to supervise such county institutions as the orphanage and poor farm and a second to administer the program of welfare grants for dependent children, old-age assistance, and aid to the blind.

Although such boards and commissions are often useful and enable a number of citizens to participate in county government through their service on such agencies, they also tend to fragment even further the already diffused county structure. Some boards and commissions are wholly or partially integrated into the general governmental structure, but others—particularly those whose members are not appointed by the county board—enjoy a degree of independence and separateness that makes overall integration of county government impossible. Fragmented governments are generally weak governments, and this is true of many contemporary county governments.

COUNTY HOME RULE

Traditionally counties have not enjoyed freedom to alter their structures or to run their own affairs. As administrative units of the state, both constitutional and legislative controls specify their structure, powers, and functions. The movement toward constitutional county home rule began in California in 1911 with the adoption of a constitutional amendment, and such home rule provisions are now available to some or all the counties in fifteen states.[11] The fifty-seven charter counties govern thirty-two million Americans; thirty-six of the charters have been adopted since 1960, indicating substantial growth in interest in home rule governments for counties. In addition, nine of the charter counties have populations of over one million and fifteen include populations greater than 500,000. The big urban counties are getting home rule charters to satisfy three needs (1) greater autonomy from uncaring state governments; (2) more executive direction through strengthened executives; and (3) demands for more representation. New York had the most charter counties with 15, followed by California with 11; Maryland, 7; and Oregon, 5.

While the 57 home-rule charters vary considerably in length and content, several points of general similarity are evident. First, the basic governing board is an elective board with membership ranging from a low of three to a high of 40 members. The smaller boards with five to nine members are the most frequent. Second, all but three of the charters provide for a chief executive officer. Thirty-five provide for the council-appointed executive form and nineteen for the commission-administrator form. Third, the structure of government generally has been simplified through a reduction of elective offices. And, fourth, administrative practices have been improved through the installation of budget procedures and the merit system.

Counties with home-rule charters are not completely free to shape their governmental structure because of state legislative and constitutional requirements. Neither does county home rule appreciably increase the power and functions of counties, which also are regulated by state provisions. However, it does give the county some discretion that might not otherwise exist so far as its structure and powers are concerned. Home rule also may be a means of working out more satisfactory arrangements for the relative sharing of power with other units of local government. The number of counties enjoying this privilege probably will increase in the years immediately ahead.

TRENDS IN COUNTY GOVERNMENT

In 1917 a revealing study of American counties was published with the provocative title, *The County, The Dark Continent of American Politics*.[12] The author presented a clear indictment against county government as then existing. He enumerated the basic problems confronting counties in the hope that his study would stimulate the rebirth of this local unit. His hope has been realized, at least partially. Not long ago many people were predicting the early demise of the county, but these units are now experiencing a revitalization.

Here are various discernible trends affecting county government.

1. The county continues to increase in importance. One reason for this is the use of the county as a base for federal grant-in-aid programs in such areas as agriculture, health, and welfare. A second reason is the expansion of population in suburban communities around major cities. As suburban communities increase in both size and number, the role of the county in coordinating some services and in providing others is enhanced. Many county

regimes represent the last hope of these one-class communities against central city dominance or metropolitan government arrangements.

2. The services carried out by counties are increasing in number and importance. The traditional functions are improved through programs of federal and state grants, and new functions are encouraged by such programs. Citizen demands for new and improved services are also falling on more receptive ears at the county level, thus making strong county government an alternative to larger and larger cities.

3. County reorganization, while advancing slowly, continues to move ahead. County executives are growing in number, and county boards seem increasingly aware of their opportunities and responsibilities. The county executive seems to foretell an expansion of county civil service and the problems inherent in increased specialization.

4. The problem of state-county relations is emerging as a cooperative relationship rather than one primarily of state control and supervision. State legislatures appear more willing to permit flexibility among counties and to enact permissive rather than mandatory legislation in many fields.

5. The role of the county governing body is becoming increasingly significant. As the county becomes more important as a governmental unit, the new strength is reflected in the powers and functions of the county board. With this expanded board role, the benefits to be derived by making many of the presently elective non-discretionary positions appointive will become more obvious, and this power will be gradually transferred to the county board.

6. The cost of county government is growing to meet the costs of the new and expanded services rendered. As property taxes increase and additional taxes are levied, citizens become more aware of their county government and may keep a closer watch on its operations. Much of the increase in county expenditures results from the rising costs of welfare, the burgeoning payroll, and the cost of pensions for retired employees.

7. The county is less a rural stereotype than formerly as several types of counties are increasingly recognized. The rural county (which once was the form of all counties) has been joined by its more urban counterparts serving densely populated counties. Cities were never expected to fit into a common mold, but counties for much too long were so treated by state control and supervision. The greater flexibility among counties will enable some to become outstanding local units and will erase the popular stereotype of the county as an inefficient government.

8. The strengthened county is an increasingly acceptable pattern of government, particularly to citizens of suburban communities adjacent to the core city. The volatile nature of urban population divisions may tend to weaken the government of cities and make the county an acceptable unit to frustrated urban dwellers as well.

9. The county continues to be recognized as a unit with potential in the

reorganization of governments in and around metropolitan areas. This point is not further elaborated upon in detail here because it is discussed in Chapter 18. However, the reorganized Dade County in Florida; the recent city-county consolidations in Indianapolis and Marion County, Indiana and in Nashville and Davidson County in Tennessee; and the urban services offered by contract to its cities in Los Angeles County are but four examples of major new emphasis on counties as units of urban government.

In conclusion, the county continues to face an uphill struggle. The typical rural county has insufficient resources to finance efficiently the modern service programs that its limited population wants in such areas as health, education, and roads. While funds from federal revenue-sharing have helped, they have fallen far short of the needs. The urban county, although increasingly useful for suburbanites in unincorporated communities, is less emphasized than formerly as the core unit in metropolitan government because such areas tend increasingly to cross county lines. Thus, future role of the county—whether rural or urban—probably depends mainly on its willingness to join in cooperative programs with neighboring counties. The number of bicounty and multicounty activities is growing, and this direction may point the way to an expanding and more useful role for the American county.

NOTES

1. These density figures and others to follow are from Bureau of the Census, *County and City Data Book, 1972*, Government Printing Office, 1973.
2. For an expansion of this suggestion, see George S. Blair, "Population Density as a Basis for Classifying Counties," *The County Officer*, 23 (June, 1958), 121-127.
3. Bureau of Census, "Governing Boards of County Governments: 1965, Government Printing Office, 1965, pp. 3-4.
4. *Ibid*, p. 3.
5. Samuel K. Gove, "A County Executive Office," *The County Officer*, 19 (September, 1954), 190-3.
6. National Association of Counties, *From America's Counties Today, 1973*, National Association of Counties, 1973, pp. 25-46.
7. National Association of Counties, *National Survey of the Appointed Administrator in County Government*, National Association of Counties, 1973, p. iv.
8. L. H. Adolfson, "The County Clerk as Manager," *National Municipal Review*, 34 (March, 1945), 125-8.
9. Since the legislative and executive processes in local government are described more fully in later chapters, these roles of the county board are not elaborated upon at this point.
10. Clyde F. Snider, *Local Government in Rural America*, Appleton-Century-Crofts, 1957, p. 147.
11. National Association of Counties, *From America's Counties Today, 1973*, op. cit., pp. 68-70.
12. H. S. Gilbertson, *The County, The Dark Continent of American Politics*, National Short Ballot Organization, 1917.

Chapter 8

Municipal Government

Urbanization is an outstanding, continuing social development in the United States. The first federal census taken in 1790 revealed an urban population of only 5.1 percent, or a ratio of one urbanite to 20 rural dwellers. The ratio was halved and the percentage doubled by 1840 when 10.8 percent of the nation's people lived in urban communities. By 1870, one of every four persons in the United States resided in such places, and the ratio was one in every three by 1890. Urban dwellers became a majority in 1920 when the federal census revealed that 51.2 percent of the population lived in communities of 2,500 or more. The ratio of 1975 was three of each four citizens as urban dwellers, and most of them were living within the urban concentrations identified as metropolitan areas.

The increasing urban nature of our society is an uncontested fact. However, considerable disagreement exists over whether this development is a forward step or one to be viewed with alarm and distrust. The "case" for cities has been well stated by many able writers from various points of view. To Luther Gulick, nothing is quite so functional as an urban center where people come together, live in congested areas, and establish great centers. Functions served by the city are primarily trade, industry, and a way of life.[1] L.S. Rowe, political scientist, notes that the close association of city life makes possible division of labor, which increases productive power. He believes we lose sight of the fact that "the crowd, the hum, the shock of men" in the city sharpens the intellect, develops inventive genius, stirs commercial activity, and arouses the spirit of cooperation.[2]

Students of American government and history are familiar with the distrust of cities held by Thomas Jefferson and his oft quoted phrase that cities were "sores on the body politic." This same general distrust of cities is apparent in the more recent work of Elmer T. Petersen who believes the city represents an engulfing process of standardizing multiplication. Human mutual relationships and valid, well-rounded personal development become more difficult within the city.[3] In even more colorful words, anthropologist Desmond Morris describes the city as a human zoo rather than a concrete jungle:

> The modern human animal is no longer living in conditions natural for his species. Trapped, not by a zoo collector, but by his own brainy brilliance, he has set himself up in a huge, restless menagerie where he is in constant danger of cracking under the strain.[4]

In whatever way we view the concentration of people in cities, urbanism unquestionably has given rise to social, economic, and political problems unprecedented in both number and complexity. Problems that do not exist or are relatively minor in rural communities become of major importance in cities, and many of these needs may be met only by cooperative action.

FACTORS IN URBANIZATION

Although a distinction may be made between the conditions that have made urbanization possible and the factors that have caused it, an overlapping may be avoided if growth is discussed in terms of factors promoting urbanization rather than in terms of necessary preconditions and causes.[5] Any listing of such contributory factors is arbitrary, but at least four major factors may be identified. They are the agricultural surplus resulting from increased efficiency of farm production, the industrial revolution and mass-production techniques, advances in public health and sanitation, and the development of public works engineering.

With the advance and adoption of the methods of scientific farming, the farmer became a quantity producer. As the number of persons who could be sustained by the labors of a single farmer increased, larger numbers of persons were freed from agricultural work and migrated to cities. A study released by the U.S. Department of Agriculture revealed that as long ago as 1961 the productivity of a single farmer could produce enough to feed himself and twenty-five other persons.[6] However, technology cuts both ways. A major bad effect of the farm surplus is that the "surplus" farm population migrates to the city and often finds it difficult to secure employment.

The application of power and the development of labor-saving machinery removed industry from the home and brought on the rise of factories. The growth of cities is closely related to the development of power-driven machinery which lead to mass-production techniques. As industries grew in size, city populations reflected this growth as farm migrants and emigrants from other countries came to the city for their livelihood.

Before the advent of modern sanitation and enhanced knowledge of germs and their control, it was impossible for cities to approach the size they have now attained. The problems of supplying pure water, removing human wastes, and controlling epidemics were so enormous that few cities achieved populations greater than 100,000. With the beginning of public health programs to control diseases, improve community sanitation and environment, and insure a safe food and water supply, city populations grew and conditions of urban living were greatly improved. Also as a result of expanding health knowledge, a natural increase in population bolstered urban populations as the excess of births over deaths widened and life expectancy lengthened.

Closely related to improvements in health and sanitation and to the industrial revolution was the gradual advancement, of technology in municipal public works engineering. The term is used broadly here to encompass the whole range of public works programs, including water, other utilities, sewers, streets and bridges, and the development of systems of transportation and communication. As these facilities and systems were developed, conveniences and comforts of urban living were greatly enhanced.

NUMBER AND SIZE OF CITIES

The term municipality is in general usage to connote an incorporated community in an American state, but it is almost impossible to ascribe any precise physical characteristics to the approximately 18,000 municipalities operating in the United States. In size of population, the range varies from 7.8 million in New York City to zero population in a small number of places that never completed prescribed procedures necessary for dissolution. The average number of cities per state is 370, but this number is exceeded in 22 states while 12 others have fewer than 100.

In terms of land area, Jacksonville, Florida, is the biggest American city, extending over 766 square miles, followed by Oklahoma City, Oklahoma, with almost 636 square miles. New York and Chicago, the two most populous cities, possess areas of 299.7 and 222.6 square miles, respectively.[7]

As Table 5 reveals, our nation is still one of predominantly small cities. More than 70 percent of the total number has a population of less than 2,500—the minimum figure required to be classified as urban by the Bureau of the Census. Also, one-third of the total municipal population lives in communities of under 25,000.

TABLE 5
NUMBER AND SIZE OF MUNICIPALITIES

Population-size Group	Municipalities Number	Percent	Population served By municipalities Number (1,000)	Percent
1,000,000 or more	6	.03	18,766	14.2
500,000-999,999	20	.1	12,989	9.8
250,000-499,999	30	.2	10,477	7.9
100,000-249,999	97	.5	14,268	10.8
50,000-99,999	231	1.2	16,130	12.2
25,000-49,999	453	2.4	15,668	11.8
10,000-24,999	1,134	6.1	17,656	13.4
5,000-9,999	1,398	7.5	9,855	7.5
2,500-4,999	1,911	10.3	6,731	5.1
1,000-2,499	3,575	19.3	5,706	4.3
Less than 1,000	9,664	52.2	3,998	3.0

Source: Bureau of Census, *1972 Census of Governments,* Vol. 1, "Governmental Organization," Government Printing Office, 1973, p. 2; and *County and City Data book, 1972,* Government Printing Office, 1973.

PROCESS OF INCORPORATION

Although the creation of a new city should be a serious business, it is relatively easy for an area to be incorporated in most states. Several legal requirements must be satisfied; they are not major obstacles if sufficient interest and support are present in the community. The specific steps to be followed differ among the states, but the procedures outlined for incorporation in the *Government Code* of California are fairly typical. In California incorporation proceedings may be initiated in any unincorporated community of at least 500 inhabitants or of 500 registered voters in counties containing a population of two million or more.[8] The essential procedural steps in incorporating are:

1. A notice of intention to circulate a petition for incorporation must be filed with the county board of supervisors specifying the boundaries of the proposed city and signed by at least 25 voters in the area.

2. This notice of intent also must be filed with the governing board of all cities lying within three miles of any of the territory in the proposed incorporation.

3. Within ninety days after the first filing a petition must be filed with the county board asking, for the calling of an election on the issue of incorporation. This petition must be signed by at least 25 percent of the voters in the area and include the owners of at least 25 percent of the total value of the land lying within the proposed city.

4. The county board examines the petition to determine its validity in terms of number of signatures, and the reasonableness of the proposed boundaries.

5. A map showing the area of the proposed city must be submitted to the local agency formation commission which has 30 days to examine the proposal and to prepare its recommendation.

6. The local agency formation commission must hold a hearing on the proposal at least two weeks after publication of the date of the proposed hearing in a newspaper serving the area. At this point, the proceedings may be nullified if the proposal is not approved.

7. The county board sets the date of the election by giving at least two weeks' notice of the date in advance.

8. After the election and canvassing of returns, the county board must declare the results. If the proposal received a majority of the votes cast at the special election, the board declares the establishment of the new city. If the proposal is defeated by the voters, no further move for incorporation of the community may be initiated for two years.

Across the country there were 100 incorporations alone in 1973, the highest total in a decade. This trend probably will continue but possibly at a slower rate in the years ahead, particularly in areas surrounding the core cities of large metropolitan areas. In many instances, such communities incorporate as a defensive move to prevent being annexed to an existing governmental unit. In other cases, incorporation is undertaken to secure the power of local zoning to preserve existing land-use patterns or to prevent proposed changes. A third reason for incorporation may be basically financial—to qualify for either federal revenue-sharing funds or for aid in the form of state-collected but locally-shared taxes, or to take advantage of the fortuitous location of a particular industry, large manufacturing concern, or major shopping center. A fourth motivation may be a felt need for basic governmental services combined with a desire to control them locally. Since police, fire, and other services normally may be obtained only by annexation to an existing municipality or by establishing a new one, the concern for local control—particularly of the police function—may encourage a community of citizens to seek incorporation.

As large counties perform more urban-type services and sell such services to cities lying within them, a further inducement for incorporation arises. The sale of services by the county enables "a city to be born without the normal pains and labor attendant upon birth. Founding a city becomes largely a paper transaction, rather artificial or synthetic in nature."[9] This latter inducement apparently has encouraged a number of communities to change from an unincorporated status in California counties because they are able to receive county services for their citizens immediately upon establishment as a city. This plan, now commonly referred to as "the Lakewood Plan," will be examined more thoroughly in Chapter 18.

FORMS OF CITY GOVERNMENT

Probably the best known "fact" about forms of city government is the one that Alexander Pope, the famous British poet, once wrote in couplet form:

> For forms of government let fools contest;
> Whate'er is best administered is best.

But there are few who would currently agree with Pope unless such qualifications as self-government with a democratic environment were added. However, it must be readily admitted that a close and direct relationship exists between form of government and its performance. While form determines what can be done and prescribes how it can be done, the persons who fill the offices are the force behind the form and set and guide its operations. A form permitting an officeholder to do his job well should result in better government than a form that unduly binds the officeholder and restricts his actions. If this is so, then form does become important; but this should not lead us to conclude that there is one best form to be universally adopted.

Three basic forms of city government have been developed in American cities. These are usually identified as the mayor-council, commission, and council-manager plans. Two other forms—town meeting and representative town meeting—are limited to cities in New England. While each of these forms has its identifying characteristics, the varieties in the application of the basic plans are numerous. The number of cities with each form is shown in Table 6.

TABLE 6
FORM OF GOVERNMENT IN CITIES OVER 5,000 POPULATION

Population Group	Total No. of cities	Mayor-council	Council-manager	Commis-sion	Town meeting	Rep town meeting
Over 500,000	26	21	5	0	0	0
250,000-500,000	30	13	14	3	0	0
100,000-250,000	98	38	51	9	0	0
50,000-100,000	256	93	145	13	1	4
25,000-50,000	520	170	293	39	4	14
10,000-25,000	1,360	585	620	55	75	25
5,000-10,000	1,550	881	530	43	84	12
All Cities Over 5,000	3,840	1,801	1,658	162	164	55

Number of Cities With spans the Mayor-council, Council-manager, Commission, Town meeting, and Rep town meeting columns.

Source: International City Management Association, *Municipal Yearbook, 1975* (Washington: 1975), Table 3, no page.

Mayor-Council Form

The mayor-council form of government is the oldest and most prevalent type in operation in American cities. While Table 6 is limited to cities of over 5,000, a large majority of cities under this size also employ this form. This form was universal until the beginning of the present century and was a logical outgrowth of the "council government" pattern in our early cities. Under council government, as the term implies, most local powers were vested in the plural-member council. In the course of the nineteenth century, the power and prestige of the council declined for a number of reasons, and the office of mayor evolved and gradually gained strength. Today there are three major variations of the mayor-council form—the weak mayor-council plan, the strong mayor-council plan, and the strong mayor-council plan with a chief administrative officer.

The *weak mayor-council plan* still reflects the spirit of Jacksonian democracy and is a product of local government in colonial days. It evolved in the colonies from English practices when the functions of city government were few and citizen fear of strong government widespread. The structural form of this pattern still demonstrates the ideology that officeholders should be many in number, possess few powers, and checks should be placed upon their exercise of these powers.

This plan has a number of distinguishing features or characteristics. First, the council has and exercises both legislative and executive powers. In addition to its policy-determining function, the council is empowered to appoint certain administrative officers and to supervise some areas of administrative activity. Second, the council usually is a fairly large body, ranging from five in small cities to over fifty in certain large cities, and its members often are elected by wards. Third, the mayor is an elective office with few controls over administration. Normally the office has a limited veto power and a restricted appointive power, but the real weakness of the office lies in its lack of authority in administrative affairs. Fourth, the office is weak because several other administrative officers are popularly elected, often including the city treasurer, attorney, clerk, and assessor. In addition, members of important administrative boards are elected. Fifth, the ballot used is usually partisan in character and long in form. Sixth, the several departments and boards are independent of each other and no real coordination of their efforts is possible because no single office is entrusted with this responsibility.

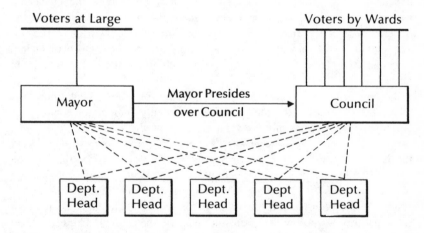

Figure 2. Weak Mayor-Council Form of City Government

These characteristics are rather vividly illustrated in Figure 2 diagramming the weak mayor-council form of government. This illustration also reveals the basis for the several major criticisms of the weak mayor-council plan. First is the lack of administrative control in the office of the mayor. He is unable to coordinate the activities of the various departments or agencies and often does not even have a voice in selecting the persons who head these agencies. A second criticism, really a byproduct of the first, occurs when the leadership is provided by a person or persons outside the government and beyond popular control. Thus, this form lends itself to political manipulation or boss control more readily than do better integrated forms of city government. Third, the long ballot unnecessarily burdens the voter and tends to confuse rather than enhance voter control.[10]

A study of Chicago's government in action found much to praise about the operation of the weak mayor-council form of government in that city.[11] Meyerson and Banfield found that political power was "highly decentralized formally but highly centralized informally." As the system worked, power over some matters was located in the city administration while power over others was left with neighborhood and ward leaders. The weakness of the city government was offset by the strength of the leading party that possessed sufficient power to run the city and passed out enough favors, protection, and patronage to keep itself in power. While such a happy wedding of a weak government and a strong majority party may exist in Chicago for the citizens benefit, it seems a dubious arrangement to encourage in other cities; it may succeed more in spite of the combination of government and party rather than because of it.

Just as there was a discernible trend to strengthen the powers of the chief executive at the state and national levels near the end of the nineteenth century, a similar development occurred at the municipal level with the development of the *strong mayor-council form*. The growth of powers for the mayor was gradual as the need for strong and active municipal administrative leadership became increasingly recognized, particularly in large cities.

The principal characteristics of this form of government show the increased role of the mayor. First, virtually complete control for administrative responsibility is concentrated in the office of an elective mayor. The mayor has the power to appoint and remove most department heads, is responsible for preparing the budget for consideration by the council, and is entrusted with a veto power over council actions that may be overridden only by an extraordinary council majority. Second, the mayor shares in the policymaking function of the council, although the ultimate responsibility for policy determination lies with the council. Third, the legal position of the mayor is such that he may exercise strong political leadership, within both the city administration and the community. Fourth, the council is usually a small body of seven or nine members who may be elected either at large or by wards and by a partisan or non-partisan ballot. Fifth, terms of both the mayor and council members are longer than in the weak-mayor form and typically are four years in duration.

The advantages of the strong mayor-council form in relation to the weak mayor organization are illustrated in Figure 3 which depicts its structure. Most apparent is the clear location of administrative authority and responsibility in the office of the mayor. The other elective offices are apt to be ministerial rather than policymaking and consist of such positions as treasurer, clerk and controller. Second, the limited number of elective offices makes the short ballot a reality in most cities using this form. Third, the office of the mayor is the focus for political as well as administrative leadership in the community.

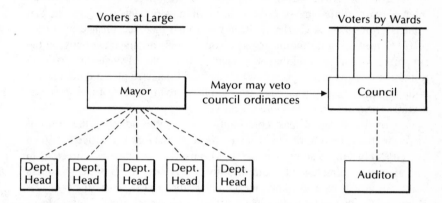

Figure 3. Strong Mayor-Council Form of City Government

The problems or disadvantages inherent in this form are also revealed in the diagram. The first is the possibility for friction between the mayor and the council, since they share the policymaking function. Strong council members may resist the mayor's leadership and attempt to restrict his role in policy matters. A second major problem emanates from the dual nature of the mayor's office; he is both the political and administrative leader of the community. This combination of leadership qualities is not easy to find. A mayor with strong political leadership may not be an expert administrator and one who is an able administrator may be a rank amateur at playing politics with political leaders. A third problem arises if the council competes effectively with the mayor, resulting in a virtual deadlock between the two branches in their efforts to check one another. In such cases, the necessary political leadership may be provided by a person outside the government in the form of a boss who is beyond citizen control and is not responsible to the citizenry.

While the strong mayor-council form of city government possesses a number of problems or potential weaknesses, it is superior to the weak mayor form because of its focus for leadership and responsibility in one person. This form has provided good results in numerous cities and remains the pattern in a large number of them, including both large metropolitan centers and smaller communities across the nation.

To offset the weakness resulting from combining political and administrative leadership in the office of the mayor, a number of large cities in recent years have established another form—*the office of chief administrative officer (CAO) to assist a strong mayor in his administrative duties.* This plan has become common enough in practice and described sufficiently in the literature to be considered a third form of the mayor-council government.[12] The concept of the CAO's office as an integral part of the mayor-council form of government originated in San Francisco in 1931. A charter revision movement there established the office of CAO to work with the mayor as a compromise arrangement between the supporters of the existing mayor-council form and the advocates of changing to the council-manager system. While the San Francisco plan did not receive wide notice nor early transplantation to other urban centers, it has served as a guide for other cities in more recent years.

One of the points of least conformity among cities adopting this form of government is the title of the office to assist the mayor. The office is known as city consultant-administrator in Louisville, managing director in Philadelphia, director of administrative services in Boston, business administrator in Newark, and city administrator in New York (the post was abolished in the last-named city in 1974). Los Angeles and New Orleans created the position of chief administrative officer, and a similar office has been established in a number of smaller localities. In some cities, this officer is appointed by the mayor and serves at his pleasure. In others, his appointment and removal must be approved by the council, while councils in other cities must approve removal but have no voice in his appointment.

Although the actual powers of the office vary slightly from city to city; the general powers of CAO's, may be grouped into three major categories. First, such officers have the power to appoint and remove heads of certain departments and agencies. Normally this power is exercised with the approval of the mayor but the power is specifically placed in the office of the CAO. Second, CAO's supervise the operations of the departments and agencies under their office. Usually they include only those for which he has appointive power but in some cities his office gives "general oversight" to other city agencies. Third, the office provides general advice and assistance to the mayor in many and varied matters, in preparing reports, and in recommending courses of action.

The basic purpose of the CAO adaptation of the strong mayor-council plan is to free the mayor from administrative duties so he may provide political and policy leadership and give the city effective administrative leadership through the employment of a professionally competent administrator. Support for this purpose is largely responsible for the successful development of the CAO plan. According to Wallace Sayre, political scientist, the plan is desirable because (1) it is a feasible and acceptable pattern of government for large cities that find the council-manager form unattractive; (2) it preserves the office of the mayor as the center of public leadership and government responsibility; and (3) it fits more comfortably into the traditions of the American political system by implementing the strong executive with administrative competence.[13]

While the strong mayor-council with CAO plan appears quite acceptable in large cities and seems to be operating well in both large and small cities, it is not without operating defects. An obvious source of potential conflict lies in the relations between the CAO and the mayor. An uncooperative mayor or an uncomprising CAO could find numerous occasions for disagreement. A second problem, common to all forms, is the continued possibility of a deadlock between the mayor and the council in policy matters or in the exercise of policy leadership. Although both these problems probably have arisen in each of the cities with this form, the plan of government has survived, indicating its adaptability to meet such problems when they do emerge.

The Commission Form

The pattern of municipal government known as the commission form is an American invention of the current century originating more from a historical accident than a planned reform. The plan was first adopted in Galveston, Texas, in 1901, following in the wake of a devastating hurricane the previous year that virtually destroyed the city and took 6,000 lives.[14] During the period of rebuilding, the state legislature suspended the weak mayor-council local government and substituted a commission consisting of five local businessmen. Because the five Galveston commissioners were able individuals and attacked their city jobs with great zeal, the plan was widely heralded as bringing the principles of business into the governing of cities, and the form was retained there following its successful beginning and initial operation.

The commission form is now the least used system of municipal government. The main characteristic of this form is the complete lack of separation of powers, with the commission members performing both legislative and executive functions. A second characteristic is the small size of the governing board. Five is the most common number of commissioners and typically they are selected at large for staggered terms of four years. Third, administrative powers are usually exercised jointly with the power of appointment and removal as a common prerogative of the commission rather than of any individual member. Fourth, the commission plan incorporated the principle of the short ballot movement by providing for no elective offices other than commission members. These features of the plan are highlighted in Figure 4 which portrays the structure of government in commission-governed cities. A fifth feature of the plan is the general provision for citizen use of the direct democratic devices of initiative, referendum, and recall.

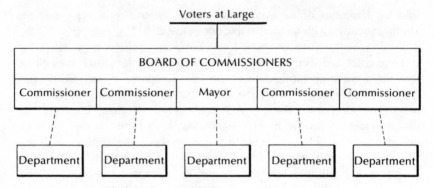

Figure 4. Commission Form of Government

The advantages claimed for the commission form largely reflected its structure. First, its organization would be simple and easily understood by citizens. Second, full responsibility would be concentrated in the commission so as to eliminate "buck-passing." Third, the plan resembled the organization of business corporations, and this, it was believed, would result in good, honest and efficient government. Fourth, the standard of officeholders would be raised since leading citizens would be willing to serve as commission members. And fifth, citizen control of government would be strengthened because of the short ballot and the provision of direct democracy devices.

What was heralded as its major strength soon became the outstanding weakness of the commission plan. In providing no organizational distinction between the policymaking and executive functions, diversity rather than unity became the operating pattern. A second difficulty arose because of the dual qualifications of legislator and administrator that each commissioner was expected to possess. The failure to provide executive leadership for the city was a third deficiency. While one of the commission members was a mayor-commissioner, he did not have powers over the other members and could not provide common leadership. The election of competent business and professional people to the commission also failed too often to materialize since the combined position of lawmaker and law-enforcer required much time. Lastly, citizen control became somewhat thwarted because responsibility could not be pinned upon individual commission members but only on the commission as a whole.

The Council-Manager Form

In the first two decades of the twentieth century, a new form of government—the council-manager form—developed in American cities. While the origin of the council-manager concept is not known for certain, one of its earliest advocates was Haven A. Mason, editor of the magazine *California Municipalities*. In an editorial appearing in the August, 1899, issue, Mason advocated a "distinct profession of municipal managers."[15] These persons should have some knowledge in such diverse fields as engineering, street construction, sewers, building construction, water, lighting systems, personnel, accounting, municipal law, police and fire services, and library management.

The practical application of the council-manager form occurred first in Staunton, Virginia, in 1908. In an effort to achieve some administrative supervision and integration in a town with a weak mayor and bicameral council form of government, the Staunton council passed an ordinance creating the position of "general manager." In a charter proposed for the city of Lockport, New York, in 1911, the concept of a manager for the city was more clearly developed. Although this specific charter did not go into effect, it served as a model for the charter adopted by Sumter, South Carolina, in the following year.

The council-manager form achieved national acclaim in 1914 upon its adoption in Dayton, Ohio, a city of over 100,000. Since that time, it has grown rapidly in terms of adoptions. In 1921, the plan was in use in 162 cities; by 1941, the number had more than tripled. Now the council-manager plan is the most prevalent among all classes of cities other than those of over 500,000 and those under 10,000.[16]

The essential characteristics of the council-manager form may be stated in this manner: (1) a small council elected at large on a nonpartisan basis; (2) the unification of all legislative and policymaking functions in the council; (3) the employment of a competent administrator to serve as city manager; (4) the location of administrative responsibility in the office of the manager; (5) the application of the short ballot with only the council members being elected by the voters; (6) the absence of a formal separation of powers and a system of checks and balances. Most of these features are evident from the governmental structure of the council-manager form presented in Figure 5.

The structural pattern of organization also shows that many weaknesses of the commission form of government are eliminated by the council-manager form. The fragmented administrative responsibility of the commission form is replaced by integrated responsibility in the office of the manager. Similarly, the combination of legislative and administrative powers in the commission is supplanted by a system in which the legislative function is with the council and the administrative function is concentrated in the manager. These are two of the strongest advantages claimed for the plan. Other advantages cited by its supporters include: (1) the simplicity of its structure makes it comprehensible to the citizen and facilitates his control over the elected representatives; (2) the presence of competent administrative leadership is assured through the appointment of a professionally trained manager; (3) the separation of politics and administration is achieved through the division of these functions between the council and the manager; and (4) the manager is a full-time employee who gives constant attention to the problems and needs of the city and its citizens.

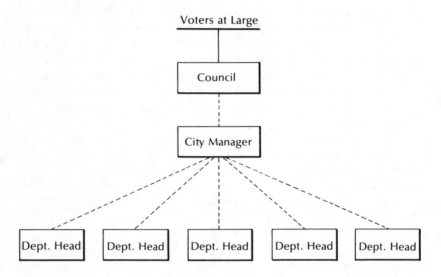

Figure 5. Council-Manager Form of Government

Realistic criticisms, however, may be directed at the plan. Making a distinction between the policymaking and administrative functions often is difficult. Yet the theory of the plan sets up this separation in very simple terms. The unrealistic nature of this oversimplification has been recognized by the International City Management Association and by students of government, but it has not yet been grasped by many citizens and, indeed, by some council members in council-manager cities. A second potential weakness of the plan lies in its provision for a council of equals. Although a council member serves as mayor, he has no stronger powers than do other members in the functioning of the council. Thus, no encouraging of leadership in the council exists because it serves only part-time. A possibility also is present that conflict will develop between a strong-willed mayor and the manager. In the event of such rivalry, the council members and the citizenry may be forced into the uncomfortable position of choosing to support one or the other in an internal struggle for power. A fourth potential weakness of the plan is its stress on nonpartisanship in regard to decisions of public policy. The plan seems to function best in communities that are not very heterogeneous in character and in which a fairly high degree of community consensus persists.

The success of the plan may be measured partly by its rapid and continuing growth and the small number of abandonments. A 1969 study listed only 115 cities that had dropped the plan subsequent to its adoption. However, in 26 of these communities, the plan was later readopted so that only 89 cities had actually abandoned the plan during its first 65 years.[17] The plan exists in many different types of cities but is found predominantly in suburban cities and white-collar or relatively homogeneous municipalities.

THE NEW ENGLAND TOWN MEETING

Few governmental concepts are imbued with the nostalgic charm and reverence ascribed to the town meeting form of direct democracy in New England. Some of the spirit and contagious appeal of the town meeting has been captured by numerous writers describing its operation—usually in glowing and picturesque terms. In the words of one writer, "Here the citizen is sovereign, and well he knows it, and so do the town officers whom he elects to perform the town chores for him."[18]

The Town Meeting

The annual town meeting is the principal governing authority of the town and every qualified voter is eligible to attend and participate in its deliberations. When assembled, the voters constitute the town's legislative body and are called upon to make a number of major and minor policy decisions.

Well in advance of the annual meeting, a warrant is prepared by the selectmen, or signed by a majority of them, showing a notice of the time and place of the meeting and its agenda. Only the items or articles included in the call of the meeting may be considered and such items are placed on the agenda by action of the selectmen or in response to a request by a prescribed number of voters. The annual meetings are presided over by a moderator who may be elected for a definite term of office, appointed by the registrar of voters, or selected by the voters in assembly. The town clerk is the secretary of the meeting and keeps records of its proceedings.

Board of Selectmen

The plural-member board of selectmen elected at the town meeting serves as the principal administrative agency of the town. As a rule, three members constitute this board, but some communities choose a greater number of five, seven, or nine. The term of office ranges from one to three years with re-election a custom of long standing.[19]

As elected representatives of the voters, the selectmen are empowered to carry on the business of the town between annual meetings and to make policy decisions necessary to implement broader policies. During their terms, they have charge of town property and manage elections. Among their other major duties are appointment and removal of various minor town officers and administrative surbordinates; granting of licenses and permits; preparation of warrants for special and annual town meetings; construction and maintenance of roads; settlement of claims against the town; and preparation of the budget for presentation at the town meeting. Selectmen, particularly in smaller towns, often serve in various other capacities such as assessors, overseers of the poor, health officers, or highway commissioners.

Other Town Officers

In towns not employing managers, most day-to-day administrative work is handled by the town clerk. Normally elected for a one-year term but traditionally re-elected year after year, the clerk is a key official and ranks immediately after the selectmen in importance. One writer describes the town clerk not only as a "general factotum but often an encyclopedia of local information."[20] The other commonly elected officers are shown in Figure 6.

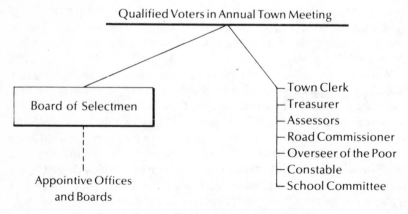

Figure 6. New England Town Meeting Plan

Modifications of the Town Meeting

As the New England towns continued to grow in population and local problems became more complex, certain weaknesses in the town meeting form became apparent. Although the basic pattern of the town meeting system has remained as the common form of town government, three significant modifications have developed. In the representative town meeting plan, the town is divided by the selectmen into precincts ranging in number from four to nine depending on its size. The voters in each precinct choose an equal number of delegates (usually thirty to forty) by popular vote. These delegates rather than the entire electorate then serve as town meeting members. Meeting with the town officers at the annual and special town meetings, these delegates and the town officers exercise essentially the same powers formerly exercised by the old town meeting.

A second modification is the finance committee plan. Members of this committee, from three to thirty in number, are often elected at the annual meeting, but in some towns the members are appointed by the moderator. Since the school budget is also prepared by the committee, school board members usually are given some committee memberships, but as a rule the committees are nonpolitical in composition, with business and professional people comprising most of the membership. The committee's function is chiefly advisory; the budget must be submitted at the town meeting for approval, but the committee recommendations carry considerable weight.

The third modification is the town-manager plan. The selectmen appoint a qualified person to the position of town manager to supervise the administrative activities under the board's general supervision. The position and powers of the town manager are similar to those of the manager in council-manager cities except that the policy-determining body is the town meeting rather than the board of selectmen. The manager, however, is directly responsible to the board and not to the town meeting.

VILLAGE GOVERNMENT

Governmental organization in villages is comparatively simple. However, the variation in organization between villages and cities differs more in degree than in kind, because the differences relate more to the complexity of organization required for functions performed than to structural principles. Just as for cities, there are the three basic forms of village government—the mayor-council, commission, and council-manager plans. Of the three, the mayor-council form is used most extensively; all three plans in villages parallel their operation in larger cities.

The principal authority in villages lies in the plural-member legislative body usually designated as the village council or board of trustees. The council typically is small, consisting of three to nine members. The chief executive officer is generally called mayor if there is a council and president of the village board if the legislative body is composed of trustees. If called mayor, the office is normally filled by popular election, while village presidents are typically selected by village boards of trustees from among their own membership.

The remainder of the governmental organization in villages is usually simple and consists of few officers and employees. It is common for marshals to exist as local law enforcement officers, and the part-time services of a treasurer or collector and of a clerk or recorder are required. The three offices are usually filled by popular election. Most villages also have an officer known as street or road commissioner and may have an assessor and solicitor. In addition, village governments may have an assortment of local boards and commissions including health boards, cemetery commissions, and boards for public utilities services such as water, sewers, and lighting if such facilities exist.

TOWNSHIP GOVERNMENT

The governmental pattern of townships in the United States fall into two main groupings. In eight states, township meetings patterned after the New England town meeting are prescribed by state legislation. Since the meetings are open to all qualified township voters and their conduct is parallel to the town meeting, their structure and operation are discussed only briefly here. Township organization in the other seven states is a miniature of county government and consists of several offices elected by the voters as well as the members of the township board.

In townships with the township meeting form of government, the board is known as a board of trustees or supervisors. One member serves as the chairperson and is known either as the board supervisor or chairman. Other common elective officers include a clerk, assessors, a treasurer, and constables or justices of the peace.

The township in the other eight states assumes a governmental pattern similar to the structure of county government in miniature. The township governing board, whose title varies from state to state, is the principal governing agency, but there are also some elective officers. The board consists of three or more members who are either elected as board members or who sit as *ex officio* members because of their other township offices. The term of office is usually for two or four years. As the general governing authority in the township, the board possesses general, but normally limited taxing powers. It commonly has a limited appointive power and may exercise some licensing and regulating authority. Other township officers vary from state to state, but the basic structure of township government is shown in Figure 7.

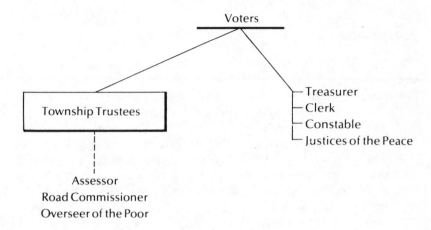

Figure 7. Rural Township Government

In charter, first-class, or urban townships, the structure of government becomes somewhat more formal and the services provided increase in number. The township board usually is increased in size as is the number of appointive officers. In contrast to their rural counterparts, functions have been expanded in these townships in recent years in several states. A number of larger townships have adopted the township manager plan by local ordinance to obtain the benefit of the full-time services of a trained administrator. In such communities, the township manager functions in a capacity parallel to that of the town manager, although his powers may be more limited because the office is established by local ordinance rather than through adoption of an optional charter.

Most present-day townships have changed somewhat from the units once described by Thomas Jefferson as "pure and elementary republics." However, townships continue to serve three important functions: (1) as units of local government; (2) as units of representation for some county governing boards; and (3) as constituent units of party machinery in some states. Despite these functions few people are strong supporters of township government as it now exists.

The local governmental forms described in towns, villages, and townships may have increasing importance in the future. It is possible such forms may serve as prototypes for the people who leave larger urban areas for a more rural and simple life-style. Often such persons seek a small community in which their participation is direct and meaningful. Thus, a revival may take place in town meetings as a governing process.

SUMMARY

Increasingly in recent years, local government structure has been emphasized as a means rather than an end in itself. As generalizations the following are discernible trends affecting municipal government:

1. The strong mayor-council with chief administrative officer form is particularly suitable for large cities. This form combines political leadership in the mayor with administrative competence in the CAO.
2. The council-manager form of government will continue to be adopted in small to medium-sized cities. This form finds special compatibility in upper- and middle-class communities, and often proves unsuitable in working-class communities.
3. The general tendency of municipal government forms to follow "business" principles will continue. A continuing indication of this tendency is the stress on managerial boosterism.
4. The governmental forms in small communities that place heavy stress on citizen participation may become increasingly important if the trend of population movement from large cities to more rural areas continues.
5. Like all human institutions, outmoded structures of governance will continue to persist in many communities. The rigidity of formal organization, the persistency of citizen apathy, and the strength of those with a vested interest in the status quo are all factors that mitigate against change.
6. Officials of local government will be under increasing pressures to meet the needs and demands of their citizens. As the number of services increases so do the pressures on the officials who provide and administer them.
7. Local government structure is important but it is only one factor that makes up the particular characteristics of a community and the type of government that will be provided.

NOTES

1. Luther Gulick, *Our Cities Today and Tomorrow*, Municipal Forum of New York, February 19, 1947, p. 5.
2. L. S. Rowe, *Problems of City Government*, D. Appleton & Co., 1908, pp. 2-3.
3. Elmer T. Petersen (ed.), *Cities are Abnormal*, University of Oklahoma Press, 1946, pp. vi-vii.

4. Desmond Morris, *The Human Zoo*, McGraw-Hill, 1969, p. 8.

5. For two excellent discussions of this general topic, see National Resources Committee, *Our Cities: Their Role in the National Economy*, Government Printing Office, 1937, esp. pp. 29-41; and Lewis Mumford, *The City in History*, Harcourt, Brace and World, 1961.

6. Department of Agriculture, "The Food We Eat," pamphlet, Government Printing Office, 1961.

7. Bureau of Census, *County and City Data Book, 1972*, Government Printing Office, 1973.

8. California Government Code, *Government of Cities*, State Printing Office, Sacramento, 1969, plus supplements.

9. Henry A. Turner and John A. Vieg, *The Government and Politics of California*, McGraw-Hill, 1960, p. 208.

10. For two examples of the actual operation of the weak mayor-council plan, see Arthur Bromage, *Councilmen at Work*, George Wahr Publishing Co., 1954, pp. 72-80; and William N. Kinnard, Jr., *Appointed by the Mayor*, ICP Case Series No. 36, University of Alabama Press, December, 1956.

11. Martin Meyerson and Edward C. Banfield, *Politics, Planning and the Public Interest*, The Free Press, 1950, especially pp. 285-302.

12. See John C. Bollens, *Appointed Executive Local Government: The California Experiment*, Haynes Foundation, 1952; Gladys Kammerer and Ruth McQuown, *The City Consultant: Plan or Expedient?*, Bureau of Government Research, University of Kentucky, 1958; Wallace S. Sayre, "The General Manager Idea for Large Cities," *Public Administration Review* 14 (Autumn, 1954), 253-8; John M. Selig, "The San Francisco Story," *National Municipal Review*, 46 (June, 1957), 290-5.

13. Sayre, *op. cit.*, 257-8. For two rejoinders to the Sayre thesis, see John E. Bebout, "Management for Large Cities," *Public Administration Review*, 15 (Summer, 1955), 188-95; and William A. Sommers, "Council Manager Government: A Review," *Western Political Quarterly*, 11 (March, 1958), 144-7.

14. Richard S. Childs, *Civic Victories*, Harper, 1952, pp. 319-21.

15. This editorial is reprinted in Bollens, *op. cit.*, Appendix III.

16. International City Management Association, *Municipal Yearbook, 1975* International City Management Association, 1975, Table 3.

17. Orin F. Nolting, *Progress and Impact of the Council-Manager Plan*, Public Administration Service, 1969 pp. 22-24.

18. L. H. Robbins, "Democracy, Town Meeting Style," *The New York Times Magazine*, March 23, 1947, pp. 24, 35, 38.

19. A study of selectmen in a Maine town revealed that one member had held office for 41 years with only a one-year break in continuity, and two former members had served for 32 and 18 years, respectively. See Lincoln Smith, "Leadership in Local Government—the New England Town," *Social Science*, 29 (June, 1954), 147-57.

20. Roger H. Wells, *American Local Government*, McGraw-Hill, 1939, p. 84.

Chapter 9
Government of Special Districts

In numbers and variety, special districts exceed all other types of local governments in the United States. Such units are found in every state except Alaska and exist in both rural and urban sections throughout the states. Of a total of about 40,000 special districts, almost 16,000 are school districts. The others—a substantial majority—represent such a variety in terms of size, function, and character that general description is very difficult.[1] However, this class of unit is deserving of careful study because it has become a significant part of the patchwork design of American local government. School districts alone account for about a fifth of all local units and the other types of special districts represent about three tenths of them. One careful student of special districts has stated that such non-school units "constitute the 'new dark continent of American politics,' a phrase applied earlier in the century to counties."[2]

As organized units of local government, special districts have the essential characteristics common to other local units. They have substantial autonomy from other units, including fiscal and administrative independence. Special districts also have official and identifying names and perpetual succession. Also, they possess the three basic rights of municipal corporations—to sue and be sued, make contracts, and to obtain and dispose of property. As mentioned earlier, the two basic types of special districts—school and non-school—have shown a contrasting pattern of development in recent years.

SCHOOL DISTRICTS

The general pattern for providing public education in the United States is through local school districts. Such independent districts have full responsibility for the operation of public schools in 25 states, the predominant responsibility in 16 other states, and partial responsibility in 4 additional states. In Alaska, Hawaii, Maryland, North Carolina, and Virginia, no independent school districts exist and public schools are administered by the local county, city, or town governments, as in true in some parts of 20 other states.

To distinguish between the two basic types of organizations for public education, the Bureau of the Census classifies the latter type as "dependent" school systems. There were about 1,500 such school systems operating in twenty-three states that operate solely or in part through this kind of organization.[3] Since dependent school systems are not separate governmental units, they are not treated further here but are discussed more fully in Chapter 15.

The number of independent school districts varies greatly among the states. In the states organized entirely into independent school districts, Nebraska has the largest number while Nevada has the fewest. The four states of California, Illinois, Nebraska, and Texas, each have over 1,000 independent school districts. The diversity in the area characteristics of school districts also shows wide variation. Many districts have the same boundaries as other general local units such as counties, cities, townships, or towns. Many other districts, however, have boundaries not conforming to those of any other governmental unit, resulting in districts extending over a very small area to those embracing more than 500 square miles.

TABLE 7
NUMBER OF SCHOOL DISTRICTS IN SELECTED YEARS

School year	No. of school districts
1971-72	15,781
1966-67	21,782
1961-62	34,678
1956-57	50,454
1951-52	67,355
1941-42	108,579

Source: Bureau of the Census, *1972 Census of Governments,* Vol. 1, "Governmental Organization," Government Printing Office, 1973, p. 4.

The school district reorganization movement which began in the 1940s has resulted in a continuing decline in the number of districts. A major factor was the closing of many one-room schools in rural areas and the consolidation of these units with the school system of the nearest town. This rapid decline is shown in Table 7.

The School Board

Paralleling the governmental pattern of general-purpose local units, the governing authority of school districts is exercised by a plural-member board commonly known as the board of education or board of school trustees. In about four of every five independent school districts, the board members are chosen by direct election by the voters of the school district. In the others, board members are appointed rather than popularly elected. The appointing authority ranges from the county governing board, the city council, the mayor, the mayor and council jointly to the grand jury, the district judge, and the governor.[4] In the township school districts of Indiana, a single school trustee is elected, but the size of the board varies from three to twenty-one members in other states. Boards most commonly consist of three, five, or seven members who are elected for terms of from three to seven years.

School board members typically are chosen without regard to party preference. Each serves for a specified term—three or four years in most cases. Board members usually are not persons whose own careers are directly concerned with education; more likely, they are business people, lawyers, farmers, or housewives.

Within the legal framework of state constitutional and legislative requirements, the school board has wide discretion in exercising its responsibilities for the scope and quality of educational services. Its financial powers include the preparation and adoption of an annual budget, determination of the district's tax rate, and the issuance of bonds after approval by the voters. Its appointive functions include selection of the school superintendent and the teaching and administrative staffs of the schools. Its educational policy powers range from determining what should be taught, the extent of extracurricular activities, the nature of the educational pattern in terms of grade divisions, or cooperation with other governmental units for school or recreational purposes, to choosing sites, and approving construction plans for new school buildings. One writer has noted that the legal powers given to school boards include

> authority to make all reasonable rules and regulations for the government and management of the schools, for the discipline of pupils and teachers, and for the admission and even exclusion of children for sufficient legal cause.[5]

The internal organization of the school board is usually fairly simple. The customary officers consist of a chairperson or president, a clerk, and a treasurer. In many districts, these three board offices are filled by direct election by the voters while in others the board selects its own officers from among or outside the membership of the board. The chairperson presides at board meetings and serves as the board's general spokesman. The clerk keeps minutes of board meetings and has custody of district records, while the treasurer receives revenues and pays out monies on orders signed by the other two board members.

The School Superintendent

To assist the school board in discharging its educational responsibilities, the board appoints a trained educator and school administrator to serve as the superintendent of schools. Unlike his counterpart in council-manager cities, the school superintendent typically is appointed to serve for a specific term. This is often for one year, but renewal is almost automatic subject only to mutual satisfaction. Like the city manager, the career pattern of the superintendent is to move from smaller to larger jurisdictions.

The responsibility for developing educational policy is largely delegated by the board to the superintendent. This officer normally plans the school curriculum for the board's approval; hires teachers to teach in the school system; purchases supplies for the school; plans the bus routes and schedules for transporting pupils to school; employs necessary administrative, clerical, and custodial employees; and suggests innovations to be implemented within the schools' educational program. In such matters the superintendent's relations with the board parallel those of the manager with the council in council-manager governed cities. The superintendent also serves as the chief planner and policy adviser to the board, and his success in directing the educational policies of the district depends mainly on his relations with the board.

The degree of delegation of responsibility by the board to the superintendent varies widely among school districts. As school administrators become a more professional group, the tendency has been for the school board to rely more heavily upon their superintendent not only for developing educational policy but also for recommendations in other aspects of school administration. Thus, the most important decision that some boards make in the course of their deliberations is their choice of superintendent. If the selection is a good one, the district's educational program moves ahead smoothly; if the choice is less fortunate, considerable friction and bickering may develop among the superintendent, the board, and the parents in the community.

School Meetings

A number of states still provide for an annual school meeting that is somewhat comparable to the annual town and township meetings discussed in Chapter 8. Such meetings are open to all voters residing in the district and the citizens in attendance give general instructions to the board members and ratify board policy recommendations. Notices of the pending meeting must be placed at conspicuous spots, usually including the schoolhouse door. Often telephone poles at the busiest crossroads serve as other posting points.

The agenda of the annual school meeting follows a fairly uniform pattern. The first order of business is the election of board members. Since such meetings are more prevalent in rural districts that tend to have three-member boards, usually only one member is selected at any particular meeting. Following the election, the board presents its policy relating to the district tax levy for the coming year. This is normally the item sparking the most discussion; if the meeting is well attended, often many people oppose a rumored tax increase for school purposes. With the two major pieces of business taken care of, the meeting then discusses such topics as the beginning of the school term, who will clean up the buildings and yards before the opening of the term, and other district policies relating to its educational program.

In more urban settings, school meetings are held periodically—one a month, bi-monthly, weekly, or even bi-weekly. These meetings are open to the public, but attendance is usually low except for official watchers representing the Parent-Teacher Association, the League of Women Voters, and other groups. Exceptions occur when controversies exist in the schools relating to the dismissal of teacher, the busing of students, the cancellation of certain programs, and the closing of certain school buildings. Like other public bodies, the school board may call executive sessions to conduct certain types of business. At these special meetings, the public is excluded.

School Reorganization

School districts were originally established in Connecticut in 1766 and grew steadily in both number and area covered up to the early decades of the present century. The common school pattern until the early 1930s in rural areas was one-teacher schools within walking distance of all homes in the district. In 1934, the Bureau of the Census reported a total of 125,627 independent school districts. The sharp decline in number during this century is clearly revealed in Table 7.

The movement toward school consolidation has resulted largely from state action to encourage the merger of small districts. In some states, such action took the form of economic incentives with local districts qualifying for financial awards under voluntary compliance. In other states, consolidation was forced on small districts by legislation affecting those failing to meet certain conditions or standards, or with too few pupils. In spite of the record of continuing school mergers across the nation, the Bureau of the Census in its most recent report shows that 2.2 percent of the existing school systems do not actually operate schools but pay tuition to other districts for the education of their pupils. Another 4.5 percent of the districts have fewer than 15 pupils and an additional 5.2 percent have enrollments of between 15 and 49 pupils.[6] Thus, nearly 12 percent of the public school systems either have no schools or operate schools with fewer than 50 pupils.

In the years right ahead, a further reduction in school districts probably will continue unless the moves for the decentralization of schools in large urban communities produces a breakup of those large school districts into a number of smaller ones. While the establishment of meaningful school district population criteria is difficult, the National Commission on School Reorganization has advanced the standard that each administrative school unit should have at least 1,200 pupils between the ages of six and eighteen to realize economy in operation and to permit needed specializations. The Commission went on to state that no elementary school should have fewer than 175 pupils with seven teachers and that no junior or senior high school have fewer than 300 pupils and 12 teachers.[7]

Some alarm has been expressed in recent years over the loss of citizen and parental interest in the public schools when the districts become very large and the members of the school board are not widely known. Only a tenth of the more than 17,000 public school systems have enrollments of 6,000 or more pupils; however, schools concentrated in large cities account for about three-fifths of the total pupil enrollment. The problem of citizen interest in schools will be commented on more fully in Chapter 15.

A continuing controversy rages concerning the status of the independent school district in our local governmental system. The core of the conflict lies in the question of whether the district should continue as an independent governmental unit or become a "dependent" school system operating as part of the program of a general-purpose local government. The question is certainly not academic because schools have the latter status wholly, predominantly, or partially in a number of states. In large part, the argument is between educators, who support the continued independent status of school districts, and political scientists, who favor the integration of education into the machinery of general units of local government. As a whole, city officials have rarely taken sides in this issue, perhaps reflecting the willingness of mayors and city managers to avoid the additional political headaches that would result from oversight of the schools.

In recent years both sides in the controversy seem to be mellowing. Instead of exchanging verbal brickbats in professional journals, both see some merits in the arguments of the other and seem to be supporting a policy of closer cooperation between school districts and other local governments. In a number of communities continuing and close cooperation has developed between the school and the municipal government in such areas as recreation, parks, libraries, use of public buildings, and adult education programs. This is a hopeful development because such cooperation in programs may produce better and more economical services to the taxpayers supporting both governmental units.

NON-SCHOOL SPECIAL DISTRICTS

The nature and variety of non-school special districts make a general description of them difficult. However, such an attempt is necessary because of their growing numbers and importance. The approximately 24,000 special districts are quite unevenly distributed among the states. Alaska, Hawaii, and Virginia have very few, while Illinois and California each has more than 2,000. Twelve other states each has over 500 of these units.

An essential first step in discussing special districts is to classify them into manageable groupings. One scheme for classification is by function and divides special districts into groups according to the services rendered. Such a division is given in Figure 8. Three types of districts—fire protection, soil conservation, and urban water supply—account for about two-fifths of all non-school special districts. A small proportion—less than 5 percent of the districts are engaged in more than one function. The services most frequently rendered by such districts providing more than one function involve urban water supply in combination with sanitation, fire protection, irrigation, or flood control.

A second basis for classifying special districts is by the area served. Under this scheme, four such groupings emerge. First, metropolitan or regional districts are created to solve or ameliorate areawide problems encompassing a number of separate governmental units. As example is the Metropolitan Water District of Southern California which supplies water to municipalities in six counties, or the Metropolitan Sanitary District of Greater Chicago. Second, coterminous special districts have boundaries identical to those of an existing general purpose local government. Such districts are often organized for such functions as housing or parks. Third, urban fringe special districts are often established in unincorporated areas bordering on cities to provide municipal-type services for the residents of these unincorporated areas. Such districts are created for such varied purposes as water, sewerage, sanitation, street lighting, and fire protection. Fourth, rural special districts are established to meet agricultural needs and provide such functions as soil conservation, drainage and irrigation. In addition to these four basic types, there are a number of other governmental entities bearing some of the characteristics of special districts. These are variably known as dependent districts, quasi-districts, or authorities. Since they are not recognized as independent units of government, being classed as departments of some recognized unit of local government, this type of district is not discussed further in this chapter, but it is essential to recognize that such entities exist in large numbers in some states and are in addition to those identified as special district governments.

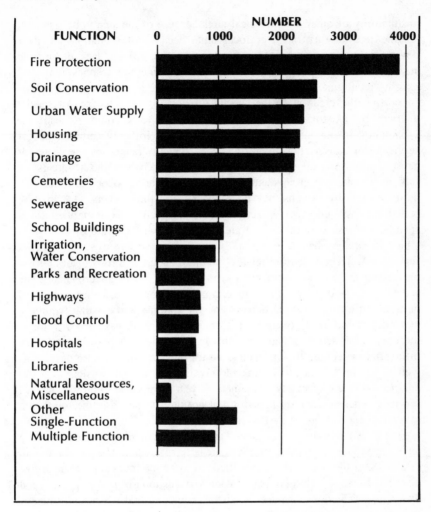

Figure 8. Special Districts by Functions
Source: Bureau of the Census. *1972 Census of Governments, Vol. 1.,* "Governmental
Organization," Government Printing Office, 1973, p. 18.

The Increase in Special Districts

Since the 1940s, the increase in numbers of special districts has been
rapid. Because of their growing importance, the reasons underlying their fast
growth are of considerable consequence to both students and practitioners of
local government. Rather than a single all-inclusive cause of growth, a
series of factors has emerged.

Seven major reasons have been identified by political scientist John
Bollens in his thorough study of special districts. He identifies: (1) the

unsuitability of other existing local units because of the area to be serviced; (2) the unsuitability of other local units because of limitations on their powers to perform and finance needed services; (3) the lack of suitable administrative machinery and willingness to assume new responsibilities by existing local units; (4) the desire for independence by the persons or groups supporting the creation of the special district; (5) the advocacy of special districts by existing governmental units to serve a common need; (6) expediency in obtaining a service and the need for only certain types of services in areas not requiring the typical range of services of general-purpose local governments; and (7) the unadorned self-interest or selfishness of some groups and individuals in creating special districts.[9] To these reasons by Bollens may be added at least three others. One may be called the psychological attraction, since a specific tax is applied for a specific purpose in a prescribed area. The taxpayer is aware of the use to which his money has been put and is sometimes willing to support such a service. A second reason relates to the general efforts of the reform movement in local government to keep "politics out of government." The special purpose district with its governing board appears to be less subject to partisan influence than a department or commission existing within a general-purpose local government. Certainly this belief has been a factor in the continuing separate status of school districts, and it probably has been influential in seeking this independence for other special purpose districts as well. The third reason concerns the creation of special districts to avoid annexation to a nearby city or the necessity to incorporate to provide needed services. These points are hinted at but not directly stated in the fourth and seventh points advanced by Bollens.

Of the ten reasons given above, the area and financing needs probably have been most important. The area factor would be important in establishing the two types classified as metropolitan and urban fringe districts. Since both these types provide services to citizens living in several different jurisdictions, the special district device provides a means whereby the existing governmental units are least affected and yet no one of them assumes the new function. The need to circumvent restrictions on the taxing and borrowing powers of existing units also is highly important. As a new unit, the special district has financing and borrowing powers of its own, and thus providing a means for obtaining the needed monies or borrowing potential to finance the essential capital improvements to render the needed services.

In most instances, a combination of the specific reasons listed above usually prevails rather than a single one in the creation of any particular special district. A number of the underlying causes are not independent but are intertwined to a considerable degree. The reasons underlying their creation also point out some potential problems of maintaining democratic local control over the districts once they have been created. These problems will be discussed in the concluding section of this chapter when the strengths and weaknesses of operating special districts are evaluated.

Creation and Organization

Since special districts are established under state rather than local authority, the state legislature holds the key position in initiating them. In most states the pertinent legal base is statutory in form, whether the authorization is by special legislative enactments or general enabling legislation. Sometimes, however, the legal basis to create such districts lies in a constitutional provision. The process of establishment usually begins with action by local residents, either in following procedures detailed in general statutes or in asking the legislature for a special legislative act authorizing the district for the affected area.

The procedural steps required to create a special district under general authorization are fairly simple and uniform, although the details of such enabling legislation vary considerably among the states. The first step is initiated with the circulation of petitions requesting the organization of a special district. The petitions must specify the type of district to be created, define the area to be serviced, and be signed by a specified number of qualified voters residing in the area or by owners of a determined percentage of the property within the area. Second, the petition is filed with a designated governmental agency, which is normally the governing board of the county or the judge of the court serving the area. In some states the petition is checked merely to confirm its compliance with provisions of the enabling law. In other states the agency conducts hearings on the proposal and is empowered to determine the desirability and suitability of the proposed district. If approval by the reviewing agency is obtained, the third step is a local referendum on the proposal. Normally the election is open to all qualified voters in the area but may be limited to property owners only. If the popular vote is favorable, the special district is established by a resolution or order of the county board or court as the final step in the process.

The organizational pattern for the governing of special districts also reflects considerable diversity. The general governing body is ordinarily a plural-membered board made up in one of four ways. First, the board may be composed of independently elected members chosen by the voters at large or from subdivisions of the district. Second, the board members may be appointed by some other governmental agency—generally the agency that supervised and proclaimed its establishment. Third, the board may be composed of *ex officio* members holding their positions on the district board because of their posts on other local governments. Fourth, the board may consist of members selected by the governing bodies of local governments within the district. In a few districts, a single district administrator rather than a board is entrusted with the general management. The size of the governing boards varies, but the most frequent numbers are three, five, or seven members who are known as commissioners, supervisors, directors, or trustees. In boards of the fourth type, the number of members depends on the number of participating local governments and their populations, since additional representation is often granted to larger constituent units. Terms of office of members ranges from two to six years, with three- or four-year terms most common.

The governing board of the special district is vested with two general classes of powers. As a unit of local government, the district possesses the general powers common to other local governments, for example, the power to sue, hold property, and make contracts. In addition, the district has the more specific authority to discharge the service or services for which it was created. This district's board has the authority to select its employees, authorize expenditures, tax and borrow, and establish policies concerning the district's operations. As is true of other local governments, the special district possesses and may exercise only those powers conferred upon it, subject to whatever statutory or constitutional limitations exist. Their sources of revenue usually are narrow and include local taxes, special assessments, service charges, and intergovernmental grants. These will be discussed more fully in Chapter 14, which concerns tax structures of local governments.

The administrative practices of special district boards also differ from state to state. Board meetings range in frequency from once a year to monthly or even weekly. Some boards handle many administrative details in their districts, but if the district services are such that full-time supervision is required, the board members usually select the person or persons so needed rather than engage in the actual operation themselves. The meetings of the board usually are attended only by board members even though they are open to interested citizens and to coverage by the local press. This lack of citizen interest in the affairs of special districts is unfortunate because the same disinterestedness is too often characteristic of the governing bodies that create or are represented on the district's governing board.

Many special districts operate with a ''low visibility'' in the eyes of the constituents they serve. A study of special districts in Texas concluded that they were undemocratic since their activities were obscured from the public eye by infrequent and little publicized meetings, meager and misleading public reporting, disguised tax and service charges, the smallness of their operations, and the omnipresence of their numbers. While the special district may be an efficient, competent, self-supporting government, it was judged not to be self-government.[10] In a similar indictment, the Advisory Commission on Intergovernmental Relations reported that

> Typically, the limited purpose special district is remote from the voters, because of the composition and method of selection of its governing body and its methods of financing. The voter has no direct control over the district's conduct. In most cases, there are several such districts in an area, and they have different boundaries, and different methods of selection of the members of the governing bodies, making the problems of voter visibility and control all but hopeless.[11]

AN EVALUATION OF SPECIAL DISTRICTS

As a form of local government of increasing numbers and significance, the special district has both ardent supporters and highly vocal critics. In a statement recognizing special districts to have both advantages and disadvantages, Bollens writes "Not all their deviations from widely known governmental molds and practices are beneficial, and in total their characteristics are a mixed blessing."[12] The nature of the "mixed blessing" will be apparent in the discussion of particular characteristics that follows because most advantages may be reworded into disadvantages, depending upon their application in particular districts.

From the list of reasons for their creation enumerated above, it is evident that special districts provide services to meet the needs of citizens in areas whose boundaries are not coterminous with those of existing general-purpose local governments. This device enables existing governments to cooperate on an acceptable basis that keeps them in control of all services except those entrusted to the special district. It also avoids the jurisdictional jealousies that would arise if one existing unit attempted to render the same service on an areawide basis. Although the provision of services is advantageous, the divisive effects of the functional approach has inherent disadvantages. As noted by the late Roscoe Martin,

> Interest and concern tend to become program-centered rather than county-city-state centered, and loyalties tend to follow interest and concern. In short, program (or administrative) loyalties tend to supplant the geographic loyalties of other days.[13]

The use of the special district to expand the taxing and borrowing power of local units is another heralded advantage that may be exaggerated. By creating the new unit, a community on its own or in cooperation with adjoining units may be able to finance some needed public service that it could not otherwise provide because of taxing and debt limitations. However, the revenue obviously must come from the pockets of the same citizens. If the financial limitations on the existing local governments are reasonable, then their circumvention through the creation of a new special district is not commendable.

Allied with the total financial picture is the question of the desirability of earmarking revenues for particular services at the local level. According to political scientist Emmett Asseff the use of the special district largely destroys the necessary flexibility of financial policy all governments must have to handle most effectively and efficiently the changing and complex problems with which they are faced. In his words,

> The dedication of any revenue to a particular function, and this results when a special district is created, means that that revenue must be spent for that particular purpose even though at a later date there is a greater need for it elsewhere.[14]

It would be possible for a local government participating in several special districts to be sadly in need of revenues when some of the single-purpose districts might have a surplus of funds on hands.

A fourth feature concerns the "out of politics" operation by boards of special districts. It is desirable to have services provided by employees chosen primarily on merit rather than on partisan influence or loyalty. However, special districts often do not exhibit any features of standard merit systems in their employment practices. Partisan loyalty is tossed aside in favor of personal loyalty, and the citizen is not afforded the safety of party responsibility as a screening device. The "out of politics" feature also indirectly implies a lack of direct citizen control, since this, too, would be political. In districts where board members are appointed by other officials, such persons are removed from the direct control of the voters and are seldom subject to removal by recall through citizen action. Thus, the lack of effective and continuing citizen control over special districts is a serious problem needing careful attention if such units are to be agencies of local democratic government.

A growing number of studies has found an unusually low rate of voter participation in elections to choose members of governing boards of special districts. Turnout rarely exceeds 20 percent of eligible participants and is often below five percent.[15] In many other districts, no candidates seek the positions on the governing board and so no elections are held. Contra Costa County, an urban county in the San Francisco Bay area, has experienced this situation:

> A dearth of candidates for special-district board seats in Contra Costa County has resulted in only nine contests on the November 4 ballot, although 34 districts have vacancies on their boards of directors. In 19 districts candidates are unopposed, so the board of supervisors simply will appoint them to the posts they filed for. In six other districts no candidates sought election and the board of supervisors will have to find people to appoint.[16]

Special districts also are often defended as devices whereby already overburdened general-purpose local governments are relieved of the responsibility of providing one or more further services. But in practice special districts have tended to be detrimental rather than helpful to general local governments. Local governments are not strengthened by bypassing them in providing certain services or in removing part of the community's financial resources from their control and placing these in single-purpose districts. Instead this process weakens these general units, so it appears desirable to lighten their responsibilities even further by creating new special districts to perform other specific functions more "efficiently." The rapid growth of special districts can only contribute to a general weakening of other units of local government, making them less responsive and responsible. Special districts often are created in response to the requests of special-interest groups rather than the general citizenry. Their large numbers contribute greatly to the fragmented governmental structure in urban areas and invite citizen disinterest and contribute to voter confusion.

The problems just referred to are summed up strikingly in this forthright statement by the Advisory Commission on Intergovernmental Relations:

> Two criticisms are so pervasive as to strike against the vast majority of metropolitan districts existing today: these allege that (1) metropolitan districts being for the most part unifunctional, prey upon an area's financial resources by unilaterally determining their budgets without being subject to a machinery for balancing allocations of these resources among the totality of competing service needs which prevail in the metropolitan area; (2) they fail to mesh their activities, their programs and policies, which demand coordination, with those of governments coexisting in the same area; this line of criticism contends that it is absurd to have a separate and independent transit authority, when such authority has no control over the very factors which should be the basis of its own programs: the planning of industrial and residential development and the establishment of competing expressways, traffic control, and parking system. [17]

The special district represents a political response to the needs of citizens for services. It also represents an attempt to innovate within the American system in a way that meets specific needs but does not seriously alter the structure of the local government system. As such units operate, they achieve the first half of their general goal quite effectively (although not very economically often in terms of duplication, overlapping, and small-scale operations), but fail on the second point. Special districts weaken other local governments and further fragment citizen responsibility and control. This is a serious price to pay for a single service or a limited number of services, and this core issue should be confronted squarely in the near future.

Once again the Advisory Commission on Intergovernmental Relations has taken leadership in this direction. The Commission has urged states to take action:

> ... 1) to limit the creation of new special districts to appropriate circumstances and provide the means for eliminating and consolidating of those which have outlived their usefulness, and 2) to increase the "visibility" and public accountability of special districts and promote coordination of their operations with those of cities and counties ... 3) to modify existing Federal categorical aid programs that promote and favor special districts rather than general purpose local governments.[18]

The implementation of these three actions would go far in ameliorating many problems of special districts. As a further result, the role and functions of those districts that are needed, efficiently managed, and effective in providing services would be strengthened and better supported by the public.

NOTES

1. Bureau of the Census, *1972 Census of Governments,* Vol. 1, "Governmental Organization", Government Printing Office, 1973, Table 5, p. 28.
2. John C. Bollens, *Special District Government in the United States,* University of California Press, Berkeley, 1957, p. 1.
3. Bureau of the Census, *op. cit.,* pp. 3-4.
4. Bollens, *op. cit.,* p. 185.
5. G. T. Contalonia, "Some Powers and Duties of School Boards," *American School Board Journal,* 129 (October, 1954), 28.
6. Bureau of the Census, *op. cit.,* p. 18.
7. National Commission on School District Reorganization, *Your School District,* National Education Association, 1948, p. 131.
8. Bureau of the Census, *op. cit.,* pp. 4-5.
9. Bollens, *op. cit.,* pp. 6-15.
10. Woodworth G. Thrombley, *Special Districts and Authorities in Texas,* University of Texas Institute of Public Affairs, No. 39, 1959, p. 118.
11. Advisory Commission on Intergovernmental Relations, *Alternative Approaches to Governmental Reorganization in Metropolitan Areas,* Government Printing Office, 1962, p. 52.
12. Bollens, *op. cit.,* p. 251.
13. Roscoe Martin, "Therefore is the Name—Babel," *National Municipal Review,* 40 (February, 1951), 70-74.
14. Emmett Asseff, *Special Districts in Louisiana,* Louisiana State University Bureau of Government Research, 1951, p. 61.
15. Institute for Local Self Government, *Special Districts or Special Dynasties?: Democracy Denied,* Berkeley, 1970, pp. 19-25.
16. *Oakland Tribune,* "A Plentiful Lack of Candidates," October 6, 1969, p. 2.
17. Advisory Commission on Intergovernmental Relations, *The Problem of Special*

Districts in American Government, Government Printing Office, 1964, p. 58. For a devastating account of these two problems in an actual setting, see Robert A. Caro, *The Power Broker: Robert Moses and the Fall of New York,* Knopf, 1974.

18. Advisory Commission on Intergovernmental Relations, *Urban America and the Federal System,* Tenth Annual Report, Government Printing Office, 1969, p. 87.

Chapter 10

The Legislative Process

Anyone who is presently serving or who has served as a member of a local legislative body may appreciate the definition of democracy once advanced by philosopher William James. He observed that democracy is a system in which the government does something and waits to see who "hollers"; then it does something else to relieve the "hollering" as best it can and waits to see who reacts by "hollering" at the adjustment so it can take further action.[1] Since the agency of local government most empowered to "do something" is the local lawmaking body, this description of democracy also is reasonably accurate for the legislative process in local government. In addition to their function of establishing major policy decisions for their community, local legislatures hold the key position in the exercise of the general powers granted by the state to the several types of local governmental units. Unless such powers are specifically conferred upon a particular officer or agency, courts have held that such general powers reside in the local lawmaking body.

THE LEGISLATIVE FUNCTION

As has been noted in the immediately three preceding chapters, the policy-determining authority in local government is customarily vested in a plural-membered, popularly-elected board variously known as a board, council, commission or committee. The principle of separation of powers, so embedded in our national and state governments, is not a feature common to all types of local units. The vital function known as the legislative process, however, is fulfilled in all units of local government. Except in communities retaining the pure town meeting form of government, the lawmaking body consists of chosen representatives rather than an assembly of all the citizens. Nevertheless the functions of local legislative bodies are the same, whether they consist of all the citizens or of their selected agents.

Broadly described, the legislative process in local government has five major aspects. These are policy leadership, enactment of ordinances and resolutions, debate, criticism, and investigation. The last four are historic prerogatives of legislative bodies throughout all of western civilization while the first—policy leadership—is primarily a product of American experience. The distrust of strong executives in colonial America encouraged legislative bodies to exercise a greater voice in community decision making and this tradition was carried over after the winning of independence from England. The frontier influence of egalitarianism also encouraged the development of legislative rather than executive power.

Local government theory holds to the traditional concept of legislative supremacy through its policymaking powers, but in actual practice the local governing board's role is often one of policy ratification rather then policy innovation. There is agreement, however, that the local governing board "determines" all municipal policies not set forth in the charter itself or specifically granted to some other officer or agency of local government. By using the verb "determine" to connote the local legislature's role, the possible conflict between theory and practice may be avoided, since this more neutral verb covers both innovating and ratifying actions. While lawmaking bodies are called upon to make a large number of policy decisions, the biggest single policy determination faced by local legislators is the adoption of the community's budget. This one decision allocates relative emphases among the several programs and services carried on within the community and apportions the community's resources to carry them out.

After agreement on questions of policy on other matters has been reached by the local legislators, the decision is implemented through the enactment of a local law. Such enactments are variously known as ordinances or resolutions. The several specifically defined procedural steps followed in the lawmaking process are described later in this chapter.

The functions of debate and criticism are traditional spheres of activity of legislative bodies at all levels of government. Debate or discussion is essential in reaching a consensus so that a policy may be announced or an ordinance enacted. John Stuart Mill assigned two important functions to national legislatures that also are highly relevant to local bodies. These are the functions of serving as a Committee of Grievances and as a Congress of Opinion.[2] In fulfilling these functions, local legislative bodies find frequent opportunities for debate and criticism as well as the chance to provide citizens with a means to express their opinions and make known their wishes.

The investigative function of local legislative bodies has assumed more importance in recent years. For one reason citizen interest in local government has risen as local tax levies have increased. Citizens thus often request more extensive hearings and investigations before new functions are assumed or older services expanded. The legislative investigation has further grown in importance as a legislative check or threat of check into the activities of local executive officers. A third reason for the increasing importance of the investigative function is the delegation of certain types of policy formulation to administrative officers or to more specialized boards or commissions. Mill's words on this point are worth consideration. He states that,

> The business of the elective body [in local government] is not to do the work, but to see that it is properly done, and that nothing necessary is left undone. This function can be fulfilled for all departments by the same superintending body; and by a collective and comprehensive far better than by a minute and microscopic view.[3]

In addition to the several aspects of the legislative function already discussed a number of local legislative bodies have administrative functions to perform. This is especially true of county governing boards and commissions in commission-governed cities. A number of legislative bodies, however, exercise administrative functions beyond those specifically required of them. This is a function Mill believed the legislative body should not undertake. In his words,

> But a popular assembly is still less fitted to administer, or to dictate in detail to those who have the charge of administration . . . The proper duty of a representative assembly in regard to matters of administration is not to decide them by its own vote, but to take care that the persons who have to decide them shall be the proper persons.[4]

THE ROLE OF THE LEGISLATOR

Representation occurs when a person is chosen to stand in place of another person or group of people. While a number of methods exist by which representatives or agents may be selected, direct election is the means most commonly used at the local level. Only the members of governing boards of some school and other special districts are chosen by different means, and popular vote is the most frequent method of selecting school board members. The concept of representation is basic to representative government because it is founded on the principle that certain individuals are chosen to act for the community on matters of policy for a fixed period of time.

Although general agreement is present about the concept of representation, no unanimity of opinion exists about the proper function or role of the representative. Yet the relationship between the chosen agent of the people and his constituency is at the very core of representational theory. Basically, there are two conflicting theories. The first holds that the representative is a free agent who should use his own judgment as to the particular decisions he arrives at, within the general concept of advancing the public interest. The second holds that the representative is merely an agent of those electing him who is bound to act in accordance with definite instructions from his electors.

These two basic role concepts are well-defined and distinguished in a study of state legislators.[5] The first type identified above is labeled a "trustee" and the second a "delegate." The trustee has two major characteristics—a moralistic interpretation and a rational conception. The delegate, on the other hand, feels committed to follow instructions when such are forthcoming from his constituents. Obviously these two roles are not always mutually exclusive nor completely inclusive. The role of the "politico" has also been advanced—a representative who "depending on the circumstances, may hold the Trustee orientation at one time, and the Delegate orientation at another time."[6] The politico is represented as being more sensitive to conflicting alternatives in role assumption and more flexible in the way he resolves the conflict of alternatives.

After a thorough study of role orientations of nonpartisan city council-members in eighty-nine cities in the San Francisco Bay region, political scientist Charles Levine explicated six role types. These are (1) the *ritualists* who focus upon the details of the policymaking process itself rather than upon long-range implications and broader relevances; (2) the *tribunes* who see the job in an external aspect and try to bring the "public will" into the decision-making process of the council; (3) the *brokers* who see the council members as middlemen in a transactional process in which interests are balanced to obtain a beneficial compromise; (4) the *directors* who feel their job is to bring leadership to the community and to direct the affairs of the community through their positions on the council; (5) the *guardians* who see themselves as defenders of community interests; and (6) the *planners* who are interested in building for the future of the city.[7] In declining order of frequency, the council members were identified as ritualists, tribunes, directors, brokers, guardians, and planners.

The responsibilities of local legislators have been considered by a number of writers. According to F. N. MacMillin, the job of a local council member consists of five principal commitments. First his policy must be to serve all citizens rather than special interests or groups. Second, as a member of the governing board, he should concentrate on broad policy matters rather than on administrative and minor details. Third, he should strive to maintain a balance among the several services provided for the citizens and apply the same standards of efficiency and adequacy in measuring particular services. Fourth, he should anticipate problems and needs rather than simply react to them. And, fifth, a councilman must have the courage of his convictions once he has made up his mind.[8] Obviously these are sane principles for all local lawmakers to adopt and follow.

In all fairness to local legislators, many of them have no conception of themselves in any particular "role" nor do they have a preconceived concept of how they are to function except to "serve the community." The nature of their service, however, may depend principally on whether they assume that their function is to reflect the views of their constituents or to represent them for the period of their term in office.

METHODS OF SELECTION

The problem of electoral areas in local government is essentially similar to that existing at other levels—how to make a fair division of territory so that the elected representatives have approximately equal numbers of citizens as constituents. Many units of local government avoid this problem by electing all their legislators in at-large elections. The frequency of such elections varies considerably with the type of governmental structure in cities. At-large elections for council members occur in 93 percent of town meeting governed cities, 90 percent of commission cities, 80 percent of council-manager cities, 75 percent of representative town meeting cities, and 51 percent of mayor-council governed cities.[9]

At-large election of local lawmakers normally operates in one of two ways. First, the election really might be at-large because all the voters may vote for the number of candidates to be elected, with the candidates residing anywhere within the boundaries of the local governing unit. This system is more common. Second, while all voters may vote for the number of candidates to be selected, district residence areas within the unit have been set up and candidates must come from these internal election areas. This pattern is found in more than fifty cities and in many counties; the three or five county commissioners or supervisors are elected by all the voters but the board members are required to be residents of particular areas within the county.

The advantages of at-large election of local legislators are several. First, this practice enables the election of the best of the willing candidates without regard to their area of residence. Second it makes possible the placing of the interests of the whole community above district or ward interests. Third, the system eliminates the possibility of gerrymandering (giving unfair advantages) and the frequent need to redraw district boundaries to keep up with population shifts. Fourth, this plan generally results in smaller governing bodies than is true of ward or district arrangements. At-large elections, however, are not without their disadvantages. The council may be so small as not to be adequately representative of a diversified citizenry. Second, a reasonably strong and disciplined minority may receive no actual representation on the council or board. Third, at-large elections lengthen the ballot and increase the voter's responsibility to inform himself about several candidates rather than one. Fourth, at-large elections increase the campaign costs of some candidates while other potential contenders without adequate financial backing may not seek election. Requiring local legislators to live in the wards or districts they represent but to be voted on by the whole community combines some good features while eliminating some possible disadvantages. This plan results in representation of the various geographical sections of the community while still encouraging the elected representatives to work for the interests of the whole community as well as for those of the areas of their own residence.

The second most common electoral pattern is to elect all local legislators by wards or districts within cities or townships within counties. This system exists in 20 percent of the cities over 5,000 population and in nearly one-third of all counties. The advantages of the ward system may be stated in this manner: (1) the chosen representative serves as the voice of his district or ward and as the point of citizen access for his constituency; (2) the representative understands the special needs of his district and may represent those interests more knowingly than an at-large legislator; (3) the system provides a better opportunity for minority representation on the governing board; and (4) the voter has fewer representatives to choose and may be better informed on their relative merits. Disadvantages of the plan include these points: (1) district needs are placed above community needs by some legislators; (2) such legislators may become "errand boys" of special interests; (3) the districts become unequal in population, resulting in unfair representation or gerrymandering; and (4) better qualified candidates may be residents of the same ward or a few wards, but only one from each ward can be elected. As a result, successful candidates in some wards may be less able than unsuccessful contestants in other wards.

A third pattern, combining election of some legislators at large and some by district, is becoming increasing frequent in cities. This system now exists in 13 percent of the cities of over 5,000 in population and 31 percent of cities of over 500,000 population. This plan seeks to maximize the potential merits of both systems while minimizing their potential weaknesses. Results to date are encouraging; voters in cities using this plan seem pleased with the results of their mixed systems.

At-large elections appear more acceptable in suburban cities or in cities not very diverse in their social and economic composition. As cities increase in size and heterogeneity, the pattern of election by ward or district is more common for the reasons cited as advantages of the plan.

A fourth electoral system of local legislators utilizes the principle of limited voting or the system of proportional representation. Both devices are essentially ways to achieve minority representation in local lawmaking bodies. The limited vote system provides that each elector may vote for a smaller number of candidates than the total number of representatives to be elected. In various counties with three-member boards, each voter is permitted to vote for only two candidates. Thus a reasonably large and disciplined minority party may elect one of the three members of the county board. This same principle is incorporated in the Philadelphia city charter which provides that each elector may vote for only five of the seven council members to be elected at large.

Several plans of proportional representation have been developed, but the Hare System is the best known and in most common use, although still not very prevalent. Essentially all plans provide for representation of political parties or groups in proportion to their voting strengths. The process of vote tabulation is time-consuming because it involves the elimination of candidates with the lowest vote totals and the transfer of their votes to the other candidates until the number to be elected have all received totals equal to or greater than the "quota" required for election.[10]

Members of local governing boards are elected on a ballot without party designation in nearly two of every three cities of over 5,000 population. Members of school boards and other special districts are also usually elected without party designation, but most county and township elections are still conducted on a partisan basis.

THE ONE-MAN, ONE-VOTE PRINCIPLE

In 1962 the Supreme Court renounced its practice of classifying issues concerning legislative representation as political questions subject to the doctrine of judicial self-restraint. Five years later the court decided its first cases relating to inequitable representation plans in local government. In a Michigan case concerning the election of county school boards by delegates from local boards rather than by the voters, the population of the units sending delegates in Kent County ranged from 99 to 201,777. The court ruled that the county board of education was "basically appointive rather than elective" and that it performed "essentially administrative functions." Therefore, the "one-man, one-vote" principle had no relevancy.[11]

A second case ruled on the same day arose from circumstances in the city of Virginia Beach, Virginia. The city had consolidated with adjoining Princess Anne County and adopted a borough form of government. Four members of the council were elected at large without regard to residence while seven were elected by the voters of the entire city but one member was required to reside in each of the seven boroughs into which the city was divided. The boroughs ranged in population from 733 to 29,048. The court upheld the borough plan stating that the restrictive candidate residence provision seems to reflect a detente between urban and rural communities that may be important in resolving the complex problems of the modern megalopolis in relation to the city, the suburbia, and the rural countryside.[12]

A major decision concerning local apportionment was handed down by the court in 1968, which was the following year. Midland County, Texas, was governed by a commissioners court of five members. The county judge was elected at large, but the other four members were chosen from districts with populations of 414; 828; 852; and 67,906, respectively. The court ruled that the apportionment was not acceptable since

the Constitution imposes one ground rule for the development of arrangements of local government: a requirement that units with general governmental powers over an entire geographic area not be apportioned among single-member districts of substantially unequal population.[13]

The applicability of the "one-man, one-vote" principle to special districts was judged by the court in 1970. Under Missouri law, separate school districts could vote to establish consolidated junior college districts governed by six trustees apportioned among the participating school districts on the basis of "school enumeration," defined as the number of persons between the ages of six and twenty who resided in each district. In this particular district, the Kansas City District contained 60 percent of the school enumeration but selected only three of the six trustees. The court invalidated the apportionment plan holding that

whenever a state or local government decides to select persons by popular election to perform governmental functions, the Equal Protection Clause of the Fourteenth Amendment requires that each qualified voter must be given an equal opportunity to participate in that election, and when members of an elected body are chosen from separate districts, each district must be established on the basis that will insure, as far as is practicable, that equal numbers of voters can vote for proportionally equal numbers of officials.[14]

The "as far as is practicable" rule formulated by Justice Hugo Black in writing the court's opinion was augmented at a later point in that opinion by these words: "mathematical exactitude is not required, but a plan that does not automatically discriminate in favor of certain districts is."[15] This rule seemed to receive special importance by the court when the next local apportionment case was heard in 1971. Rockland County, New York, was governed by a board of eighteen supervisors chosen from the five constituent towns within the county. The variance between the most underrepresented district and the most overrepresented district was 11.9 percent. The court upheld this deviation as not excessive by finding that its decision was

based on the long tradition of overlapping functions and dual personnel in Rockland County government and on the fact that the plan before us does not contain a built-in bias tending to favor particular political interests or geographic areas.[16]

The court thus seems to follow a balancing approach to local government reapportionment, weighing the magnitude of the deviation against the rationale for it, without the strong predisposition toward near zero deviation that characterizes its approach to other levels of government. Rather, the tone of the local government decisions emphasizes the need to preserve room for flexibility and experimentation in local government arrangements.

STRUCTURE OF LOCAL COUNCILS

The basic structure of local governing bodies was discussed in pertinent sections in Chapters 7-9. While county boards vary in size from one to over 100 members, by far the most common size is boards of three to five commissioners or supervisors. The median number of council members in cities of over 5,000 population and the median number of such members in the most numerous forms of municipal government are shown in Table 8.

TABLE 8
SIZE OF COUNCIL IN CITIES OVER 5,000

Population group	Number of council members				
	1-4	5-10	11-15	Over 16	Median
Over 500,000	0	6	4	6	12
250,000-500,000	4	15	3	2	8
100,000-250,000	15	48	6	5	7
50,000-100,000	45	108	16	11	6
25,000-50,000	110	203	37	6	6
10,000-25,000	225	446	42	2	6
5,000-10,000	131	353	16	1	6
Form of government					
Mayor-Council	33	261	62	15	7
Mayor-Council with CAO	82	326	37	14	6
Council-Manager	306	558	23	3	5
Commission	95	15	1	0	4
Town meeting	14	19	0	1	5

Source: International City Management Association, *Municipal Yearbook 1972*, Washington, 1972, p. 17.

The median number ranged from four members in cities with the commission form of government to seven in mayor-council governed cities. Boards of selectmen in New England towns with town meeting government varied from under four to over sixteen with five the median number. Village boards parallel those of New England towns in size, with three to five the most common numbers. Three is also the most frequent number of members found on governing boards of townships, school districts, and special districts, although the range in each case includes some boards of five, seven, and nine members.

A tendency exists for councils to increase in size of membership as the population increases. Thus, the median number of councilmen in cities of over 500,000 is twelve in contrast to six for all cities of over 5,000. The same generalization holds true for counties in which the board consists of township representatives and for New England towns. A second variable concerning size of local councils is the form of government in the community. Councils in mayor-council cities are larger than those in council-manager cities, which in turn have more members than boards in commission-governed cities.

Terms of office of local legislators range from one to six years. One-year terms are found in cities with the town meeting form while six-year terms are in use in some counties and in a few commission and council-manager cities. By far the most frequent lengths of terms are two and four years, with the latter becoming more general recently. With four-year terms, staggered terms of office are common so that half of the positions on the local governing board are filled at each biennial election.

The bicameral council, which was a common feature of city governments in the eighteenth and nineteenth centuries, has virtually disappeared. Only Everett, Massachusetts, now has a bicameral council with the larger chamber composed of council members elected by wards and the smaller house consisting of aldermen elected at large. The Board of Estimate in New York City also functions as an upper chamber. The city council there is composed of members elected by wards, while this board has an *ex officio* membership consisting of the mayor, controller, the president of the council, and the president of each of the city's five boroughs. The powers of the Board are both financial and ordinance-making. It receives the city's budget, holds hearings, and is free to alter the proposed budget. After approval by the Board, the budget goes to the city council which has more limited financial powers and may only reduce or delete budget items. According to a study of New York City government, the city council has ''no important power in adopting local laws which the Board does not share on equal terms; the Board is, in effect, the upper chamber in a bicameral city legislature.''[17]

COUNCIL ORGANIZATION AND OPERATION

The internal organization and procedures of local legislature bodies varies considerably among the several types of local units and among various sizes of units, but several general principles may be identified. The first is the need for and functions of a presiding officer. This person may be elected to the position of chairperson of the board as in the case of the supervisor in townships, the mayor in commission cities, and the board chairman in some counties. More typically, the chairperson or presiding officer is elected by the members of the legislative body itself. The functions of this officer are to conduct the council meetings, appoint members of committees, and serve as the general spokesman for the governing board. In "weak executive" forms, the chief executive is likely also to be the presiding officer of the council.

In general, little use is made of committees in councils consisting of five or fewer members because the board is sufficiently small to handle community affairs as a group. However, as the size of the local council increases and as the population of the community rises, council committees become important agencies for transacting the work of the legislative body. In counties with boards composed of township supervisors and in mayor-council governed cities, an elaborate system of standing committees often exists.

Where the committee system prevails in local government, the local council as a whole becomes chiefly a ratifying body for approving the actions of its committees. Before matters are considered by the whole body, they are referred to the appropriate committees for consideration and recommendation; it is rare for the council to override a recommendation of one of its committees. In some communities, and particularly on some matters such as zoning neither the committee nor the governing group as a whole would ordinarily act contrary to the views of the representative from the area most substantially affected.

Meetings of local legislative bodies may be classified into four basic types. The first is the regular session held at intervals prescribed by statute or council rule. Meetings of county, township, and school district boards usually are held monthly as is true of small towns and villages. As the size of cities increases, the meetings occur more frequently. In large cities, council members may meet at least weekly and sometimes almost daily for committee work. The city councils of Los Angeles and Detroit meet in formal session each weekday throughout the year—a distinction believed unique among local legislative bodies in the United States. The second type of meeting is the adjourned session, which is used to convene the council at some date following a regular meeting and before the next regular meeting. This type of session is most often used when regular meetings are held at lengthier intervals. County boards in Illinois, for example, are limited to two regular sessions a year, so other meetings are known as adjourned sessions of one of these two regular meetings. The third type is the special session, which may be called in various ways and for a number of reasons. Usually such meetings are convened by the presiding officer at his discretion, in response to a request by a certain number of board members, or in response to a request from a prescribed number of citizens within the community. The fourth type might be called the "conference session," which is an executive session called before regular meetings when the members consider informally many matters to come up for full discussion at the regular meeting.

Forms of board or council decisions normally are taken in one of three types of actions—motions, resolutions, or ordinances. Motions usually are internal actions pertaining to such substantive matters in the conduct of council business as adopting reports, instructing officers, and authorizing council proposals for future actions. Resolutions are less important and less authoritative in form than ordinances and are commonly used to accomplish an administrative action. Examples are an expression of sentiment by the board on a matter beyond its authority, such as a bill before the state legislature, an expression of appreciation for the services of an individual or group, or an expression of sympathy upon the passing of a local official or long-time employee. Ordinances are the form of action used in laying down a rule that applies generally throughout the community. Typical uses include ordinances setting tax levies, approving appropriation requests, changing the rules or regulations pertaining to some community project or service, and all the more important acts of the local council.

The legislative procedure involved in enacting a local ordinance follows a fairly common pattern in all types of local government units. Proposals are introduced in writing by a council member and copies are filed with the clerk or secretary or presented on the floor to each member. This step is known as the first reading of the bill. At this time, the bill is referred to the appropriate committee, if the board operates with a committee system, and also to pertinent administrative officers for the information necessary to weigh the merits of the proposal. During its study of the bill, the committee may hold public hearings or study the bill on its own. Upon the reporting out of the bill, the committee's recommendations include any amendments to the original bill deemed desirable. At this point, the bill is given its second reading.

Final or third reading of the bill is usually listed on the council agenda so that interested citizens will be aware that the measure is coming up for discussion and may appear before the council to endorse or oppose it. At this third reading, debate or amendment of the bill is possible before final council action is taken. Upon passage of the bill, it becomes an ordinance and is published in local newspapers and made a part of the codified ordinances of the governmental unit, thus becoming a local law. The process may be speeded up considerably by the local council with a motion to suspend the rules. Approval of such a motion dispenses with the three-reading rule, but this is customarily done only for "emergency" bills.

In the conduct of a meeting of a local legislative board or council, eight steps are followed in the normal order of business. First, the council is called to order and the presence of a quorum of members is determined. The names of those present are recorded in the minutes by the clerk or secretary. Second, minutes of the previous meeting are read, corrected or amended if necessary, and then approved. Third, the presentation of petitions, memorials, and remonstrances is called for. Such matters usually are presented by the clerk or secretary unless a delegation of citizens is present who wish to present matters before the council. Fourth, the reports of officers, standing committees, and special committees are received. Following each report, motions are made to adopt them if they contain a recommendation. If they do not have a recommendation, the reports are merely filed without action. Fifth, unfinished business not settled when the last meeting adjourned, if any, is taken up for action. Sixth, the call for new business is made. The order of new business ordinarily is taken up in this sequence: (a) introduction of ordinances and resolutions; (b) first reading of ordinances generally by caption only with the introducers briefly explaining their content; (c) second reading of ordinances by caption only; (d) third reading of ordinances with reading in full (any changes or amendments are offered at this time); (e) council action on ordinances. Seventh, announcements are requested following the completion of business. Eighth, the adjournment of the meeting is called for. If the business of the meeting has been completed, no motion for adjournment is necessary. If the body wishes to adjourn before completion of its business, a motion to adjourn must be made and receive a favorable vote. The procedural steps throughout the meeting usually are adapted from *Robert's Rules of Order*, the customary guide used by all local legislative bodies.

In an analytical study of city councils in eighty-four cities in the greater San Francisco area, Peter Lupsha, political scientist, identified three major types of local decisional structures. They are (1) the unipolar structure where a great deal of decisional unanimity is present with each member seeing himself allied with every other member; (2) the bipolar structure where the council is divided into two rival and hostile factions that contend for decisional dominance; and (3) the multipolar structure where shifting coalitions develop. In the first type, leadership is based on many personal and external attributes associated with the leaders' image and prestige in the community at large. In the second type, leadership is principally provided by the majority faction; and in the third type, leadership depends upon instrumental and integrative qualities by emergent leaders. Lupsha concludes that leadership "like many other aspects of council life, is influenced by the degree of conflict and stability which underlie the decisional structure of these groups."[18]

The bipolar structure in many cities results from a division between members with longer service and those recently elected. A struggle between the so-called "old-timers" and the "young Turks" appears to be a growing phenomenon as former community activists campaign successfully for elective office. The city council in Austin, Texas, was recently described as "an affirmative action program gone beserk" since it consisted of a 30 year old Jewish mayor, a black man, a brown man, a blind white millionaire, and three women.[19]

POWERS OF LOCAL COUNCILS

As mentioned previously, the local legislative body holds a crucial position in the exercise of the general powers granted to local governments. If these powers have not been conferred upon a particular officer or agency, they reside in the local legislative body. The actual authority of any local council depends upon the distribution of powers within the local unit's organization. However, several broad categories of power are retained and exercised to some degree by all local councils.

The first category of powers may be characterized as legislative and involve the determination of public policy for the community. While legislative powers include both fiscal and regulatory actions, the fiscal powers of the council are discussed as a part of financial rather than legislative powers. In this more limited context, the legislative powers include those relating to public improvements and to the regulation of the health, safety, and morals of the community.

Financial powers comprise the second category of general powers. These include the power to approve the local budget, levy taxes, raise revenues, appropriate monies, and incur indebtedness. Other financial powers are buying and selling government property, passing upon local contracts involving major expenditures, and in many communities serving as the board of tax equalization. Although many state limitations are imposed concerning financial transactions of local governments, including rate of tax levy, types of taxes that may be levied, and the extent of indebtedness, no money may be raised or spent without council authorization. In addition to being a financial document, the budget is the most important public policy decision the council makes since it allocates relative emphases among the programs and services of the community.

The third category consists of the administrative powers of local councils. These powers vary widely among the several types of local units and their forms of government. In local units without a central executive officer, as in the case of most counties, the council exercises broad administrative powers. In units with central executive leadership as provided by city and county managers, school superintendents, and strong mayors, the council exercises fewer administrative functions. However, such bodies give general supervision to their executive officers, receive financial reports, obtain the reports of auditors, and use their powers of investigation when the occasion demands, even as do the councils exercising broad administrative functions. Thus, the careful exercise of its administrative powers consumes much of the council's time whatever the form of government.

Judicial powers, broadly interpreted, constitute a fourth broad type of council function. Many county boards, particularly those composed mainly or partly of judges or justices of the peace, still exercise judicial duties. Local councils typically are empowered to punish contempt actions and to enforce obedience of their orders by attachment or other compulsory process. A council exercises quasi-judicial functions when sitting as a board of tax equalization or tax appeal board. The investigatory powers of a local body also have some characteristics of a quasi-judicial function since in addition to serving the end of producing a better legislative product, they also serve to keep administrators honest and to uncover any wrongdoing. The investigatory power of local boards has been misused on occasion but is a desirable part of the process in local government. One writer has pointed out that,

> The greatest protection in the future, as it has been in the past, is the election of council members who are interested in the furtherance of the general welfare by the determination of wise public policy.[20]

The final category of council powers pertains to its activities in the field of public relations. The council as a whole and its individual members serve both as "middlemen" or "brokers" between the individual and his local government. As middlemen between the city and the individual, the council has public-relations functions that neither it nor its members may fail to provide. One commentator has described the council member in these graphic words,

> If he tries to envade his former friends and neighbors, he is highhat; if he says he will try to fix things up and does not deliver, he is incompetent; if he makes promises that are not fulfilled, he is a liar.[21]

As a representative of the city, a council member is a salesman of the community's needs to the citizenry and exerts a major role in securing popular acceptance of necessary changes in local regulations and policies and voter approval of bond issues.

In general, the public-relations function of the local legislative body may be described as those activities resulting in a community consensus evolving from conflicting points of view. Failure to accept this role and to work to achieve this goal may produce both community factionalism and factionalism on the governing board itself. Agreement or harmony for its own sake is not necessarily a good thing, but united council action after thorough study of a problem or course of action assists greatly in achieving community support for the undertaking.

PROBLEMS OF A LOCAL LEGISLATOR

The task of the conscientious local legislator is not easy. Five major problems confronting the council or board member were identified by a political scientist at the midpoint of his first four-year council term in a community of 20,000. They were: (1) trying to determine the public's real opinion on a controversial issue, (2) learning to roll with the inevitable verbal punches and criticisms of his stand on issues; (3) ascertaining what things are to be taken on faith and which "expert" advisers to trust; (4) informing the public on what the council is doing and why; and (5) not taking a position too quickly on a major issue. Nelson McGeary concluded that

> serving on council is a headache. But democracy is based on the supposition that some citizens will be willing to endure headaches. Actually the travail is not unbearable. And sometimes, for brief periods, it is forgotten—believe it or not—in the knowledge that some little service is being offered.[22]

The National League of Cities recently conducted a survey of municipal elected officials. A total of 1,031 responses were received in this mailed questionnaire. One point of the inquiry related to the "Elected City Official Frustration Index"—the things irritating city councilmen about their jobs. In declining order of frequency of their listing, the following items represent the major frustrations: (1) excessive time spent away from family; (2) long hours required for "part-time" job; (3) inefficient use of elected officials' time; (4) information glut—too much paper to wade through to make decisions; (5) too many meetings to attend and excessive time spent away from private business (tied); (7) expensive election campaign spending; (8) low public salary; (9) late night calls from constituents; and (10) lost private business due to conflict of interest legislation. Other frequently mentioned complaints included incompetent, glory-seeking, nonworking council members; public apathy; red tape; national-state mandates; attitude toward elected officials; and hassle with news media.[23]

This "frustration index" is revealing, but some other recurring problems are characteristic of many local governing bodies. One is the strong sense of localism that may prompt a member to stress the interests of his district above the broader interests of the community. The political mobility from local legislative office to citywide post or office at higher governmental levels is quite limited. This factor may have a dampening effect on encouraging the candidacies of potentially effective council members. Despite heralded fanfare, most local ordinances are incremental in nature and promote only minor deviations from the status quo even in controversial matters. A fourth problem is the increasing demands for action by local legislators and the increasing blame heaped upon them for acting too cautiously or too daringly. Such "heat" from the community probably will increase the number of one-term legislators and the number of council resignations.

NOTES

1. T. V. Smith, *The Promise of American Politics*, University of Chicago Press, 1936, pp. 199-200.
2. John Stuart Mill, *Representative Government*, Everyman's Edition, 1948, pp. 239-40.
3. *Ibid.*, p. 351
4. *Ibid.*, pp. 231, 233.
5. Heinz Eulau, John C. Wahlke, William Buchanan, and Leroy C. Ferguson, "The Role of the Representative: Some Empirical Observations on the Theory of Edmund Burke," *American Political Science Review*, 53 (September, 1959), 742-56.
6. *Ibid.*, p. 750.
7. Charles F. Levine, "Purposive Role Orientations of Non-Partisan City Councilmen," paper presented at American Political Science Association meeting, Chicago, September, 1967.
8. F. N. MacMillin, "The Job of an Alderman," *The Municipality*, 45 (June, 1950), 117.
9. International City Managers' Association, *Municipal Year Book*, 1968, p. 59.
10. For a thorough study of proportional representation see George H. Hallett, Jr., *Proportional Representation: The Key to Democracy*, National Municipal League, New York, 1940.
11. *Sailors* v. *Board of Education of the County of Kent*, 387 US 105 (1967).
12. *Dusch* v. *Davis*, 387 US 112 (1967), 117.
13. *Avery* v. *Midland County*, 390 US 474 (1968), 485-6.
14. *Hadley* v. *Junior College District of Metropolitan Kansas City*, 397 US 50 (1970), 56.
15. *Ibid.*, p. 58.
16. *Abate* v. *Mundt*, 403 US 182 (1971), 187.
17. Wallace S. Sayre and Herbert Kaufman, *Governing New York City*, Russell Sage Foundation, New York, 1960, p. 627. Each of the five borough presidents has two votes, while the mayor, controller, and council president each has four votes.
18. Peter A. Lupsha, "Leadership, Expertise, and Decision-making in Small

Legislative Bodies," paper presented at American Political Science Association meeting, Chicago, 1967, p. 28.

19. Neil R. Peirce, "Some Activists Join City Hall," *Los Angeles Times*, February 22, 1976.
20. Alice L. Ebel, "Investigatory Powers of City Councils," *Marquette Law Review*, 38 (Spring, 1955), 223-36.
21. Harold F. Alderfer, *American Local Government and Administration*, Macmillan, 1956, p. 333.
22. M. Nelson McGeary, "The Councilman Learns His Job," *National Municipal Review*, 43 (June, 1954), 284-7.
23. Raymond L. Bancroft, "America's Mayors and Councilmen: Their Problems and Frustrations," *Nation's Cities*, 12 (April, 1974), 14-24, at page 22.

Chapter 11
The Executive Function

The characteristic features of the local executive office differ widely among types of governmental units and among various size units of a single type. In authority, these officers vary from mere figureheads to powerful chief executives with wide variation in specific powers and functions. Such diversity exists because four basic patterns of the executive role in local government evolved in the United States and remain a feature of our contemporary local government scene.

Two of the fundamental executive patterns in local government developed in colonial America. In some classes of local units, no one official served as the chief executive in any real sense, nor was all administrative authority vested in the local governing board. This fragmented executive authority developed in county, township, and town governments and may be described as the plural or divided executive form. In cities, the general pattern was a mayor-council form of government patterned after the English system. The mayor was usually appointed by the governor although selected by the council in a few communities. His term was normally for one year, but reappointments were common. Early colonial charters conferred few executive or administrative powers upon the mayor. While he had neither the veto nor appointing power, he did preside over council meetings. He usually was a person experienced in municipal affairs, and because of his position and status he "became something more than a dignified figurehead, and was a real force in municipal government."[1] This pattern of executive leadership is labeled the weak executive form, because of the limited legal authority of the office.

With the establishment of state governments following the Revolutionary War, most states provided for the selection of the mayor by the city council, although this office continued as an appointment of the state executive council in New York until 1821. By 1825, however, the pattern of locally-chosen mayors was common throughout the existing American states. In the early 1820s, the mayor became an elective office in Boston, St. Louis, and Detroit, and this was the common practice by the end of the next decade. A steady increase also took place in the powers of the mayor during this period. As presiding officer of the council, his power to appoint committees became increasingly important. A new charter in New York City adopted in 1830 gave the mayor the veto power. By 1850 the mayor was generally granted the power to appoint administrative officers with council approval and confirmation.

In addition to the plural or divided executive and weak executive forms of executive leadership, two other patterns have developed. During the last half of the nineteenth century, the strong-mayor plan emerged, gradually becoming the accepted form for larger cities where active and forceful administration was needed. Then in the first decade of the present century, the concept of the appointed local executive developed. This form has resulted in the creation of the positions of manager and chief administrative officer in cities, counties, towns, and townships across the nation. These four patterns form the basic character of the executive function in local government today. How the executive fulfills his functions in each of the four will be examined after a discussion of the essential features of the executive process in local government.

DEFINING THE EXECUTIVE FUNCTION

The executive function in local government recently has been increasingly described as a role of leadership rather than a role of specific functions. Where once it was assumed that the activities of the executive in any organizational setting conformed to a fairly well-defined pattern, now greater emphasis is placed on the personal qualifications of the effective leader and his ability to guide and direct the operations of the governmental organization toward agreed-upon objectives.

Illustrative of the pattern of duties concept was the work of Luther Gulick in coining the word "POSDCORB."[2] The letters in this term designate the different elements of the executive's seven-fold task—planning, organizing, staffing, directing, coordinating, reporting, and budgeting. The expansion of the executive's role is evidenced by the coinage of a new word—POSIDDOCEM—by Ordway Tead. Here again, each letter represents a component of the administrator's functions, which, in order, are planning, organizing, staffing, initiating, delegating, directing, overseeing, coordinating, evaluating, and motivating.[3] The change in executive emphasis from doing things to getting them done is apparent from the addition of new words and substitution of words for those comprising the Gulick concept.

A more current view of the local executive's leadership role describes it as more complex because

He faces multiple pressures and problems as complex as our society. His life is complicated by the fact that he must be one part institutional leader, one part political leader, one part educator, one part scapegoat, and some other part for whatever purpose his community wishes to use him. Of his various roles, however, that of institutional leader stands out as basic and crucial.[4]

To describe the institutional leadership role of mayors, Henry Maier, who served as the chief executive of Milwaukee, developed his "D-Stepp" formula. The letters in the formula state that Decision-making is accomplished through the sequential use of Strategy, Tactics, Enrollment, Power, and Philosophy. He defines these terms as follows:

1. Strategy is the mayor's total planning perspective, the overall design of his objectives.
2. Tactics is his procedures to implement the strategy.
3. Enrollment is both his specific and his broad efforts to enlist people in support of his objectives.
4. Power is his capability to effect results.
5. Philosophy is his system of leadership as exercised through his understanding of the demands of institutional leadership and the ways of people.[5]

Numerous helpful statements concerning the major attitudes, skills, or qualifications essential to administrative leadership have been made. Four such prerequisites have been identified by political scientist Stephen Bailey. They are: (1) a sense of organizational relevance by which the administrator gets the feel of his precise role in the common purpose of the enterprise. In Bailey's words, "The successful administrative leader, like the successful pilot, is the one who always takes account of what's above him, what's below him, and what's on both sides of him, in relation to what is in front of him;"[6] (2) a capacity for human warmth and understanding; (3) a spirit of enthusiasm coupled with courage—a person who exudes contagious excitement about his work and who is never entirely satisfied with the way things are going and has the courage to say so; and (4) a technical proficiency in the procedural and substantive aspects of his job.

In viewing the administrator's role, Ordway Tead advances a fivefold classification of personal qualities that appear to be almost universal prerequisites. They are: (1) sheer physical and nervous vitality and drive; (2) ability to think logically, rationally, with problem-solving skills that get the point quickly; (3) willingness to take the burdens of responsibility for executive decisions and actions; (4) ability to get along with people in a sincerely friendly, affable, yet firm way; and (5) ability to communicate effectively by voice and pen.[7] While the attributes of effective leadership are situational, certainly a person with the personal qualities listed above would be able to exercise discretion to achieve concrete action in any given administrative situation.

A more politically-oriented way of looking at the local executive's many roles has been advanced by Paul Ylvisaker, formerly with the Ford Foundation. His baker's dozen of executive functions is as follows:

1. Winning elections.
2. Leading—or deciding when not to lead.
3. Persuading.
4. Developing ideas of what to do and strategy for doing it.
5. Performing and getting performance.
6. Trouble-shooting, making peace, and raising hell.
7. Winning elections.
8. Surviving friends and enemies.
9. Getting informed and being challenged and needled.
10. Keeping intact family and sense of humor.
11. Finding good people to help.
12. Realizing his ambitions.
13. Winning elections.[8]

Notwithstanding the increasingly important responsibilities of the local executive in formulating and initiating policies, however, the primary responsibility for determining the direction of action and the policies to attain the accepted goals remains a function of local legislative bodies. The degree and types of controls exercised over the local executive vary considerably among legislative bodies. The discretion and powers of the local executive obviously vary with the type, nature, and intimacy of legislative councils. This relationship is worth examining in some detail in the following discussion of the four basic patterns of executive leadership in local government.

DIVIDED EXECUTIVE FORMS

The pattern of divided executive leadership in local government often is referred to as the no-executive type. This does not infer that the executive function is not performed—only that it is not centered in any one office or single agency. Thus, in county government the administrative function is performed in part by the county governing board, but this power is shared with certain separately elected officers—such as sheriff, treasurer, clerk, recorder, surveyor, assessor, solicitor, superintendent of schools, clerk of court, and coroner. Since the duties of these several officers were briefly described in Chapter 7, they are not repeated here. The excessive use of popular election in county government has prompted one writer to describe county administration as a ''hydra-headed monstrosity.''[9]

The fragmented nature of the executive function in the government of most counties is evident. Because the officers just listed are popularly elected and derive their authority from state constitutions or statutory provisions rather than from county ordinances, the county governing board exercises only limited control, if any, over them. The treasurer runs his office, for example, as he interprets his powers, and the same is true of the other county administrative officials. The administrative powers of the county board itself are numerous and varied, and it is still probable that the board's administrative work constitutes its greatest task.

The same pattern of fragmented executive leadership exists in most townships and is less of a problem there only because of a smaller number of township officers who undertake fewer services and activities. Divided executive leadership further characterizes government in town meeting-governed communities where the administrative responsibilities are divided among the board of selectmen and the several separately chosen town administrative officers.

The divided executive form also is a feature of the commission plan of city government. Under this form, each member of the governing board additionally operates as the head of an administrative department. Usually five commissioners exist, and the administrative function is divided among them with no overall guidance and direction except that offered by the five administrators when they change hats and sit as members of the governing board. The common tendency of the individual commissioners is not to interfere in the provinces of their colleagues because reciprocal "independence" is then more likely. However, often one commissioner is in charge of finance and accounts, and this could give an energetic and forceful person in this office a vehicle for exercising a degree of control in such affairs. A second source of leadership in commission cities may come from the commissioner who serves as mayor. An energetic leader in this position is able to exercise the functions of his office in a manner to overcome the inherent structural weaknesses of the plan. He does so, however, because of his personality rather than the powers of his post.[10]

Along with the issue of the divided executive, local government faces the dilemma of finding among its executives the proper balance between the generalist who has a broad understanding of government but little technical skill and the specialist who possesses technical knowledge but only a limited appreciation of the broader problems and procedures. As Roscoe Martin points out, with special reference to rural government, the smaller the unit or area, the less meaningful is the distinction among politics, government, and administration, for the lines separating politics from government and both from administration blur and grow dim in small governments. Thus the differentiations in process common in big government are hardly known in small units.[11]

WEAK EXECUTIVE FORMS

The weak executive form is the oldest of the main types of city government in the United States. Although losing ground in larger cities since the turn of the present century, it still is the predominant pattern of government among smaller cities, villages, and towns, and is a feature of government in a small number of counties that have an elective executive. The distinguishing features of the executive function in this form are (1) the limited role of the executive in the administrative process because of his restricted appointive and financial powers and the absence of a veto; (2) the existence of several popularly elected administrative officers, often including treasurer, attorney, clerk, and assessor; (3) independence of these elective officers from direction and control by the executive; and (4) a relatively strong council endowed with administrative functions as well as its policy-determining authority.

At this point it seems helpful to point out how this form differs from the divided or no-executive forms discussed above, because many of the administrative problems are commonly shared. In those forms, no single officer is present to whom the executive functions could be entrusted; in the weak-executive form, the office of mayor or county supervisor exists but the administrative function is still shared with the governing board and with other elected officers. This is a product of colonial fear and distrust of concentrated executive power. In addition, weak executives in both city and county governments have certain legislative powers. They have the right to recommend policy actions to the governing board, attend meetings of the council, and in some communities to preside over council meetings. In certain communities, they vote in the event of an even split on the governing board and in some policy areas they have a veto power that the council can override. These legislative powers, even though sometimes quite limited, give the so-called weak executive an opening to exercise influence in matters of administration which is not a feature of the divided executive form.

To have effective power over administration and to coordinate administrative activities, the mayor or county supervisor, at a minimum, should have general powers to shape fiscal policies and to appoint key officials and hold them accountable. The mayor in the weak executive plan has neither of these basic powers. The budget in such cities usually is prepared by a committee of the council, and the controller, if the latter office exists, is either a council appointee or is popularly elected. The financial powers of the weak executive are so restricted as to provide no means of real influence in determining either fiscal policy or in controlling municipal expenditures. The appointive power of the weak mayor is similarly restricted with the popular election of some administrative officers and council appointment of others. A general rule in such cities gives the mayor the right to nominate people for unpaid positions while nominations of paid administrative officials is lodged in the council or other city boards or commissions.

The weak executive plan in county government is illustrated by the office of elected county supervisor in a small number of New Jersey counties. Elected for a three-year term, the supervisor is normally responsible for supervising subordinate officers and employees. He may remove county employees for neglect of duty or insubordination, but he lacks the power of appointment. In practice, few employees have been removed by the supervisor because the employee so removed may appeal to the state civil service commission or to the courts. The fiscal powers of the county supervisor are similarly restricted since he neither prepares the budget nor controls the expenditures. Thus, the administrative powers exercised by the elected county supervisor largely parallel those of his counterpart in city governments with the weak-mayor form.

Chicago is one of the last large cities with the weak-mayor form of government. A study of that city in 1955 noted that the city formally had a "weak-mayor" form of government but it also had a powerful mayor and a powerful leader of the council. The paradox of a "weak" government that was strong was explained by the presence of the Democratic machine, an organization parallel to but outside the city government. The weakness of the city government in Chicago was offset by the strength of the party.[12] As mentioned earlier, a shortcoming of the weak mayor-strong council form of government is that the policy leadership essential for the welfare of the citizen sometimes goes by default to some person or group outside the formal machinery of government because often no person is present within the framework of the government to provide it.

The weak executive form of local government has few supporters among students of government. Its inherent structural disadvantages far outweigh the possible advantages of keeping government close to the people through popular election of a number of officials and protection against the abuses that may result from the concentration of too much power in one office. However, no one seriously questions that the form will continue to exist, especially in smaller cities, for the foreseeable future.

STRONG EXECUTIVE FORMS

Governments in large cities in recent decades have followed the general trend in American government of strengthening the powers of the chief executive officer. The same development has occurred in a small number of counties where an elected executive serves as the real head of county administration. Four characteristics distinguish the strong executive form from the plural- and weak-executive types. In the first place, much stronger controls over administration are vested in the chief executive office. Second, this officer is empowered to appoint and remove his department and agency heads. Third, the strong executive officer prepares the budget, or a budget officer responsible to and appointed by him prepares it. And fourth, the executive has both the general and the item veto power. In communities with this form, the council exercises its policy-determining power, but is expected to leave administration to the executive and his subordinates within the general policy guides it determines.

The strong executive form is not limited to large cities, although their need for forceful, imaginative, executive leadership has made its growth and development there particularly striking. The Report of the National Advisory Commission on Civil Disorders is outspoken on this point. In its words,

> Now, as never before, the American city has need for the personal qualities of strong democratic leadership. . . . In most cities the mayors will have the prime responsibility. . . . As leader and mediator, he must involve all those groups—employers, news media, unions, financial institutions and others—which only together can bridge the chasm now separating the racial ghetto from the community. His goal, in effect, must be to develop a new working concept of democracy within the city.[13]

The coordinative, appointive, and fiscal powers of the strong mayor give him a significant influence over and important sanctions that he can bring to bear upon the administrative process in his city. His coordinative powers include general supervision over the activities of the departments and agencies, while his powers in the preparation and administration of the budget give him influence over their activities. His appointive powers extend to department heads and in many cities even to the major subdivisions within the departments. While approval of the council is necessary, the mayor, in most cities, definitely exercises the leadership in the selection of his subordinates and "consults" with the council rather than shares this important responsibility. The mayor's basic fiscal power is found in the preparation of the budget, but its administration also gives him important powers over both his subordinates and agencies independent of his general control.

The same pattern of strong executive powers and sanctions is found in the office of an elected executive in more and more counties. The major responsibilities of the county executive include preparation of programs for approval by the governing board, implementing the policies approved by the board, responsibility for daily county administration including budget and personnel control, and submission of the county's operating and capital budgets. An appraisal of his office finds him "both an administrator and a leader in the true executive sense of the word."[14] Among the counties with such executive are Dade County, Florida; Cook County, Illinois; Baltimore County,

Maryland; Erie, Nassau and Suffolk Counties, New York; and King County, Washington.

The mayor's term of office ranges from one to six years, with two-year terms the most common in both mayor-council and council-manager governed cities. Four-year terms occur in two of every three commission-governed cities. One-year terms are still surprisingly common in council manager cities with one in every five having such an abbreviated term.

TABLE 9
METHOD OF SELECTING MAYOR

Population Group	Council Selects	People Elect	Council Member Receiving Highest Vote
Over 500,000	1	15	0
250,000-500,000	4	19	0
100,000-250,000	18	53	1
50,000-100,000	51	120	1
25,000-50,000	119	221	2
10,000-25,000	201	469	7
5,000-10,000	99	369	3
Form of Government			
Mayor-Council	12	344	2
Mayor-Council-CAO	42	405	1
Council-Manager	401	428	7
Commission	25	77	4

Source: International City Management Association, *Municipal Year Book, 1972*, Washington, 1972, p. 24.

Table 9 shows the variations in methods by which the mayor is selected. Methods of selection vary considerably among the major forms of city government. The mayor is elected directly by the voters in most mayor-council cities, in three of each four commission-governed cities, and in slightly more than half of the cities with the council-manager form.

The mayor's veto power is both strongest and most frequent in cities with the mayor-council form of government, and weakest and least frequent in commission-governed cities. In about half the cities of both forms, the mayor has veto power over all measures while the veto is limited to selected items in the other half. The selective veto is found nearly twice as often as the general veto power in council-manager government cities.

The problem of securing able and effective leaders to serve as strong executives in city and county governments persists. Seymour Freedgood has identified the four major challenges facing the big city mayor as he strives to exercise his powers of policy leadership. These are the staff experts and the civil service bureaucrats who attempt to increase their own authority at his expense; the growing "external bureaucracy" in the form of public corporations and authorities; the state legislature with its controlling voice in the fiscal affairs of his city; and the continuing struggle between the mayor and the suburbs surrounding his city.[15]

The challenge to the mayor from staff experts and civil service bureaucrats listed by Freedgood has been elaborated upon in more recent studies. In colorful but insightful words, one writer zeroes in on middle-level bureaucrats. In his words,

> The growth of highly specialized bureaucracies leads to self-contained guilds which monopolize their areas and, like trade unions, become more and more averse to any but their members performing functions that they have stamped as their own.[16]

The problem beginning in the 1970's was further complicated by the fact that urban executive power has to be shared. One writer notes that "the mayor must deal, sometimes as friend but more often as antagonist, with increasing numbers of actors" including economic actors (banks, municipal unions), social actors (racial, religious and ethnic groups), professional actors (in governmental and private service), political actors (other elective officials), and intergovernmental actors representing the state and federal levels. Jewel Bellush, political scientist, concludes, "At the very least the city's citizens need a strong mayor able to deal with these other actors—to bargain, to challenge and to muster coalitions for the tough struggles."[17]

APPOINTED EXECUTIVE FORMS

In the strong executive form discussed above, the control over administration usually is vested in an elective official. In other local units, this power is entrusted to an appointive administrator who is generally known as a manager or chief administrative officer. Both plans are more common in cities than in counties, but the number of county adoptions of strong appointive executive plans is rising.

Two basic features of the manager plan in both city and county government are the unification of authority and political responsibility in an elected governing board, and the centralization of administrative responsibility in the manager who is appointed by and responsible to the council. A corollary characteristic of the centralized administrative responsibility in the manager is the understanding that the governing board normally deals with administration only through the manager, the manager has power to select and direct the department heads, and neither individual council members nor council committees undertake administrative functions.

While city and county charters vary considerably in their prescription of the duties of the manager, rather common agreement exists that these duties are to include: enforcing all laws and ordinances; appointing and removing department heads and employees on the basis of merit; exercising control and supervision over all departments; making such recommendations to the council concerning city affairs as he may deem desirable; keeping the council informed of the financial condition of and the future needs of the city; preparing and submitting the annual budget to the council; preparing and submitting such other reports as may be required by the council; informing the public through reports to the council, regarding the operations of the city government; and performing such other duties as may be prescribed by the charter or required by ordinance or resolution of the council.

In addition to the manager, cities with this form have a mayor with legislative, political, and ceremonial functions. He presides at council meetings and is a leader in the development and determination of municipal policies. With the other council members, he interprets municipal policy to the people and shares the responsibilities of local political leadership. He represents the city in ceremonial functions and maintains contact with civic groups. He also appoints citizen advisory committees and commissions and coordinates their efforts in studying problems of the community. In counties these functions are provided, in a more limited way, by the president of the board.

When the manager plan first developed, a sharp distinction was made between the policy functions of the manager and those of the mayor in mayor-council cities. The changing concept of the manager's function in this regard is evident from this recent assessment. According to John Bollens and John Ries, managers are and always have been major actors in urban politics. As the only full-time professional with broad executive powers and considerable political resources in the community, a manager cannot avoid coming to terms with dominant local interests. The extent to which the manager is able to translate his resources into "leadership" depends upon the characteristics of the political environment and upon his professional values and personality.[18]

In a perceptive study of managers and councils in more than eighty cities in the San Francisco area, it was found that the two held varied views about the manager's role. The managers saw themselves as strong political executives expected to exert policy leadership on most demands or issues on the civic agenda. They believed they should be involved in the initiation, fixing of priorities, and bargaining for the acceptance of policy proposals as well as in implementing council policy decisions. The council members, on the other hand, saw the role of the manager as staff officer hired to give advice and information on city affairs and to implement policy once it passed by the council.[19]

According to another study, the adoption of the council-manager plan in a community is likely to result in both administrative and fiscal changes. Responses from sixty-nine cities revealed that major changes in budgeting procedures occurred in 77 percent of the reporting cities; major changes in departmental organization in 75 percent; better use of revenue in 89 percent; major increases in expenditures for capital improvements in 70 percent; manager more accessible than previous chief executive in 76 percent; and weakening of influence of political parties in 21 percent.[20] In a before and after study in these cities, 91 percent had centralized purchasing compared to 16 percent before adoption; 90 percent had a master plan compared to 37 percent before; 98 percent had satisfaction of public with services compared to 29 percent; and 89 percent expressed public satisfaction with the community's plan for growth and development compared to 25 percent before adoption.[21]

The problem of leadership and accountability also is a significant factor in governing urban counties. A recent report advocates that the elected county executive plan is particularly suited to urban counties with substantial differences of opinion over policy and where group and sectional diversity exists, thus creating the need for strong and decisive leadership to get things done. The council-strong executive form of government is particularly applicable to highly urbanized or rapidly growing jurisdictions that have social and economic cleavages and disparities and substantial political competition, thereby necessitating strong political leadership to get things done.[22]

The chief administrative officer or general manager idea for large cities and counties began in the consolidated City and County of San Francisco with the adoption of a new charter in November, 1931. Two differences distinguish the chief administrative officer (hereafter referred to as CAO) and manager plans. Instead of acting directly as does the manager, the CAO makes recommendations that are reviewed by the governing board before implementation. This supports the basic theory of the plan that the CAO is the agent of the board, acts for it and in its name in carrying out his assigned duties. Second, the assignment of duties of the CAO are generally more limited than those entrusted to the manager.

The following list of duties assigned to CAO's is fairly common. It includes: supervising, coordinating, and reporting on designated activities and operations; carrying out administrative policies and rules adopted by the governing board; making suggestions on departmental activities to increase overall efficiency; recommending changes in annual departmental budget estimates; administering the adopted budget; supervising expenditures; controlling expenditures; developing and assisting in carrying out public improvement programs; serving as public relations officer. The list further includes cooperating with community organizations; itemizing all property owned by the local governmental unit; recommending purchase, transfer, and disposal of equipment and supplies; suggesting abolition or consolidation of positions; handling routine administrative business; and performing other duties assigned by the governing board, including recommendations on personnel.[23] This is a more lengthy list of duties than those comprising the core functions of the manager, but they are more confined in scope, thus bearing out an essential difference between the two plans of appointed local executive government. While the manager plan establishes a professional administrator who is free from control by the mayor, the CAO plan creates a position but makes it responsible to the mayor. The success of the plan depends mainly upon the relationship between the mayor and the CAO. The key problem concerning the successful operation of the CAO plan is that "of finding a mayor who is willing to delegate responsibility for administrative detail to a CAO and of finding a CAO who can secure the confidence of the mayor."[24]

The existence of a large number of executive officers in the plural- and weak-executive forms has already been noted. However, the discussion of the strong and appointed executive forms has been limited to the role and responsibilities of the chief executive officer and the mayor in appointed executive forms. In cities and counties governed by these two forms, usually one or more other administrative officers are either elected by the voters or appointed by the governing board and thus somewhat independent of the chief executive officer's control. In cities, the officers most likely to be elected are one or more of the following: clerk, city attorney, treasurer, or controller. In counties, the positions of attorney, clerk, sheriff, and assessor are most often elective. The basic responsibilities of these officers have been discussed in Chapter 7.

EXECUTIVE LEADERSHIP

The need for strong executive leadership in local government has been touched upon at several places in this chapter. The need is so great, however, that to reiterate the point in this closing statement seems relevant and necessary.

In a discussion of the changing and emerging role of the mayor in New Haven, Robert Dahl concluded that the executive centered order was not a neat hierarchical system with the mayor at the top operating through subordinates in a chain of command. Rather, he described the mayor as sitting at the center of intersecting circles.

He rarely commanded. He negotiated, cajoled, exhorted, beguiled, charmed, pressed, appealed, reasoned, promised, insisted, demanded, even threatened, but he most needed support and acquiescence from other leaders who simply could not be commanded. Because the mayor could not command, he had to bargain.[25]

The mayor, however, had a number of political resources to utilize in his bargaining. As mayor, he had the resource of legality. This gave him control over jobs and easy access to the press and other mass media. The media resource is important in molding public opinion in support of favored policies and in opposition to those not wanted. The mayor also possessed significant informal powers in mediating between and among groups and in coalition-building to back his policies and programs.

Centralized executive leadership also is essential to utilize the mass media sources effectively. These media—newspapers, radio, television, magazines, and journals—enjoy an immediacy and directness in their contact with citizens. Dahl described control over these media a political resource of great potential importance. "Dictators and democratic leaders alike recognize this fact, the one by establishing, the other by trying to prevent a monopoly of control over the mass media."[26] On one day, the media in Milwaukee had thirteen reporters who demanded the mayor's time for many questions since, in that issue, the mayor had become a "news source" exclusively. In these situations, the mayor must direct his time and energies to control, insofar as possible, the image these media give to the public. Henry Maier believes a mayor's public standing is assessed by the citizens through signs in the press and television and radio comment.[27]

A recent role thrust upon the local executive is that of "diplomat" to the state capitol and Washington, D.C. In these frequent visits, the local executive more often wears the hat of a "pleader" for funds and needed policy enactments rather than the more usual hat of booster and boaster. In his relations with these intergovernmental actors, the mayor often is at a disadvantage. For example, the voice of the mayor is actually muted when federal programs bypass city hall to encourage local citizen involvement and participation. Similarly, states have expanded their intervention in local governments under the guise that it is for the welfare of local citizens. Fiscal crises are almost certain to re-emphasize the fact that local governments are creatures of the state. Sometimes fiscal aid is granted at a heavy price in home rule.[28]

A final problem of increasing concern for the local executive is the field of labor relations and the growing militancy of public employee organizations. Organized employee groups present the local government with certain advantages and opportunities and often are a source of support for needed changes in personnel administration. However, they also represent the increasing self-perceived needs of public employees for job security and adequate compensation. These goals may be difficult for the local executive to meet in times of budget crises, and the recent result has been a large number of strikes. This particular problem is elaborated upon in Chapter 13.

Many people still believe that strong local executive forms—whether the administrative head is elected or appointed—are a serious threat to democracy in local government because too much power is concentrated in the hands of one individual. While many of these persons are sincere in their belief, the evidence of strong executive plans in practice is hardly on their side. The role of the governing board in holding the executive responsible has been pointed out in several sections of this chapter as well as in previous one. When the local executive is responsible to the elected representatives of the people, or directly to the people, as are the managers, mayors, CAO's, county presidents, and county executives, there is no real danger to democracy. Such forms are not only compatible and reconcilable with effective democracy; they are conducive to it.

NOTES

1. John A. Fairlie, *Municipal Administration*, Macmillan, 1901, p. 74.
2. Luther Gulick and L. Urwick, *Papers on the Science of Administration*, Institute of Public Administration, 1937, p. 13.
3. Ordway Tead, *Administration, Its Purpose and Performance*, Harper, 1959, p. 31.
4. Henry W. Maier, *Challenge to the Cities: An Approach to a Theory of Urban Leadership*, Random House, 1966, p. 29.
5. *Ibid.*, p. 33.
6. Stephen Bailey, "Administrative Leadership in Local and State Government: Its Meaning and Educational Implications," in S. B. Sweeney and Thomas J. Davy (ed.), *Education for Administrative Careers in Government Service*, University of Pennsylvania Press, 1958, pp. 329-32.
7. Tead, *op. cit.*, p. 59.
8. Paul Ylvisaker, "Administrative Assistance for Mayors," address presented at National Municipal League Conference on Government, Cleveland, November 20, 1957.
9. Roger Wells, *American Local Government*, McGraw-Hill, 1939, p. 81.
10. For an interesting case study of the activities of such a strong mayor in a commission-governed city, see John H. Vanderzell, "Mayor Joseph T. Moriarty" in Richard T. Frost (ed.), *Cases in State and Local Government*, Prentice-Hall, 1961, pp. 28-33.
11. Roscoe C. Martin, *Grass Roots*, University of Alabama Press, 1957, p. 40.
12. Martin Meyerson and Edward C. Banfield, *Politics, Planning and the Public Interest*, Free Press, 1955, p. 287.
13. *Report of the National Advisory Commission on Civil Disorders*, Bantam, 1968, pp. 298-9.

14. National Association of Counties, *From America's Counties Today, 1973*, Washington, 1973, p. 22.
15. Seymour Freedgood, "New Strength in City Hall," in Fortune Magazine (ed.), *The Exploding Metropolis*, Doubleday, 1958, pp. 64-65.
16. Norton Long, *The Unwalled City, Reconstituting the Urban Community*, Basic Books, 1972, p. 148. See also Wallace S. Sayre and Herbert Kaufman, *Governing New York City*, W. W. Norton, 1965, pp. 447-9. Among such guilds, Long identifies the police, the teachers and the medical industry.
17. Jewel Bellush, "A Bicentennial Resolution: Let the Mayor Be," *National Civic Review*, 64, No. 9 (October, 1975), 459-63.
18. John C. Bollens and John C. Ries, *The City Manager Profession, Myths and Realities*, Public Administration Service, 1969, p. 34.
19. Ronald O. Loveridge, *City Managers in Legislative Politics*, Bobbs-Merrill, 1971.
20. Walter E. Mardis and W. Donald Heisel, "When the Manager Plan Comes to Town," *Nation's Cities*, 9 (May, 1971), pp. 20-23.
21. *Ibid.*, p. 22
22. National Association of Counties, *op. cit.*, p. 19, in evaluating William V. Musto, *County Government: Challenge and Change*, Official Report of the New Jersey Municipal Government Study Commission, April 1969.
23. John C. Bollens, *Appointed Executive Local Government*, Haynes Foundation, 1952, pp. 12-13.
24. Charles R. Adrian, "Recent Concepts in Large City Administration," in Edward C. Banfield (ed.), *Urban Government, A Reader in Administration and Politics*, revised edition, Free Press, 1969, pp. 512-24, at p. 524.
25. Robert A. Dahl, *Who Governs?* Yale University Press, 1961, p. 204.
26. *Ibid.*, p. 256.
27. Maier, *op. cit.*, pp. 133-4.
28. Bellush, *op. cit.*, 461-2.

Chapter 12

The
Justice Process

The problem of the administration of justice begins and ends with people. While many individuals have no occasion year after year to use the services of courts, others are not so fortunate. Some may be stopped by police officers for exceeding the posted speed limits; others may be victimized by or be accused of victimizing a fellow citizen; still others may fail to conduct their place of business in keeping with established norms of cleanliness, safety, or decency.

THE ROLE OF THE COURTS

The essential role of the courts is to interpret and apply the laws regulating relationships between individuals and between citizens and their government in such a manner as to approximate justice. In other words, the courts are to administer justice. Justice is a relative concept, which is difficult to define in substance or essence very satisfactorily. A procedure thus has been established by which a person involved in a dispute receives a fair hearing and the benefit of a judgment by an impartial judge or jury of his fellow citizens. The spirit of this process is well illustrated by our symbol of justice which depicts a blindfolded woman holding a balance scale in her hands. As the three main features of this symbol, the woman represents gentle protectiveness, the blindfold insures impartiality, and the scale reflects the desire to determine the merits of the case objectively.

In a typical judicial proceeding, the court performs three basic functions. First, it must determine the facts in the case before it. Second, it must determine which rules of law are relevant. And third, it must apply the pertinent law or laws to the relevant facts to arrive at a judgment. Broadly speaking, law represents the community's rules of conduct that are backed up by the organized force of that community. Law is an important necessary device for social control complementing but also going beyond the mores and folkways of the community.

The two main types of law that have evolved in our society are statutory and common. The former is law established by lawyers or legislators and is written and codified. Common law, on the other hand, is decreed by judges, appears first as case law, and is based upon custom. In one of his well-known decisions, Mr. Justice Holmes defined common law in these words, "The common law is not a brooding omnipresence in the sky, but the articulate voice of some sovereign or quasi-sovereign that can be identified."[1] Case precedents in common law, while not codified, exist as a matter of record in courts of record, and previous judgments are not ignored by judges in cases coming before them.

In addition to interpreting the law, courts have a significant role in the whole local governmental process. The wording of a local ordinance may be somewhat ambiguous and the court will need to clarify its meaning and intent. Another local ordinance may be contrary to state law, and the court may declare it null and void because of its conflict with the higher law. Courts also have an effective role in protecting the rights of a citizen against unwarranted actions by local officials or other citizens. The role of the courts therefore is much broader than that of applying and interpreting the law. Courts may also clarify local law, overrule it, and check its overenforcement or unreasonable application. According to Herbert Jacob, political scientist, courts in America daily make "political" decisions settling conflicts that otherwise would have to be decided by legislative or executive action. Courts not only mediate disputes but also formulate policy in the same manner. In Jacob's words,

> It makes little difference to those affected whether desegregation is the consequence of a legislative act, an executive order, or a court decision. It is a governmental policy that must be obeyed at the risk of imprisonment.[2]

Lower courts are the true "work-horses" of the judiciary in terms of volume of work handled.

The main functions of courts are to: (1) investigate and determine facts; (2) apply law to the facts thus determined; (3) determine and construe law; (4) prevent the infraction of law and the violation of rights; (5) advise the legislative and executive branches with respect to law; (6) act as public administrative agencies; (7) administer property; (8) act as agencies to enforce decisions; and (9) determine rules of judicial procedure.[3]

TYPES OF LOCAL CASES

Before examining the structure of the local court system, the several common types of cases heard by the lower courts should be differentiated. The jurisdiction of particular courts is often limited to civil or criminal cases or to cases in equity. By defining each type, we should make the discussion of court authority clear.

A civil case normally is between private persons and/or private organizations; it deals with actions concerning the rights and duties of individuals in their relationships with each other. Proceedings, as a general rule, are initiated by a party or organization known as the plaintiff, while the party against whom the action is brought is the defendant. Civil cases include such actions as defamation of character, divorce, trespassing on private property, personal injury resulting from being struck by a bicycle or automobile, breach of contract, and suits to collect unpaid bills or overdue payments. Although most civil cases do not involve governmental units, cities as municipal corporations may sue and be sued in much the same manner as persons or private corporations.

The most common type of offense that may involve a local government is a civil suit known as a tort, which has been defined as a civil wrong not arising out of a breach of contract. The majority of tort cases, as in civil cases generally, concern government only as an umpire providing facilities for settling disputes. On occasion, governmental bodies may be liable for damages for injuries to individuals or their property. Also, the possibility exists that the official committing the injury may be personally liable. While it is difficult to generalize, the tendency is to modify by statute or court decision the old rules that created a broad immunity from suit.

A criminal case is usually brought in the name of the "people" with the governmental unit serving as the prosecutor. The case involves an accusation stating that the defendant has violated some specific law regulating the conduct of individuals with the infraction being punishable by penalties provided in the law. Criminal acts fall into one of three major categories—treason, felonies, or misdemeanors. Treason, which is the most serious offense against the state, is carefully defined. As found in the national constitution and in most state constitutions, treason consists of "levying war against them (the United States), or in adhering to their enemies, giving them aid and comfort." In recent years, a number of treason cases have grown out of urban disorder situations, and the term no longer may be viewed only as disloyal activity in time of war.

While the concept of a felony is used to connote a major or serious crime, it is not uniformly defined by statutes in the fifty states. It typically includes such acts as murder, manslaughter, arson, larceny, burglary, rape, and aggravated assault. Misdemeanors, too, are not uniformly defined, but the term is reserved for less serious offenses such as public drunkenness, traffic violations, disturbance of the peace, rowdiness, and violation of local health ordinances. Sometimes the term misdemeanor is limited to lesser indictable offenses whereas non-indictable actions are known as petty offenses. However, two useful distinctions may be made between the two types of crimes. Felonies in most instances are breaches of a major crime defined by state law while violations of local ordinances ordinarily are only misdemeanors. The possibility of a prison confinement is a further distinguishing characteristic of a major criminal action in contrast to an award of money damages in a civil suit and a monetary fine in minor criminal cases.

Cases in equity involve the application of rules and principles supplementing common law and providing a remedy to prevent an injustice in cases where common law fails to do so. It enables a judge to hand down an order to prevent an injustice and is remedial in character. The decision of the judge in such cases is known as a decree rather than a judgment, and it usually is in the form of a writ such as a writ of injunction, mandamus, or prohibition.[4] Over the years, the rules of equity have become increasingly rigid in contrast to its original concept of being preventive justice where the common law failed to provide an adequate remedy. Two reasons for this change are the growth of the "litigation industry" as the number of lawyers has increased and the expansion of the middle class in society, which has become more demanding in its role as a consumer.

COURT ORGANIZATION AND JURISDICTION

Generally speaking, a fairly simple heirarchy of four levels of courts has been organized in most state judicial systems. The bottom level is known as the minor judiciary and includes such courts as those headed by justices of the peace, magistrates, recorders, or aldermen. A number of specialized municipal courts (such as police or traffic courts) are also a part of the minor judiciary. The second rung of the judicial ladder is comprised of general trial courts known variously as county, district, or circuit courts. Next in line comes the court of appeals, which serves as an intermediate court. At the top of the pyramid is the state supreme court. In the following discussion, only the first two levels are treated, because they are the only two that may properly be described as local courts.

The Minor Judiciary

The best known and the traditional court for rendering community justice are the courts of the justices of the peace. In some rural sections of the nation, they are headed by squires and in cities by magistrates or aldermen. As courts of limited jurisdiction, they exercise three main types of authority. First, they possess the authority to hear and determine minor criminal cases. Second, these courts are generally empowered to hold preliminary hearings where persons are accused of more serious crimes. Following the hearing, the judge may release the defendant for lack of evidence, release him under bail pending a future trial or grand jury investigation, or hold him in jail custody to await his trial. Third, the minor judiciary also has jurisdiction in civil cases involving limited amounts of money including small claims, torts, and common law suits. Judges of these courts usually are authorized to render other services such as performing marriage ceremonies and attesting certain documents.

In general, these courts of the minor judiciary—often called inferior courts—are not courts of record and their judges are not trained in law. As courts of record, no permanent records of proceedings, which are usually quite informal and without jury, are kept. The judges are elected by the voters of the township, borough, village, or city ward serving as the jurisdictional area of the court. By and large, they serve only part-time in this capacity and in many areas are paid from fees derived from the cases they hear. In larger cities, these inferior court judges are commonly on a salary basis, are usually trained in law, and work full-time at their judicial duties. They thus present a sharp contrast to their rural counterparts.

Increasingly in recent years, the justice of the peace courts have been widely criticized, and in some states the character of the office has been improving. One of the biggest criticisms concerns the lack of qualifications for the judges who preside over these minor courts in many states. They are not required to have legal training and many do not.

A second criticism concerns the court facilities of the minor judiciary. While some justices are provided with courtrooms, many hold court in their homes or in the place of their other and primary occupations. The records maintained by these justices are often scanty and inaccurate and sometimes do not even exist. But the greatest criticism of justice of the peace courts is the fee system of compensation. The penchant of these judges to decide in the plaintiff's favor has caused Clyde Snider to suggest that ''J. P.' (the usual abbreviation for justice of the peace) means ''judgment for the plaintiff.''[5]

The urban counterparts of the justice of the peace are quite unlike their more rural associates. But neither they nor their courts are shining lights in the overall judicial structure in many cities. While salaried, the judges are not paid enough to attract many high quality candidates and the courtroom facilities are often shabby and overcrowded. Frequently these judges ignore fine points of law and otherwise intimidate their main workload of lower class citizens. A definite trend seems under way, however, for cities to establish under state enabling legislation special courts designed to improve administration of justice in minor cases. Such courts have various names, including magistrates courts, courts of common pleas, traffic, and police courts. A further trend is evident in large cities where cases are segregated according to the nature of the question involved. Types of cases are assigned to a particular judge or judges who are organized in specialized branches or divisions of the court. The main criticism of city judges has to do with their handling of juveniles. The judges appear to be disinterested or delegate decisions to others who are supposedly in charge of the young offenders. The result in too many cases is the release of delinquents to commit further acts of mayhem and even murder.

General Trial Courts

The next higher level in the state court system is the county court, which might aptly be called the workhorse of the judicial system.[6] Known in some states as the district, superior, or circuit courts, or the court of common pleas, the term county court is used here to embrace these court titles as well because in large part they have parallel jurisdiction. This court's jurisdiction extends to four types of controversy; ordinary civil cases, cases in equity, criminal cases, and probate or inheritance cases. Typically, this general trial court consists of one judge, who is chosen by popular election on a partisan ballot. In about one-fourth of the states, this judge is appointed by the governor or selected by the state legislature, and about an equal number of states provides for his election by nonpartisan ballot. His term of office ranges from two years to life, with four- or six-year terms most common.

As indicated by the types of cases heard by general trial courts, their jurisdiction is extensive and normally includes both original and appellate authority. Their appellate power extends to appeals from municipal and justice courts on which they have the authority to make final decision. This pattern of authority is common for general trial courts. In addition, many such courts are authorized to review, on appeal, the actions of certain local administrative agencies.

Although general trial courts try many non-jury cases, they also make substantial use of the jury in both civil and criminal cases to serve as a fact-determining agency. The essential duty of the trial or petit jury is to decide, on the basis of the evidence presented before it, the arguments of counsel, and the instructions of the court, whether the accused in a criminal case is guilty or innocent of the offense charged, and in civil actions whether judgment should be in favor of the plaintiff or the defendant. State constitutions almost universally contain broad guarantees to citizens of a right to trial by jury, and even though the use of the jury is voluntarily waived by the parties involved in some cases, the trial jury continues to play an important part in judicial administration.

Many states now provide for the trial of misdemeanor offenses and some civil cases by juries of less than twelve members, but the jury of twelve still is almost universally required in trials of more serious crimes and still is widely used in other cases as well. The list of jurors is usually chosen at random from either local tax assessment rolls or voter registration lists. When a jury panel is needed, the court clerk draws a designated number of names from a box, and these persons are summoned to appear for service. The jury hears the case and then retires to arrive at its verdict.

An application of the common law rule holds that a valid verdict in either a civil or criminal case must be based on unanimous agreement of the twelve jurists. About half the states have modified this unanimity rule in civil cases and in trials of lesser crimes by requiring a vote of two-thirds, three-fourths, or five-sixths of the jurists. This change has produced many fewer "hung" juries—the term used when a jury fails to agree, resulting in a new trial or the dropping of the case.

The jury system has long been criticized on two main counts. The first relates to the qualifications of persons comprising the jury and the second to the unanimity requirement in jury decisions. Because of the ease of obtaining an excuse from jury service, many persons qualified by education, experience, and temperament avoid this service. The legal qualifications for jury duty are fairly uniform and consist of lower and upper age limits, citizenship, and residence requirements. The question of the unanimous verdict makes it twelve times as difficult to secure a conviction as it does to prevent one, since every member of the jury must be convinced, beyond a reasonable doubt, of the guilt of the defendant. Few would disagree with our principle that an accused person is presumed innocent until proven guilty and that the burden of proof lies with the state. However, use of the unanimous verdict probably will continue to decline except in cases of capital offenses.

Although the grand jury has fallen into partial disuse in some states, it continues to be a judicial device in wide use. A grand jury differs from the petit or trial jury in both size and function. In size, it varies from twelve to twenty-three members and its function is to determine whether or not sufficient evidence exists to bring a person to trial. The defense does not have an opportunity to present its side to the grand jury. As a consequence, the grand jury does not return a verdict but decides whether or not the evidence presented deserves an indictment of the accused so that he must stand trial.

The return of indictments was historically the primary function of the grand jury, but this no longer is the common procedure in some states for bringing a person to trial. An alternative procedure involves a preliminary hearing in an inferior court, followed by the filing of an "information," a sworn statement, by the district attorney in a general trial court. A major advantage of the grand jury proceeding is its secrecy. Accordingly it is still ordinarily used when a case is weak or doubtful to protect the accused against unfounded public accusations, or in cases of a sensational nature.

As the percentage of time spent by grand juries in considering criminal indictments lessens, they have more time to devote to "watchdog" activities. In California a grand jury of nineteen citizens is impaneled annually in each county in the state. A considerable portion of its time is spent in looking into the conduct of public officials, the expenditure of public funds, and the functioning of local government. While grand juries have been accused of unwarranted harassment of public officials and of being cumbersome, amateurish, and time-consuming in their performance, they do seem to serve as a potentially powerful arm of direct democracy and many have rendered valuable service through studies and investigations. A number of district attorneys use grand juries as their springboard for selecting which cases to prosecute and which to ignore. In many cases, the choice is made to make the district attorney look good and to further his political aspirations for higher office.

DUE PROCESS OF LAW

The deeply-cherished safeguards secured for American citizens by the Fifth and Fourteenth Amendments to our national Constitution are also guaranteed by our state constitutions. As a result, we are twice assured that no person shall be deprived of life, liberty, or property "without due process of law." This is not an easy concept to define and possibly it becomes more meaningful by considering the several procedural steps that occur in the trial of a person charged with an offense. These steps represent the procedural safeguards that must be followed and, when taken together, they comprise the major elements of the due process principle.

Because the major procedural steps differ in civil and criminal cases, they are listed in outline form in Table 10. A legal officer of the state serves as the prosecuting attorney since the state is the plaintiff in criminal cases while in civil cases the plaintiff is the person bringing the suit. Defendants in criminal cases have a number of general rights which include: a preliminary hearing in the case of a felony charge, the right to legal counsel, the right to know the charges against him, the right to trial by jury, the right to confront witnesses against him, and the right to summon witnesses on his own behalf.

TABLE 10
MAJOR PROCEDURAL STEPS IN CIVIL AND CRIMINAL CASES

CIVIL	CRIMINAL
1. Plantiff, or his attorney, files complaint with court stating facts upon which claim against defendant is based.	1. Defendant commits an action which violates a specific law that makes such action a crime.

CIVIL	CRIMINAL

2. Court issues summons for defendant allowing him a period of ten days in which to answer complaint. At this point, defendant has one of three options: decide not to contest suit and thus allow plaintiff to win by default, seek to settle dispute out of court, or decide to contest action and file formal answer to stated charges; in in some cases he may file a countersuit.

3. Assuming defendant takes the third course of action, judge reviews statements to decide whether or not there is sufficient cause for action. If he determines there is, a time is set for the trial.

4. Both parties and their attorneys appear in court. (Evolution of "pre-trial procedures" in civil cases has tended to expedite administration of justice by wide departures from common-law practice of trial by surprise, debate, etc. Essence of these procedures is conferences with judge in which issues are narrowed, some facts admitted, and the precise matter in dispute is clarified.) Trial begins before a judge, or if either party prefers a jury trial, before judge and jury.

5. Both sides present cases with witnesses appearing and attorneys for the plaintiff and defendant present arguments before court.

2. Defendant is properly arrested with or without a warrant.

3. The accused person is "booked" at police station or sheriff's office and is informed of specific charges against him.

4. Accused is brought before judge of an inferior court for preliminary hearing to determine if evidence against him is sufficient to hold him for trial or to require posting of a bond for release.

5. Accused is held for trial either upon basis of an information signed by district attorney or indictment voted by grand jury.

6. Trial begins in general trial court. Accused has right to counsel of his own choosing or is assigned counsel by court. At this point, accused pleads either innocent or guilty. If he pleads guilty, he is sentenced without trial. If he pleads not guilty, trial commences, and, unless waived by accused, a jury of 12 is impaneled to hear proceedings.

7. Next comes the trial proper with presentation of evidence both for and against accused, examination of witnesses, and arguments and counterarguments by prosecutor and counsel for accused.

8. With submission of evidence and argument completed, judge instructs jury in questions of law and it retires for deliberation.

CIVIL	CRIMINAL
6. If jury has been waived, judge takes case under consideration for decision. If it is a jury trial, judge instructs jury which then leaves courtroom for its deliberations.	9. Jury presents its findings to court. Its decision for conviction must be unanimous vote of jury panel. If verdict is guilty, judge pronounces sentence upon accused. If verdict is not guilty, accused is released and he may not be tried again on the same charge. If jury cannot reach a unanimous decision within a reasonable period of time, it is dismissed and new trial is ordered or accused is freed by virtue of a "hung" jury.
7. Judgment is rendered by court as a decision of the judge in a nonjury case or in a judgment by judge based on findings of the jury in favor of plaintiff or defendant.	
8. Either party may appeal to a higher court on grounds of a procedural error, misdirection of jury, or other errors which might result in miscarriage of justice.	10. Defendant has right to appeal to higher court if he believes he has been deprived of justice because of a mishandling of laws or evidence.
9. If appeal is accepted, case is tried again in a higher court with steps of trial repeated in the court of appeal.	11. If appeal is not granted, judgment of the general trial court is carried out. Following completion of his sentence, the person may not be tried a second time for the same offense.

WHO USES THE COURTS?

According to political scientist Kenneth Dolbeare, the local trial court is the judicial institution of the local political system. It is the means to power for some, the key to profits for others, and the avoidance of burdens for still others.[7] While our democratic tradition and heritage hold that the courts are open to any citizen who wishes to use them, the operation of the courts themselves encourage some categories of people to use them while other groups are discouraged. The availability of the court structure to secure delay encourages those who seek to defend the *status quo* to utilize courts and court procedures.

In a study of cases initiated during a fifteen-year period in an urban county in New York, Dolbeare found that individuals, on their own behalf or on behalf of a group, initiated 43 percent of zoning and land use cases and 61 percent of all other cases. Businesses were responsible for 41 percent and 27 percent of the cases in the two categories. Local governmental units accounted for 12 percent of the zoning and land use cases and for only 2.5 percent of all other cases.[8]

Another feature of court operation that treats low-income persons less preferentially results from the overcrowding of lower court calendars. The result is "assembly-line" justice for many users. Herbert Jacob points out that

> The most significant fault in our present system of criminal justice is that in those areas where it comes in contact with the average citizen . . . its performance is poorest. Mass-production techniques in traffic courts and misdemeanor arraignment courts are apt to create disrespect for law and the judicial process. Scant regard for human dignity and the worth of the individual can be evidenced where judges face daily calendars in the hundreds.[9]

While free legal assistance is available to persons whose income falls below the poverty level, many people still face economic barriers in obtaining access to the courts. Apparently the greater a person's wealth, the more likely it is that he will be able to use the courts successfully.

ESSENTIALS OF A SOUND JUDICIAL SYSTEM

Observers, critics, and experts who have examined the organization and operation of our lower courts have commented on many imperfections in their structure and practice. Since court systems vary widely among the states and between sections within a single state, it would not be very meaningful to enumerate a number of specific and needed reforms. It is possible, however, to present a checklist of the essentials of a sound judicial system, and the lower courts in any particular state may be measured in terms of meeting the prescribed essentials.

Here is a checklist of such essentials:

1. A simple system of courts embracing (a) a local court of limited civil and criminal jurisdiction; (b) a trial court of general statewide jurisdiction; and (c) an appellate court or courts depending on the needs of the particular state. There should be considerable specialization by judges in trial courts rather than the establishment of courts with special jurisdictions.
2. A corps of independent judges beholden only to the law and constitution who are knowledgeable in the field of law, experienced at the bar, industrious, and believed to be honest.
3. Juries representing a cross-section of the honest and intelligent citizenry.
4. Honorable and well educated lawyers and an effective bar organization.

5. Competent court clerks, stenographic reporters, and bailiffs, and an administrative judge to give general supervision to the judicial system.
6. Elimination of unnecessary delays in bringing cases to court and in the procedure of the courtroom.
7. Decisions based on merit rather than legal shenanigans. This involves restoration of power to preside effectively in the trial judge, careful review of judicial rules, and the use of pre-trial procedures.
8. Elimination of judicial discourtesy by increasing the decorum of courtrooms and dignifying the role of the judge.
9. Fair division of work among judges by assigning judges of courts without backlogs to assist those who have work overloads.
10. Compilation of weekly and monthly reports by the administrative director of the courts from statistics supplied by court clerks and in the weekly reports from judges.
11. The use of these reports in assigning judges, supervising their work, and investigating complaints from individuals or bar associations.
12. The selection of an administrative director to assist the administrative judge in the many details of running the court system effectively.
13. An abiding conviction that the law and the courts exist for the benefit of the litigants and the state rather than for the benefit of judges, lawyers, and court officers.[10]

While the record of the court system as a whole is one of continuing, if slow, progress toward meeting many of these essentials, the need for continuing improvement remains. The National Advisory Commission on Civil Disorders reports that

> We have found that the apparatus of justice in some areas has itself become a focus for distrust and hostility. Too often the courts have operated to aggravate rather than relieve the tensions that ignite and fire disorders.[11]

The most general criticism leveled against the court system is that it is essentially a conservative institution. Its procedures are costly in terms of both money and time, making the institution less available to the poor. A second complaint relates to the wide discretion entrusted to the judges and their wide latitude in its exercise. Third, the credibility of the accused often is perceived as less than the credibility of the arresting officer testifying against him.[12]

THE INCIDENCE OF CRIME

Crime is a major social problem in the United States in both rural and urban areas. No one actually knows how much crime costs the nation in either money or misery, but estimates of the financial cost have been placed as high as $20 billion yearly. While the rate of crimes in all major categories has increased in recent decades, whether this has resulted from increased criminality or better enforcement and reporting is not clear. The basic and primary source of data concerning crimes is the *Uniform Crime Reports,* issued by the Federal Bureau of Investigation from statistics submitted by local police departments throughout the nation.[13]

While urban crime rates are considerably higher in most categories than are those in rural areas, urban police facilities for detection and apprehension are also much better. Comparative rates of crime arrests known to police in urban and rural areas are presented in Table 11. In this compilation, violent crimes include offenses of murder, forcible rape, robbery, and aggravated assualt whereas property crimes consist of offenses of burglary, larceny of $500 and over, and automobile theft. The crime rate is expressed in terms of number of crimes per 100,000 inhabitants. A general pattern of decline of crime as measured by the crime index is evident as population decreases from largest cities to rural areas, with the exception of total crimes and property crimes being fewer in cities over a million than in cities between 100,000 and a million.

TABLE 11
CRIME RATES, OFFENSES KNOWN TO THE POLICE,
BY POPULATION GROUPS

Population group	Crime Index Total	Per 100,000 Inhabitants	
		Violent Crime	Property crime
1,000,000 and over	6,961.4	1,363.1	5,598.3
500,000-999,999	8,029.4	961.0	7,068.4
250,000-499,999	7,755.4	853.4	6,902.0
100,000-249,000	7,111.0	600.0	6,511.0
50,000-99,999	5,747.4	405.8	5,341.6
25,000-49,999	5,151.6	330.6	4,820.9
10,000-24,999	4,417.8	249.7	4,168.1
Less than 10,000	3,818.2	217.8	3,600.5
Rural areas	2,001.4	161.6	1,849.8

Source: Federal Bureau of Investigation, *Crime in the United States, 1974,* Government Printing Office, 1975, Table 14, pp. 160-61. "Population Group" represents cities except for final entry.

THE POLICE FUNCTION

The police function in local government may be defined in terms of police objectives since the organization varies from the constable system in small towns and townships to the elaborate and complex organization of a big-city police department. In general, however, police objectives are the same and include the maintenance of peace and order, control and prevention of crime and vice, traffic control, and police duties involving a number of regulatory responsibilities.[14] As identified by the Institute for Training in Municipal Administration, the major police activities are (1) prevention of criminality, (2) repression of crime, (3) apprehension of offenders; (4) recovery of lost or stolen property, and (5) regulation of non-criminal conduct.[15] The last is a growing activity, embracing such varied activities as traffic control, enforcement of health and sanitary regulations, and compliance with safety precautions.

In a pioneering study of local police, James Wilson classifies three different styles of strategies of police administration. The first is the watchman style, which emphasizes the order maintenance role of the police. The police tend to judge the requirements of order differently depending on the character of the group that caused the infraction. The second is the legalistic style, which stresses the law enforcement role under which the police act on the assumption that a single standard of community conduct exists. The third style is that of service under which police take seriously all requests for either law enforcement or order maintenance.[16]

URBAN POLICE ORGANIZATION

The problem of police organization in urban areas ranges from the simple arrangements in small cities with a one- to three-member police force to the complex and intricate law enforcement organizations in large cities composed of several thousand employees. As the size of the police force increases, both specialization of functions and subdivision of levels of activity become essential. The first characteristic implies that not all duties are performed by all members of the department. Some perform traffic control duties, others detective functions, others work primarily with juveniles, and so on. The second characteristic means that higher ranks direct the performance of those of lower ranks. Thus, a large police department is organized along quasi-military lines.

As mentioned previously, the basic purposes of police are to prevent crime, suppress criminal activity, apprehend criminals, preserve the peace, regulate conduct, and protect life and property. To carry out these functions, the department is organized in several divisions, all responsible to the head of the department, usually called the chief. He normally is a professional officer, but in large cities the chief may be subordinate to a lay department head known as the police commissioner.

The core of police operations centers in a patrol division, which is usually the largest subdivision of the department. Its functions broadly consist of crime prevention, juvenile delinquency control, crime repression, protection of life and property, and the provision of advice, information, and assistance to the public. Patrol activities are carried on by uniformed police who serve both as "cops" on the beat and in patrol cars. Among their specific duties are observing conditions while patrolling, controlling public gatherings, checking locks on commercial buildings after closing hours, settling minor complaints, answering emergency calls, and testifying in courts.

The second largest unit in an urban police department is often the detective division. Primary functions of this division include the investigation of crimes, recovery of property, and the identification and apprehension of offenders. Because of the nature of their work, detectives are not in uniform. This division normally is equipped with scientific and technical aids including equipment for microscopy, photography, finger-printing, lie detectors, and impression casts.

Another large unit is the traffic division. As the name implies, members of this unit enforce traffic regulations, staff busy traffic intersections, enforce parking laws, give first aid at accidents, furnish accident records, and help in the trial of traffic violators. Since this police activity most directly affects the largest number of citizens, the personnel of this unit greatly influences the concept of many citizens of their police department. Recognizing the importance of the public relations aspect of this unit, many police departments now demand high standards of appearance, conduct, and impartial performance of duties by the members of its traffic division.

The enforcement of laws on such activities as gambling, prostitution, narcotics, and liquor is known as vice control. In most cities, these laws are enforced either by a vice division or by vice squads in the patrol and detective divisions. Vice operations are sometimes highly organized in cities, but this function involves problems and techniques differing from those of normal patrol and investigation. Because of occasional revelations of collusion between vice ring leaders and some policemen, the public often has a rather low regard of vice squads and their work.

Curbing juvenile delinquency is another major task of police departments carried on by specialized officers of the patrol division or by officers of a separate juvenile division. The work of these officers is largely preventive and seeks to prevent and correct conditions inducing criminality by teen-age boys and girls. Delinquency is a broad social problem rather than a police problem, and members of this unit therefore work closely with schools, recreation departments, health and welfare agencies, and probation officers. A well rounded program of a juvenile division, according to O. W. Wilson, police scholar and administrator, includes: (1) the eradication of conditions promoting criminal activities, of elements inducing criminal activities, and of elements inducing criminal tendencies in youth; (2) the discovery and treatment of the delinquent, the near-delinquent, and those exposed to high-risk situations; and (3) the planning, promotion, and direction of activities providing wholesome influences on youth.[17]

Comparative data on the average number of police department employees per 1,000 inhabitants and the range in number of employees per 1,000 inhabitants are shown in Table 12. In general, the number of police declines as the size of the city decreases.

TABLE 12
AVERAGE NUMBER OF POLICE DEPARTMENT EMPLOYEES AND RANGE IN NUMBER OF EMPLOYEES, PER 1,000 INHABITANTS

City population size	Average number per 1,000	Range in number per 1,000
More than 250,000	3.5	2.2-3.5
100,000-250,000	2.3	1.8-2.5
50,000-100,000	1.9	1.5-2.2
25,000-50,000	1.9	1.5-2.1
10,000-25,000	1.9	1.5-2.2
Under 10,000	2.1	1.4-2.7
All cities	2.5	

Source: Federal Bureau of Investigation, *Crime in the United States, 1974,* Government Printing Office, 1975, p. 235.

INTERGOVERNMENTAL RELATIONS

A new era of intergovernmental relations in police administration began in 1968 with the passage of the Omnibus Crime Control and Safe Streets Act and the resultant creation of the Law Enforcement Assistance Administration to manage the new program. The 1968 Act requires that before action funds can be made available to state and local units of government a state comprehensive law enforcement plan must be prepared. The plan must reflect the state and local criminal justice needs as well as programs for meeting them. Planning funds are made available to the states on the basis of population, and the states, in turn, must make at least 40 percent of these funds available to local units of government alone or in combinations. The three largest grant areas have been detection and apprehension, upgrading law enforcement, and riots and civil disorders. Areas receiving relatively little support included community relations, research and development, and organized crime.

The National Advisory Commission on Criminal Justice Standards and Goals was created by LEAA and the Department of Justice in 1971 to formulate the first national criminal justice standards and goals for crime reduction and prevention at the state and local levels. After nearly two years of work, the Commission issued a summary volume entitled *A National Strategy to Reduce Crime* and five task force reports. The Task Force Report on Police contains recommendations to divert juveniles, drunks, and mental patients from the criminal justice system; to consolidate or eliminate police departments with fewer than ten full-time officers; to increase the use of civilian personnel; to require a college education for new police officers; and to promote police minority hiring by employing such individuals in proportion to their number in the population. The Task Force Report on Community Crime Prevention calls for citizens patrolling their neighborhoods; the renovation of slums; career education in elementary and secondary schools; improved physical design of buildings, parks and thoroughfares to reduce criminal opportunities; ethics codes of conduct for government officials; and improved neighborhood streetlighting programs.[18]

The range of activities covered by the term public safety includes a number of aspects and functions in which the national and state governments cooperate with and assist local units. In addition, local governments negotiate interjurisdictional agreements to assist each other in times of need. A number of these agreements are formal but an even greater quantity is informal. These relationships often develop quite voluntarily because of the recognized need for assistance and cooperation in the important activities of protecting the person and property of the citizenry.

SOME CURRENT CONCERNS IN LAW ENFORCEMENT

The National Advisory Commission on Civil Disorders, in its report assessing the causes of the riots in 1967, advanced five principal problem areas in police-community relations. They are: (1) the need for change in police operations in the ghetto to ensure proper individual conduct and to eliminate abrasive practices; (2) the need for more adequate police protection of ghetto residents to eliminate the present high sense of insecurity to person and property; (3) the need for effective mechanisms through which the citizen may have his grievances handled; (4) the need for policy guidelines to assist police in areas where police conduct can create tension; and (5) the need to develop community support for law enforcement.[19] To overcome or ameliorate these problem areas, it was recommended that the recruitment, assignment, and promotion of minority officers be speeded up; police should stress community service functions and establish community relations programs; and police should have a strong internal investigative unit and a fair and effective means to handle citizen complaints.

One of the new areas of concern of local police is their new activism or their greater politicization. Jerome Skolnick chronicles a number of events and occurrences involving illegal police strikes, lobbying, and political organizing. In his words, there is a "growing tendency of the police to see themselves as an independent, militant minority asserting itself in the political arena."[20] Skolnick sees the transformation of the police fraternal and social organizations into effective interest groups seeking to advance what the police conceive to be their proper concerns and to work for or against candidates and issues.

A further concern in local police administration is the question of decentralization of large police forces to enhance community control. An eloquent spokesman of the need for community control is Arthur Waskow. He bases his argument on the assumption that "In almost every American metropolis, the police no longer are under civilian control—that is to say, democratic public control." He proposes a "Formal restructuring of metropolitan police departments into federations of neighborhood police forces, with control of each neighborhood force in the hands of neighborhood people through election of commissions."[21] Waskow suggests a population of 100,000 as the ideal size of the community to be entitled to its own police force. James Wilson, on the other hand, opposes community control—if this means each neighborhood is allowed to determine its own style of law enforcement. Wilson prefers to keep the authority governing large police forces centralized but favors certain administrative changes to decentralize the functions of the police. The goal for Wilson is a "decentralized, neighborhood-oriented, order maintenance patrol force."[22]

For most police forces, discipline is maintained by an internal review board composed of police officials who hear citizen complaints against individual officers. In recent years, increasing criticism about such boards has come forth because complainants often did not appear to receive a full and open hearing of their felt injustices. A proposed remedy is to eliminate such internal boards and replace them with civilian review boards or add civilian members to the internal review boards. While both reforms have been implemented in some communities, neither has produced the hoped-for reforms of its advocates nor resulted in the shams predicted by police and other groups opposing them. Another suggested plan is to establish a municipal ombudsman who would handle complaints against police as one of the functions of his office.

Another recent development is the increasing use of policewomen in local government. A study based on matched groups of eighty-six male and eighty-six female patrol officers of the Metrolpolitan Police Department of Washington, D.C., reached these interesting conclusions: (1) women made fewer arrests and gave fewer tickets than men; (2) men were more likely to engage in unbecoming conduct; (3) injuries to women did not cause them to be absent from work more often than men; (4) arrests made by male and female officers are equally apt to produce convictions; (5) no difference between the two groups developed in the number of driving accidents in which they were involved.[23]

NOTES

1. *Southern Pacific Co., v. Jensen,* 244 U. S. 205 (1916), p. 222.
2. Herbert Jacob, *Justice in America,* Little, Brown, 1965, pp. 3-4.
3. W. F. Willoughby, *Principles of Judicial Administration,* Brookings Institution, 1929, Chap. XVI.
4. Henry J. Abraham, *Courts and Judges, An Introduction to the Judicial Process,* Oxford University Press, 1959, p. 3.
5. Clyde F. Snider, *Local Government in Rural America,* Appleton-Century-Crofts, 1957, p. 309.
6. Because terminology varies so much among the states, there may be a "county" court with relatively limited jurisdiction between the minor judiciary and the general trial court. In urban areas, there often is more than one judge for the general trial court, while the court's boundaries may include several counties in less populated areas.
7. Kenneth M. Dolbeare, *Trial Courts in Urban Politics* New York: Wiley, 1967, p. 3.
8. *Ibid.,* p. 38.
9. Jacob, *Justice in America,* op. cit. p. 143.
10. Arthur T. Vanderbilt, "The Essentials of a Sound Judicial System," *Northwestern University Law Review,* 48 (March-April, 1953), 1-15.
11. National Advisory Commission on Civil Disorders, *Report,* Bantam Books, 1968. p. 337.
12. For an excellent summary of these and other charges, see Herbert Jacob, *Urban Justice,* Prentice-Hall, 1973.
13. A brief caveat should be entered that these reports are neither uniform nor a reporting of all crimes. The statistics are compiled from reports prepared and submitted by individual cities.
14. V. A. Leonard, *Police Organization and Management,* Foundation Press, 1951, p. 2.
15. International City Management Association, *Municipal Police Administration,* 6th ed., International City Management Association, 1969, p. 3.
16. James Q. Wilson, *Varieties of Police Behavior, The Management of Law and Order in Eight Communities,* Harvard University Press, 1968.
17. O. W. Wilson, *Police Administration,* McGraw-Hill, 1950, pp. 210-1.
18. *Nation's Cities,* "New Directions in the Criminal Justice System," special report, Vol. 12 (June, 1974), pp. 23-24.
19. National Advisory Commission on Civil Disorders, *Report,* op. cit., p. 301
20. Jerome H. Skolnick, *The Politics of Protest,* Ballantine Books, 1969, p. 278.
21. Arthur I. Waskow, "Comment: Community Control of the Police," *Transaction,* 7 (December, 1969), p. 4.

22. Wilson, *op. cit.*, p. 293.
23. *Nation's Cities*, "Study Finds Policewomen as Competent as Policemen," Vol. 12 (June, 1974), p. 48.

Chapter 13

The Administrative Process

The administrative process is both an extension and a part of the local political process. While the distinction commonly made between the two processes—that policies are formulated through the political process and executed through the administrative process—is valid in part, their overlapping is inevitable and their complete separation impossible. In determining local policies, the local legislative body and the executive delineate in varying degrees how they are to be carried out and the policies are modified somewhat in their execution by the administrative officers who shape the general policies to specific cases.

The intermixture of the political and administrative processes has been vividly described by Arthur Bromage, political scientist, in the terms of America's favorite sport—baseball.

> Once the people have elected mayors and councilmen, these officials, together with the administrators, take the field in the municipal ball park. The municipal team plays against crime, fire, disease, poor housing, inadequate public parks, insufficient water supplies, inadequate recreational programs, pollution of our water resources, problems of planning and zoning, and many other heavy hitters. The citizens, if they are alert, fill the bleachers from week to week to see how the local team is doing. On the municipal ball team we have both councilmen and administrators, including clerks, attorneys, fiscal officers, public officers, police and fire chiefs, public works superintendents, planning officials, and many others. The administrators do the infield work, handling the hot grounders, and the councilmen patrol the outfield, handling anything that gets by the infielders. When something gets by the outfielders on this municipal team, there will be jeering from the bleachers, and there is likely to be a change in administration of the ball club.[1]

Numerous definitions of the term "public administration" have been developed. Two typical and common ones are: (1) public administration is the organization and management of men and materials to achieve the purposes of government; and (2) public administration is the art and science of management as applied to the affairs of state. Neither, however, is very useful in explaining what public administration is. A more meaningful definition holds, "The central idea of public administration is rational action, defined as action correctly calculated to realize given desired goals."[2]

The process to achieve the "rational action" called for in the definition above may be described as the administrative process. Two key elements in this process are the structural or organizational pattern in local government to realize the desired courses of action, and the techniques of management utilized to guide and control these actions. The first part of this chapter discusses the organizational aspects, and it will be followed by a consideration of the basic management aspects practiced in the local administrative process.

LOCAL ADMINISTRATIVE ORGANIZATION

According to Dwight Waldo, "Organization is the structure of authoritative and habitual personal interrelations in an administrative system."[3] Sociologist Amitai Etzioni offers a more detailed description holding that organizations are those social units characterized by three traits. First, divisions of labor, power, and communications responsibility are deliberately planned to enhance the realization of specific goals. Second, one or more power centers control the concerted efforts of the organization and direct them toward its goals. These centers must review the organization's performance and repattern its structure, when and where necessary, to increase its efficiency. And third, personnel are substituted through removal or reassignment to expedite the achievement of goals.[4]

Considerable disagreement is present concerning the existence and utility of principles of administrative organization, but several general rules for local governments may be advanced. First, administrative responsibility should be centralized in a single chief administrator who is given sufficient authority to perform his responsibilities and is aided by an adequate staff. Second, the number of departmental units and governmental agencies reporting to the chief administrator should not be so numerous as to make him unable to exercise effective direction over them. Third, related functions should be logically grouped into departments and agencies. This is essential because the number of functions and activities is greater than the number of departments and agencies. Fourth, the factor of public convenience should be given careful attention in determining local administrative structure. Fifth, the use of boards and commissions for administrative purposes should be carefully considered. The more proper uses for plural-member boards is discussed later in this chapter.

TYPES OF AGENCIES

Of the several schemes for classifying administrative agencies, one of the most meaningful is a threefold division into line, staff, and auxiliary agencies, based on the primary purpose for which they exist. Line agencies are concerned with the primary purposes for which the governmental unit exists and thus serve citizens directly by providing basic services or by regulating their conduct. Typical local government activities classified as "line" include police and fire, health, welfare, utilities and public works, education, and recreation.

Staff agencies, on the other hand, carry on activities of service to other agencies of the government rather than directly for citizens. Their function is to advise but not act, to plan but not implement, and to inform but not enact. Thus, they are thinking, planning and advisory—but not operating— agencies. Among local governmental activities properly labeled staff are those of planning commissions, budget officers, accountants, legal officers, zoning boards, research agencies, bill-drafting agencies, and public relations personnel.

The third type of agency—an auxiliary agency—combines one aspect of each of the other two. Like a line unit, the auxiliary agency has operating responsibilities, but these are performed for other governmental agencies rather than for the citizens. Thus, their clientele is similar to that of the staff organization rather than a line agency. The basic function of an auxiliary agency is to maintain other existing agencies. It does this by fulfilling specialized functions common to a number of operating units, but removed from them for reasons of economy, coordination, and specialization. Typical examples are central personnel agencies, central purchasing and disbursing agencies, central fiscal control units, and central custodial services. In large jurisdictions, there often is a subordinate office in each major agency that carries on these activities within that agency under the general direction of the head of the auxiliary agency.

Administrative Departments

The major administrative agencies in local government are the operating and service departments differentiated above. There is generally recognition of the desirability of keeping the number of departments reasonably small to permit their effective control and supervision. This desire leads to a problem in the grouping of functions and activities within departments, because it is also recognized that only similar functions should be grouped together in a single agency. Since the objective sought through administrative agencies is the efficient and economical execution of policies determined by the local executive and legislature, their organization should be planned with this goal in mind.

Several principal bases are recognized for the organization of departments and the assignment of functions within them. They are the concepts of organization by purpose, process, clientele, and area. Organization by purpose is based on what is to be done; by process, how it is to be done; by clientele, the persons to be served; and by area, where it is to be done. The four bases are not exclusive and divisions within a single agency may be variously organized to reflect two or more. A health department illustrates a purpose agency—to protect health and prevent the spread of disease. A licensing bureau or a legal department is based on process. A department of welfare, which deals with persons needing aid, is organized on a clientele basis. Precinct stations of a police department and station houses of a fire department both represent area organization with each serving a distinct geographic area. Each of these examples is an agency with a purpose and all utilize certain processes in carrying out their functions. However, they illustrate both the non-exclusiveness of the four basic concepts and the fact that local agencies have varying organizational patterns reflecting the nature of their assignments.

To give a specific numerical answer to the question of the number of departments most desirable in a local government is not possible. A study of the government of New York City advises, "Make certain that there is one main function for every major department, and one department for every major function." To place all activities in a few departments, the report adds, "would turn many departments into bushel baskets," each with various and unrelated functions resulting in many orphan activities.[5] The number of departments tends to vary directly with the size of the community. This is logical since the larger the unit, the more functions and activities it provides for its citizens. Effective coordination can be achieved in part through executive supervision as well as through organization. Thus some local governments with effectively functioning staff and managerial aids for their executive may have more departments than communities in which the executive is weaker in powers of supervision and coordination. However, this is far from a universal practice and some of the strongest local executives have very few administrative departments operating under them.

While most departments have a single head, some still are directed by a plural-member board or commission. If the department is empowered to determine policy, issue rules and regulations, or exercise quasi-judicial or quasi-legislative functions, then a plural head has merit. Policies should be the result of deliberation, and rules are normally more readily accepted if issued by a board rather than by an individual. Thus, the board is still used in some health and personnel departments as well as in library and school administration. However, unless the department has these functions, a single head is preferable, as executive supervision is simplified, the head may act with greater speed, and no opportunity exists for "buck-passing."

Boards and Commissions

Although boards and commissions do not usually function effectively in operating a department, they are useful in an advisory capacity and are widely used by local governments for this purpose. They provide an opportunity for some citizens to participate directly in their government and are valuable in selling governmental proposals for action to the citizenry. Usually board service is uncompensated, with the members thus being persons interested in serving the community. Their opinions and recommendations thus are usually accepted more readily than those coming directly from public employees who have a more recognizable stake in the success of the incumbent officials or political party.

Citizen boards in local government carry out a number of functions: (1) they study complex problems that the local legislative body does not have time to study in depth; (2) they serve as a buffer to protect the local executive and legislature from certain types of political pressures; (3) they provide a considerable amount of staff work at little cost; and (4) they offer effective and useful aid to the local officials and the community. On the negative side, such boards (1) do not remove important problems from the arena of politics; (2) often perceive their functions narrowly; and (3) sometimes they feel they are not consulted often enough, their advice is too freely ignored, or they are not sufficiently informed of the outcome or the use made of their recommendations.

ADMINISTRATIVE MANAGEMENT

As defined by Waldo, "Management is action intended to achieve rational cooperation in an administrative system."[6] Thus, it is the kinetic force in administration while structure represents a somewhat more static element. Although such a distinction between administrative organization and management (often referred to as "O" and "M") is valuable as a means of analysis, they are not independent aspects in practical situations. The close relationship between "O" and "M" at the operating level is evident in agencies combining the purpose and process bases of organization. The methods used in rendering the processes may directly influence the organizational structure of that agency. Similarly, the assignment of duties may directly determine the specific methods to be utilized within that organization.

A second definition of management holds that it concerns the leadership and direction of groups of individuals to the accomplishment of desired objectives. ''The art of management is therefore simply the administrative means of getting the 'job done.''"[7] Since the entire leadership and direction of these groups cannot be unified and provided by a single executive, he has a number of aides, depending on the size of the community and the number, variety, and level of services provided.

Leadership

Proper organization is important, but leadership is a prime essential of effective management. Successful administrative leadership is an elusive quality not adequately definable in listings of duties to be performed or described in terms of personal character traits. Leadership is not autocratic rule but the solution of problems and accomplishment of results. John Pfiffner and Robert Presthus define leadership as the ''art that stresses the attainment of mutual ends through the coordination and motivation of both individuals and groups.''[8]

As identified by Herman Pope, longtime head of a management consulting firm, the essential elements of effective administrative leadership are: (1) an intelligent and effective handling of personnel transactions and regularized patterns for doing so; (2) an adequate organization so that each member knows his job, authority, and responsibility; (3) a general understanding and appreciation of specialized programs and problems; (4) an opportunity for participation by subordinates in deciding how things are to be done; (5) an ability to time administrative decisions and action so that many problems can be anticipated and avoided. Pope concludes that an

> administrative leader is more like his subordinates than different from them. In this age of specialists he too is a specialist. His specialty is the art of furnishing leadership and coordinated purposes to other specialists.[9]

The literature on leadership includes a number of efforts to classify leadership styles. Three basic styles are singled out most frequently—the authoritarian, the democratic, and the participative. In broad terms, the authoritarian leader insists upon holding and exercising personally all the decision-making power placed in the unit he heads within the organization. Usually a hard-worker himself, this type of leader demands much from his subordinates and expects their unfaltering compliance with his commands. The democratic leader, in sharp contrast, refrains from personal decision-making and often delegates substantial portions of this responsibility to others. This leader often is concerned with the needs and welfare of his fellow workers and strives for acceptance by his subordinates. As an intermediate position between the two extremes, the participative leadership style shares some decision-making with his subordinates but retains the ultimate responsibility in his own hands. This leader expects positive response to his leadership and often uses positive incentives to secure achievement of goals as well as adherence to prescribed rules and procedures.

A major leadership responsibility of the administrator is to make appropriate decisions for and within his agency. Decision-making is the process by which an individual or a group of persons chooses among alternatives. The process may vary between elementary to highly complex, but procedurally it consists of various identifiable steps: (1) the recognition of a problem; (2) identification of the factors involved; (3) identification of the available alternatives; (4) weighing and testing of alternatives; (5) choosing a course of action; and (6) implementing the choice.[10] As mentioned in the discussion of leadership styles above, decisions are not made only at the top. William Gore, political scientist, has phrased the process aptly by stating

> The roots of the decision-making process are deep in the subsoil of an organization. Hidden from common sense observation, they lie far below the forms and rituals of formal organizations and the crust of rationality.[11]

Another significant responsibility of the administrator is the undertaking of administrative planning for his agency—deciding in advance what is to be done, who is to do it, and how it is to be accomplished. Administrative planning ranges from that carried on so routinely as to be hardly recognized as planning to the truly difficult decisions that must occasionally be made in the life of any agency. The administrative planning process may be described as consisting of seven elements. The process need not progress smoothly and directly through each of the steps and may be terminated at any point in the process. These elements are (1) the decision to plan; (2) description and prediction through the statement of assumptions; (3) definition of objectives; (4) setting of priorities; (5) development of action programs; (6) implementation of action programs; and (7) evaluation and revision of plans. John Parker, management consultant, has summarized the administrative planning process as a "vital tool of management. It provides the means for translating community needs and policies of the city council and top administrators into action."[12]

The Public Interest

The concept of the public interest figures prominently in discussions of the leadership and responsibilities of an administrator. General agreement exists that government, at whatever level, must serve the interest of the public rather than any small portion of it, but no real consensus is present as to what constitutes the public interest, either among administrative theorists or practitioners.

According to Charles Adrian, four basic assumptions concerning the nature of the public interest are shared by most administrators. These are: (1) the public interest is identified with the expectations of the professional peers of the administrator. The local recreation director is likely to consider the standards of his professional association as right and in the public interest of the community he serves; (2) the public interest is interpreted by the administrator as reflecting the expectations of his administrative superiors; (3) the public interest is rationalized by the administrator as the extension of his own personal value system; and (4) the public interest is identified by the administrator with the wishes of the interested public or publics.[13]

The commonality of the above views, however, does not make them necessarily sound. By injecting the necessity for ethical or moral considerations, a process for determining the public interest may be arrived at more easily than defining the concept itself. Thus, the public interest may be considered as resulting when an ethical administrator follows good procedures, since decisions should reflect his highest ethical judgment based on an examination and a careful analysis of facts. Although the public interest is sometimes considered only a useful myth, decisions based on it are a goal worthy of the conscientious efforts of every administrator.

Accountability

Keeping citizens intelligently informed is a major problem of local government. Information is necessary if the citizenry is to have a legitimate and knowledgeable basis for holding its public officials accountable to the mandates recorded in local elections. Reporting to the public, however, should spring from the desire to inform the citizenry so intelligent decisions may be made, rather than from the desire to advance the political fortunes of certain local officers or a political party.

Government officials, whether elected or appointed, are subject to a number of restraints. Chief among these checks are the periodic expressions of the citizens in local elections and on questions of policy submitted to them for decision. Other restraints exist in the structure of the local government. The division of powers and functions among different officials and agencies constitutes a check on the actions of a single one. A third major check lies in the division of the citizenry into a number of small publics rather than its grouping into a single monolithic public. For example, the basic interest of a citizen in his government may come from his occupation, his area of residence, his tax bill, the level of services received, personal friendships with public officials, or from other reasons. Rarely does the entire citizenry hold a single point of view on any question of policy, and the divergent interests of its several divisions operate as brakes on the wishes of any one group in settling that question.

Citizen direction and control of the local bureaucracy, however, are sporadic and limited. While they may function effectively in small communities, the problem of accountability goes far beyond citizen control in large governmental units. Recent studies even suggest that effective direction and control are not or can not be provided by the local executive and governing board. One reason often presented is that public employees are organized into front-rank pressure groups. The importance of the political support of these groups in future elections may prompt elected officials to forget about controlling them.

The importance of big county or big city personnel as a political fact lies not only in the services they are expected to provide, but also in the increasing strikes called by local government employees. The public payroll is a major source of jobs and the number of seekers for these positions increases particularly in times when hiring in the private sector is down.

Many grievances of minorities are directly related to the obstinate or hostile nature of local agencies and their employees in the field. A study of public welfare programs and policies concludes that the growth of bureaucracies has resulted in a diminished influence of low-income persons in public spheres. The bureaucracies have intruded upon and altered public decision processes so that low-income groups have fewer opportunities for exercising influence and fewer effective means for doing so. The bureaucracies also have come to exert powerful and inhibiting controls over their clients—low-income groups.[14]

The inability of elected officials to control the local bureaucracy has prompted one writer to describe the administrative apparatus as the "New Machine" in urban government.[15] While the old political machine was corrupt, it was people and service oriented. The "New Machine" is not corrupt, but neither is it people or service oriented. Rather it appears more interested in self-protection and self-perpetuation and is more likely to seek rewards for itself than to be primarily concerned with providing service. In such situations, accountability becomes a serious problem.

The Concept of Standards

Administration cannot be wholly scientific or neutral. The interrelationships of the political and administrative processes have been noted previously, and it need only be mentioned here that it is not yet possible to replace political considerations completely with objective criteria and administrative standards. But while no one best way exists to administer programs or organize local governments, certain guides have been developed to assist local officials.

Possibly the first administrative standard developed was the concept of official honesty. Reaction to the exposure of local corruption and inefficiency at the turn of the present century resulted in the development of a number of techniques to insure honesty of local officials. Among these were legal restraints on actions of local officials and such procedures as the annual audit, accounting system, operating and capital improvement budgets, purchasing systems, and regularized personnel practices.

Today citizens expect their local governments to be both honest and reasonably efficient. Administrative efficiency has been described as measurable "by the ratio of the effects actually obtained with the available resources to the maximum effects possible with the available resources."[16] As this definition implies, efficiency is difficult to evaluate because, in the last analysis, it is largely a matter of point of view. What seems to be the best way to one official may seem to be a poor way to another.

Increasing efforts are being made to establish criteria for appraising governmental activities at all levels. According to Clarence Ridley and Herbert Simon, "The appraisal of administration can take place only after the objectives of administration have been defined in measurable comparable terms."[17] Thus, a comparison of gross expenditures by comparable units of local government is no longer a meaningful method for determining very much about these communities or the efficiency of their services. When expenditures are broken down into more specific categories, such as personal services, equipment and materials, police and health services, they become more helpful.

A measurement technique meaningful for various activities of local government is cost accounting. A useful definition of cost accounting describes it as

> the process of searching out and recording all the elements of expense incurred to attain a purpose, to carry on an activity or operation, to complete a unit of work, or to do a specific job.[18]

If costs for work units in specific service areas is determinable, for example, miles of streets cleaned, tons of refuse collected, gallons of sewerage treated, then more meaningful data exist for measuring the comparative performance of local governments.

A recent concept in organizational management is the systems approach, which has two basic characteristics. First, objectives are stated in terms of measurable performance standards; and second, relationships within the system are emphasized. When properly utilized, the systems approach provides the administrator with a comprehensive framework within which he can exercise his knowledge of how to manage the organization to achieve objectives or goals. A second recent development has been the widespread use of electronic computers by local governments. Computer utilization can result in a reduction of administrative and clerical costs, permit increasing administrative work loads, improve the quality and speed of service without substantial increase in costs, and expedite the flow of information among departments and agencies.[19] John Parker concludes

> It is already clear that the computer has become a major tool of modern management. . . . it is likely that the impact of the computer and related techniques will far exceed that of any previous technological development.[20]

A number of professional organizations set standards for appropriate areas of governmental activity. For example, the National Recreation Association advances standards for numbers, types, and sizes of needed recreational facilities, and the American Public Health Association suggests standards in terms of types of services and personnel needed and minimum citizen financial support. In general, standards of such organizations should be considered as ''optimum'' because they are usually set so high that few governmental units are able to meet them. However, they do serve as stimuli in communities where officials and citizens alike are interested in improving particular services.

PERSONNEL ADMINISTRATION

In addition to the various elected officials and their top appointees, local governments require large numbers of employees. There are more than eight million public employees in local governments across the United States. Since 1900 the number of local employees (excluding those in school districts) increased by more than thirteen times. Local public employees exceed the number of state and federal employees combined. The reason is that local governments are far more involved in providing direct services than are the higher levels.

Various acceptable definitions for the term personnel administration have been developed. One author defines it in these words:

> Personnel administration is that phase of public administration which is concerned with the ''handling of persons'' . . . that is, the employment, placement, and motivation of people within an organization, to the end that the objectives of that organization can be achieved most effectively and economically and with the maximum utilization of all employees.[21]

Personnel administration, so defined, covers all aspects of employment, including recruitment, selection, placement, training, promotion, tenure, and separation.

Every unit of local government has some employees and hence has some types of arrangement or process for hiring and firing employees. In communities without a formal system, the regularly elected officials are free to employ and dismiss employees without restrictions. Formal systems are identified as civil service or merit systems. Some writers make a distinction between the two, but both imply selection on the basis of merit through competitive examination, the retention and promotion of employees on the basis of performance, and the absence of political affiliation as a major test for fitness for a position. Thus, the terms are used interchangeably in this section.

Not much uniformity exists in the legal bases for local personnel systems. In some states, mandatory state laws apply to local employees. More commonly, states enact general "civil service" provisions applicable to various classes of local governments, often depending upon their size; and in some communities, the local personnel systems are provided by special acts of the state legislature. Home rule charters, where authorized, normally include authorization for local merit systems. Although less binding than the above legal bases, some personnel arrangements are governed by local ordinance or by local executive or administrative orders.

Characteristics of Local Personnel Administration

Personnel administration in local government has a number of identifiable features. The first, which is organizational, pertains to the independent status of the agency administering the personnel system. Developed historically to keep politics out of the merit system, the independent civil service commission still is the most common type of administering agency. Appointed by the local legislative body or the chief executive officer, the board normally consists of three or five members who serve overlapping terms of office. The commission and its staff recruit and test applicants and certify lists of eligibles to the authorities who appoint employees to fill vacancies. In recent years, some governmental units have replaced the plural-member commission with a single-headed personnel agency responsible to the chief executive, but the older organizational pattern continues to prevail in most local governments. Most commissions are composed of laymen who serve on a part-time basis. Technical functions are performed by a personnel director and his staff, while the commission represents the public interest in the administration of the local civil service law.

The "position" concept is a second important characteristic of local personnel administration. A position consists of a group of duties and responsibilities assigned to one employee. By describing positions in terms of duties and responsibilities, jobs may be grouped into classes because of their similarities, and pay schedules may be established, resulting in equal pay for equal work. The concept of the position as the unit for recruitment distinguishes the American system from the British system which recruits persons to broad classes of positions of the basis of educational attainments.

A third feature is the generally accepted principle of open competition for positions in local public service. Any person meeting the minimum qualifications established for a given position is eligible to compete for that post by taking the examination. Announcements of available positions must be posted, stating the time and place of the examination, and interested persons meeting the qualifications are eligible for the examination whether or not they are currently employees of that local government. Such open examinations are less frequent at higher levels and occasionally promotional examinations are held with only current employees of prescribed grades, qualifications, and experience eligible to seek the position.

A fourth characteristic of local personnel systems also pertains to the nature of the examination. Testing for fitness of the candidates is for a specific position. This feature logically follows from the position concept described above and is emphasized by the common requirement of local civil service laws that examinations must be practical in character and based upon the nature of the work or duties to be performed. An examination for typists thus consists, at least in part, of a speed and accuracy test of typing skills.

The "rule-of-three" remains a common feature of local personnel systems. This rule pertains to the certification of eligible candidates after the examinations have been scored. Usually the names of the top three candidates are certified to the appointing officer who is free to select any one of them for the opening. If for some reason none of the three persons is eligible or acceptable, the appointing officer may return the list and request three other names. Some local governments use the concept of the eligible list rather than the rule-of-three. Under this arrangement, the names of all persons passing the examination are certified to the appointing officer who may select any person on the list. Other communities use the rule-of-one or the rule-of-five, both operating in the same manner as the rule-of-three. The rule-of-three has been criticized increasingly in recent years as giving the appointing officer discretion to discriminate against otherwise impartial hiring standards.

The probationary period is the sixth common characteristic. Once appointed to a particular job, the employee is on probation for a period of time—usually six months. This is a trial period and the agency may reject with reason any employee who does not perform satisfactorily. In actual practice, the probationary period weeds out few employees. It is opposed by taxpayer groups as too short to serve as a practical means for getting rid of potential problem employees, and no effective means exists for removing them after the probationary period.

Professionalization of employees is a seventh important feature of local personnel systems. While the association of persons engaging in similar duties is more likely among higher-level than lower-level employees, organizations now exist for most employees if they wish to join with other employees engaged in similar tasks in other jurisdictions. Thus, associations for city managers, recreation leaders, engineers, clerks, housing officials, public works employees, among others, have been established. One value of such associations is that the person who belongs usually feels an obligation to do his best because of his dual loyalty to his community and to his professional group.

An eighth characteristic is the parallel existence of career and political services. The features described above pertain to the former group consisting of persons appointed through a competitive merit system. The political service, on the other hand, embraces elective officials and the persons appointed by them on a noncompetitive basis such as the inflated staffs of mayors and council members often constructed largely from federal funds. Even the most inclusive merit systems almost always exclude department heads and their chief deputies. Other career systems find it impractical to include laborers in a formal merit system and exclude such employees. Employees in the political service serve at the pleasure of their appointers because they are responsible to them and are not covered by the same restrictions on removal as are members of the career service. Critics claim that such employee cadres are simply miniature "machines" in the service of the particular politicos they serve.

The recognition of distinctive differences between the rights of employees in the public service and workers in private industry is a ninth characteristic feature. The rights of public employees to join unions and to bargain collectively are generally accepted, but public employees are denied the ultimate weapon of their counterparts in private industry—the right to strike. This may seem a strange statement to make because of the increasing number of strikes by public school teachers, nurses, and other hospital workers, police and firemen, and sanitary workers. But the right to strike has been expressly renounced in the constitutions of some public employee organizations, and similar prohibitions are expressed in many state laws and local ordinances. Two principal arguments are made against striking by public employees. First, a strike against the government would be a disloyal act since the government is the entire people and its interests must be placed above those of any part of it. Second, the public service is so closely connected to the health and welfare of society that continuity of these services is paramount in the interest of all citizens. On the other hand, James Belasco concludes that it is "impossible to separate collective bargaining from politics" in the modern community and that some officials may approach the matter as one of trading economic benefits for political benefits. In his words,

The collective bargaining relationship is a swapping of political power assets. The Mayor grants salary and benefits to the employee organization in return for their support in a variety of political activities. The trading of votes and support for salaries and benefits is the heart of the negotiation process.[23]

TABLE 13
NUMBER OF AGREEMENTS AND WORKERS COVERED, BY UNIT OF GOVERNMENT, POPULATION SIZE, AND AFFILIATION, 1974

	County Population		City Population			
	Million	500,000	Million	500,000	250,000	Special
Affiliation	Plus	Plus	Plus	Plus	Plus	District
AFL-CIO	20	72	22	57	42	13
unions	22,058	64,651	80,938	57,507	27,887	21,128
Independent	1	-	1	3	1	-
unions	60	-	1,065	982	400	-
Associa-	14	26	11	12	15	1
tions	23,651	43,616	16,297	6,504	6,718	90
Unions and	-	4	-	-	-	-
assn's	-	9,694	-	-	-	-
Totals	35	102	34	72	58	14
	45,769	117,961	98,300	64,993	35,005	21,218

Source: Bureau of Labor Statistics, *Characteristics of Agreements in State and Local Governments, January 1, 1974,* Bulletin 1861, Government Printing Office, 1975, Table 9, page 7. Reading down, the first number in each pairing is the number of agreements; the second, the number of workers covered. Note: only the most populous counties (over 500,000 population) and the most populous cities (over 250,000) are included.

Unionization of public employees is most common in the local governments in the Pacific, East North Central, and Middle Atlantic states, and least frequent in the West South Central, Mountain, and East South Central states. Four of the largest employee organizations (not in order of size)—the American Federation of State, County, and Municipal Employees; International Association of Fire Fighters; Laborers' International Union of North America; and Service Employees International Union—are affiliated with the AFL-CIO. Three other large employee organizations are the Fraternal Order of Police, International Brotherhood of Teamsters, and the Building Trades Union.

BUREAUCRACY AND THE PUBLIC

Although advocates of the merit system have won victories in most large cities and the larger counties as well as in many smaller cities since the start of the present century, the argument between them and the defenders of a purely amateur class of public employees continues to be waged. Proponents of the latter insist that the best interests of democracy cannot be served by a professionalized public service. In this regard, they re-echo the fears of President Andrew Jackson, often called the father of the spoils system. In Jackson's words,

> The duties of all public officers are, or at least admit of being made, so plain and simple that men of intelligence may readily qualify themselves for their performance; and I cannot but believe that more is lost by the mere continuance of men in office than is generally gained by their experience.[24]

Some methods for watching the local bureaucracy were briefly discussed in the section on accountability earlier in this chapter. But too constant and too critical citizen control is not a complete good. As Woodrow Wilson pointed out in his pioneering essay on administration in 1887,

> The problem is to make public opinion efficient without suffering it to be meddlesome. Directly exercised, in the oversight of the daily details and in the choice of the daily means of government, public criticism is of course a clumsy nuisance, a rustic handling delicate machinery. But as superintending the greater forces of formative policy alike in politics and administration, public criticism is altogether safe and beneficient, altogether indispensable.[25]

It is interesting to note the kindred testimonies of Jackson and Wilson in regard to bureaucracy. Jackson is often called the "father" of the spoils system and Wilson is called the "father" of meritocracy. Just as it may seem a paradox that these two men would complement each other's views, the problem of bureaucracy in contemporary local government is somewhat of a paradox. Many citizens want additional or expanded services from their governments but fear a loss of control over that government if the non-elective segment of the public service grows. This fear is not entirely ungrounded because most new positions are technical and require specialists rather than persons who can be appointed from the ranks of the citizenry. Adrian describes this paradox in these words, "People like the product of government; they do not like the means that seem necessary in order to deliver the product."[26]

The "means" to deliver the product has been described by Theodore Lowi as the "New Machine" in urban government. The trappings of this "machine" are perhaps best noted in the several characteristics which in combination comprise the "New York syndrome." First, the local citizenry demands new services and increased levels of existing services. Second, provision of these services requires a large bureaucracy. Third, the bureaucracy demands wage increases to keep pace with high inflation rates. Fourth, the city is forced to float bonds to meet the increased costs of services and salaries. Fifth, the city's debt expands and interest payments increase, thus causing a fiscal crisis. The net result is a citizen backlash against city hall and the local bureaucracy, which produces a renewed role of the citizen as local watchdog.

NOTES

1. Arthur W. Bromage, "The Art of Governing American Cities," *Horizons for Modern Pennsylvania Local Government*, 3 (March 1956), 3-4.
2. Dwight Waldo, *The Study of Public Administration*, Random House, 1955, p. 11.
3. *Ibid.*, p. 12
4. Amitai Etzioni, *Modern Organizations,* Prentice-Hall, 1964, p. 3.
5. Mayor's Committee on Management Survey, *Modern Management for the City of New York*, Vol. 1, 1953, p. 17.
6. Waldo, *op. cit.*, p. 12.
7. John H. Ames, "The Art of Management," *Public Management*, 32 (January, 1950), 2-6.
8. John Pfiffner and Robert Presthus, *Public Administration*, Ronald Press, 5th ed., 1967, p. 88.
9. Herman G. Pope, "The City Manager as a Leader in the Administrative Organization," *Public Management*, 30 (October, 1949), 294-7.
10. David S. Brown, "Making Decisions," in James M. Banovetz (ed.), *Managing the Modern City*, International City Management Association, 1971, p. 135.
11. William J. Gore, *Administrative Decision-Making: A Heuristic Model,* John Wiley & Sons, 1964, p. 36.
12. John K. Parker, "Administrative Planning," in Banovetz, *op. cit.*, p. 254.
13. Charles R. Adrian, *Governing Urban America*, 2nd ed., McGraw-Hill, 1961, p. 321. For an alternative view of public interest, see Edward C. Banfield, *Political Influence,* Free Press, 1961, pp. 264-70. Banfield's concept stresses the notions of compromise between contenders and organizational aggrandizement in determining the public interest.
14. See Francis F. Piven and Richard Cloward, *The Politics of Turmoil, Essays on Poverty, Race and the Urban Crisis*, Pantheon, 1974; and Piven, *Regulating the Poor, The Function of Public Welfare*, Pantheon, 1974.

15. Theodore Lowi, *The End of Liberalism, Ideology, Policy and the Crisis of Public Authority*, Norton, 1969, chap. 7.
16. Clarence E. Ridley and Herbert A. Simon, *Measuring Municipal Activities*, 2nd ed., International City Managers' Association, 1943, p. 3.
17. *Ibid.*, pp. 2-3.
18. International City Management Association, *Municipal Finance Administration,* 3rd. ed., 1948, p. 142.
19. See Edward F. R. Hearle and Raymond J. Mason, *A Data Processing System for State and Local Governments*, Prentice-Hall, 1963.
20. John K. Parker, "Tools of Modern Management," in Banovetz, *op. cit.,* p. 237.
21. Kenneth O. Warner, "A Common Sense Personnel Program," *Tennessee Town and City*, 2 (April, 1951), 13.
22. James Belasco, "Collective Bargaining in City X," *Government Labor Relations in Transition*, Public Personnel Association, 1966, p. 50.
23. *Ibid.*
24. Quoted in Leonard D. White, *Introduction to the Study of Public Administration,* rev. ed., Macmillan, 1939, p. 280.
25. Woodrow Wilson, "The Study of Administration," *Political Science Quarterly*, 56 (December, 1941), 499.
26. Adrian, op. cit., p. 324.

Chapter 14

Local Government Finance

Faced with the contradiction of the demands of citizens for new and improved services at present or lower total costs, local governments find monetary problems difficult indeed. Thus, while fiscal management is part of the administrative process, it is treated in a separate chapter because of its importance.

The changing nature of the financial focus in local government has been noted by James Jernberg, political scientist, in these words:

> The traditional discussion of financial administration has focused primarily on the procedural and control methods with which the administrator could most efficiently and honestly conduct the internal fiscal affairs of the city administration. . . . Now the administrator's financial horizon extends beyond internal management to the financial leadership demands created by his attempts to provide a meaningful public contribution to the quality of urban life.[1]

In this chapter emphasis is placed on local fiscal organization, the budgetary process, custody of funds, accounting, purchasing, reporting, financial planning, and revenue sources and major expenditures. Because successful administration of local finance depends upon sound fiscal organization, this aspect is examined first.

ORGANIZATION FOR FISCAL MANAGEMENT

Existing patterns of fiscal organization vary widely among size and types of local governments. It may be readily appreciated that the fiscal machinery of a city of over seven million would be more complex than that in a city of a few hundred persons. Similarly, the machinery of fiscal management in a large urban county differs from that in a small rural county. However, every government unit has a form of organization and a type of process involved in its fiscal management—with both ranging from the highly integrated and complex to the highly decentralized and simple.

In most local governments, fiscal functions and responsibilities are shared by a number of officials and agencies. Such a condition is known as decentralized administration in contrast to the centralized pattern where all fiscal officers are subject to the direct supervision of the chief executive officer. The integrated pattern is found in a number of cities with strong mayor-council or council-manager forms of government. While the number of fiscal officers and agencies varies, four types are usually found. They are (1) the local legislative body; (2) the local chief executive; (3) other administrative officers; and (4) overseers or checkers on the fidelity and legality of expenditures after completion of the transactions.

The fiscal responsibilities of local legislative bodies have been discussed in Chapter 10. Nonetheless, it bears repeating that the governing board in any unit is the supreme fiscal authority because it adopts the basic financial policies for that unit. The budget is often presented by the local executive, but the governing board must ratify it on behalf of the people. Moreover, the local legislature determines the local tax rate, demands an accounting of funds spent by agencies and officers of the unit, and may conduct investigations into the handling of public monies.

Except in cases where the governing board is both the chief legislative agency and the principal administrative agency, the chief executive also is the major fiscal officer and usually plays a significant role in the fiscal process. Increasingly, the executive takes a leading part in establishing policies for raising and spending money through his preparation of the local budget. Even in communities where his budget role is limited, the executive is responsible for its administration. He assists in allocating funds, oversees their spending, and supervises their accounting.

In the third category of fiscal officers are such officials as the treasurer, who serves as the custodian of public monies; the controller, who performs fiscal control functions; the assessor, who values property for determining the general tax rate; the purchasing agent, who procures materials and supplies; and the board of tax appeals to whom aggrieved citizens may carry their complaints about the taxes levied against their property. As an agent of the legislature, the auditor is charged with determining the fidelity and legality of the manner in which money has been spent.

In the past fifty years, a clear trend toward a more centralized or integrated pattern of fiscal management has emerged. As strong executive plans for cities and counties have developed, fiscal officers have been placed in subordinate positions and are responsible to the chief executive officer. The concern has shifted from a concentration on accounting and auditing to a new focus on budget decision-making, its implementation, and its evaluation.

The Budget Process

It is almost a truism that no local government ever has sufficient money to satisfy all the needs of its citizens. Thus, the adoption of a budget serves as a guide to the community in estimating its needs and planning to raise the necessary funds to meet these needs. More technically, the budget serves as an economic plan reflecting the allocation of scarce resources among alternative uses, a political document recording the preferences of "who gets to spend what the governmental unit has to spend," and as a decision process in which interest focuses on the reduction of complexities to manageable proportions.[2]

Possibly no other field of local management has experienced as many important technical advances recently as the budget process. Budgeting developed first in municipal government at the start of the present century and the intervening years have witnessed a series of improved budgetary processes and techniques. No longer is it feasible to speak of a "local budget" since it may be an executive or legislative budget, an operating or a capital budget, a line-item or a program budget. The basic budget is the operating budget which represents a financial plan for the operation of a local government for a specified period of time known as the fiscal year.

Originally the local budget was a legislative document. The legislature proposed expenditures with the executive forced to accept this financial plan except in communities where he had the veto or the item veto power. As an outgrowth of the general efficiency and economy movement in the early years of this century the budgetary roles have been interchanged in a number of local governments. Now the executive proposes the financial plan and the legislature disposes by accepting, amending, or rejecting it. A budget so prepared is known as an executive budget in contrast to the legislative budget, but the latter is still the more common in county and township governments.

A capital budget is a long-term financial plan embracing a program of capital improvement projects rather than the daily expenditures of the operating budget. A line-item budget places emphasis upon the things to be acquired—such as typewriters, fire trucks, police radios. This type of budget specifies the exact amount to be spent for each item. A performance or program budget, on the other hand, emphasizes the services to be rendered by stressing what is to be accomplished rather than the particular items to be purchased.

The process of budget preparation begins in the office of the responsible local officer or agency. This office may be the governing board as in most counties and townships, a legislative committee as in some counties and cities, or the chief executive as in many cities and special districts and in a small number of counties. The first step is a general request for the operating agencies of the government to prepare their expenditure estimates for the forthcoming year. This request comes from the responsible agency and contains a general statement of policy as a guide in the development of these estimates.

The second phase of the budget process begins with the collection of the several separate budget requests in the appropriate agency. This may be a legislative committee, a budget office, or the office of the chief executive. The major task of the budget officer is to shape the individual requests into a preliminary budget and to measure the requests against the expected revenues. Since the total amounts of the former are almost certain to exceed the expected revenues, either a plan for increasing revenues or one for cutting proposed expenditures must be made at this stage. At this point of the process, close cooperation between the officials heading the agencies and the budget officer is essential. Most local government budgets are documents reflecting incrementalism. If the community is enjoying prosperity, the budget will show an increase reflecting this condition of growth. If the local economy is shrinking, the budget will reflect this condition with declining requests. Even more individual budget items indicate this same policy of incrementalism based on the previous year's request.

The budget plan emanating from the second phase is in a form for transmittal to the legislature. With its submittal, the second stage of the budget cycle—adoption—begins. If the local legislature operates with committees, the usual practice is to refer the budget to the finance committee. During its deliberations, the committee holds hearings where interested citizens and groups may appear and department or agency heads attend to answer questions. Individual citizens rarely attend these hearings unless the budget includes some controversial proposal, but representatives of citizen organizations often appear to give support to or to oppose certain proposals. Although the legislators seldom acquire new information from these sessions, they are an important part of the democratic process and allow groups and individuals to express points of view and criticize existing or proposed programs.

In general, the legislative body is free to change the submitted budget as it sees fit. It may add to, reduce, delete, or modify any part of the budget. It also is free to accept, modify, or reject proposed new sources of revenue and increase or decrease suggested tax rates. There is a general limitation on the board's budgetary powers; the budget it approves must be balanced with a revenue program sufficient to meet approved expenditures. In many communities, other limitations also exist, such as requiring more than a simple majority vote of the council to approve changes, or limiting the board's power to reduction only. The legislative body's final action is taken by approving the budget as either transmitted or amended. Approval takes the form of an ordinance relating to appropriation measures, revenue proposals, and borrowing—if necessary—to carry out the budget.

The degree of state control over local budgeting differs widely. In some states, local governments are required to prepare their budgets on forms provided by the state. In other states, review of local budgets by a state agency is provided to check their legality and compliance with state regulations.

The third phase of the budget cycle—execution—begins after legislative approval of the budget document. The first step in the actual administration is a device for controlling expenditures and involves the submittal of work programs by agency heads to the chief executive for sanction. Work programs usually are on a monthly or quarterly basis and show how much of the total appropriation of an agency is desired for each period of the fiscal year. This device is known as the "allotment system," which provides a means for keeping expenditure programs under constant review to prevent the disbursement of funds at a pace that will result in deficits later in the fiscal year.

Two major considerations are involved in the pre-audit control function. First, the legality of the proposed expenditure is checked, and second, the adequacy of funds to meet the obligation is assured. This control also is of an executive nature and aims to achieve the double objective of realization of program goals and preservation of legislative intent.

The third step in the process of budget administration is the post audit, which comes at the close of the fiscal period. After the monies have been spent, the auditor is concerned with the honesty and legality of the completed transactions and the accuracy of accounts. The auditor may be a public officer or a private person or private firm hired to perform this function. He normally reports his findings to the local legislative body and frequently also to the state auditor. In some states, the auditing function is performed through a state bureau of supervision of public offices.

As described above, the budget cycle may appear to consist of a series of interrelated but not overlapping steps. But this is not so in practice. As monies are being spent, checks are operating and plans are being laid for possible changes in next year's budget. New programs are under study and methods for reducing costs are also under consideration. Thus, the budget process is a continuing and unending operation rather than a short interval of heavy pressure coming once a year.

Custody of Funds

The custodian of funds in local governments is the treasurer, often an elective officer. As custodian, the treasurer is responsible for depositing funds other than small amounts needed for daily operations in banks known as depositories. The most common practice for selecting depositories is for the council or an *ex officio* board of which the treasurer is a member to select the bank or banks in which local funds are to be deposited. Obviously safety should be the prime consideration in choosing certain banks as depositories. Commonly funds are divided between two or more local banks which are required to provide for the deposits.

To protect the public against loss of funds through dishonesty, negligence, or mistake on his part, the treasurer is usually under an indemnity bond. The basic purposes of such bonds are (1) to protect the local government against monetary loss by such officials, and (2) to guarantee faithful performance of duty by such bonded officials. Not many local officials misuse public monies today, but the requirement of the indemnity bond was enacted in some states only under pressure from local governments following experiences of official dishonesty.

The treasurer's office continues to be a widely coveted elective office in many counties. In some states, county treasurers are prohibited from succeeding themselves in office or from holding the office for longer than two successive terms. Such provisions concerning reeligibility are less needed now than earlier when regulations providing for checks on the custodian of county funds were few and poorly enforced. Today the duties of the treasurer as custodian of public monies are ministerial only and are primarily of a bookkeeping nature. Little or no discretion is entrusted to this officer, and the justification for its retention as an elective office is no longer as valid as previously.

Accounting

Accounting has been described as the heart of fiscal management because it records financial information and makes that data available to administrators, legislators, pertinent employees, and interested citizens. Accounting activities usually are placed in the office of the controller, often an elective position. As "watchdog of the treasury," it is hoped that his election will make him independent of both the tax levying and spending authorities so that he may be a true representative of the public.

There are several important purposes for maintaining government accounts. They are (1) to provide information about past operations and present conditions; (2) to serve as a basis for future operations; (3) to establish controls over the acts of public bodies and officers in the use of public funds; and (4) to publicize the financial operations and conditions of government for the benefit of interested citizens.

The two principal bases for the maintenance of local accounts are known as cash and accrual accounting. Under the cash system, revenues are recorded only upon receipt and expenditures only when paid. In the accrual system, revenues are accounted for when earned or billed, as in the case of taxes, while expenditures are recorded when the liability has been incurred. The accrual system places emphasis on a fiscal period and gives a more accurate picture of the local financial condition for the period but may give a misleading picture at any one time. The cash system, on the other hand, gives a daily picture but is not very helpful in seeing conditions over a longer period.

Since both systems have advantages and disadvantages, small units in particular may find it best to use the cash basis for revenues and the accrual basis for expenditures. Such a combined system would make it impossible to incur more liabilities than revenues could cover. By accruing revenues, property tax receipts would be recorded at the time the bills were sent out since they represent an asset to be received. Unfortunately, taxes on some pieces of property may not be received and yet these amounts are also shown as assets under this system. By recording expenditures only when paid, the local government may seem to have more assets than it actually has and it may overextend its funds.

As the concept of performance budget has gained wider usage in local government, a third basis of accounting—cost accounting—has developed. This method of accounting records all expenditures incurred in the performance of some unit of work that can be enumerated. Cost accounting seeks to achieve a distribution of direct and indirect expenses to arrive at an accurate total cost. Normally four basic types of costs occur—labor, equipment, materials and supplies, and overhead charges. As far as possible, standard work units are established for the various activities to which the cost accounting system applies. Examples of such standard units are miles of streets cleaned, patient days in a hospital, tons of refuse collected, gallons of sewage treated, and square yards of street patched. By establishing these standard work measures, unit costs can be determined and future work programs can be based upon these unit costs.

Reporting

A financial report of some type is prepared by all units of local government. Such reports may be defined as statements that set forth the government's financial condition. Internal reports are made to the chief executive by his financial aides, and he in turn makes periodic financial reports to the local board or council. These reports are made primarily to assure that budget administration is proceeding legally and in accordance with the general directions prescribed by the local legislative body.

The most important of the local financial reports is the annual financial report, of which there are two common types. The first is a complete financial report with detailed data. Such complex reports truly defy citizen comprehension, and in some governmental units this may be a recognized factor in their continued preparation in such form. The second type of report is more usable because it attempts to show what the citizenry is getting for its money as well as the general condition of local finances. In addition to essential data on the sources of revenue and the costs of local services, this report typically gives a brief description of functions performed, a chart or charts showing the organization of the local government, information on current, past and projected costs, a directory of local officials, and a statement of plans for the year ahead.

Purchasing

Local governments today ordinarily have purchasing or procurement officers or establish this function as the basic purpose of a division or bureau within the local finance agency. This is in sharp contrast to the earlier practice under which purchasing was largely individual and decentralized. Since the turn of the present century, many local governments have introduced centralized purchasing systems as a means to greater economy and efficient administration. Central purchasing is the delegation of the authority to one office to purchase needed supplies, materials, and equipment for use by all the operating divisions of that government.

Among the advantages claimed for centralized procurement are: (1) lower prices derived from purchasing in larger quantities and increased competition among suppliers; (2) additional savings accruing from expedited payments, fewer purchase orders and vouchers, and simplified accounting procedures and controls; (3) purchases are made only from qualified vendors, preventing the acquisition of inferior supplies or equipment; (4) the development of standard specifications for items bought in large quantities facilitates bidding by competing suppliers; (5) the removal of vendors whose records of service are poor from the list of qualified vendors; and (6) centralized inspection of materials and supplies helps to prevent the purchase of inferior items.

In the eyes of the heads of operating departments and agencies, centralized purchasing is a mixed blessing. Among the objections with some validity are the "red tape" and delay involved in securing supplies, the dictatorial nature of some purchasing officers, the time consumed in developing adequate specifications for items used by various departments and agencies, and the stockpiling of certain items which may result from bargain buying. In addition, many agency heads feel they are better able to determine the nature and quality of the items most suitable to their own needs.

The purchasing procedure typically begins with the preparation of a requisition sent to the purchasing agent by the using department. The purchasing officer attempts to get competitive bids on most items by advertising to secure bids, by letters to suppliers requesting quotations of cost, or by telephone calls to prospective suppliers. After bids have been received, the purchase is awarded to the "lowest responsible bidder." Upon receiving the goods, the purchasing agent records its receipt and notifies the using department. Many local governments give preference to local vendors but this practice is being increasingly limited to instances where the price, quality, and services offered locally are equal to those realizable from outside sources.

Financial Planning

If local fiscal plans are limited to each annual budgetary period, the result often is a somewhat haphazard allocation of the financial resources of that unit. Since revenues are seldom sufficient to meet all needs, funds are apportioned annually on an "emergency" basis since no serious effort has been made to foresee either operating or capital needs beyond the current year. Pressures both inside and outside the official government circle may result in unwise and stopgap expenditure plans because no orderly pattern or plan of priorities has been established.

An important step to prevent such short-term developments is careful preparation of a long-range comprehensive fiscal plan. Such a plan might be developed for a period of sixteen to twenty years, with four-year installments or subplans of the total plan. In the development of such a plan, estimates should be prepared in four major areas. They are: (1) needs for local services in such functions as education, health, safety, transportation, water, and sanitation; (2) capital improvements needs in major public buildings and service facilities such as freeways, sewage disposal plans, and water systems; (3) schedule of priority of needs in terms of timing since all the programs and projects cannot be instituted or built at any one time; and (4) methods of financing the services and facilities to be developed. Without a plan for getting the financial support needed to carry the specific projects and services to fruition, the plan is not worth the time and effort devoted to its preparation.

As in the case of the operating budget, the preparation of the long-range fiscal plan is decentralized at first, with departments and agencies submitting estimates of programs to be expanded or developed and capital facility requirements. These are combined in the overall plan, and then the council or governing board establishes priorities or programs to be embraced in the four-year installments. It is essential that flexibility characterize all aspects of the long-range plan. It is also desirable to prepare a number of alternative approaches so that unforeseen events will not effect the total plan too adversely.

LOCAL REVENUE PATTERNS

Once the "bill of goods" for the government-unit has been drawn up, a major question arises: how will the bill be paid? Budget politics often is very different than taxation politics. The former is advanced by employee groups who seek higher salaries, new positions, and expanded services. Conversely, taxation politics are often spearheaded by taxpayer associations and senior citizens with both groups agreed upon the curbing of expenditures.

The local revenues picture is not generally healthy or promising. The main problem relates to the pre-emption of major revenue sources by the national and state governments, leaving only relatively small revenue producers (except for the property tax) for local governments. A second element is the redistribution problem when portions of the same local government or adjoining local governments differ so widely in their financial resources. A third element is the "ripple effect" that all local governments experience when a few local governments face financial crisis.

But in spite of these enormous and unsolved fiscal problems, local government costs have risen sharply in recent years, increasing more than sevenfold since 1942. In large part, the reasons for this increase parallel those for a similar growth in state and national expenditures. These include the rise in the general price level, the decline in the purchasing power of the dollar, the increase in population, rising concentration of people in urban areas, citizen demands for new and expanded services, and the high cost of capital facilities to provide many newer services.

As creatures of the state, local governments have no inherent powers to tax and possess only such authority as the state confers upon them. For the most part, the local taxing power is granted by the state legislature; however, some local units in strong home-rule states may possess certain constitutionally granted taxing powers. Limitations on local taxing authority are both statutory and constitutional and differ considerably among the states. Constitutional limitations commonly concern the exemption of certain classes of property from taxation (such as property used for educational, religious, and charitable purposes); require uniform and equal tax rates; and impose rate limitations on some kinds of taxes. Legislative limitations generally parallel constitutional ones and also relate to rate limitations, withholding or granting specific taxing powers to certain types of local units, and preventing taxing by local units of items already taxed by the state.

The changing pattern of local government general revenues is shown in Table 14. Intergovernmental revenues have increased for all types of local units except townships since 1957, while the property tax has declined as a source for all types of units during this same period. Intergovernmental revenues rose from 29.6 percent to 37.5 percent for local governments, while the property tax declined from 48.7 to 39.9 percent as a general source for all local governments. The income tax shows a slight increase as does the revenue from current charges. The sales tax has decreased slightly as has the category ''all other'' sources.

TABLE 14
PERCENTAGE DISTRIBUTION OF LOCAL GOVERNMENT GENERAL REVENUES BY SOURCE AND BY TYPE OF GOVERNMENT, 1957 AND 1971

Year	Intergovernmental	Total	County	City	Town-ship	Spec. dist.	School dist.
1957	Intergovernmental	29.6	38.0	18.9	24.8	14.1	42.1
	Property tax	48.7	46.5	46.3	63.6	29.1	50.1
	Income tax	0.8	0.0	1.9	0.3	0.0	0.1
	General sales	2.6	0.9	6.5	0.0	0.0	0.0
	Current charges	10.0	9.3	10.3	3.9	49.9	5.9
	All other	8.3	5.2	16.1	7.4	6.9	1.8
1971	Intergovernmental	37.5	41.8	31.7	22.3	26.4	46.1
	Property tax	39.9	37.4	32.8	62.8	19.7	45.7
	Income tax	1.9	0.8	4.6	0.8	0.0	0.4
	General sales	2.5	2.9	5.4	*	0.8	0.2
	Current charges	10.7	11.3	11.7	4.8	41.6	5.6
	All other	7.5	5.7	13.7	9.3	11.4	2.0

*Less than 0.05 percent.

Source: Advisory Commission on Intergovernmental Relations, *Federal-State-Local Finances: Significant Features of Fiscal Federalism, 1973-74.* Washington, 1974, Table II, p. 19. Intergovernmental revenues are those provided the local government by the federal and state governments.

The Property Tax

The property tax still serves as the largest single source of local revenues. In the early years of our nation, this tax was a fairly good measure of ability to pay, since a close relationship existed between property owned and income received. Now property is commonly divided into two kinds for local taxing purposes: real and personal. Real property includes land, buildings, and permanent improvements, while personal property embraces all other kinds—clothes, furniture, automobiles, stocks, bonds, and jewelry. Because of its varied nature, personal property is further divided into tangible and intangible properties. The term tangible is used to describe such belongings as furniture, cars, and jewelry, while stocks and bonds are examples of the intangible type.

Even from this brief description of the elements of property obviously it is no longer a measure of one's ability to pay taxes. Some properties produce income for their owners; others do not. Many Americans own no tangible and perhaps little intangible property and yet have sizable incomes. Thus, even while the property tax is the most productive source of local revenues, several serious criticisms have been raised against it. E.R.A. Seligman once suggested that there is nothing wrong with the property tax except that it is wrong in theory and does not work in practice.[3] Table 15 gives an answer to the question of who pays the local property tax by showing its major sources.

TABLE 15
WHO PAYS THE LOCAL PROPERTY TAX?

Type of Property	Percent
Non-farm residential realty and personalty	48.9
Commercial and industrial realty and personalty	33.5
Public utilities	7.5
Farm realty and personalty (land and improvements)	5.7
Farm residential realty and personalty	2.3
Vacant Lots	2.0

Source: Adapted from Advisory Commission on Intergovernmental Relations, *Federal-State-Local Finances: Significant Features of Fiscal Federalism, 1973-74*, Washington, 1974, Table 102, p. 173.

In addition to the unsoundness of the property tax in principle, it is difficult to administer, resulting in inequities among taxpayers. Determining the value of property is not an easy task because of the great variation in its types and worth. A third major objection relates to the ease of hiding intangible personal property. Here the problem of valuation is one largely of uncovering stocks, bonds, and other securities. A fourth problem is raised by the persons who serve as assessors. In many local governments, they continue to be elected and have no special competence for their positions.

The property tax is defended on the basis that many benefits of local government go to people living on property in the area. In most places, the idea of a general property tax has been attenuated in various major respects. Under these changes, personalty not used to produce income may be exempt and intangibles may be taxed through some form of income tax. Twenty-two states have enacted programs of relief for persons of certain ages and for those with low incomes. Known as "circuit-breaker" programs, these operate as a state-financed property tax relief program in which the state rebates that part of the tax deemed excessive in relation to household income.[4] Also, a number of states grant exemptions to senior citizens and have programs for farm land exemptions for land actually utilized in farming.

INTERGOVERNMENTAL REVENUES

Revenues for local governments from federal and state subsidies and grants have increased markedly in recent years. The "State and Local Fiscal Assistance Act of 1972," discussed in part in Chapter 4, was a logical culmination of a series of programs and policies providing for interlevel funding for services where the three levels share interest and concern.

By fiscal year 1971-72, the year before passage of the above mentioned act, local governments received nearly $4.5 billion from the national government, an amount equal to 4.3 percent of the total general revenues of local government. State aid for that fiscal year totaled $34.5 billion, or 33.4 percent of the total general revenues of local governments.[5]

In the same year state aid to local governments averaged $158.82 per capita. The grants were in four major areas and, again on a per capita basis, averaged $93.87 for education, $28.03 for public welfare, $15.85 for general local government support, $12.20 for highways, and $8.87 for all other programs.[6] The per capita grant in individual states ranged from $320.42 in New York to a low of $21.49 in Hawaii. The next four highest per capita grants were in the states of Alaska ($261.12), Minnesota ($252.09), California ($247.63), and Wisconsin ($220.03). The four states with the next lowest per capita grants to local governments were New Hampshire ($64.27), South Dakota ($65.80), Maine ($78.14), and Missouri ($78.43).[7]

State financial assistance to local government takes two major forms—grants-in-aid and shared taxes. Grants-in-aid are payments from one level of government to another; like federal grants-in-aid to states, state grants to local governments are allocated according to a formula and normally are made with conditions attached. The basic elements in the formula vary with the end purpose of the appropriation. Thus, a formula for aid for highways generally includes mileage as a component and number of pupils figures in the formula for aid to education. Conditions attached to the grant usually include matching of funds in some ratio, the use of trained personnel in administering them, the right of the state to audit local accounts relating to expenditures of the funds, and the use of the money only for certain stated purposes.

Shared taxes are collected by the state and apportioned among local governments according to a formula that is commonly a fixed percentage of the yield. The amount received by each local government customarily is in direct ratio to the amount of the tax collected within its area or is a per capita grant with local receipts determined by population. Here are examples of the two common bases for state sharing of these taxes. Revenues returned to a county or city from a state-imposed liquor tax may depend on the income collected by the state from liquor sales in that community. Revenues returned to a local government from a state gasoline tax is more likely to be on a population basis than on a local sales basis. Other taxes commonly shared by the state with its local governments are those on motor fuels, motor vehicles, liquor, income, and general sales.

Income and Sales Taxes

Of recent vintage on the local level, income taxes may be one of the major local taxes in the future. First assessed in Philadelphia and Washington, D.C., in 1939, local income taxes are now levied by some local governments in ten states.[8] In some states, only the largest city or cities are permitted to levy an income tax and the rate of the local income tax is low, ranging from 0.25 percent to 3.5 percent.

Local income taxes have three characteristics that contribute to their increasing use. First, they provide much-needed revenue. Second, they are relatively easy and economical to administer. And, third, they are assessed in the community where they are earned rather than in the community in which the earner resides. Hence, they enable a local government to exact contributions from both nonresidents and residents and thus may be of increasing use, particularly in metropolitan areas where the residency and place of work of many citizens lie in different communities within the metropolitan complex.

New York City adopted the first local sales tax in 1934 as a ''temporary'' expedient to produce badly needed revenues. The tax served its purpose well, but New York has never outgrown the need for its revenues and this temporary tax appears to have become a permanent revenue source there. Twenty-five states have authorized some or all of their local governments to impose a sales tax. Rates range from 0.5 percent to 3 percent. All states except Alaska that permit local governments to impose a sales tax also have a state sales tax. Typically the state collects both taxes and returns the local portion to the local governments. This practice retains the collection and administration of the tax at the state level, thereby assuring uniformity in these features. The tax's major disadvantage is its regressiveness which produces a greater proportional burden on lower income people than on wealthier individuals. To overcome the worst aspects of this feature, the necessities of life—food, medicine, and essential items of clothing—are sometimes exempted from the tax. The rate of growth of this tax is reflected in these figures. It existed in 60 counties and 1,300 cities in 1960, but thirteen years later the tax was being utilized in 632 counties, 3,780 cities and 49 school districts.[9]

Other Sources

For a long time many local governments have secured some revenue from business taxes and licenses. They may be sufficient only to pay the cost of supervising a business, or they may produce excess revenue. An example of the first type might be a restaurant license fee to finance health inspections of such businesses. License taxes upon retail liquor establishments and commercial amusements are illustrative of revenue-producing licenses. Among the variety of business and commercial enterprises licensed in some form are hotels, apartment houses, food and department stores, beauty and barber shops, pawnshops, taxicabs, and vending machines.

Local taxes on admissions to various types of entertainment and sports events have grown more common in recent years. Resort areas expand this concept a bit, since tourists and vacationers are favorite objects of taxation. Such areas usually enact taxes on accommodations for their visitors as well as on the attractions pulling them there, in the form of either admission or use taxes.

Service charges are often imposed by local governments for certain services. These are particularly prevalent in utility services such as water supply and sewage disposal. Recently, however, the service charge concept has been extended to such fields as street lighting, parking, and garbage and refuse collection. Various bases or formulas are used to determine the amount of these charges. For example, the charge for sewage disposal is computed on such varied bases as water consumption, number of water outlets, assessed valuation, and front footage. But in general, service charges are based primarily upon the principle of benefits received.

While service charges often are described as a means of avoiding tax increases and making the tax level appear lower than it actually is, a case may be made that such charges promote greater equity in local taxation. Placing some services on a charge basis makes possible the assessing of these charges against properties exempt from the local property tax. Similarly, they are a useful device to obtain revenues other than the property tax from properties consuming large amounts of water or contributing a disproportionate amount of sewage or other waste to the local sewerage system.

A special assessment is an extra levy against pieces of real property made in rough proportion to benefits received by that property. It is used to defray the costs of services or conveniences of particular value to those properties. Frequent uses of special assessments include the financing fully or partly of the costs of new street paving, building sidewalks, installing water or sewage lines, street lighting, constructing off-street parking, or establishing parks and playgrounds.

EXPENDITURE PATTERNS OF LOCAL GOVERNMENT

Just as the revenues of local governments have risen enormously in recent decades, a similar growth in local expenditures has occurred. In a satirical vein, Northcote Parkinson would say the latter is inevitable since his second ``law`` states that expenditures rise to meet revenues—whether personal or governmental. In Parkinson's words, ``It is widely recognized that what is true of individuals is also true of governments. Whatever the revenue may be, there will always be a pressing need to spend it.`` His solution is to ``Put an absolute limit to the revenue, and let expenditures rise to meet it. These are the profits of experience and from these profits we should derive our law.``[10]

This solution is not very practicable for local officials on the receiving end of citizen demands for new and improved services and state-issued directives for higher standards for services. There are many reasons for expanding local costs and rising expenditures, but three in particular may be singled out. These are changes in our social and economic order resulting from population growth and its concentration in urban areas, our changing theory about the proper role of government, and a changing concept of democracy that now recognizes social and economic needs of citizens as well as the goal for political equality.

Although comparing expenditures of local governments over a period of years has limitations, it does point out the marked expansion of expenditures at this level. At the turn of the century, expenditures of local governments totaled one billion dollars. By 1929, this amount has risen sixfold to a little over six billion dollars. In the next twenty-four years, expenditures trebled to a little over 19 billion dollars. By 1960, these costs had doubled again, soaring to over 38 billion dollars. During the next fourteen years, these expenditures rose to 124.7 billion in fiscal 1973-74.[11]

While comparative expenditures by types of local governments for four major services and for interest on general debt are presented in Table 16, the data provided are not very revealing as to the total spending patterns of types of local units. In every case except for school districts, the amounts shown for ``all other`` expenditures comprise a large percentage of the total.

TABLE 16
SELECTED ITEMS OF LOCAL GOVERNMENT FINANCES BY
TYPE OF GOVERNMENT, 1973-74 (Millions of dollars)

Item	All local govts.	Counties	Cities	Townships	School dists.	Special dists.
Education	56,080	4,224	6,392	1,497	43,770	196
Highways	7,310	3,012	3,306	808	0	184
Public welfare	9,576	6,074	3,444	58	0	0
Police and fire protection	9,181	1,401	7,203	496	0	80
Health and hospitals	8,451	3,794	3,180	54	0	1,424
Interest on General debt	4,803	695	1,918	132	1,167	892
All Other	29,267	7,883	16,477	1,305	0	3,602
Total	124,668	27,083	41,920	4,350	44,937	6,379

Source: Bureau of the Census, *"Governmental Finances and Employment at a Glance"*, Government Printing Office, January, 1976, p. 4.

Table 16 shows, excluding the "all other" category, the three largest expenditures for counties are welfare, education, and health and hospitals; police and fire protection, education, and welfare for cities; education, highways, and police and fire protection for townships; and health, interest, and education for special districts. The contrasts in the spending patterns of local governments are considerable.

LOCAL DEBT ADMINISTRATION

Every local government theoretically enjoys the choice of paying for its capital improvement projects by increasing taxes and paying cash, or by issuing bonds to be paid off in future years. This statement assumes the acceptance of the principle that borrowing should not be used to meet current operating expenses, although this often has been done in the past, either in times of depression or as a means of keeping current taxes low—particularly in years of local elections.

Borrowing to finance permanent or capital improvements differs from issuing bonds to pay for current or continuing public operations. If the life of the bonds is such that they will be paid off before the improvement or facility becomes obsolete or unusable, a good case can be made for financing these undertakings by this method. In addition to borrowing to finance major public improvements, local governments often incur debts for two other reasons. They are to meet unanticipated emergencies and to obtain funds in anticipation of revenues to be received a short time later. Borrowing for the latter reason is sometimes necessary because taxes and other revenues do not come into the treasury sufficiently early in the fiscal year to meet current expenses. This type of borrowing is known as "short-term indebtedness" since it is normally repaid within a matter of months.

Local bonds may be classified in various ways. One frequent classification is based on the method for paying off the indebtedness and divides issues into sinking fund and serial bonds. Sinking fund bonds generally all mature at the end of a definite period, and money is set aside in a sinking fund to retire the bonds when they are due. Serial bonds, on the other hand, have staggered maturity dates, and money is appropriated directly for their payment. In recent years, serial bonds have gained in favor and are now the more commonly used. A major reason for the decreasing use of sinking funds is their frequent mismanagement, resulting in past failures to have the funds to pay off the bonds at the time of their retirement.

A second classification of bonds relates to time of maturity and consists of callable and no-callable bonds. If the bonds have a "call" feature, they can be paid off at any time prior to the date of maturity at the option of the debtor, subject to whatever time restrictions are placed on the issue. For example, an issue for twenty-five years might include the condition that none would be redeemable before a period of ten years. Non-callable bonds, as the name implies, have a definite maturity date and cannot be paid off before that time.

A third classification pertains to the four major types of local bonds, which are general obligation, limited obligation or special assessment, revenue, and mortgage bonds. General obligation bonds are guaranteed by the taxing capacity of the issuing local government and often are called full faith and credit bonds. A community issuing this type promises to use any and all of its revenue sources to pay the interest on and to retire these bonds. Limited obligation or special assessment bonds are backed by income from one or more specific sources instead of by the full faith and credit of the community. Revenue bonds frequently are issued to pay for public improvements directly benefiting only a part of the community. Revenue bonds are secured by the pledge of revenues from self-liquidating projects such as toll bridges or roads, waterworks, and public transit systems. Mortgage bonds usually are used in connection with the acquisition or construction of utilities and are in essence mortgages on the utilities, with the plant and the revenues to be realized from the sale of services as the security. When such bonds are issued, they generally require a higher rate of interest than general obligation bonds and therefore have been less popular with local officials. A pledge of full faith and credit is also used to back some mortgage and revenue bonds to reduce interest rates.

In general, there are three major types of local debt limitations—those dealing with the purposes of local debt issues, amounts of local debt, and kinds of bonds that may be issued. These limitations are found in three primary sources, which are state constitutions, state statutes, and local charters. The specific limitations found in most state constitutions are to (1) prohibit public aid to private enterprise, (2) fix debt limitations as a percentage of assessed value of taxable property, (3) prescribe maximum periods for life of bonds, (4) require referendum on bond issues. Statutory requirements often prescribe maximum interest rates, length of bond periods, and other limitations. Local charters often reiterate the state-imposed limitations but sometimes contain additional limitations. Most often these concern the debt limitation of the unit prescribing it in terms of a fixed percentage of the assessed valuation of taxable property, a fixed sum, or prohibiting an amount in excess of the current revenues of the unit.

In an effort to overcome some shortcomings of a system of such rigid controls, various states have established administrative agencies to pass upon debt proposals by local governments. State administrative control should not displace local discretion entirely, but it can prevent local abuses of borrowing power and provide aid to local governments by developing a borrowing policy that will avoid the recurrence of the financial disasters occurring at the local level in the past.

TABLE 17
INDEBTEDNESS OF LOCAL GOVERNMENTS, 1973-74

Item	Dollar Amount (in millions)
Debt outstanding total	141,320
Long-term	128,256
Full faith and credit	80,095
Nonguaranteed	48,161
Short-term	13,064

Source: Bureau of the Census, *"Governmental Finances and Employment at a Glance,"* Government Printing Office, January, 1976, p. 3.

An example of such a state agency is the Municipal Assistance Corporation (often called "Big Mac"), created in 1975 to help New York City meet its financial crisis. The agency was established to float long-term bonds to replace the burdensome short-term debt of the city. When "Big Mac" bonds did not sell, the agency was authorized to review and limit the city's budget so its bonds would be more attractive. As a result, the mayor was stripped of important budgetary powers and large cutbacks were made in public services. While New York's financial problems are more extreme than those in most other cities, the conditions that brought on this fiscal crisis exist in many other governmental units. Even the spill-over effect of loss of confidence in large urban governments was clearly apparent as many cities were forced to pay higher interest rates on their bond issues after the New York crisis became well publicized.

TABLE 18
CITIZEN ATTITUDES ON LOCAL TAXES

City	What do people in the city think about local taxes?			Do people get their money's worth from their local taxes?*	
	Too high	About right	Too low	Yes	No
Albuquerque	27%	57%	11%	47%	46%
Atlanta	35	50	9	39	53
Baltimore	68	28	4	27	72
Boston	67	22	7	21	70
Denver	38	50	4	46	44
Kansas City, Kan.	53	39	5	25	65
Kansas City, Mo.	35	48	13	26	62
Milwaukee	67	27	3	35	56
Nashville	27	47	19	36	58
San Diego	28	60	6	64	29

Source: *Nation's Cities,* "City Taxes and Services: Citizens Speak Out," An Urban Observatory Report, Vol. 9, August, 1971, p. 13.
*"No responses" are not shown; therefore data do not always total 100 percent.

CITIZENS AND TAXES

The Urban Observatory Program has conducted in-depth interviews with citizens in ten cities to measure their feelings and perceptions about basic governmental services in their cities. The responses to two key questions asked in the interviews are shown in Table 18. It is important, however, not to read into these responses more than they actually show. As the report states,

> what people think of their city's service system and their government is real, and it constitutes one of several possible criteria for evaluating services provided by municipal governments.[12]

The special fiscal problems of metropolitan areas are discussed in Chapter 18. It is important to note that many of these problems are redistributive in nature and thus, very political. The struggles between the "haves" and the "have nots" is similar whether it occurs between a wealthy suburb and a depressed center city or between a high income area and a ghetto both within the center city.

NOTES

1. James Jernberg, "Financial Administration" in James M. Banovetz (ed.), *Managing the Modern City,* International City Management Association, 1971, p. 347.
2. *Ibid.,* pp. 351-52.
3. Charles R. Adrian, *State and Local Governments.* 4th ed., McGraw-Hill, 1976, p. 383.
4. For information on these programs, see Advisory Commission on Intergovernmental Relations, *Federal-State-Local Finances: Significant Features of Fiscal Federalism, 1973-74,* Government Printing Office, 1974, table 108, p. 187.
5. *Ibid.,* table 9, p. 15.
6. *Ibid.,* table 58, p. 83.
7. *Ibid.*
8. *Ibid.,* table 150, pp. 291-4.
9. *Ibid.,* table 136, pp. 252-3.
10. C. Northcote Parkinson, *The Law and the Profits,* Houghton Mifflin, 1960, pp. 5, 246.
11. Bureau of the Census, "Governmental Finances and Employment at a Glance," Government Printing Office, January, 1976, p. 3.
12. *Nation's Cities.* "City Taxes and Services: Citizens Speak Out." An Urban Observatory Report, vol. 9, August, 1971, p. 10.

Chapter 15

Life-Style Services

There are several possible classification plans for analyzing local public services. A common division is to consider services as either social-centered "software" programs or brick and mortar "hardware" services. A second grouping divides services into "life-style" and "system-maintenance" functions.[1]

Life-style policies connote a value cluster associated with a daily living pattern and consist of a set of preferences pertaining to the frequency, character, and context of social interactions. Education and zoning are two prominent examples of such services. System-maintenance policies, on the other hand, are neutral with regard to life-style values and generally facilitate the choice of interactions rather than structure them. Transportation, water, and sewerage are examples of this class. Oliver Williams, political scientist, concludes that

> Assuming no outside interventions, policy areas which are perceived as neutral with respect to controlling social access may be centralized; policies which are perceived as controlling social access will remain decentralized.[2]

This distinction seems useful and helpful in discussing local government services. Life-style services emphasize the importance of local values while system-maintenance services stress economic values. Certainly various, suburban communities have incorporated precisely to control the first group of services while they "cooperate" in the provision of the second set. Bridge building is less controversial than busing of students, and even large jurisdictions seem to favor the distributive policies of the system-maintenance services over the redistributive policies of life-style services. Often the latter are shifted to higher levels of government or face budget cuts before the hardware types of services are curtailed.

This chapter discusses five of the major life-style services provided by local governments while the next chapter considers four major system-maintenance services.

PUBLIC HEALTH

Although local health organizations exist in many forms, the main objectives of public health administration are essentially the same at all levels of and in all types of local government. Broadly conceived, public health is the art and science of preventing disease, prolonging life and promoting physical and mental efficiency through organized community effort. Public health administration has been defined as "that responsibility which rests upon the community for the protection of life and the promotion of the health of its people.[3] Typically, these services are provided through a department of city and county governments.

Originally local health functions were primarily twofold—quarantine measures when communicable diseases were in the community and the abatement of nuisances. Functions have expanded over the years, however, with the newer emphasis on services rather than on controls. Public health people and local government officials generally agree that local health departments should provide certain basic services. They are:

1. Collection and analysis of vital statistics, including the recording, tabulation, interpretation, and publication of the essential facts of births, deaths, and reportable diseases.
2. Communicable disease control, including tuberculosis, venereal diseases, malaria, and hookworm disease.
3. Community sanitation services, including supervision of milk and milk products, food processing, public eating places, and maintenance of sanitary conditions of employment.
4. Public health laboratory facilities and services for local physicians.
5. Maternal and child health services, including child hygiene and maternal care.
6. Public health education for the citizenry.[4]

The National Advisory Commission on Civil Disorders reported some sobering statistics on health services and needs in our urban communities. It found that residents of the racial ghetto suffered from higher mortality rates, higher incidence of major diseases, lower availability and utilization of medical services, and higher admission rates to mental hospitals.[5] As a result, about 30 percent of all families with incomes less than $2,000 annually suffer from chronic health conditions that adversely affect their employment as compared with less than 8 percent of the families with incomes of at least $7,000.

Other significant health facts reported by the Commission related to maternal mortality, infant mortality, life expectancy, and utilization of health services. Maternal mortality rates for nonwhite mothers are four times as high as for white mothers, while infant mortality rates among nonwhites are 58 percent higher than among whites under one month of age, and almost three times as high among those from one month to one year. Life expectancy at birth is 6.9 years longer for whites than for nonwhites. At age twenty-five, the white person can look forward to 48.6 more years of life while a nonwhite can expect only 43.3 years. Nonwhite families in the lower-income groups spend less than half as much per person on medical services as white families with similar incomes. The discrepancy narrows in higher income groups but nonwhite medical expenditures per person in a family whose income is $10,000 annually spend, on the average, 74.3 percent as much as a white family with a similar income.[6]

While America's rural communities were once considered more healthful than urban places, the situation has changed substantially. With advances in preventive medicine and municipal sanitary engineering, cities have gained in healthfulness and are making more rapid progress in the prevention and treatment of disease than rural communities. The problem of adequate health care in rural areas is of a dual nature. First, the problem persists of getting physicians to locate their practice in small communities so that ample medical care is available to private patients, and, second, finding physicians who on either a part-time or full-time basis can be utilized by public health authorities.

AIR POLLUTION CONTROL

Polluted air is an expensive byproduct of the economic growth of America. For Americans in the nineteenth century, living in sooty cities was the price to be paid if they hoped to get rich, since it was there that the nation's industrial plants had concentrated. Americans in the twentieth century, however, are not happy that this industrial might and its products—automobiles, freeways, skyscrapers and so on—are filling the air with visible and invisible gases, smoke, and dust particles. Although no accurate records of the costs of polluted air are in existence, it has been estimated that the direct yearly economic costs for the nation as a whole are $30 billion. In individual terms, it is estimated that air pollution now costs an average of at least $65 per year for each person in our nation to replace damaged goods, repair and repaint discolored surfaces, and launder and clean soiled clothes.[7]

While the magnitude of the air pollution problems has increased greatly, it is actually an old problem to humankind. In England, coal smoke and fumes forced Queen Eleanor to move from Nottingham in 1257, and the first smoke abatement law was enacted there sixteen years later under Edward I. The first known smoke abatement organization was formed by members of Parliament in 1306 in an effort to improve conditions of the air over London.[8] In the 1940s, the cities of St. Louis and Pittsburgh began cleanup campaigns and stringently reduced the smoke pollution resulting from the burning of solid fuels. In 1947, the now well known efforts of Los Angeles to abate its smog problem were started with the creation of an air pollution control district following the passage of state enabling legislation.

The eye irritation produced by air pollution is an unpleasant nuisance, but the real concern is with the nature and extent of the relationship of smog to the increase in chronic respiratory diseases, including asthma, bronchitis, emphysema, and lung cancer. In 1948, nearly 6,000 persons were made ill in Donora, Pennsylvania, during a three-day period of fog, air inversion, and excessive air pollution. Twenty deaths were attributed to that occurrence and followup studies were conducted about its effects on the health of others. During a heavy smog seige in Los Angeles in 1955, nearly 1,000 excess deaths occurred. The incidence of smog coincided with a period of unusually hot weather, and the latter is usually blamed for these excessive deaths. In both cities, however, the majority of the deaths and illnesses took place among the elderly or persons with pre-existing heart or lung conditions that made them more susceptible to the irritants in the air interfering with oxygen use.[9]

The need to clean up the air over our big cities is evident from the following statement concerning an individual's relative need for food, water, and air.

> Man can live five weeks without food and five days without water. But he perishes after five minutes without air. Every day the average adult eats about 2¾ lbs. of food and drinks 4½ lbs. of water. But his lungs draw in and expire 30 lbs. of air. Although oxygen requirements are the most critical of man's daily physical needs, he does less to control the purity of the air than he does to ensure the wholesomeness of his food and water.[10]

Air pollution is a complex problem that varies from place to place, from season to season, and even from hour to hour. Photochemical smog, the particular problem of Los Angeles, does not occur at night. Sulfurous pollution is most serious in northern communities because large amounts of sulfur-bearing fuels are used to heat buildings and generate electricity. Thus, it is very difficult to compare air pollution in different areas.

A recent survey reveals that air pollution control is an assigned function of government in 139 counties, or in 37 percent of all counties with populations in excess of 100,000.[11] Typically, the county governing board also acts as the governing board of the special agency or district entrusted with this important function. The Los Angeles County Air Pollution Control

District was established in 1947 under general state enabling legislation that established such districts in each California county. Districts were activated, however, only after a public hearing and a resolution passed by the county board declaring the need for such an agency.[12] The administrative structure of the Los Angeles agency was organized into six divisions—enforcement, engineering, technical services, evaluation and planning, special services, and administrative services.[13]

EDUCATION

About $56 billion dollars are expended annually by local governments to finance educational programs for close to fifty million Americans. Public education is the largest operation of local governments, viewed in terms of capital investments, current operating expenditures, and number of employees. Considered in terms of objectives, public education is also the most important and vital service of local governments. Our system of democracy depends on the capacity of citizens to make informed, rational choices. An aim of our educational programs is to equip citizens to participate in community affairs in an informed manner, and these programs for widespread education constitute the foundation of our free institutions.

The objective of education, according to one writer, "presupposes that each individual be mentally, socially, and emotionally competent to the fullest possibility of his inborn capacities."[14] Political participation by citizens so equipped strengthens the institutions of a democratic society. Since it is essential that educational opportunities be available to all, the provision of school facilities logically becomes a public service. Many private and sectarian educational institutions exist and have an important share in this great undertaking, but nearly 85 percent of our students attend schools maintained at public expense. These schools are the focus of this discussion.

The concept of free public education is accepted everywhere in the United States, but considerable variety is present among public school systems. An interesting countertrend to the smaller number of public schools resulting from consolidation in recent years has been the rise in the number of private and church-supported schools. While the number of public elementary schools decreased from 247,581 in 1930 to 87,392 in 1972, the number of private elementary schools increased from 9,275 to 14,900 in the same period. Enrollments in private schools also have increased more rapidly in recent decades, partly as a reaction to increased busing to achieve integration in public schools. Oddly enough, the Calvinists who were leaders in the movement for public education systems in colonial times are now among those maintaining a number of parochial schools because of the almost complete secularization of the public schools.

Local Units of School Administration

Public education is a state function, but it has been primarily a local responsibility. State constitutions and statutes set forth the general outline and objectives of public school systems, but local governments have been authorized to control curriculum content within the state's general policy guides.

Four types of local governmental units are concerned with providing education. The most numerous are the school districts that are created only for school purposes and have a board with basic powers of control over their operations. Such independent districts number about 16,000 and are the sole or predominant unit responsible for operating public schools in twenty-five states and had partial responsibility in four others. The county is employed to administer some or all schools in about a third of the states. Relationships between county boards of education and county school superintendents and the general-purpose county governing board vary from state to state, but typically the school officials are relatively free from control by the county board. Cities form independent school districts in most states. While the boundaries of the school district are often coterminous with those of the city, the school district is often completely independent, or largely free, of any municipal controls. Towns and townships also have school responsibilities. In New England, the towns serve both as the unit of general government and for school purposes. The same situation exists in regard to the township in all or part of six states. About 1,500 such "dependent" school systems are operated by the state, general-purpose local units, or agencies acting on behalf of groups of school districts.

Most states do not employ a single type of local government for administering its schools. In a number of states, all four units—the independent special district, the county, the city, and the town or township—share in this important public undertaking. Whatever the types of units, two traditions greatly influence our educational system. They are the tradition of local determination in educational matters, and that of independence of officials concerned with public schools from control by general governing bodies.

One writer, commenting on the durability of our school system, states:

> What the schools do may be altered, in kind or in degree; how they are run—the administrative and political structure of the typical American school system—will remain largely as it is today. Each community's stake in its own school system is so firmly grounded, and the general faith in local control is so deeply held, that only a cataclysmic upheaval would quickly change the general structural pattern. [15]

Not all commentators view the current pattern of school governance with such calm. A recent book on the New York City schools concludes that forces within the school bureaucracy keep the schools from responding to change.

The failure of the schools is also conditioned by the failure of many other urban institutions. Restructuring of the school system must therefore be part of a total urban development strategy that involves the simultaneous revitalization and reform of transportation, recreation, cultural facilities, housing, and the economies of such communities throughout the city.[16]

The Task of Public Schools

Public education faces enormous contemporary challenges. The nation's population has risen to well over 200 million and is still climbing. While the trend in birth rates in the immediate future cannot be predicted with any certainty, all signs point to a decrease in school populations. A second factor is the mobility of our society. It is estimated that at least a fifth of our people change their address each year. Such mobility results in severe strains on some school systems and drains on others. Another factor of mobility is the drift of population northward and westward to the great metropolitan centers, producing even greater stresses on already over-burdened school resources there.

In addition to the problems of numbers of students, our schools are faced with the difficulty of meeting the changing demands of society for their graduates. Organization in modern society depends upon an increasing range of skills and complexity of tasks. While the demand for better trained talent has been a continuing trend since the start of the present century, it is expected to accelerate in the years ahead. Thus the task of the school system is to educate many students and to equip them with increasing skills to fill more demanding tasks within the labor force.

The difficulty of establishing meaningful population criteria for school districts was discussed in Chapter 9. However, a valid generalization would be that a small number of schools have too many students and a large number of schools have too few students. This picture is likely to continue at least in the immediate future because of the mobility noted above and the continuing trend toward suburbanization.

The question of how well our schools are doing their job has been asked with increasing frequency in recent years. A sense of urgency about our schools began developing shortly after World War II, and widening concern crystallized after the successful launching of the first Sputnik by the Soviet Union in 1957. The question is important because of the magnitude of our public school system and the seriousness of the goals entrusted to it. It is doubly important to ask ourselves this question about our schools in a period when respected authorities are making broad criticisms of their current performance.[17]

A survey of public attitudes determined the most commonly felt complaints about and satisfactions with public education. The complaints in order of frequency are (1) lack of discipline, (2) integration/segregation problems, (3) lack of proper financial support, (4) difficulty of getting good teachers, (5) use of drugs, (6) size of schools and classes, and (7) poor curriculum. On the positive side, the public listed in order (1) the curriculum, (2) the teachers, (3) school facilities, (4) extracurricular activities, (5) up-to-date teaching methods, (6) absence of racial conflict, and (7) good administrators.[18]

The long controversy between educators and political scientists concerning the independent status of school districts was discussed briefly in Chapter 9. While teachers and school administrators often prided themselves that schools were "beyond" politics, the adjective public before public schools implied that they were very much in the mainstream of politics. This point was well made by Thomas Eliot, political scientist, with these words:

> School systems cannot be considered usefully on the assumption that they operate in a kind of aspetic enclave, protected by high walls from the distempers of politics. Public schools are public businesses. Running them is a governmental and hence a political process.[19]

In a recent article describing how big-city mayors have been coming increasingly involved in the issues of urban education, Jerome Ziegler concludes:

> The chief issues of the schools are political in the deepest and broadest sense, engaging citizens' passions and affecting the economic and social life of the city. Because these issues are political and because the mayor cares about the future of the city, he will have a new relationship and a new impact upon the public education system, whatever the final form.[20]

The Teachers

An extensive nationwide survey of public school teachers has produced a composite picture of the average female and male members of the profession. According to this study, public school teachers are younger and better educated than in earlier years. The median age of all teachers is about thirty-five. Less than 3 percent of the teachers lack a bachelor's degree, and 27 percent have earned a master's degree. More than 60 percent of the teachers indicated that they were "conservative" or "tended to be conservative" in their political opinions and leanings.[21]

As an earlier Rockefeller study states,

> Perhaps no profession has suffered such a general neglect of specialized talents as that of the teachers. Teachers at the pre-college level tend to be handled as interchangeable units in an educational assembly line. The best teacher and the poorest in a school may teach

the same grade and subject, use the same textbook, handle the same number of students, get paid the same salaries, and rise in salary at the same speed to the same ceiling. Clearly, if the teaching profession is to be made more attractive, this will have to be changed.[22]

Determined and successful efforts have been underway in recent years to improve teacher salaries. While salary scales show a great diversity among states, the common stereotype of the underpaid school teacher is not very accurate today. One writer has advanced the view that the acceptance of a status as hirelings by teachers creates one of the chief obstacles to better schools.[23] Myron Lieberman urges teachers to regard themselves as professionals rather than as civil servants and wants them to establish a new national organization to become more effective as a group and as individuals through the development of standards of excellence, securing adequate salaries and improved working conditions, and reducing the harassment of local pressures. His overall program calls for federal support and would necessitate serious rethinking of our conventional system of local controls.

Financing Schools

Challenges to the pattern of school financing are being raised in a number of states. In a California case in 1971, evidence was presented to show that the average expenditures per student in one system were more than $1,200 while the school tax rate was only $2.38 per $100 of assessed valuation. In another system, only a few miles away, a tax rate of $5.48 produced funds for an average expenditure of slightly under $580. The California Supreme Court ruled that "... this funding scheme invidiously discriminates against the poor because it makes the quality of a child's education a function of the wealth of his parents and neighbors."[24] Similar verdicts have been handed down by courts in other states indicating that a change in the financing base of education is likely. Heavy reliance on the property tax, however, will probably continue since the U.S. Supreme Court ruled in 1973 that such a base of support did not infringe on a fundamental right protected by the Constitution.[25]

Federal aid for education has been largely limited to special programs such as financing school lunches, helping areas where federal military or other installations bring an influx of students into the schools, and pre-school preparatory programs. Proponents of more general federal aid emphasize that (1) the present mobility of our population makes education a matter of national concern; (2) the national government is the only agency capable of effecting an equitable distribution of educational opportunities; (3) numerous precedents of federal aid exist without the onus of controls in other service areas; and (4) the national government is partly responsible for general education since the preservation of our democracy depends upon the existence of a high standard of education. Principal arguments of opponents of federal aid include the points that (1) the responsibility for education is reserved to the states; (2) education is better controlled to suit local needs by local and state authorities; (3) the federal aid would further unbalance the budget and increase the national debt; and (4) such aid would increase the dangers of federal centralization and regimentation of our schools.

Another line of reasoning to support federal aid for education concerns the leadership of the national government in advancing the status of blacks and other minorities. The bestowal of citizenship following the Civil War on blacks brought forth problems in states with large black populations and created a responsibility for understanding and assistance by the national government. This concern and responsibility were increased by the decision of the Supreme Court in 1954 in *Brown* v. *Board of Education of Topeka*.[26] This historic decision overruled the legal doctrine of separate but equal facilities established in 1896. Recognizing the vast changes necessitated by this policy, the Court did not order prompt integration of schools but decreed that integration should proceed ''with all deliberate speed,'' under the general supervision of the United States district courts. Although progress toward integration seems to have emphasized ''deliberation'' rather than ''speed,'' delaying action and legislation by states have not succeeded in preventing but have deterred desegregation.

The need for a plan of federal aid is becoming more apparent as bond issues are more commonly defeated in local communities across the nation. These rejections seldom occur because the citizens feel that new schoolhouses are not needed; instead, the voters turn down the issues because they know approval will produce an increase in property taxes. The fact that poorer states, judged on the basis of the proportion of tax revenues spent on education, are making a greater effort to support education than wealthier states is also gaining wider recognition and acceptance. A program of federal aid would be paid for by all the nation's taxpayers, including those in districts needing no new schools and able to finance educational programs without assistance.

THREE CURRENT PROBLEMS

Among various contemporary problems facing public school decision makers, three are receiving much attention in America. They relate to school decentralization, unionization of teachers, and continuing efforts to achieve equality of educational opportunity. Each is discussed briefly.

School Decentralization

Decentralization is an ambiguous term but in reference to schools it generally means a meaningful shift in power from central agencies to local schools and communities. It has resulted from the efforts of big-city schools to provide greater community participation. As Mario Fantini, educator, and Marilyn Gittell, political scientist, point out,

> Because participation under decentralization increases the voice of the educational consumer in educational decision-making, this alternative is *political* in nature. Decentralization deals with the *governance* of urban school systems. Since politics deals with *power*, it is not surprising that this pattern of participation produces controversy.[27]

As a concept in the mid-1960s, decentralization first publicly emerged in New York City. After much controversy, a school decentralization law was passed by the New York state legislature in 1969. By four years later thirty-one elective local community school boards were operating. Similar action by the Michigan legislature resulted in the creation of eight elective regional boards in Detroit. In both cities, the decentralization plans called for local elective school boards empowered to choose their own superintendents under prescribed standards of qualification. The results of local elections in both cities seem to reflect the point that mere election of local boards is not a satisfactory guarantee of a redistribution of power. Of the 279 board members in New York, only forty-seven were Black and thirty Puerto Rican yet the system has about 57 percent Black and Puerto Rican enrollment. Suprisingly, a total of approximately 53 percent of the board members sent their own children to parochial rather than public schools. In Detroit, only 30 percent of the members were Black in a city where school population is 63 percent Black.[28]

Fantini and Gittell are guardedly hopeful that decentralization efforts will be successful. They recognize that this movement for decentralization or community control must focus on the creation of new community forces that challenge the bureaucratic power structure and overt racism in the American city and produce a balance between citizen participation and professional roles in the policy process. Certainly public education is a primary target for change and both the efforts toward and the results of this movement merit careful consideration and concern.

In a study concluded a few years earlier, Basil Zimmer, political scientist, and Amos Hawley, sociologist, sought to answer the question "What are the roots of the resistance to change in school reorganization?" They found resistance so strong that they predicted any proposals for reorganization would face overwhelming odds. In their words, "For as long as change is to be decided either by public officials or by a referendum, the chances for success decline sharply as size of area increases."[29]

Teacher Unionization

The rise of militant unionism among teachers is a fairly recent development. The National Education Association, the oldest and largest professional group, continued to stress professionalization and, until the 1960s, opposed the organization of teachers into trade unions and opposed teachers' strikes. A competitive union, the United Federation of Teachers, the local New York City branch of the American Federation of Teachers, an affiliate of the AFL-CIO, won an impressive victory in that city in 1962. In the period 1960-62, the UFT held two strikes, won a collective bargaining election, and secured substantial salary increases. As a result of these victories, the membership ranks of the UFT climbed from 60,000 in 1960 to over 200,000 ten years later.

In his careful study of unionization in New York City, Stephen Cole offers an explanation for its rise. The key factor was the increase in male teachers. A second reason was the growing proportion of Jewish teachers who were "more favorably predisposed than [the non-Jews] to accept the union and the programs of its leadership."[30]

Salaries have represented the most common battleground between organized teachers and the school board and administration. But teachers also want to achieve more power in the decision-making of their educational systems. Since teachers usually employ expert negotiators to represent them in bargaining sessions, their organization generally can compete successfully with the board and administration. Teacher groups may become even more politically active and militant in the future because of their recent successes.

Equality of Opportunity

In the years since the *Brown* v. *Board of Education* decision in 1954, continuing debate has been under way over the kinds of local policies needed to satisfy the requirements for school desegregation. While progress toward full integration was slow in being realized in many communities, segregated housing patterns made it difficult to integrate school facilities in the traditional neighborhood schools. Community support often rallied around the neighborhood school concept in both the white and minority populations in the drive for neighborhood control of the school.

Various alternative proposals to establish integrated school facilities in urban areas have been made and attempted. Busing of students has worked reasonably well in a number of small and medium-sized communities but has been very expensive on the large scale needed in big urban communities. It also has proved highly controversial in some large cities. The paired-school concept also has proved acceptable in some communities, but segregated housing patterns have made in infeasible in large urban centers. This plan utilizes two elementary schools (grades one through six), for example, with different racial compositions in their student bodies; grades one through three attend one school and grades four through six the other.

It soon became clear to all concerned parties that equality of opportunity was a laudable principle that escaped easy realization. The number of participants in educational decision-making has expanded but the range of acceptable and feasible solutions has remained few in number and has differed from community to community.

PUBLIC WELFARE

Local governments have played an important part in providing public welfare services since the early years of our nation. The concept of public welfare held by English colonists was based on the Elizabethan Poor Law of 1601 that placed responsibility for welfare activities on the individual, his family, and his local government. This basic law recognized and provided for three classes of indigent persons. They were: (1) those who were poor because of physical disability and required some type of permanent relief; (2) those who become needy as the result of injury or temporary illness and required temporary assistance; and (3) persons who were thriftless or vagrant and for whom certain penalties were imposed by law. The basic approach of colonial "poor" or "pauper" laws remained largely the same until the Great Depression of the late 1920s and the 1930s brought a fundamental change in the public attitude toward welfare. This change was aptly phrased in one study as moving from one in which recipients of relief were "objects of disgrace and humiliation" to one where the public has "come to realize that poverty, particularly in times of economic stress, is unavoidable and that the individual who needs help should not be subjected to indignity and public disgrace because of circumstances beyond his control."[31]

Our more charitable attitude toward the unfortunate has brought on three important modifications in our approach to welfare problems. First, welfare is a service in which all three levels of government cooperate in financing and administering. Second, greater emphasis is given to ascertaining the causes of indigence and to rehabilitating persons. And third, recent programs reveal a greater interest in preventive than remedial measures. New terminology in the welfare field indicates the changes in the public attitude. For instance, "pauper laws" are now "public assistance codes," "paupers" have become "needy persons," "poor relief" is now "public assistance," and "inmates" of institutions are presently known as "patients" or "residents."

Public welfare is not a precise term and, as indicated above, its meaning has changed in recent years. Broadly conceived, public welfare may be defined as a "helping hand at public expense." This helping hand is available to a number of groups, such as aging citizens, children, the blind, disabled and injured workers, and the unemployed. While many programs are not primarily programs of local government, they directly affect citizens living in communities across the nation. Thus, a discussion of public welfare programs deserves a consideration of its intergovernmental aspects.

The United States annually produces nearly a trillion dollars worth of goods and services—about $5,000 worth a person. And yet, there is a serious problem of poverty in the United States despite this seeming abundance. Four groups of persons do not have a sufficiently productive role to provide an adequate income for themselves: (1) the aged, (2) small children and the mothers who care for them, (3) the physically and mentally disturbed or disabled, and (4) the unemployed and the underemployed.

A report of the Department of Health, Education and Welfare, *Portrait of Median City,* presents a capsule view of social welfare programs in the United States. The characteristics for this imaginery city of 200,000 were determined by locating the median in a list of the 130 American cities with populations of over 100,000. Thus, a brief recounting of welfare programs in action in Median City are fairly typical of programs operative throughout the United States.[32] The major programs are:

1. A total of 20,900 people (10.45 percent) receive monthly benefits under old-age, survivors, and disability insurance programs. About 14,200 of these beneficiaries are retired workers and their qualified dependents; 5,000 are survivors of deceased workers; and 1,700 are disabled workers and their dependents.

2. Public assistance is extended to five categories of needy persons: (a) the aged, (b) the blind, (c) the permanently and totally disabled, (d) families with dependent children, and (e) the unemployed and unemployable who do not fit into any of the other four categories and received general assistance support. The national government participates in financing the first four programs and the fifth is financed entirely by the states and their local governments. In Median City, 8,000 persons are helped by these five programs. The largest group is 1,100 parents and 3,200 children receiving support under the Aid to Families with Dependent Children program. The second largest group—2,200 aged persons—receive aid under Old Age Assistance. A further 225 elderly persons not on public assistance are medically indigent and receive aid from the Medical Assistance to the Aged program. Another 600 residents receive aid from the Aid to the Blind and Aid to the Permanently and Totally Disabled programs. In the fifth category, 350 cases involving 800 persons qualify for and receive General Assistance support.

Over and above these five programs, other groups in Median City also receive financial aid. These include Unemployment Insurance Compensation for 4 percent of the adults who are unemployed; Workmen's Compensation and temporary disability insurance payments for a small number; 2,000 veterans with service connected disabilities; 1,200 veterans receive pensions; and 800 widows, children, or parents of veterans receive death pensions;

and surplus agricultural products are distributed to 2,000 persons.

Public welfare services call for true partnership roles by the three levels of government. Generally, the principle of cooperative partnership seems to function fairly smoothly, but causes of potential friction are numerous and sometimes erupt into open controversy and direct conflict. While these controversies were largely between the state and national governments in earlier years, much of the present conflict develops between the state and its local communities.

An approach to the problem of helping persons rise above the poverty line and to meeting the problem of unemployment due to technology is the guaranteed annual income. In the words of Robert Theobald, economist, "A guaranteed income provides the individual with the ability to do what he personally feels to be important."[33] Such a program allows risk-taking and innovation in areas where existing and emerging needs of society are not being adequately met by the free enterprise system. Unemployment, redefined as the condition of not holding a job, therefore is viewed as less undesirable since the individual is free to develop himself in society.

Although the exact nature of the guaranteed annual income program depends on the concept of its overall social function, the concept received support during the Nixon administration and may represent a new approach to poverty in the years ahead.

PUBLIC RECREATION

Recreation has been an important segment of life throughout most of recorded history. The athletic games of the Greeks, the circuses and public baths of the Romans, and the tournaments and hunts of the Middle Ages are all well known as integral parts of life in those earlier eras. The energies of early Americans were mainly absorbed by their work but quilting bees and house warmings were social events of some significance in colonial times. Before 1900, however, leisure hours and recreation opportunities were greatly restricted, and the modern recreation movement grew out of the period following World War I.

To provide recreation service in accordance with the criteria advanced by the International City Managers' Association, at least an acre of park and recreation space is needed for each 100 people. Recreational opportunities should be provided for persons of all age groups rather than just for pre-school and school age children. A well-rounded recreation program offers year-round opportunities to spend free time profitably and enjoyably for all persons from toddlers to senior citizens.

While the discussion above emphasizes space requirements of a balanced recreation program, many other problems are found in this important service. One concerns the financing of areas and programs. Less than 3 percent of the direct expenditures of local governments are expended for parks and recreation. In view of the public health and public welfare benefits accruing from recreation programs, this seems a small investment that pays off handsomely. To some others, however, the expenditures of public monies for facilities such as zoos, museums, golf courses, or botanical gardens seem wrong since they never personally make use of them.

To many persons, recreation is a form of education and is its own reason for being. The need for even closer cooperation between these two public activities becomes apparent when it is realized that youngsters have an amount of free time daily about equal to the time spent in school. Yet, as one writer has commented,

> We spend billions annually in highly refining the regimen for the hours in the classroom and devote almost nothing in most communities to the free hours. From the most expensive tuition in the world the youngster is dismissed without rapport into whatever happens to be his environment, however squalid it may be, however depraving.[34]

NOTES

1. For an expanded discussion of these categories, see Oliver P. Williams, *Metropolitan Political Analysis, A Social Access Approach*, The Free Press, 1971, pp. 86-93; and his "Life Style Values and Political Decentralization in Metropolitan Areas," *Southwestern Social Science Quarterly*, 48 (December, 1967), 299-310.
2. Williams, *Metropolitan Political Analysis, op. cit.*, p. 93.
3. W. G. Smillie, *Public Health, Its Promise for the Future*, Macmillan, 1955, p. 1.
4. Haven Emerson and Martha Luginbuhl, *Local Health Units for the Nation*, Commonwealth Fund, 1945, pp. 1-2.
5. National Advisory Commission on Civil Disorders, *Report*, Bantam Books, 1968, p. 269.
6. *Ibid.*, pp. 270-1.
7. Howard Simons, "Per Capita Air Pollution Cost Put at $150 a Year," *Washington Post*, (June 26, 1964).
8. Hazel Holly, *What's in the Air?* Public Affairs Pamphlet No. 275, 1958, p. 5.
9. *Los Angeles Times* (January 8, 1961).
10. Public Health Service, *Where We Stand on Smog Problem, What's Been Done, What's Ahead*, Government Printing Office, 1961, p. 13.
11. National Association of Counties, *From America's Counties, 1973*, Washington, 1973, pp. 31-5.
12. County of Los Angeles, Air Pollution Control District, *APCD, History and Function*, Los Angeles, May, 1972.
13. *Ibid.*
14. Arthur B. Moehlman, *School Administration*, Houghton Mifflin, 1951, p. 11.
15. Thomas H. Eliot, *Governing America, The Politics of a Free People, State and Local Supplement*, Dodd, Mead, 1961, p. 156.

16. David Rogers, *110 Livingston Street, Politics and Bureaucracy in the New York City School System*, Random House, 1968, p. 497.

17. Among the many studies that may be cited are: Robert Bendiner, *The Politics of Schools, A Crisis in Self-Government*, Harper & Row, 1969; Marilyn Gittell (ed.), *Educating an Urban Population*, Sage Publications, 1967; David Rogers, *op. cit.*; Julius W. Hobson, *The Damned Children, A Layman's Guide to Forcing Change in Public Education*, Washington Institute for Quality Education, 1970; and Jerome M. Ziegler, "Should the Mayors Run the Schools?", *City*, 6 (Winter, 1972), 15-19.

18. George H. Gallup, "Fifth Annual Gallup Poll of Public Attitudes Toward Education," *Phi Delta Kappan*, 45 (September, 1973), 29.

19. Eliot, *op. cit.*, p. 164.

20. Ziegler, *op. cit.*, p. 19.

21. National Education Association, *Status of the American Public School Teachers*, 1970-71, National Education Association, 1971.

22. Rockefeller Brothers Fund, Inc., *The Pursuit of Excellence, Education and the Future of America*, Doubleday, 1958, p. 26.

23. Myron Lieberman, *The Future of Public Education*, University of Chicago Press, 1960.

24. *Serrano* v. *Priest*, 5 Cal. 3rd 585, 487 P 2nd 1241 (1971).

25. *San Antonio Independent School District* v. *Rodriguez*, 411 U.S. 1, (1973).

26. 347 U.S. 483 (1954).

27. Mario Fantini and Marilyn Gittell, *Decentralization, Achieving Reform*, Praeger, 1973, p. 45.

28. *Ibid.*, pp. 49-50.

29. Basil G. Zimmer and Amos H. Hawley, *Metropolitan Area Schools, Resistance to District Reorganization*, Sage Publications, 1968, p. 307.

30. Stephen Cole, *The Unionization of Teachers: A Case Study of the UFT*, Praeger, 1969, p. 94.

31. Tax Foundation, *Improving Public Assistance: Some Aspects of the Welfare Problem*, 1953, p. 6.

32. Frances A. Koestler, *Portrait of Median City*, Government Printing Office, 1966.

33. Robert Theobald (ed.), *The Guaranteed Income*, Doubleday, Anchor Books, 1967, p. 57.

34. James C. Charlesworth, "An Attitude Toward Recreation," *The Daily Pennsylvanian*, May 4, 1959, p. 3.

Chapter 16
System-Maintenance Services

As mentioned in the introduction to Chapter 15, systems-maintenance services are less political in nature than are life-style services. This does not mean that they are non-political, however. A wide range of considerations in laying out a transportation route may be controversial and pits interest against interest and community against community. Similarly, the location of an airport, a sewage treatment plant, or a public housing site also may be very political and divide the local citizenry into supporters and opponents. Communitywide interests usually prevail against more local interests in the provision of systems-maintenance services because such services require some overall structure and planning.

PUBLIC HOUSING

Since poor housing generally is recognized as a detriment to the community, local governments are empowered by state law to improve housing conditions. They may regulate housing through building and housing codes, sanitation laws, and zoning ordinances. Laws pertaining directly to housing are now comprehensive and deal with both construction and maintenance. The principal construction provisions relate to requirements for light and ventilation, sanitation, and fire protection. Maintenance provisions of housing codes vary widely from community to community, but generally concern requirements of cubic feet of air space, the keeping of animals, and maintenance of such items as cellars, roofs, and fire escapes.

Although this approach to housing problems is still important, a new way of attacking the evils of poor housing began in 1937 with the passing of the Housing Act establishing the United States Housing Authority. Under this act and its subsequent amendments, the national government stimulated action in low-cost housing by loans and grants and by actual operation of housing projects. Slum clearance programs were authorized by the Housing Act of 1949; federal aid thereby became available for tearing down old buildings in slum areas and building new housing on the cleared site. The Housing Act of 1954 extended federal aid by authorizing urban renewal projects to prevent and eliminate urban decay.

The extent of the low-rent housing program is evidenced by the growth of the number of units supervised by the Public Housing Administration. In 1950, there were 302,146 such units, but this total had risen to 1,155,300 by twenty years later. The programs of low-rent public housing or rental subsidy housing requires local initiative and action with federal approval and assistance.

A need exists for close and cooperative relations among the three levels of government in the field of housing. Local governments acting alone cannot possibly provide an adequate housing policy for the nation. The resources and sanctions of state and national governments are needed to assist and urge local governments to act in this area, and it is essential for these intergovernmental relations to be coordinated effectively. Typically, local governments have great difficulty in enforcing housing codes applicable to private housing and do not have sufficient resources to undertake major slum elimination or new construction projects on their own.

FIRE PROTECTION

Fire protection services of local governments consist of a number of important functions, the most colorful and best known being fire fighting. Probably the most important function of fire departments, however, is fire prevention by correcting common hazards that result in fires and by educating the citizenry in the careful use and control of fire. Closely related activities include keeping loss of life and property to a minimum in case of fire, investigating causes of fires, and salvaging operations. Activities of importance within the department are installation and maintenance of a fire alarm system, repair and maintenance of equipment, and training of personnel.[1]

The magnitude of fire department activities may be shown in a number of ways. More than 12,000 men, women, and children have been killed in fires in each of several recent years. The hazardous nature of the fire fighting profession is reflected in the death annually of about 200 firefighters in the line of duty and injuries to about 40,000 others. In terms of cost, citizens spend about $2.7 billion a year on fire protection while the value of property lost totals about $3 billion. In terms of employees, approximately 25,000 professional and volunteer fire fighting departments employ about 200,000 professional firefighters and utilize one million volunteers.[2]

Fire Prevention

It is a truism that most fires could have been prevented with proper regulations and enforcement. It also is true that local governments have become more concerned with programs of fire prevention. An effective fire prevention program has three primary methods—inspection, enforcement, and education. The inspection program has the purposes of preventing fires and familiarizing firefighters with the layout of buildings and the general area of their district. Inspections cover such items as rubbish burners, incinerators, fire doors, heating devices, chimneys, fire extinguishers, storage of combustible materials.

Enforcement begins where inspection ends. If hazards are discovered, they should be reported and the property owner forced to correct or remove the potential hazard. A second aspect of enforcement relates to granting permits, licenses, and certificates of approval where hazards are involved or might develop, as in the use of dry-cleaning materials, licensing of motion picture operators, and installation of oil burners. In such cases, the adherence to prescribed standards and inspection for compliance often become conditions for the issuance and retention of licenses.

Fire prevention education is effective only if the public cooperates. Many communities annually sponsor a fire prevention week when special efforts are made to inform the public of safety regulations and the dangers from their misuse. Safety education should be a continuing operation, however, utilizing the public schools, the press, radio, television, posters, and other means to educate the public. Other communities have cleanup campaigns that serve to remove potential fire hazards while informing the citizenry about their danger. In large cities a trained public relations expert often is employed to spearhead the program of fire prevention education.

Police-Fire Integration

Police and fire services still have some essential differences, but the recent strong emphasis on prevention in both fields has drawn the two closer together. In a number of cities the recognition of this development has brought forth the establishment of a single department of public safety. One form of integration is administrative only; within a single department of public safety headed by a lay commissioner are a bureau of police and a bureau of fire headed by professional careerists. A second type of integration recognizes that some duties are so similar as to warrant integration. Police officers walking the beat also check on fire hazards and those on patrol function are on guard against the outbreak of both an act of violence and a fire. In communities using this system, the patrol car often is a patrol wagon equipped with a fire extinguisher and other basic fire-fighting equipment. A third type of integration has positions known as public safety officers—individuals trained to perform both police and fire-fighting functions.

The first and second kinds of integration exist in some large cities; the third has been limited primarily to small communities. Among the advantages claimed by proponents of full integration are (1) it increases the supply of trained personnel available in emergency situations; (2) it provides full-time activity for the personnel; (3) it reduces overhead needs of equipment, personnel, and buildings; (4) it simplifies keeping of safety records; (5) it simplifies the administrative organization of local government; and (6) it often results in more economical protective services for the community.[3]

Integration of public safety services remains the unusual pattern of operation, even in small cities. An analysis of certain police-fire integrations reports successful operations in Ft. Lauderdale, Florida, and Dearborn, Michigan, both cities of over 100,000 population; Grosse Point Woods, Michigan, a place of 25,000; Huntington Woods, Michigan, a center of 9,000; and Sewickley Heights, Pennsylvania, a city under 5,000.[4]

PUBLIC WORKS

The public works department generally is one of the largest in city or

TABLE 19
PROGRAM DIVISIONS IN PUBLIC WORKS DEPARTMENTS: SURVEY OF 429 CITIES OF OVER 25,000 POPULATION

Program	Frequency
Street Maintenance	378
Engineering	338
Refuse collection and disposal	231
Building inspection	224
Equipment maintenance	210
Sewer maintenance	192
Building maintenance	146
Street construction	117
Water and sewers utilities	103
Water distribution	99
Sewer treatment	98
Water treatment	38
Airports	30

Adapted from Table 3.1 in International City Management Association, *Municipal Year Book, 1971*, pp. 172-78.

county government in terms of expenditures, range of activities, and number of employees. The number and diversity of its activities are more elastic than those of any other department in local administration and vary considerably from jurisdiction to jurisdiction. A typical strand of unity among the activities of public works departments is their need for personnel trained in engineering. Public works activities have been defined as those "concerned with the installation, construction, operation, and maintenance of physical plant and equipment used to service the needs of the people of the community."[5] Activities that we will consider as public works operations include streets and highways, traffic, and refuse collection and disposal.

The frequency of program divisions within the department of public works, based on a study of 429 cities of at least 25,000 population, is shown in Table 19. In general, the survey found that public works departments are quite centralized organizations. Most departments have been functioning for many years and are headed by veteran government personnel.[6]

Streets and Highways

Highway mileage in the United States totals about 3.75 million miles. Nearly 20 percent is under state control, and another approximate 185,000 miles, mostly roads in national forests and on Indian reservations, are under national control. The remainder—about 80 percent—is under local control. The total rural mileage is nearly seven times larger than the total municipal mileage.

The county is the most important unit for highway administration at the local level, controlling nearly half of the nation's total highway mileage. The governing board of the county has the general responsibility for locating, planning, and financing county roads and bridges. The direct management of construction and maintenance is usually lodged in the office of a single administrative official, variously known as the highway commissioner, superintendent, or engineer. However, in some counties the governing board itself supervises the details of road and bridge construction, maintenance, and repair.

The administrative organization for streets and highways in city government is complex in comparison to that in county government. Most common in larger cities is a line department under the direction of a single head. A second common plan places the public works department under board or commission control. In small cities, supervision commonly is a function of the city engineer.

In addition to serving as travel ways from one point to another for pedestrians and vehicles, urban streets perform four other important functions. First, they provide access to abutting property by providing for pedestrian, vehicular, and utility access to the properties along them.

Second, they serve as automobile storage space by providing for short-term, long-term, and overnight parking. Third, they provide light and air for urban dwellers and buildings. And, fourth, they are a collector and carrier of storm drainage as an important element in the storm water runoff system.

Today a tripartite relationship is present among the three levels of government in highway administration—a pattern of cooperation likely to be extended even further in the decades ahead. For instance, the Federal Aid Highway Act of 1956 provided for a super network of 41,000 miles of expressways of two, four, six, and eight lanes. Known as the Interstate Highway System, these major highways crisscross the nation, connecting 209 cities of more than 50,000 population and 42 state capitals, and wind through all forty-eight continental states. These highways represent only 1.2 percent of the nation's total mileage and were completed in 1970, but they probably will carry about 20 percent of the total traffic.

The prevalence of state aid to local governments for streets and highways has been previously noted. This aid takes two principal forms—a share of highway user taxes and grants-in-aid. The former is more important to local governments generally, but state grants are of major importance to particular units from time to time.

Although streets and highways may appear to be a technical field where engineers would be expected to be in control, local governing bodies still commonly reserve to themselves formal approval of roadwork to be done. Local governments performing their own construction and maintenance functions have a number of contracts to let, and these usually are actively competed for by local business firms. In units without a formal merit system, a number of positions in this section of the public works department can be filled by patronage appointments.

Traffic Congestion

Both the growth of population and the increasing concentration of people in large urban centers contribute to the traffic problem. Related factors are the increased number of motor vehicles and the expansion of vehicular movement. Commuter living results in increased traffic because of the travel patterns of persons to and from work. Daylight populations of our largest urban centers are often as high as 20 percent above official census counts, and smaller suburban communities with one or more large industrial employers frequently have daylight populations two or three times their resident populations.

Despite the amount of traffic engineering and street improvement and the large number of freeways and expressways built in recent years, most cities are not making real progress in meeting their traffic problems. The three "E's" of a traffic control program have been identified as "Engineering,

Enforcement, and Education.''[7] Engineering, of course, is the technical and physical approach to the problem by attempting to eliminate or reduce the effect of the several immediate causes of congestion listed above. These efforts include the rounding of corners, increasing street width, use of traffic signals and other control devices, establishing one-way streets, posting of speed limits, and parking bans during rush hours.

Enforcement of traffic regulations is principally the responsibility of the police and the courts. A growing percentage of the time of the average police officer is devoted to traffic problems, and police departments in large communities have traffic divisions with specialized officers and individuals whose primary concern is traffic regulation and enforcement. This is an important responsibility because a traffic violation introduces many citizens to both the police department and the lower courts.

Traffic education is the capstone of a traffic control program, which recognizes that the most effective way to bring about improvement is to attack the problem at its source—the driver. In recent years, driver education courses have been offered in many high schools which also offer instruction in pedestrian and bicycle safety. The development of safe driving and safe walking habits also is a function of traffic police and other community organizations such as automobile clubs and citizen safety councils. Schools have been established for traffic violators in some communities with the final disposition of cases sometimes depending on the progress of the violator as reflected in his attitude and performance in class. A few judges have elected to pass out unusual sentences rather than imposing fines on traffic violators. Among the more common sentences are to require the violator to spend a certain amount of time at the emergency ward of local hospitals to witness the admission of victims of traffic accidents; to pick up trash and debris along streets; to sweep streets; or to spend a designated number of hours reading to hospitalized victims of other traffic accidents. The problem of traffic education has been receiving increasing attention from schools, traffic police, and other community organizations.

Refuse Collection and Disposal

Refuse collection and disposal represent other functions performed by a division of the local public works department. However, in a number of communities these activities are rendered by a private firm under contract with the local government. In other communities special districts have been established to provide these services. Interlocal cooperation is common because of economies and the lack of suitable areas for disposal sites in some localities.

The refuse collection and disposal functions consist of the pickup of wastes at households, business properties, and institutions, its transport to a disposal site, and its ultimate disposition so that nuisances are not created. Refuse, as the term is here used, includes garbage, rubbish, ashes, street refuse, industrial wastes, and dead animals. Although some communities provide for a combined refuse pickup, many others have three separate pickups, one each for garbage, rubbish, and ashes. Sanitation trucks generally are used for garbage collection in urban areas to reduce the health menace and often are employed for rubbish and trash as well. Collection pickups usually are at least once a week in residential areas and as often as daily in commercial areas and at major institutions.

Disposal of refuse is accomplished by various methods, depending upon the soil and climatic conditions, availability of sites, and other circumstances. Incineration is a common method used for combined disposal. Under this method, refuse is transported to incinerators and destroyed in furnaces. Recent improvements in incinerator design and operation now make it possible to reduce the odors and eliminate the gases that once were a major problem of this method. A second popular method for combined disposal is known as the sanitary-fill method. Refuse is deposited in trenches or low areas and then covered with dirt. This method has the advantage of low cost, but its major drawback is the size of the area required for disposal. Eight to ten acres are required for each 100,000 persons. This method is not a reasonable solution to many communities with no ready access to open space that can be used for this purpose.

There are a number of other disposal methods still in use in some places. One is barging refuse out to sea, a method obviously limited to cities along shore lines. The open dump, which has been condemned as both a health menace and a public nuisance, remains in use in many highly rural areas. Landfill is a third method permitting combined disposal; it is similar to sanitary-fill except that low areas rather than trenches are used. When the hole is filled, it is covered with dirt, usually scraped off an adjoining high area. Other methods for disposing of garbage include its feeding to hogs, garbage grinding in homes or in community grinders, reduction to retrieve the grease content of garbage, and fermentation. This last-named method consists of placing garbage on large trays and applying heat to them to stimulate bacterial action. After a period of thirty days, the garbage has dried to resemble humus and the liquids have drained off.

There are various arrangements for intermunicipal cooperation in refuse collection and disposal. Probably the most widely used is the creation of a special district or authority, which takes on the independence of a private corporation but enjoys the tax exemption of a governmental entity. Some counties assume responsibility for collecting and disposing of refuse for the municipalities within it by establishing a countywide system. Smaller communities often enter into contractual arrangements with other localities for these services. Whether the cooperative arrangements are for disposal by incineration, landfill or some other method, they enable the participating communities to solve a common problem through joint efforts that reduce costs.

PUBLIC-SERVICE ENTERPRISES

Public-service enterprises or public utilities have been identified by one authority as "industries, properties, corporations, or other business concerns that furnish recognized public services through private forms of organization."[8] The concept that certain businesses were affected with a public interest was presented in a decision of the U.S. Supreme Court in 1887 which stated that property is

> clothed with a public interest when used in a manner to make it of public consequence, and affect the community at large. When, therefore, one devotes his property to a use in which the public has an interest, he, in effect, grants to the public an interest in that use, and must submit to be controlled by the public for the common good, to the extent of the interest he has thus created.[9]

While the concept seems clear at first reading, it presents considerable difficulty when applied as a criterion to determine the extent of public interest of particular business enterprises. Obviously some such as water or electricity are more important to the general public than are others. Bauer points out two distinguishing characteristics identifying the public nature of utilities. First, the services rendered are essential and virtually indispensable to modern business, industrial, and community life. Second, they are natural monopolies "in which competition is either physically or financially impossible, or publicly undesirable."[10] Early experience with competition in these services proved devastating to both consumer rates and service quality.

Several other characteristics usually are associated with public utilities. They enjoy special privileges such as the power of eminent domain and the right to use public property. Utilities have unusually high capital investments and require continual additions of capital for expansion of their physical plants and equipment. Because the services of the utility companies are affected with the public interest, they are subjected to detailed public regulation whether under public or private ownership and management. Such regulation is designed to protect the interests of consumers, investors, and utility enterprisers alike, and is aimed at assuring proper service at reasonable rates and financial stability.

The question of public versus private ownership of businesses affected with the public interest is more often answered by emotion than reason or empirical study. As one writer has pointed out:

> Local politicians have coupled its affirmative answer with life, liberty,

equality, and votes for themselves. The utility executives, giving free lectures at "institutes" financed by their own industries, have pointed out so many evil principles in municipal administration that one wonders how they dare drink from municipally owned and operated water systems. One orator is raising the rabble while the other is raising the rates and dividends, and neither contributes to the public service. The arguments of one are entirely positive, while the contributions of the other are entirely negative; when, added, they produce zero.[11]

Although a number of advantages and disadvantages of public ownership have been presented by proponents and opponents of municipal ownership respectively, existing data are insufficient either to prove or to disprove most of these claims. By the careful selection of favorable statistics and considerations and de-emphasizing the unfavorable, strong cases are made by both sides. In reality, there can be no categorical answer either in favor of or in opposition to municipal ownership.

Both sides in the ownership controversy claim that their position tends to eliminate politics from the management of the utility. The inference, of course, is that politics is harmful; it may well be if policy is based on political rather than economic and technical considerations. On the other hand, the intrusion of political considerations may curtail irresponsible activities and the maximizing of profits at the expense of adequate service. In summary, there is neither intrinsic good or evil in public ownership, nor is public ownership the first step on the path to socialism. Individual cases must be decided on their merits because public ownership has worked well in some communities and fared badly in others.

Auditoriums and Stadiums

Although auditoriums are not yet found in most cities, a growing interest is present among cities in constructing and operating them. As a rule, auditoriums are handsome and spacious structures used for staging concerts, circuses, conventions and other public attractions. The term convention center seems to be increasingly used and is a more logical description than auditorium. Cities with such centers usually consider them excellent community facilities and aids to local business and citizen groups through the types of events they hold and the conventions attracted to the city.

With the recent expansion of franchises in the major sports of baseball, basketball, and football, many large cities have constructed stadiums and sports complexes to house home games and other major sports attractions. Often these facilities are promotional projects and big business ventures rather than in response to taxpayer demands. Typically, the construction of such facilities face huge costs over the original estimate and sometimes are not financial successes.

Water Supply

The sources of all our water supplies are rivers, lakes, and underground reservoirs. Communities located along rivers or lakes often obtain their water supply from these sources, and a few coastal cities are beginning to use ocean water processed by desalting plants. Many communities depend upon underground sources such as wells and springs for their water supplies. Other communities are forced to bring water many miles from inland sources. Water for the city of Los Angeles is carried 400 miles from the Colorado River through aqueducts as large as sixteen feet in diameter.

To meet the overall water needs in a community, its water plant must supply 140 gallons of water per person a day. An average of 50 gallons per person goes for residential uses including drinking, cooking, laundering, bathing, flushing toilets, lawn or garden watering, and other home uses. Another 50 gallons for each person goes for industrial users, 20 gallons for commercial uses, and 10 gallons for public uses including fire fighting, street washing, swimming pools, public fountains, and water for public buildings. The other 10 gallons each day is a loss from leaks and breaks in underground pipes.[12]

Water supply is the most common of municipally-owned utilities. Water utilities are administered by independent water boards or commissions in some communities. Others are administered by boards of special districts and authorities, with the facilities financed by the revenues received from the sale of water. In smaller localities, a committee of local governing board often administers the water supply and supervises the engineer in charge of the plant operations. Some large cities have departments of water functioning as important line departments. A fifth administrative arrangement occurs in communities where a popularly elected director of public works has water supply as a responsibility.

A major recent political issue in water supply has been the controversy over fluoridation. This involves adding controlled amounts of the chemical fluoride to water supplies as a means of reducing tooth decay. Although fluoridation has been opposed for various reasons including that it is "un-American," virtually all major health organizations, including the American Dental Association and the American Medical Association, have endorsed controlled fluoridation programs. In many places, citizens have taken the lead in bringing about fluoridation because its reduction of dental decay has been verified by conclusive research findings of half a century. About one-half of all Americans are drinking water with either natural or added fluoride.[13]

There are many perplexing problems in the field of water supply. Those of supply, administrative management, and fluoridation have been discussed above. Another relates to rate charges for water use. The most common practice is to charge all classes of users on the basis of amount used.

Another problem of charges concerns rates for residents and institutions outside the incorporated limits of a community. Charges outside the city sometimes are as much as three times as high as those within the city. Health considerations are the major technical problems, since chlorination and purification are usually essential processes to eliminate possible pollution.

The responsibility of providing an adequate and pure water supply is shared by all three levels of government—local, state, and national. Because water resources do not follow local or state boundaries, the national level of governmental authority must often be called upon to arbitrate both interlocal and interstate disputes. According to lawyer Bernard Frank, "you could write the story of man's growth in terms of his epic concern with water."[14]

The dependence of humankind upon water makes its supply and conservation a highly important domestic problem. They will help to shape the patterns of future development in the United States.

Sewage Disposal

Sewage may be defined as a community's combined liquid wastes including those from residences, business establishments, and surface water. It is carried from its sources by a system of drains, sewers, and pumps that make up the sewerage system to a disposal plant or other suitable disposal site. In some communities a single sewerage system carries all three types of waste. Other communities have separate storm sewerage systems for disposing of the waters from rains and melted snows. While a combined system offers the advantage of a single set of expensive sewerage installations, difficulties often arise at the treatment plant, in cleaning the system in dry periods, and some danger exists of backflow of contaminated water in times of heavy rainfall.

In 1823 Boston became the first American city to install a system of sanitary sewers. At this time the common practice was to dump the sewage into a nearby body of water. If a sufficient supply of moving water existed and if cities were sufficiently distant from each other, this method of disposal was safe. However, as population and numbers of cities grew, sewage had to be treated before disposal in most communities. There are several sewage treatment processes. The primary treatment removes the solids in suspension in the sewage, decomposes and then disposes of them by burning, by using them as fertilizer, or by some other means. Oxidation is a second process. This process utilizes bacteria to oxidize the organic material, either in solution or after its removal from the tanks. The third method is known as sterilization or disinfection, which aims to kill the remaining germs. Chlorine is a germicide commonly used for this purpose.

Sewage disposal is an expensive operation and financing it exclusively from property taxes is no longer as common as before. These costs in many localities are increasingly borne by the householder and other users. Most communities assess the abutting property for sewer construction, charge fees for sewer connections, and levy special taxes for sewerage facilities. Two common bases are used to determine the charges for householders. One is computed on water consumption, with the bill normally a fixed prcentage of the water rate. The second method is a flat rate charge on some unit, such as front feet of the property, number of sewer connections, types of plumbing fixtures, number of persons in the household, or various combinations of these or other factors.

Nearly all urban places own their sewerage systems. The potential hazards to health in case of failure of the system are indeed fearful to contemplate, and this probably accounts in part for the almost universal recognition of sewage disposal as a municipal function. Nearly half of sewage treatment plants are not publicly owned, however.

Electric Plants

Electric power continues to be a field dominated by private plants. Most publicly-owned systems are in smaller municipalities, but there are a few major exceptions such as Los Angeles, Seattle, and Detroit.

Since the majority of publicly-owned electric utilities are in smaller communities, the most common administrative arrangement is to place the utility directly under the control of the council or the chief executive officer who appoints the utility superintendent or director. Utility boards appointed by the council or chief executive are also common, and in a few centers members of the utility board are popularly elected.

Airports

Airports have been accepted as a municipal utility since the 1920s when local governments were authorized to construct them and usually to operate them, too. Local units interested in airports have received two big stimulants since World War II. First, over 500 military airport facilities constructed during that war were turned over to cities, counties, and states for airport use. Second, the Federal Airport Act of 1946 called for the development of a "nationwide system of public airports" to meet present and future needs of civil aeronautics.

Local airports, as most other utilities, are administered in various ways. Some are directed by an airport manager appointed by the local governing board or chief executive officer. Others are managed by semiautonomous airport boards and commissions or by special districts. Various line departments including public works, public service, and utilities control airports in some communities, and the staff department of finance supervises their operations in some other cities.

A significant problem in providing airport facilities is the location of the airport. Most citizens do not want the airport near their homes for safety reasons, and the amount of space needed often is unavailable in or adjacent to the municipality. Airports are usually constructed some miles from the heart of the area served, thereby inconveniencing many users. Such distant locations from large cities are necessary, however, because of the noise generating from jet propelled planes. A second problem is financial and centers on the public subsidy usually necessary for their support. Other problems pertain to traffic congestion, noise, dirt, and the threat of accidents.

Public Transportation

The need for concern over the problems of mass transportation has been succinctly phrased by one writer in these words:

> Every morning thousands—perhaps millions—of people travel from their homes in the outskirts to their places of employment in the center of the city. Every evening they reverse the process. . . . At every hour of the day and night there is some crosstown travel.[15]

While large numbers of people have automobiles and get along without public transportation, it remains a necessary utility for many others— particularly in our largest urban centers. Virtually all transit systems, however, whether publicly or privately owned, have been running deficits in recent decades.

Among the "pat" solutions to the economic problems of mass transportation are the opposite demands that cities sell their systems to private companies and that private companies be taken over by public ownership. However, recent experiences in Chicago, Boston, and other cities have shown that operating deficits remain although patterns of ownership change. The pattern of national-local cooperation in airport construction holds some promise of a similar relationship in the construction of mass transit facilities. Federal programs of aid to transit systems became available only in the late 1960's following the creation of the Department of Transportation, but the amount of aid so far has been disappointing to transit system supporters.

The problems created by a mass transit system, or the absence of one, are difficult indeed. Since movement of people between the central city and its suburbs is involved, the core city has a legitimate complaint in believing it should not bear all the costs. Thus, a number of metropolitan areas may seek to follow the action taken in San Francisco in the 1950's when voters approved a very large bond issue to help finance a mass transit system.

Others may follow the lead of New York where a special tax on business was levied to help support its transit system, which is recognized as a convenience to business. The relocation of business and industry in outlying areas has lessened the transportation problem in some areas but created new problems as a result of the loss of public and private investments in the central business district.

As with many other problems, solutions in public transit must be tailored to the individual community. Where solutions are found, they likely will combine public subsidy, business support through special taxes, and continuing educational campaigns to encourage the use of transit facilities. Municipal bus drivers, for instance, may even adopt the Greyhound slogan and encourage persons to "take the city bus, and leave the driving to us." The slogan of the rapid transit district in the Los Angeles area describes its buses as "your extra car" and special programs to induce new riders have been at least partially successful.

THE ENERGY CRISIS

The current and projected energy crisis is not a product of local governmental action or inaction, but the impact of policies and programs of higher governmental levels will continue to be felt most immediately in the consumption and commuting patterns of citizens in their local communities. The darkened "Strip" in Las Vegas, the voluntary ban on outdoor Christmas lighting in 1974, the decision to enforce the fifty-five mile an hour speed limit and to sell gasoline to owners of cars with even or odd license plate numbers on even or odd days are examples of how national policies when implemented affect the local citizen.

The achievement of essential goals at reasonable costs in such areas as environmental protection, nuclear safeguards, energy conservation, and adequate energy supplies are important national priorities. To make maximum progress toward their realization will require not only farsighted decisions by higher governmental levels with supporting local enactments but also faithful compliance with these decisions and enactments. The enforcement of these policies, of course, will be felt most at the local level and will have a strong impact on local public works programs and the activities of public-service enterprises.

NOTES

1. International City Managers' Association, *Municipal Fire Administration,* 5th ed., International City Managers' Association, 1950, p. 63.
2. Raymond L. Bancroft (ed.), "City Fire Chief Speaks Out," *Nation's Cities,* 10 (June, 1972), 9.
3. For a fuller account of integrated public safety programs, *see* Charles S.

James, *Police and Fire Integration in the Small City*, Public Administration Service, 1955.

4. James H. Barnett, *A Study of Police and Fire Department Integration in Selected Cities of North America*, Bureau of Governmental Affairs, University of North Dakota, 1973.

5. Harold F. Alderfer, *American Local Government and Administration*, Macmillan, 1956, p. 546.

6. Jerome Hanus, "A Profile of Public Works Departments," in International City Mangement Association, *Municipal Year Book, 1971*, Washington, 1971, pp. 170-1.

7. Henry G. Hodges, *Municipal Management: Theory and Practice of Municipal Administration*, Crofts, 1939, p. 456.

8. John Bauer, *Transforming Public Utility Regulations*, Harper, 1950, p. 3.

9. *Munn* v. *Illinois,* 94 U.S. 113, 126 (1887).

10. Bauer, *op. cit.,* p. 5.

11. Hodges, *op. cit.,* p. 538.

12. American Water Works Association, *The Story of Water Supply*, New York, 1955, p. 3.

13. For an interesting study of the politics of fluoridation, see Robert L. Crain, Elihu Katz, and Donald B. Rosenthal, *The Politics of Community Conflict: The Fluoridation Decision*, Bobbs-Merrill, 1969.

14. Bernard Frank, "The Story of Water as the Story of Man" in Alfred Stefferud (ed.), *Water*, Government Printing Office, 1955, p. 1.

15. Austin F. MacDonald, *State and Local Government in the United States,* Crowell, 1955, p. 642.

Chapter 17

Planning and Land-Use Controls

Planning has been described as the oldest of the arts of humankind—the one distinguishing humans from other animals. Thus, there is no such thing as not planning, for someone in the community will begin to "plan" when a problem is perceived. There are hundreds of variations on the single theme of what planning means, but most definitions center on two central points. First, planning is the process of making rational decisions; and second, these decisions concern actions directed toward the attainment of predetermined community goals. Local planning is both a process and a technique applied through local governments to the shaping of the physical environment and to the spatial distribution of activities within the community. Its effectiveness depends on the systematic and continuing application of organized knowledge and foresight in the pursuit of clearly defined and properly related community development objectives.

THE DEVELOPMENT OF LOCAL PLANNING

While local planning in the last half of the twentieth century is proving to be much broader in scope and more intricate and involved than in earlier periods, planning of some kind has existed throughout our nation's history. Notable examples of early planning were the checkerboard street system designed by William Penn for Philadelphia in 1682, the system of squares developed by Oglethorpe for the city of Savannah, and the combination of rectangular and radial streets around a central hub by L'Enfant for Washington, D.C. in 1791. In spite of deviations through the years, the important principles of the original plans of these three cities are still visible.[1]

Accepting the point that planning of a sort has existed since the early years of our nation, two events have been singled out as important stimuli to local planning. The first was Chicago's World's Fair of 1893 which featured an orderly arrangement of monumental buildings, streets, and parks. Men and women from all over the United States saw this site, publicized as the "City Beautiful," and were spurred to action by these words of Daniel Burnham:

> Make no little plans; they have no magic to stir men's blood and probably themselves will not be realized. Make big plans; aim high in hope and work, remembering that a noble logical diagram once recorded will never die, but long after we are gone will be a living thing, asserting itself with every growing insistency.[2]

The idea of the city beautiful became a dominant concept in communities across the nation, expressing itself in civic centers, civic buildings, parks, fountains, and street plantings.

The second stimulus occurred in 1909 when the first national conference on city planning was held in Washington. The economic rather than the aesthetic aspects of city planning were stressed at this meeting as were the value of a comprehensive technical survey to the development of plans and the need for coordination in the treatment of related problems. As described by one writer, "This conference was in many ways a confluence of the several urban reform movements ... It was, however, more the precursor than the true beginning of the organized planning movement."[3] The American City Planning Institute was started in 1917 as a technical organization of the National Conference on City Planning, a movement given considerable encouragement by Herbert Hoover as Secretary of Commerce.

Planning activities in local communities were largely carried out by self-constituted committees of bankers, realtors, and other businessmen, or similarly composed committees appointed by the local public executive or governing board. In many communities the early efforts were too grandiose, and planning was more rampant speculation than careful development. In other communities land speculators made careful planning in the early stages of development impossible. One writer has characterized this era in these words:

> ... The stamp of the early speculator remains, however, upon most of our cities. At a pace a hundred times slower than the original development, and at enormous expense, modern city planners now are attempting to erase the worst blotches spilled across the country by the boomers, the townsite promoters, and the speculative builders of yesterday. It is an aspect of our urban history in which Americans can take little pride.[4]

The concept of comprehensive planning emerged in the 1920s, embracing the six elements of zoning, streets, transit, transportation (rail, water and air), public recreation, and civic appearance.[5] A decade later, the seven elements of community land planning were identified as streets, parks, sites for public buildings, public reservations, zoning districts, routes for public utilities, and pierheads and bulkhead lines.[6] As Robert Walker observed in 1950, public planning should be "as broad as the scope of city government,"[7] and the planning concept has been expanded to include housing, slum clearance, location of business and industry, urban renewal, and redevelopment in our larger communities. But because the scope of government is still relatively narrow in more sparsely populated rural communities, planning if it exists at all there as a governmental function, is still narrowly conceived and implemented. Enlightened rural communities, however, often have a form of zoning ordinance designed to prevent some of the adverse consequences of unplanned land use.

LOCAL PLANNING AGENCIES

The first permanent planning commission as a municipal agency was established in Hartford, Connecticut, in 1907. This pattern of organization has been followed almost universally since that time as evidenced by the existence of official planning commissions in more than 90 percent of American cities of 10,000 or more population. A few communities have entrusted the planning function to a department under a full-time professional director responsible to the chief executive officer. The relative merits of a staff agency versus an independent planning commission will be discussed after the organization and functions of the typical local planning commission are characterized.

The official local planning agency in most local governments is a plural-member commission that carries on planning activities of a communitywide nature, and coordinates the plans of public departments and agencies. The organization of the planning commission varies considerably among local units. Its typical size is five or seven members, but it may have as many as fifty. The members may be *ex officio*, that is, composed of designated public officials, or they may be citizen appointees serving without pay, or a combination of *ex officio*, and citizen appointees. In most communities, the power to appoint citizen members lies in the local executive officer. In some, however, planning is viewed as a legislative rather than as a staff responsibility, and citizen members are appointed by the local governing body.

Powers and duties of city and county planning commissions also vary greatly. In general, their responsibilities parallel those suggested for such an agency in the *Model County Charter*. It proposes that the commission (1) report its recommendations and advice to the governing board on all proposals submitted to it, and on such other matters pertaining to planning as the commission desires or the board requests; (2) formulate and develop planning proposals for submission to the board whenever requested to do so by the board or upon its own motion; (3) keep informed on all matters pertaining to planning and hold hearings concerning such matters whenever necessary; (4) promote public interest in and understanding of the county plans and related matters; and (5) perform such other advisory functions and duties and exercise such other powers as the board may establish.[8]

Recognizing that planning commissions assisted by professional staffs are often well equipped to carry out additional functions, Martin Meyerson has suggested that they be given expanding responsibilities. Labeling these proposed additions as "middle-ground community planning functions," he believes they would bring planning and policy closer together in the community. These new functions are those of (1) a central intelligence function to facilitate market operations for housing, commerce, industry, and other community activities through the greater issuance of market analyses: (2) a pulse-taking function to alert the community through periodic reports to danger signs in such areas as blight formation, economic changes, population movements, and other shifts; (3) a policy-clarification function to help frame and regularly revise development objectives of local government; (4) a detailed development plan function to phase specific programs—both public and private—as part of a comprehensive course of action covering a period of time of up to ten years; and (5) a feed-back review function to analyze carefully the consequences of programs and activities as a guide to future action.[9]

Not everyone, however, is convinced of the need or desirability of continuing planning commissions. According to Richard Babcock, a zoning authority,

> . . . The planning commission, except, perhaps in the smallest communities is a dodo . . . today it is the principal deterrent to more meaningful communication between the professional planner and the politically responsible decision-maker. Planning should be as much a part of the municipal staff responsibility, with direct accountability to the politician, as fire or police protection.[10]

Two other writers evaluate independent planning commissions as being less adequately related to the execution of planning than to the distribution of resources and means of access to decision-makers.[11]

The most common task of local planning commissions is to prepare a comprehensive or master plan to serve as a blueprint for the future development of the community. Upon approval by the local governing board, this plan becomes "official." In the words of one writer, the master plan is "nothing more than the easily changed instrumentality which will show a commission from day to day the progress it has made."[12] The zoning plan for the community, which also is prepared by the planning commission for approval by the governing board, will be discussed later in this chapter.

A second type of organization for planning is as a staff aide to the chief executive as a full-fledged department head. A planning commission advises and assists the planning director, but the commission is less important than the semi-independent commission described above. A third type of organization for local planning holds that the agency should serve as a policy making activity of the city or county governing board itself because that body is the final policymaking authority. This arrangement also keeps a planning commission, but that body serves only as advisory to the governing board. In support of this type of organization for planning, T. J. Kent, Jr., professor of city planning, has stated

> The concept of the role of city planning as a policymaking activity of the city council regards the city council not only as the body which must be relied upon to make all the final decisions on major policy questions, but it also regards the members of the council as being capable of understanding what it is that they must do if effective civic-improvement programs are to be developed and sustained.[13]

LOCAL PLANNING DIRECTORS

In general, planning implies something to be done in the future. It seeks to correct or minimize the effects of past mistakes and, if possible, to avoid them in the future. As such, it is a sizable undertaking involving an array of professional skills and commitment of time that the commission members are unable to contribute. Therefore, in most communities a full-time director of planning and a planning staff are present in addition to the planning commission. A full-time resident director and staff indicate that planning is a continuing rather than a periodic process, a condition that is highly desirable and needed in most communities. When the community is too small or feels it cannot afford a permanent staff, outside specialists often are consulted to assist the planning commission on a contractual or per diem basis. The resident planner usually becomes a major adviser to the policy innovator for the executive officer or the governing board to which he is responsible. He also has advantages in seeking and securing public support for the plans he and the commission propose. Too often the work of the consultant is placed on the shelf to collect dust because he is not present to defend and conduct a sustained sales campaign to translate the plan into reality.

The planning director is selected in various ways. He is usually an appointee of the local executive officer or local governing board. In communities with the council-manager form, he is generally selected by the manager, while he is appointed by the commission in commission-governed communities. In some communities, he is appointed by the planning commission itself, and in others the functions of planning officer are assumed by some other local official, such as the manager, mayor, engineer, or director of public works.

Turning again to the proposals of the *Model County Charter*, it recommends the appointment of the director of planning by the manager with the approval of the governing board. His recommended powers and duties are to (1) serve as the chief planning officer and regular technical adviser of the manager and board on all planning and related matters, and to direct the activities of the planning staff; (2) coordinate the planning and related activities of the county with similar activities of the municipalities within the county, confer with and advise officials and agencies of such municipalities on planning matters, and cooperate with state, regional, and other local planning agencies; (3) maintain an up-to-date file of municipal plans, zoning ordinances, official maps, building codes and subdivision regulations, and amendments to any of them, of municipalities within the county; (4) supply technical planning services to any municipality of the county upon such agreement between the affected governing boards; (5) assist the county manager in preparation of the capital program; and (6) perform such other duties and exercise such other powers as the manager or board may establish.[14]

Obviously the contribution of the planner in community planning is major and also should be unique because of his special perspective. The planner should be equipped with special technical skills, should take a long-range view of his evolving community, and should have been trained to perceive the community in its entirety. Some interesting insights into the planner's job are as follows:

> The town planner (laymen or professional) must of course look at the town as it is. If he is true to his calling, he cannot stop at this. He must look backward, to see how it got that way. He must look around him, to see what the greater public interest demands of his town. He must look ahead, to see what his town is likely to become and what it should become. After he has done these things, if he is a wise planner, he will be guided in what he proposes by a simple rule: *No town is an island, no time is forever.*[15]

Based on her study of planning in New Jersey municipalities, Francine Rabinovitz, political scientist, suggests three primary roles for the local planner. First, he can serve as a technician giving technical and policy advice to community leaders. Second, he can serve as a broker, specifying alternatives and negotiating solutions. Or, third, he can serve as a mobilizer, who generates *ad hoc* support on particular issues.[16]

The planning literature contains many accounts of special problems of local planners. The job of the local planner is to propose courses of action, not to execute them. Standards prescribed by elected officials for his guidance sometimes are contradictory, ambivalent, or non-existent. Another problem is "to give the bold planning director room in which to maneuver, to encourage him to take the risks of initiating."[17]

Although planners continue to use the rhetoric of "planning with people, not for them" their actions often belie the desire for active citizen participation. Some authorities recently have proposed "advocacy planning" for and by citizen and interest groups. Planners are retained by those organizations and groups to prepare plans for them and to argue for their adoption before the planning commission somewhat in the manner of a lawyer pleading for his client. A proponent of advocacy planning believes citizens should be included in the planning process by being staffed to evaluate planning proposals and to offer alternatives rather than the more limited role of protesting plans presented to them.[18]

THE COMPREHENSIVE PLAN

A major function of a local planning commission is to prepare a comprehensive plan to project the future development of the community. Planning must be based upon facts that can be collected and made known, and the collection and assembling of information represent the first stage in the development of a comprehensive plan. At this point the planning commission usually relies heavily upon professional help. The principal sources of the planning data needed are the community records that provide such information as general population, school population, existing land-use patterns, tax rates, bonded indebtedness, capacity of utilities, subdivision regulations, housing, and parks. After the data are assembled, they are used in various ways. Base maps are prepared, showing such things as existing land-use patterns, population densities, age of population, racial compositions, and other characteristics of the community and its citizenry.

The second stage of work on the comprehensive plans consists of careful study of the existing land-use patterns within the community. From this study, judgments must be made concerning the adequacy of certain patterns, needed projections in certain areas, and the allocation of space for various types of land use. Economic forces are usually given considerable weight because most communities have an economic reason for their existence. Further plans are intricately related to projected populations which, in turn, depend closely on what happens to the community's industrial and commercial growth.

The third stage in the development of the community plan involves the actual preparation of the blueprint for development. This shows recommended uses of private land and the proposed location of all necessary and desirable public facilities. In most communities, the plan as it finally emerges is a compromise of the recommendations of the professional staff, the sober judgments of the members of the planning commission, and the demands of various interests within the community.

The plan, when completed, usually consists of a series of maps supplemented by descriptive reports outlining and explaining the principal reasons for the plan and its component elements. In many communities the comprehensive plan is given the force of law upon its approval by the governing body. It is a flexible "law," however, since before some of its proposals can be realized community conditions will change, requiring modifications in the plan.

The development of the comprehensive plan, like planning itself, is a continuing process. The plan must be subject to change but alterations should be approved only after the same careful study that went into the preparation of the plan itself. Because of the recognized need for flexibility, many communities never adopt the comprehensive plan formally as a single document but the governing board adopts its various features when they can be implemented. This method has the advantage of not requiring formal action of the governing board if any changes must be made after its adoption.

The comprehensive plan cannot remake most communities; it can only make adjustments. The existing situation of the community must be accepted and changes may be made only gradually and against community inertia and vested interests. But changes are possible, as evident from the experience of many communities that have slowly transformed themselves into more desirable places for residents, commercial enterprises, and industries through harmonious development of public and private land uses.

To implement the community plan, most local units must acquire considerable amounts of land for public uses. Employing foresight through planning and proper legal devices can save a community considerable money. Most of the land required by the local government for public use is acquired through purchase. Normally, the community and the land owner are able to agree on a reasonable purchase price for the property. When agreement is unattainable, the local government may exercise the power of eminent domain, under which property can be taken for a public use upon payment of fair compensation. The proceedings are settled in court if the landowner refuses to sell or demands an unreasonable price. The use of eminent domain before the construction of private buildings on the needed property, of course, is less costly to the community than its exercise after such construction.

REGIONAL PLANNING

Considerable progress has been made in local planning, but awareness is growing of the limitations of planning on a small-area basis. This restriction is especially noticeable in metropolitan areas where to most people the physical division between local governments means only the inevitable sign reading "city limits." However, even for a community geographically separated from others, regional planning is logical and beneficial. Such a community usually is a center of an economic area and the system of streets and highways—incoming and outgoing—require coordination beyond its own boundaries.

In addition to highways, planning for the location of parks and recreation facilities, utilities, industrial areas, and a number of other urban matters is more logically approached on a regional than an individual community basis. To fill the gap between the need for regional planning and its political practicality, a number of cooperative planning commissions, groups, and agencies have been recently established. In some states, such joint planning efforts are encouraged through the passage of state enabling legislation. In other communities, such agencies are private and unofficial and may be composed primarily of business firms. When such agencies are public, they usually are composed of representatives of the local governments in the region. Councils of government (discussed in Chapter 3) and the substate districts required by the national government (considered in Chapter 4) represent two major thrusts to achieve coordinated regional planning.

The major functions of regional planning are to help communities within the area (1) identify their many competing wants; (2) understand compatibilities and incompatibilities among these wants and between these wants and resources; (3) identify and then examine the alternative, internally consistent set of goals that fall within the range of choice; (4) gain agreement upon an internally consistent set of long-, middle-, and short-range goals for the qualities of living and working environments; and (5) develop courses of action whereby the community's resources may be rationally and economically allocated to meet best the deliberately selected goals.[19]

Some progress has been made in regional planning, but such joint or cooperative agencies usually are merely advisory. Their recommendations are followed only if acceptable to and approved by the participating local governments. Too often, of course, one or more of the member communities are unwilling to accept the recommended plans and they are never implemented. While noting the American preference to plan on a small-area basis, one planner has commented that "if piecemeal planning is to be the rule, it is evident that the pieces are getting bigger and that a larger variety of factors are being taken into accord than ever before."[20]

LAND-USE CONTROLS

The police power of local governments permits them to regulate and limit the use of private property when necessary for the "public health, safety, welfare, or morals" of the community. The use of this power does not require compensation to property owners because their property is not taken for public use as in the exercise of eminent domain. The police power of the community thus is the means by which private property is controlled in local planning. Three primary means of such control are building codes, subdivision regulations, and zoning.

Building Codes

A building code is a legislative set of principles for administrative guidance in regulating original construction and improvements. The code provides for minimum standards of building construction and condition and for human occupancy, and concerns such factors as lighting, ventilation, heating, sanitation, plumbing, electrical work, types of building materials, and fire prevention and protection. Smaller cities may have a single code setting standards in each of these fields; larger cities usually publish sections of their building codes as separate documents. For instance, the sanitary code in a large community may run to several hundred pages. It covers a variety of commercial businesses such as bakeries, barbershops, drugstores, hospitals, and hotels. It also may regulate noises, nuisances, and morals.

Building codes are not a recent development in most cities. For a long time they have been utilized for enforcement of subdivision and zoning regulations and to attain desired housing standards by requiring permits to build, renovate, or install equipment. Building codes in some communities are quite restrictive and require materials of a quality beyond what is reasonable, resulting in higher building costs. More often, such codes lag somewhat behind the needs of the times. Communities with outdated codes permit construction of substandard housing and/or the conversion of old homes into apartments that are inadequate for accepted standards of human living. Other codes fail to allow modern building techniques because they are not kept up-to-date.

In addition to the requirement of the building permit, most building codes provide for inspection of the premises to determine whether or not standards are being met. According to Donald Webster, political scientist, the building inspector "can destroy the effectiveness of the code by overlooking violations or permitting exceptions to the regulations. The integrity of such officer is, therefore, most essential."[21] As more local units recognize that the reputation and the physical appearance of their communities depend principally on the provisions and enforcement of their building codes, stricter codes and more careful enforcement may be expected.

Subdivision Regulations

The necessity for control over subdivision development if the community plan is to be realized is apparent. However, this need was learned from bitter experience in a great many communities. The tremendous expansion into the countryside around almost every large city has produced the parceling of open land into lots for homes. Much of the expansion was unplanned and unregulated because of the profit motive of real estate and other private interests seeking to maximize returns on investments without regard for planning safeguards. In some cases developers did not even provide such necessities as streets, water supply, or adequate sewerage facilities. Homeowners in such subdivisions found themselves unable to finance the necessary improvements on these properties. The adjustments often proved costly and inconvenient to the community and citizens of the subdivision alike.

With subdivision control, communities are able to prevent the development of land without provision for necessary services. The laying out of subdivisions is regulated through the power of the local government to withhold the privilege of recording parcels that do not meet required standards or do not have official approval. If the plat is not recorded, lots within it are sometimes more difficult to sell. They cannot be sold by lot number but only by ''metes and bounds'' descriptions of their boundary lines. Because the danger of future title disputes may be greater than with recorded plats, such unapproved and unrecorded homesteads may be less attractive to would-be purchasers.

State enabling acts granting local governments the right to regulate land subdivisions generally give this authority directly to local planning boards or permit local governing bodies to delegate this function to them. The conditions that the planning commission requires before granting approval to have the plat recorded are those which will prevent the property from becoming a liability to the community and purchaser alike. In general, the layout and width of streets, length and depth of blocks, width and depth of lots, provision of open space, and the provision of water and sewerage are the conditions checked.

In many communities acceptance of subdivisions is a county function. The board with this power of approval may be limited by law to accepting only those subdivision plans meeting prescribed standards and approved by the planning authority, where one exists. This sanction is a rough equivalent to a building permit. Problems occasionally arise when the subdivision is outside a municipality and, in the eyes of the municipality, county control is inadequate. Some states have granted cities extraterritorial powers over subdivisions built in adjacent areas with the extent of this grant commonly ranging from three to seven miles.

Zoning

Zoning is a form of governmental regulation providing for the orderly social and economic development of a community. According to Harold Alderfer, political scientist, zoning is

> the division of the community into districts for the purpose of regulating the use of the land and buildings in each district in accordance with the desired character of the district, for the purpose of regulating the height and bulk of buildings, the proportion of the lot that can be covered by them, and the density of population.[22]

These zoning restraints were for health reasons to assure adequate sunlight, free flow of air, and the like.

Early examples of the use of restricted zones in American communities exist, but there was little progress in zoning until the enactment of a New York City ordinance in 1916. There it was feared that the construction of a new transit system might further intensify the congestion it was intended to relieve, and committees studied the practicality of regulating the height and area and the use of buildings under the police power of the state. Now zoning is a major means by which private land use is integrated into the overall community plan.[23]

To insure the efficient use of land and achieve the goals of the comprehensive plan, the community normally is divided into subcategories of residential, commercial, and industrial zones. Residential districts may include zones for single-family residences, two-family residences, four-family residences, and multi-family or apartment residences. Commercial districts are of two types—the central business district and neighborhood shopping centers. Typical divisions for industrial zones are for light industry, heavy industry, and unrestricted districts. Most communities do not permit a lower use in a zoning district but permit a higher use in lower zoned area. For instance, no plural family residences would be allowed in an area zoned for single-family homes, but the latter would be permitted in areas zoned for plural-family residences.

Zoning on the basis of use is a major type of land-use regulations. A second type restricts the height of buildings in relation to the width of the street, size of side yards, and the use to which the area is put. The single-family residential districts are the most restricted zones in terms of height. Height limitations are sometimes expressed in terms of stories or in maximum number of feet. Apartment house and commercial zones usually have the least restrictive height limitations.

A third type of zoning restriction limits the amount of the lot area to be occupied, with the amount varying by type of district. This requirement specifies the building line as a prescribed number of feet back from both the front and rear of the lot and its side lines. Area regulations also include such factors as maximum permitted density of population, the percentage of the lot that may be built upon, the minimum size of courts, and provisions of garage and parking areas.

THE ZONING ORDINANCE

The zoning ordinance includes regulations other than those pertaining to land-use restrictions. A good zoning ordinance can be prepared only after careful painstaking study and cannot be lifted from sections of laws of other communities. The ordinance usually is complemented by the preparation of a zoning map marking out the lines of the several types of use districts. In addition to protecting property values, the zoning ordinance also insures access to all property and the availability of adequate light and air to protect public health and minimize fire hazards.

Following its adoption, the zoning ordinance is enforced by the building commissioner, engineer, manager, or other local official responsible for issuing building permits. Appeals against the ordinance's administration are taken to the planning commission or to the board of zoning appeals or adjustment. The major functions of the appeal agency are (1) to hear appeals alleging error of the administrative officer in enforcing the ordinance; (2) to pass on exceptional cases as required by the basic ordinance; and (3) to grant departures or variations from the strict letter of the law if enforcement would cause a needless hardship.

Members of the board of zoning appeals usually are appointed by the local executive officer with the approval of the local governing body but, as mentioned above, the planning commission serves *ex officio* as the zoning board in some communities. The principal device for implementing the community plan is lost unless the zoning board exercises its authority free from favoritism and undue political pressure.

Zoning serves a number of functions. It protects health, safety, morality, and welfare; it protects residential neighborhoods; it ensures property values; and it effectuates the goals of planning. In a 1974 decision, the Supreme Court stated that zoning

> may indeed be the most essential function performed by local government, for it is one of the primary means by which we protect the sometimes difficult to define concept of quality of life.[24]

This decision upheld the right of local zoning ordinances to prevent communes in a community.

A second decision in the same year resulted from a suit brought by the United States against the city of Black Jack, Missouri. This all-white community of 3,000 incorporated in 1970 in opposition to an integrated housing development sponsored by a religious organization. Upon its incorporation, the new city adopted a zoning ordinance that legislated out of existence the proposed housing project. The federal circuit court upheld the national government's challenge of this local zoning law, holding that the use of incorporation to zone out blacks was unconstitutional.[25]

A third landmark decision grew out of litigation initiated in 1974 by builders against the city of Petaluma, California. Petaluma enacted a community growth-control ordinance restricting larger projects to 500 new housing units a year. A U.S. district court in that year ruled the ordinance invalid because it placed unconstitutional restrictions on the right of citizens to free movement. But a circuit court of appeals in 1975 reversed the lower court, holding that

> The concept of the public welfare is sufficiently broad to uphold Petaluma's desire to preserve its small-town character, its open spaces and low density of population, and to grow at an orderly and deliberate pace.[26]

Nonconforming Uses

While courts have sustained retroactive exculsion of nuisances from certain types of zoned districts, it is not probable that exclusion of nonnuisances would be upheld. The usual plan in communities is to allow for nonconforming uses—a term applied to uses contrary to the zoning ordinance that were established before the enactment of the zoning law. Examples of such uses are the existence of a corner gasoline service station in a residential district or a fraternity house in a district zoned for single-family residences.

The generally accepted method for handling the problem of nonconforming uses is to allow the continuance of such use subject to certain limitations. The usual restrictions include prohibitions against enlargement of the noncomforming use, repair of structure up to a stated percentage of its value if it is destroyed or damaged, and renewal of nonconforming use after discontinuance for a stated time. While it was anticipated that nonconforming uses would gradually die out and remove the problem, experience has not been too satisfactory in this regard. In some communities, quite the reverse has actually occurred through the granting of use variances permitting the establishment of new nonconforming uses.

A relatively recent approach to the problem of eliminating such uses is to establish a policy for their abandonment over variable periods of time. This allows the private detriment to be amortized over time, thereby producing less hardship on the property owner. For example, the period of amortization for a ''five-and-dime variety'' store in a residential district might well be relatively short because such stores anticipate a fairly rapid turnover of merchandise. On the other hand, the amortization period might be considerably longer for other types of commercial uses that experience slower rates of merchandise turnover. The period of amortization also might relate to the nature of the structure housing the non conforming use. The period of time could be considerably shorter for a dental office or beauty salon in a residential building than for a similar use in a building constructed for such purposes.

Misuse of Zoning

As an exercise of the police power, zoning should be used to further the general welfare of the community. When employed properly, it can remedy some mistakes of the past and control private land use in the interest of the community. Attempts have been made in some local governments, however, to obtain ends through zoning that are incompatible with a proper exercise of the police power. One misuse of zoning is to exclude undesirable but necessary uses from the community. Garbage disposal plants, sewage disposal plants, laundries, and dry-cleaning establishments, may have disagreeable effects on abutting properties, but they are essential services in most urban areas.

A more serious misuse of zoning occurred in communities that once attempted to achieve racial segregation through the exercise of police power. The technique utilized was to establish certain residential zones within which specific racial groups would be forbidden to settle. Ordinances to this effect have been held as an unconstitutional limitation upon property rights under the Fourteenth Amendment and as an unreasonable exercise of the police power. Attempts by subdividers to place restrictive covenants in deeds whereby the purchaser would agree never to sell to particular racial groups have been less operative since 1948. In that year, the Supreme Court held that such agreements are not enforceable in state courts when the parties to the transaction are willing buyers and sellers.[27]

In addition to racial zoning, some communities have been overly enthusiastic in their efforts to protect property owners from depreciation of the value of their homes by the construction of "cheaper" homes in the immediate neighborhood. Such efforts are sometimes known as "snob" zoning, and their protective regulations have imposed minimum building costs, minimum floor area or cubic content of homes, and minimum lot sizes. Zoning on the basis of cost has not received court approval, but the courts have disagreed over the legality of minimum floor area and lot size restrictions. The general test that the court imposes is the reasonableness of such restrictions in relation to health, safety, and general welfare. As long as the minimum requirements of floor size and lot area are reasonable, the courts probably will be more responsive in approving them.

A further question on which the courts have not agreed relates to restrictions on the use of property for aesthetic reasons. The Supreme Court indicated qualified approval of the use of police power for aesthetic reasons in a 1954 decision by stating

The concept of the public welfare is broad and inclusive. The values it represents are spiritual as well as physical, aesthetic as well as monetary. It is within the power of the legislature to determine that the community should be beautiful as well as healthy, spacious as well as clean, well-balanced as well as carefully patrolled.[28]

A real difficulty in using the local power of zoning to achieve aesthetic goals is the problem at arriving at these goals in a reasonable, acceptable manner.

Regional Zoning

In zoning, as in planning, considerable progress has taken place in individual communities and awareness has grown of the desirability of zoning on a larger areal basis. Th need is essentially greater in metropolitan areas.

The political practicality of zoning beyond the confines of a single community received a considerable assist in a 1954 decision of the New Jersey Supreme Court. This court held that the proposition of the responsibility of a municipality stopping at its boundary lines

cannot be tolerated where as here the area is built up and one cannot tell when one is passing from one borough to another. . . . At the very least Dumont owes a duty to hear any residents and taxpayers of adjoining municipalities who may be adversely affected by proposed zoning changes and to give as much consideration to their rights as they would to those of residents and taxpayers of Dumont. To do less would be to make a fetish out of invisible boundary lines and a mockery of the principles of zoning.[29]

The implementation of the obvious need for interlocal cooperation, however, is difficult to achieve.

The most dramatic state action to overcome local parochialism was the creation of the Urban Development Corporation (UDC) in 1968 to identify and redevelop target areas in New York cities. It was given authority to override local zoning and building controls when necessary since as a state enterprise it was beyond the control of either local officials or local voters. The UDC was given one billion dollars in bonding authority, eminent domain powers to enhance its ability to acquire land, and complete authority to develop a project from planning to completion. Considerable progress had been made in the construction of housing until the UDC defaulted on a bond issue in 1975. It will be interesting to see whether the progress of the UDC will encourage other states to create such enterprises or whether its financial problems will discourage similar action in other states.[30]

ENVIRONMENTAL QUALITY

Decades of concern about our deteriorating environment brought forth the passage of the National Environmental Policy Act in 1969.[31] Encouraged by NEPA's objectives and accomplishments, fifteen states have adopted state environmental policy acts. While the precise wording of these laws differ, the general provisions as they relate to local governments in general parallel those found in the California Environmental Quality Act of 1970:

> All local agencies shall prepare, or cause to be prepared by contract, and certify the completion of an environmental impact report on any project they intend to carry out or approve which may have a significant effect on the environment.[32]

The provisions were extended to private applications to construct projects with a significant effect on the environment by the California Supreme Court in 1972.[33]

According to the American Society of Planning Officials, an environmental impact statement.

> is an attempt to inject environmental sensitivity into the decision-making machinery. It is, however, a tactical approach rather than a strategic one. It suggests that environmental quality as a public policy has not been institutionalized into the decision-making framework, and, until it is, proposals will have to be reviewed for their effect on the environment.[34]

The contents of the typical environmental impact report (EIR) are both general and specific. The project is described in terms of its exact location, characteristics and objectives, and both short-term and long-term effects of the project on the local and regional environments must be presented. Other EIR features include alternatives to the proposed action, and the growth-inducing impact of the project. A result of the EIR requirement is a general slowdown in growth and development in many communities. Many citizens support this policy but many interest groups are opposed and typically cite their opposition in such terms as its effect on the economy, the loss of jobs, and the decline in sales.

Although the California Act does not require formal public hearings at any stage, the guidelines for its implementation state

> it is a widely accepted desirable goal of this process to encourage public participation. All public agencies adopting implementing procedures in response to these Guidelines should make provisions in their procedures for wide public involvement, formal and informal, consistent with their existing activities and procedures, in order to properly receive and evaluate public reactions, adverse and favorable, based on environmental issues.[35]

As a recent innovation in state and local decision-making, the environmental impact statement holds real promise for orderly future development of our landscape and resources in a manner that will not harm the environment. The concern for the environment should be a common interest of all levels of government as well as a deep interest of the citizenry.

NOTES

1. John W. Reps, *The Making of Urban America, A History of City Planning in the United States,* Princeton University Press, 1965.
2. Quoted in Harold F. Alderfer, *American Local Government and Administration,* Macmillan, 1956, p. 596.
3. Robert A. Walker, *The Planning Function in Urban Government,* 2nd ed., University of Chicago Press, 1950, p. 11.
4. Reps, *op. cit.,* p. 380.
5. Theodora K. Hubbard and Henry V. Hubbard, *Our Cities Today and Tomorrow,* Harvard University Press, 1929, p. 109.
6. Edward M. Bassett, *The Master Plan,* Russell Sage Foundation, 1938.
7. Walker, *op. cit.,* p. 10.
8. National Municipal League, *Model County Charter,* Art. VI, Sec. 6.04, 1956, p. 36.
9. Martin Meyerson, "How to Bring Planning and Policy Together" in Edward C. Banfield (ed.), *Urban Government, A Reader in Administration and Politics,* Free Press, 1961, p. 491.
10. Richard F. Babcock, *The Zoning Game,* University of Wisconsin Press, 1969, p. 40.
11. Francine F. Rabinovitz and J. S. Pottinger, "Organization for Local Planning: The Attitudes of Directors," *Journal of the American Institute of Planners,* 33 (January, 1967), p. 28.
12. Bassett, *op. cit.,* p. 5.
13. T. J. Kent, Jr., *The Urban General Plan,* Chandler, 1964, p. 16.
14. National Municipal League, *op. cit.,* Art. VI, Sec. 605, p. 27.
15. Virginia Curtis (ed.), *Planning Cities: Selected Writings on Principles and Practices by Frederick H. Bair, Jr.,* American Society of Planning Officials, 1971, p. 25.
16. Francine F. Rabinovitz, *City Planning and Politics,* Atherton Press, 1969, pp. 80-98.
17. Alan A. Altshuler, *The City Planning Process,* Cornell University Press, 1969, pp. 1, 390-1.
18. For a fuller discussion of advocacy planning, see Paul Davidoff, "Advocacy and Pluralism in Planning," *Journal of the American Institute of Planning,* 31 (November, 1965), 332; Alan S. Kravitz, "Advocacy and Beyond," in *Planning, 1968,* American Society of Planning Officials, 1968, pp. 38-51; and Marshall Kaplan, "Advocacy and the Urban Poor," *Journal of the American Institute of Planners,* 35 (March, 1969), pp. 96-101.
19. Remarks of Melvin H. Weber, Department of City and Regional Planning, University of California, Berkeley, as reported in Stanley Scott (ed.), *Metropolitan Area Problems,* Report of the Pacific Coast Conference on Metropolitan Problems, University of California, Berkeley, 1960, pp. 152-3.
20. Richard L. Meier, "Systems and Principles for Metropolitan Planning, *Centennial Review,* 3 (Winter, 1959), 79-94.
21. Donald H. Webster, *Urban Planning and Municipal Public Policy,* Harper, 1958, p. 424.

22. Alderfer, *op. cit.*, p. 608.
23. The validity of use of police power for zoning was sustained by the U.S. Supreme Court in 1926 in *Village of Euclid* v. *Amber Realty Co.*, 272 U.S. 365. The Court held, however, that the reasonableness of a particular zoning ordinance is always open to question.
24. *Village of Belle Terre* v. *Boraas*, 416 U.S. 1, 13 (1974).
25. *U.S.* v. *City of Black Jack*, 508 F. 2d 1179, 8th cir., 1974.
26. *Construction Industry Association of Sonoma County* v. *City of Petaluma*, 375 F Supp 574 (N.D. Calif., 1974) and *ibid.* 522 F 2d 897.
27. *Shelley* v. *Kraemer*, 334 U.S. 1 (1948).
28. *Berman* v. *Parker*, 348 U.S. 26 (1954).
29. *Borough of Cresskill* v. *Borough of Dumont*, 15 N.J. 247, 104 A 2nd 445 (1954).
30. See Donald Canty (ed.), *The New City*, Praeger, 1969, p. 122, and Alan E. Bent, *Escape From Anarchy: A Strategy for Urban Survival*, Memphis State University Press, 1972, p. 149. For the financial problems of the Urban Development Corporation, see *New York Times*, March 16, 1975, sec. 8, p. 1.
31. P.L. 91-190, 83 Stat. 853.
32. California Environmental Quality Act (1970), Sec. 21151.
33. *Friends of Mammoth* v. *Board of Supervisors of Mono County*, 8 Cal. 3d 247.
34. Statement found in a project narrative of a proposal submitted by the American Society of Planning Officials to the Environmental Protection Agency as quoted in Edward Haworth and Anthony Anderson, *Implementation of the Minnesota Environmental Policy Act*, December, 1974, p. 115.
35. Guidelines for the Implementation of the California Environmental Quality Act of 1970, Sec. 15164.

Chapter 18

Metropolitan Areas and Their Governments

The continuing urbanization of American society was noted in Chapter 8 as one of the most significant and spectacular population trends of our national history. In the period stretching from 1790 to 1975, we grew from a nation with only 5.1 percent of its population living in urban communities to one with three of four citizens classified as urban residents. And estimates indicate the urban trend is continuing.

The United States has experienced three great changes in its population patterns within the span of the last century, all of which have persisted to the present. The shift from a predominately rural to a definitely urban society was accomplished by 1930, when 56 percent of our population lived in urban communities. Since 1930, the second change, a shift from an urban to a metropolitan society has occurred. In 1930, 49.7 percent resided in metropolitan areas. The percentage climbed to 62.9 percent in 1960 and rose to 68.6 percent in 1970. The third shift began occurring in 1940, recasting us as a suburban rather than a metropolitan society. In 1940, 38.2 percent of the population of metropolitan areas lived outside the central cities. Between 1960 and 1970, the suburban ring experienced an increase of 28 percent in contrast to a 5 percent growth for center cities. In fact, territory added to center cities by annexation actually accounted for 3.1 million of the 3.4 million increase experienced by core cities.[1] The impact of the population shifts of that decade is vividly shown in this statement:

> In 1960, the population of the United States was divided almost equally among central cities, suburbs, and nonmetropolitan areas, each of which contained approximately 60 million persons. By 1970, the population of nonmetropolitan areas had grown to 63 million and that of central cities to 64 million (each comprising 31 percent), but the population of the suburbs exceeded 76 million and made up 38 percent of the nation's total.[2]

Actually the movement of persons to the suburbs is not totally a recent phenomenon. Philadelphia was the first American city to have a pattern of independent suburban communities. Instead of Philadelphia growing as expected, clusters of population formed along the Delaware River just beyond the established limits of the city. Four contiguous suburbs containing a third of the population of the area existed by 1790, and six suburban communities contained more than three-sevenths of the area's population by 1810. Forty years later Philadelphia was a city of 121,000 population huddled in an area of two square miles. However, it was the metropolis of an area of 140 square miles embracing 422,000 people and thirty political subdivisions.[3]

METROPOLITAN AREA DEFINED

While many colorful descriptive definitions of a metropolitan area have been devised, a meaningful operational definition is more difficult to come by. The one most common today was established by the United States Office of Management and Budget and followed by the Bureau of the Census in its compilation of data. More fully, these areas are known as "standard metropolitan statistical areas." Such an area is defined as involving two considerations:

> First, a city or cities or specified population to constitute the central city and to identify the county in which it is located as the central county; and second, economic and social relationships with contiguous counties which are metropolitan in character, so that the periphery of the specified metropolitan area may be determined.[4]

The complete definition of a standard metropolitan statistical area (SMSA) involves four criteria. The first relates to population; each SMSA must contain at least one city of not fewer than 50,000 people or a population concentration of at least 50,000 (including a municipality of 25,000 or more) that constitutes a single community for general economic and social purposes. The second criterion pertains to the metropolitan character of the SMSA; it refers basically to the urban attributes of a county adjoining the central county, requiring that at least 75 percent of the resident labor force must be engaged in nonagricultural occupations. The third standard relates to the possible integration of the central county with an adjacent county or counties, based on the existence of economic linkages with the central county, as demonstrated by the intercounty flow of workers, for instance. The fourth criterion relates to the title appropriate for the SMSA, making use of the names of the central city or central cities and the state or states in which it is located.[5] (In New England the units making up a metropolitan area are cities and towns instead of counties.)

In 1950, the number of urban communities meeting these criteria and thus designated as SMSAs were 168, while 212 such areas were recognized ten years later. By 1970, the number had risen to 243, and it has now increased to 264.

DISTRIBUTION, SIZE, AND TYPE OF SMSAs

The 264 SMSAs are distributed in an irregular geographical pattern among forty-seven of the fifty American states, with only Alaska, Vermont and Wyoming having none. Texas with twenty-four has the largest number of metropolitan areas while six states each have only one SMSA. The District of Columbia also meets the necessary criteria for inclusion as an SMSA.

There is a tremendous range in population size. As the two extremes, New York has a population of 11.5 million while Meriden, Connecticut, has less than 56,000. Thirty-two SMSAs have populations exceeding one million, while twenty-eight areas were under 100,000. Slightly less than half of the SMSAs have populations between 100,000 and 300,000.

Types of Metropolitan Areas

In addition to grouping metropolitan areas into classes according to their population, they can be meaningfully classified in terms of their geographical limits. A metropolitan area containing the territory of a single county is an intracounty area, while an area embracing two counties would be a bicounty area. If the metropolitan area extends over three or more counties, it can be classified as a multicounty area. The three areas with eight counties are Philadelphia, Indianapolis, and Providence, while the two nine-county areas are New York and Washington, D.C.

A sizable number of bicounty and multicounty areas have a further characteristic—they are also interstate metropolitan areas. All but four of these thirty areas are bistate in nature. The Cincinnati, Huntington-Ashland, and Wilmington SMSAs extend into three states, and the Washington, D.C., area extends into Maryland and Virginia as well as the District of Columbia.

Four other metropolitan areas are actually international urban communities. These are El Paso, Texas, and San Diego, California, both of which are met by urban communities of Mexico; and Buffalo and Detroit, which border Canadian urban communities. In addition, several other metropolitan areas bordering on the Great Lakes face problems of international significance in such service areas as water supply and water pollution.

TABLE 20
CLASSIFICATION OF SMSAs BY TERRITORY

Number of counties	SMSAs of 200,000 population or more	SMSAs with less than 200,000
1	51	72
2	42	14
3	25	6
4	13	2
5	6	1
6	4	0
7	2	0
8	3	0
9	2	0
Totals	148	95

Table based on the SMSAs as recognized in 1970.

PROBLEMS OF METROPOLITAN AREAS

The term "metropolitan problem" has become familiar as students and practitioners of government, club speakers, researchers and writers, league of women voters, and other study groups have expressed deep concern with existing and projected future problems. The term itself has been variously defined, but there is general agreement that such a problem or problems exist. To Luther Gulick, the metropolitan problem is

> millions of human beings who want to do something effective to solve the rising difficulties they are experiencing from the new pattern of urban settlement, but who do have the clear ideas, the teamwork machinery, or the leadership with which to proceed.[7]

To others, the metropolitan problem lies in the multiplicity of units within the metropolitan area and the absence of any governmental agency with regional authority. Sociologist Scott Greer notes that the metropolitan community reflects a social and economic unity which "is not reflected in government. The problems created by contiguity and mutual dependence are not allocated to any government which includes all of those affected and affecting others."[8] The governmental dichotomy of the metropolis and fragmentation of suburbia results, as Greer sees it, in a "schizoid polity" with serious consequences for both the political and governmental processes.

Another view equates the metropolitan problem to the service needs of the central city and its suburbs. The Committee for Economic Development lists as the major problems of central cities those of handling a daylight population in excess of the residential population, building expressways and providing parking space, adapting newcomers to the urban environment, and halting the spread of blight and obsolescence. Suburban communities, on the other hand, feel the brunt of demands for new schools, water systems, sewage disposal plants, fire stations, streets and utility lines.[9]

A few writers have attempted broader definitions. James Coke states

> a problem is metropolitan if all of the following conditions are satisfied: (1) if the problem is urban in character; (2) if it transcends the boundaries of a single political subdivision, and (3) if it is thought to be an appropriate subject for community decision-making.[10]

The second aspect of this definition emphasizes that the involvement of more than one unit of local government is an essential characteristic of a metropolitan problem and it is this factor rather than sheer size which so identifies a metropolitan problem.

While admitting there are urban problems, political scientist, Edward Banfield is more optimistic than most other writers concerning the nature of the metropolitan crisis resulting from problems. As he sees it, most of the "problems" that constitute the urban crisis could not conceivably lead to disaster. Some of them are important in the sense that a bad cold is important, but they are not critical in the sense that a cancer is critical. They have to do with comfort, convenience, amenity, and business advantage rather than the essential welfare of individuals or the good health of the society.[11] Continuing the medical analogy used by Banfield, it might be noted that the untreated symptoms of a cold can lead to pneumonia and untreated pneumonia normally results in a more rapid death than cancer because the latter is often a lingering disease.

INADEQUATE GOVERNMENT STRUCTURE

The close relationship between the governmental pattern and the metropolitan problem has been noted by almost every observer. The problem is actually a dual one which Gulick identifies as a governmental vacuum on the one hand and a fractionalization of assigned duties on the other.[12] The governmental vacuum exists because there is no governmental body with authority to cope with the major problems affecting the whole area. The fractionalization of duties occurs because each local unit has limited jurisdiction. Thus, while all of the metropolitan community is under some form of governmental control, no single governmental unit can exercise any degree of control over the whole—except when the metropolitan community is contained within the limits of a single county.

The pattern of local government in metropolitan areas is almost unbelievably complex. The 264 metropolitan areas contain a total of 22,185 separate governmental units—an average of 84 units per SMSA. The average number of units, however, is deceiving in some specific areas. The Chicago SMSA contains a total of 1,172 units and there are 852 separate governmental units in the Philadelphia area. Five other SMSAs have more than 300 governmental units, and six others have in excess of 250 units.

While few modern writers would consider the problem of illogical boundaries and inadequate governmental areas as the source of all metropolitan problems, they are recognized as an important element. One survey points out four ways in which the boundary-jurisdictional problem is important. These are:

1. Inadequate governmental areas mean that there is no agency large enough to cope with needs affecting the whole of a metropolitan community.
2. The small areas of many local units sometimes cause inefficiency and often greatly aggravate the problem of financing public services.
3. In the suburban portions of metropolitan areas, the absence of municipal government has often meant inadequate zoning and other controls, as well as substandard public services.
4. The tangle of governments found in most metropolitan areas has been a real barrier to the public understanding and participation which insures effective democratic control.[13]

APPROACHES TO METROPOLITAN GOVERNMENT

The problem of metropolitan government stems largely from the contradiction between the underlying unity of a metropolitan area and its fragmented governmental structure. A web of interrelationships creates a community of interest that is fractionalized among a number of separate governmental units. To meet this problem, a number of approaches are being tried. Some involve few or no changes in the structure of government within the area, while others call for fundamental alterations in the jurisdiction, structure, and functions of existing units. Devices in the first category are interjurisdictional agreements, annexation, single-purpose special districts, functional transfers, metropolitan planning and councils of government, and extension of administration by state and national governments. Six approaches involving governmental changes are city-county consolidation, city-county separation, multi-purpose special districts, metropolitan counties, federation, and metropolitan city states.

Interjurisdictional Agreements

Interjurisdictional agreements are defined here to include both formal or written compacts and informal or clearly understood unwritten compacts by which two or more governmental units voluntarily attempt to solve a mutual problem. As a cooperative device, the interjurisdictional agreement has various characteristics which largely account for their popularity. The device (1) permits joint action by the participating units on problems of common concern, (2) usually involves financial savings, and (3) normally the problem is met more efficiently than it could be through separate efforts. In addition, the device (4) maintains the corporate identity of the participating units, and (5) permits their elected officials to retain a degree of control over and responsibility for the functions provided cooperatively.

The interjurisdictional agreement is a widely utilized method for the amelioration of problems by adjoining communities. They are negotiated in a wide variety of service areas and involve every type of local government. A recent study identified municipalities as the most frequent participants in such interlocal agreements and found a direct relationship between the population size of a city and the number and quantity of its interjurisdictional agreements.[14] An earlier study concluded that the interjurisdictional agreement device "can only be a stop-gap arrangement to meet a current problem and it can only ameliorate—not solve the problem."[15]

The amelioration of problems in a metropolitan area is not to be belittled, however. The frequency and range of interjurisdictional agreements among neighboring communities indicate that this approach is acceptable and feasible and will be relied upon for the foreseeable future. Two common uses of such arrangements pertain to relations among local police departments to come to the assistance of the police in any one community in need of aid and to similar relationships among fire departments in adjoining communities.

Annexation

Annexation means the addition of new territory to an established governmental unit—to the core city in metropolitan areas, for example. At first glance, this method seems the most obvious one to adopt, but it has become increasingly unsatisfactory and holds little promise for the future. The basic reason for its decline is the requirement in most states that areas may be annexed only upon approval by the voters in the unincorporated areas affected as well as in the annexing city. Thus, except in a few states, notably Virginia, Texas, and Missouri, constitutional or statutory provisions make the annexation of incorporated municipalities almost impossible and the annexation of unincorporated territory most difficult.

Annexation may still be desirable and is still utilized occasionally, but it was never a permanent solution to the problems of fringe settlements around a city. Population growth outran annexations in almost every community. A second problem is that most state laws prohibit annexations across county lines, and annexations across state boundaries are impossible. Yet modern urban developments flow over into areas of adjoining counties and states. A third factor is the increasing tendency of territories in and around center cities to incorporate as separate municipal entities.

A comprehensive study of annexation since 1950 reports that 19 cities have added not less than 100 square miles to their areas while another 21 have gained between 40 and 100 square miles through annexation.[16] The procedure is utilized in some states much more successfully than in others. Of these forty cities with major annexations since 1950, nine are in Texas; three each in Tennessee, Virginia and California; and two each in Florida, Oklahoma, Arizona, Missouri, Georgia, Ohio, Alabama, Kansas, and North Carolina.

Single-Purpose Special Districts

Since special districts were discussed in Chapter 9, they are considered only briefly here. However, their importance in metropolitan areas is attested to by their continuing growth in numbers. Almost 8,000 single-purpose districts now operate within standard metropolitan statistical areas. A breakdown of their major purposes is provided in Table 21.

TABLE 21
NUMBER AND TYPE OF SINGLE-PURPOSE
SPECIAL DISTRICTS IN SMSAs, 1972

Type of special district	Number
Fire protection	1,547
Natural resources	1,371
Urban water supply	888
Sewerage	866
Housing and urban renewal	731
School buildings	619
Parks and recreation	378
Other	1,092
Total	7,492

Source: Bureau of the Census, *1972 Census of Governments,* Vol. 1, Governmental Organization, Government Printing Office, 1973, p. 10.

One writer evaluates special districts in these words:

> As presently used, the district approach lacks sufficient compre-
> hensiveness to deal with the general metropolitan problem. Its limited
> functional nature leads us to further proliferation of government units, to
> more widespread citizen confusion and to inadequate popular control of
> the governmental system. . . . they may tend to lull local residents into a
> false sense of satisfaction that the total metropolitan problem, which
> consists of many deficiencies, has been solved.[17]

Functional Transfers

Transfer of functions is a mild approach to the metropolitan problem, and
yet it can be reasonably effective in one-county metropolitan areas. This
approach involves reallocation of a service or services by transferring them
from municipalities to the county or from the county to the central city of
the SMSA.

One of the most significant reassignments of local functions occurred
between Atlanta and Fulton County, Georgia, in 1952, following the
preparation of the Plan of Improvement to eliminate overlapping and
duplication. Under the reassignment of functions, certain services were to be
provided by Atlanta for the area—fire and police protection, inspections,
garbage collction, parks and recreation, airports, water, sewers, library,
auditorium, and traffic engineering. The county, in turn, assumed the
functions of public health, public welfare services, courts, and surveying.
Both city and county provide public education, road and street maintenance
and construction, planning and zoning, and law enforcement. The Georgia
state legislature appropriated money to pay for an appraisal of all property in
the county, resulting in the merger of the city and county offices of tax
assessment and collection.[18]

A marked change in functional arrangements has taken place in the recent
city-county governmental reorganizations in the areas of Miami, Jacksonville, Indianapolis, and Nashville. In general, these reorganizations expanded
services both in the core city and in the fringe areas. Each of these arrangements
is analyzed in later sections of this chapter because a major reorganization
prompted the functional transfers that did occur.[19]

Decisions relating to the transfer of functions between and among local
governments are an important consideration in any government reorganization effort. The topic is regularly under study and consideration in both
communities that have experienced some functional transfers as well as in
those where a major reorganization has been experienced.

Metropolitan Planning and Councils of Government

To fill the gap between the need for metropolitan planning and its political practicality, a number of metropolitan planning commissions have been established in recent years. Although planning is necessary for effective legislation and administrative action on metropolitan problems, it is not a reasonable substitute if no machinery for implementing its recommendations exists.

Metropolitan planning commissions most commonly are established by joint action of the participating units under state enabling legislation. A few cross state lines, such as the Tri-State Regional Planning Commission established by interstate compact among Connecticut, New Jersey, and New York; and the Metropolitan Council of Governments, serving the District of Columbia, and parts of Maryland and Virginia. In some areas, the planning is the responsibility of an areawide government as in the Nashville-Davidson County, Tennessee, and Jacksonville-Duval County, Florida, areas. In the Boston area, the Metropolitan Area Planning Council serves ninety-six municipalities.

Although regional planning agencies already numbered about 300 by 1966, the process itself was substantially enhanced by a requirement in the Demonstration Cities and Metropolitan Development Act enacted that year. This Act specified that all applications by local governments for federal grants and loans in a wide range of programs must be submitted to an areawide "clearinghouse" for review. The federal Office of Management and Budget was authorized to designate these clearinghouses. Regional planning was further enhanced by OMB Circular A-95, issued in 1967, which required that the clearinghouses comment on "the extent to which the project is consistent with or contribute to the fulfillment of comprehensive planning. . . ."

A sharp distinction once existed between a metropolitan planning commission and a council of governments (COG). The distinction began to blur in the late 1960s and is now almost impossible to draw. By 1971 there were 560 recognized COGs.[20] Several metropolitan planning commissions have been converted into councils of governments. For example, the Detroit Metropolitan Area Regional Planning Commission has become the Southeast Michigan Council of Governments, and the Metropolitan Washington Council of Governments replaced the former planning commission that served the District of Columbia and portions of Maryland and Virginia. The planning function has been included as an original responsibility of some COGs, such as the Association of Bay Area Governments operating in the San Francisco area and the North Central Texas Council of Governments functioning in the Dallas-Ft. Worth area. Planning has been added as a responsibility for other COGs that did not originally undertake this function.

Direct Action by Higher Levels

The shifting of power from a lower level of government to a higher level has been a subject of much concern in the past few decades. While the weight of expressed opinion seems to be against this trend, the movement itself is unmistakable. As even larger percentages of the American people become concentrated in metropolitan areas, we may expect both the state and national governments to become more directly involved in a number of service problems, including those of water, transportation, air pollution, water pollution, and health.

Recognizing the probable increasing roles of higher levels of government in concern for metropolitan problems, Gulick calls for the working out of appropriate assignments of the three "extensions" of government under the principle of intergovernmental cooperation. He states

> In the process of assignment we will deal with "aspects" of functions, not with the allocation of whole functions. We will look at highways, at water supply and sewers, at pollution control, at education, at crime control, at planning and zoning, and at every other service and governmental activity, and decide what "aspects" of these functions shall be done by the federal government, what by the state, and what by the local constituency.[21]

Although no metropolitan area has experienced extensive integration through action by higher levels (with the obvious exception of Washington, D.C.), there are a number of specific examples of state and federal influence and leadership. Federal programs now encourage and require regional planning for such programs as housing, urban renewal and redevelopment, and highways. Most federal grants-in-aid are funneled through the county government, thus strengthening it as the administrative unit of local government in metropolitan areas. Examples of state assumption of services previously exercised by local governments are more numerous. The specific services assumed vary among the states but include such services as welfare, highways, health, and hospitals. In addition, New York State assumed leadership and direction for correcting the financial ills of New York City.

City-County Consolidation

City-county consolidation, as the term implies, consists of a partial or complete merger of the area and government of a county with that of the city or cities lying within it. Theoretically, this seems a reasonable approach to governmental integration in one-county metropolitan areas.

City-county consolidation seemed an approach of the past until 1947 when a consolidation charter was adopted by the voters of the City of Baton Rouge and East Baton Rouge Parish by the narrow margin of only 307 votes. The legal identities of the two units were retained, but their governments were interlocked in several ways.

A second modern city-county consolidation occurred in 1962 when the voters of Nashville and Davidson County, Tennessee, passed such a proposal. This consolidation establishes a two-zone or district arrangement—one district is the urban services district (the city of Nashville) that may be expanded and the second is the general services district covering the entire county including Nashville and the six incorporated municipalities that existed at that time. The government is headed by an elective metropolitan mayor and a 41-member council, six elected at large and the rest elected from individual districts.[22]

TABLE 22
STRUCTURE OF CONSOLIDATED GOVERNMENTS
IN THREE SELECTED AREAS

Item of information	Nashville-Davidson County	Jacksonville-Duval County	Indianapolis-Marion County
Effective date of consolidation	4/1/1963	10/1/1968	1/1/70
City area prior to consolidation	72.5 sq. mi.	39 sq. mi.	84 sq. mi.
Area of consolidated government	533 sq. mi.	841 sq. mi.	402 sq. mi.
City population before consolidation	255,000	198,200	525,000
Population of consolidated government	410,000	507,200	742,000
Number of municipalities in county not incorporated in new government	6	4	3
School districts included in consolidation	Yes	No	No
Form of consolidated government	Mayor-council	Mayor-council	Mayor-council
Mayor elected	yes	yes	yes
Size of legislature	41	19	29
Elected by district	35	14	25
Elected at-large	6	5	4

Since 1967 five other major city-county consolidations in SMSAs have occurred—Jacksonville-Duval County, Florida, in 1967; Indianapolis-Marion County, Indiana, in 1969; Columbus-Muscogee County, Georgia, in 1970; Lexington-Fayette County, Kentucky, in 1972; and Las Vegas-Clark County, Nevada, in 1977. A recent study by the National Association of Counties reports that the feasibility and desirability of city-county consolidation were under consideration in thirty-six areas.[23] With the exception of the Indianapolis-Marion County and the Las Vegas-Clark County consolidations, which were effected by acts of the state legislatures, the other consolidations resulted from voter-approved referenda in the affected communities.[24]

Comparative information relating to three of the recent city-council consolidations as they pertain to the structure of the reorganized government is presented in Table 22.

City-County Separation

City-county separation involves the detachment of a city, sometimes after territorial enlargement, from the rest of the county with the new city government performing both municipal and county functions within its territory. Current city-counties that resulted from such separation movements exist in Baltimore (1851), Denver (1902), St. Louis (1876), and San Francisco (1856), and in a number of Virginia cities. In Virginia, the city-county separation occurs through an automatic legal process, while in the other four states it resulted from local sponsorship of state enabling legislation.

In Virginia, the process of separation is automatic, applicable to cities of at least 5,000. Cities of 10,000 or more population are completely separated from the county and perform all the functions of both city and county governments within their boundaries. Cities of 5,000 which separate from the county are equally independent except for sharing the circuit court of the county. There are thirty-eight such city-counties in Virginia.

There is current discussion in Los Angeles County, particularly by suburban office holders, of the possible desirability of breaking the county into five counties. One of the new counties would consist of the present city of Los Angeles while the remainder of the county would become four new counties. If this suggestion were to be successfully implemented, then in essence the city of Los Angeles would become a form of city-county separation.

Multipurpose Metropolitan Districts

The multipurpose metropolitan district is a method to ameliorate metropolitan problems, combining the advantages of the special district and broadening the purposes it serves and the services it can render. Thus, it meets, at least in part, the problem of the limited functional nature of single-purpose districts. However, in undertaking to solve a few critical problems, such multipurpose districts tend to divert interest away from more thorough efforts at reorganization.

The Boston experience with special districts is interesting. The Metropolitan District Commission in the Boston area grew out of three separate commissions—the Metropolitan Sewer Commission, the Metropolitan Water Board, and the Metropolitan Parks Commission. The water and sewer commissions were merged in 1901, and this body was merged with the Parks Commission in 1919. The Metropolitan District Commission is an agency of the Commonwealth of Massachusetts rather than a direct instrument of the local governments it serves. Its five commissioners are appointed by the governor, and the expenditures of the Commission are included in the annual Commonwealth budget established by the state legislature. However, most of the amounts of money spent by the Commission are later recovered by a levy on the participating units.

In one capacity or another, the Metropolitan District Commission serves Boston and more than forty suburban communities. Not all cities subscribe to all three services, with parks the most frequently subscribed to service and water the least in terms of numbers of governmental units. Boston itself is included in each. The Commission serves as a "wholesaler" to the participating governments for water and sewers. It procures and sells water to the local units, which in turn sell it to their residents in locally-owned and –operated distribution systems. Collection of sewage is similar in that the local units pump it to the district which collects, treats, and disposes of it. Newer metropolitan functions have not been assigned to the Commission but have been placed in other agencies such as the Metropolitan Transit Authority and the Port Authority Agency.[25]

The Port Authority of New York and New Jersey probably is the outstanding example of a multipurpose special district. It now operates programs in the areas of airports; port facilities; bridges; tunnels; helioports; bus, motor truck and railroad freight terminals; and the World Trade Center. Two other illustrations are the Bi-State Development District around St. Louis, which provides mass transit and port facilities, and the Municipality of Metropolitan Seattle which furnishes sewage disposal and mass transit services.

The governing boards of such multipurpose districts are usually constituted in one of three ways. First, their members are appointed by the governor or other state officials. Second, their members are appointed by local officials or are composed of local officials *ex officio*. And, third, the composition reflects a combination of the other two methods.

Metropolitan County Plan

Because about half the metropolitan areas are contained within a single county, well-organized and well-governed county governments have real possibilities as the best units to achieve metropolitan integration. There have been numerous proposals and some action in recent years to establish urban counties. In 1947, voters in Erie County (Buffalo), New York, approved several measures aimed at making the county an instrument or urban government. Similarly, Milwaukee County has assumed a number of functions qualifying it as an urban county.

Voters in Dade County, Florida, in 1956, approved a plan creating an urban county. Because of the federated nature of the plan for composing the governing board, this plan is discussed in the section on federation that follows. More modern charters have also been adopted in St. Louis and Baltimore counties, establishing these suburban counties that adjoin but are not part of the cities with the same names as modified urban counties.

The development of the urban county in California is epitomized by the expansion of services rendered by Los Angeles County. The county acts as a coordinator by five principal means. They are (1) performing certain services directly on a countywide basis; (2) directing activities of certain special districts that have countywide significance; (3) performing functions transferred from other local governments; (4) performing municipal services for cities on a contractual basis; and (5) exercising leadership influence because of its size and the recognized qualities of its administration.[26]

One of the first and best known examples of county service to cities in Los Angeles County is the contractual arrangement for the assessment and collection of taxes. All but three of the seventy-eight incorporated municipalities utilize this county service. Other examples among the more than fifty different services performed by the county for varying numbers of municipalities include health administration, personnel administration, enforcement of industrial waste ordinances, issuance of building permits, election administration, fire protection, law enforcement, library services, parks, planning and zoning, sewer construction and maintenance, and street lighting. The county has approximately 1,600 agreements involving all municipalities, with the number of services ranging from seven to forty-five.[27]

The logical development of the county contract program in Los Angeles County reached fulfillment in 1954 in the so-called "Lakewood Plan," named for the city of Lakewood. As a newly incorporated city, Lakewood negotiated a master contract with the county for all its administrative services. Its local officials have served primarily as negotiators with the county government and as liaison agents with the various county departments to arrange for services requested by the local city council. More recently incorporated cities have tended to follow the Lakewood pattern and contract, at least initially, for many services from the county.

Federation

The basic element of federated forms of metropolitan government is the division of functions between a newly established metropolitan government and the existing local governments. The metropolitan governing body consists of representatives of the local units, who are either elected to serve on the metropolitan board or serve on it in an *ex officio* capacity because of their position in their home communities. While this device has been much heralded as the most promising device for metropolitan integration, there have been few serious efforts to implement it.

A plan for a federated metropolitan government in Toronto, Canada, was prepared after extensive hearings by the Ontario Municipal Board. Becoming operative on January 1, 1954, the action established the Municipality of Metropolitan Toronto, an areawide unit of government overlying the territory of thirteen municipalities. The city of Toronto and the twelve suburban communities continued to exist and handled all functions not allocated to the metropolitan unit. The original governing board consisted of twelve from Toronto, a member from each of the twelve suburban communities, and a chairman. A major reorganization occurred in 1967, resulting in the consolidation of the twelve suburban communities into six and a restructuring of the council so that twenty of its thirty-three members came from the suburban communities. Several reassignments of functions also have taken place since the original allocation in 1954.[28]

Federation was implemented in the Toronto area without needing to satisfy two requirements, one or both of which have proved to be insurmountable obstacles to the few attempts to achieve federation in the United States. Neither constitutional authorization nor local voter consent was necessary, because the plan was submitted to the provincial legislature by the Ontario Municipal Board, a quasi-judicial body with wide jurisdiction over municipal affairs.

The Dade County metropolitan government is not strictly a federation since it combines features of the urban county with those of a federation. Voters approved a locally-prepared home-rule charter in 1957 that redistributed functions between the strengthened county and its twenty-six municipalities. The charter established a governing body of the county as a board of commissioners of flexible size. Five members were to be chosen by countywide vote from districts, five to be elected by and from districts, and each city of 60,000 or more was authorized to elect one member of the board. The board now consists of thirteen members because the three cities of Miami, Miami Beach, and Hialeah have each qualified to have their own representative on the county board.

Among the functions assigned to the metropolitan government are mass transit, major streets and highways, planning, water and sewer systems, port facilities, major parks and public beaches, hospitals, welfare services, assessment and collection of taxes, flood control, and water conservation. Additional functions may be transferred to the county from time to time, with traffic engineering and penal functions already so transferred. In addition, the county government is responsible for setting minimum standards for the services performed by the municipalities. If the standards are not met, the county is empowered to take over and perform the services in the noncomplying municipalities.[29]

The two major problems in realizing metropolitan federation in urban areas relate to the assignment of functions between the areawide governing body and the local governmental units, and the problem of representation of people and local units on the newly constituted areawide governing board. These are not easy problems to solve and no common pattern of arrangements may be prescribed as "ideal." It seems likely that federation proposals will continue to be prepared for specific metropolitan areas and at least some will win voter support and approval in the years ahead.

Metropolitan-City States

The proposal for the creation of metropolitan-city states has received some support among academicians and reformers as an alternative worthy of consideration by policymakers. The general concept advances the proposal that any consolidated metropolitan region whose population reaches a specified total should be separated from the state and admitted to statehood. Richard Burton, an early supporter of this concept, advocates one million as the population minimum,[30] a figure currently surpassed by thirty-three SMSA's.

Burton claims several advantages for the concept of metropolitan states. First, local governments within their consolidated regions would be kept intact. Second, the metropolitan state could provide a fiscally and constitutionally viable form of government. Third, such states would redress the city-suburban imbalance of political power presently existing in many state legislatures. Fourth, these metropolitan states would provide functionally meaningful state boundaries within which comprehensive planning could be realized. Fifth, such states would preserve the local political gains of blacks and other minority groups. And, sixth, such states would assume responsibilities for the problems of the urban crisis and obviate the need for "direct federalism."[31]

A proposal somewhat like that of the metropolitan state was made by John Lindsay when mayor of New York City. He recommended that "national cities" be instituted on the order of other federal corporations. He advocated such charters for cities of over 500,000 so that these urban centers could deal directly through their own senators on matters of finance, welfare, and other program supports. Lindsay suggested that these units might give urban interests more leverage in shaping federal policies.[32] He also believed such status for New York would enable it to get back more money from Washington and enable it to short circuit Albany completely.

While the idea at first seems far-reaching, its ardent supporters regard it as a politically realistic and far less fanciful prescription for major metropolitan reform than some of the alternate proposals.

AN EVALUATION OF APPROACHES

Evaluation of the alternative approaches to the problem of metropolitan government is possible in a number of ways. One of the most fruitful methods is to measure the approach with respect to the objectives sought in governmental reorganization. One statement of such objectives holds that metropolitan government should be so organized that it

1. Is easily adaptable to current and future problems that arise from changes in social organization, technology, and public attitudes.
2. Is capable of making long-range plans for the area and of implementing area-wide policy.
3. Provides for reasonable citizen control and participation.
4. Maintains a system of strong local governments.
5. Provides an adequate level of urban public services, of acceptable quality, at reasonable unit costs, and without overlapping and duplication of services.
6. Distributes tax burdens fairly among all classes of citizens.
7. Receives adequate consideration by state and federal administrative agencies.
8. Provides an orderly means for the attainment of commonly agreed upon objectives and for the reconciliation or adjudication of conflicting interests.[33]

In view of these criteria, federation currently seems the most promising of the several approaches discussed. It provides for a two-layer system of government, with the metropolitan agency composed of representatives chosen by the citizens of the several community units. However, metropolitan areas continue to provide new frontiers for new solutions, and probably various new approaches will be devised in the future.

NOTES

1. Bureau of the Census, *General Demographic Trends for Metropolitan Areas, 1960-1970,* Government Printing Office, 1971, p. 3.
2. *Ibid.*
3. Stephen B. Sweeney and George S. Blair (eds.), *Metropolitan Analysis, Important Elements of Study and Action,* University of Pennsylvania Press, 1958, pp. 81-2.
4. Bureau of the Census, *County and City Data Book, 1972,* Government Printing Office, 1972, pp. xxi-xxii.
5. *Ibid.,* p. xxii.
6. Bureau of the Census, *1972 Census of Governments,* Government Printing Office, 1972, p. 9. The number 264 excludes the four SMSA's identified for Puerto Rico.
7. Luther H. Gulick, *The Metropolitan Problem and American Ideas,* Knopf, 1962, p. 163.
8. Scott Greer, *Governing the Metropolis,* Wiley, 1962, p. 56.
9. Committee for Economic Development, *Guiding Metropolitan Growth,* New York, 1960, pp. 21-22.
10. James G. Coke, "The Objectives of Metropolitan Study" in Sweeney and Blair, *op. cit.,* p. 21.
11. Edward C. Banfield, *The Unheavenly City Revisited,* Little, Brown & Co., 1974, p. 4.
12. Luther Gulick, *Metro: Changing Problems and Lines of Attack,* Governmental Affairs Institute, 1957.
13. Government Affairs Foundation, *Metropolitan Surveys: A Digest,* 1959, pp. 5-6.
14. Joseph F. Zimmerman, *Intergovernmental Service Agreements for Smaller Municipalities,* International City Management Association, Urban Data Service, 1973.
15. George S. Blair, *Interjurisdictional Agreements in Southeastern Pennsylvania,* Fels Institute of Local and State Government, University of Pennsylvania, 1960, p. 124.
16. John C. Bollens and Henry J. Schmandt, *The Metropolis, Its People, Politics and Economic Life,* Harper & Row, 3rd ed., 1975, pp. 242-3.
17. Council of State Governments, *The States and the Metropolitan Problem,* Council of State Governments, 1950, p. 122.
18. M. C. Hughes, "Annexation and Reallocation of Functions," *Public Management,* 34 (February, 1952), 26-30.
19. Advisory Commission on Intergovernmental Relations, *Governmental Functions and Processes: Local and Areawide,* Government Printing Office, February, 1974, p. 49.
20. *Regional Review Quarterly,* 4 (January, 1971), 2.
21. Gulick, *The Metropolitan Problem and American Ideas,* p. 130.
22. Among the growing body of literature about the Nashville area experience, see Daniel R. Grant, "Metropolitics and Professional Political Leadership: The Case of Nashville," *Annals of the American Academy of Political and Social*

Science, 353 (May, 1964); Grant, "A Comparison of Predictions and Experience with Nashville 'Metro'," *Urban Affairs Quarterly,* 1 (September, 1965), 38-48; C. Beverly Briley, "Nashville-Davidson County," in *Guide to County Organization and Management,* National Association of Counties, 1968, 22-28; Brett Hawkins, *Nashville Metro: The Politics of City-County Consolidation,* Vanderbilt University Press, 1966; and David A. Booth, *Metropolitics: The Nashville Consolidation,* Institute for Community Development and Services, Michigan State University, 1963.

23. National Association of Counties, "Consolidated City-County Governments in the U.S.," *The American County* (February, 1972).

24. For accounts of the specific areas, see Richard A. Martin, *Consolidation: Jacksonville-Duval County,* Crawford Publishing Co., 1968; Advisory Commission on Intergovernmental Relations, *Regional Governance: Promise and Performance,* Government Printing Office, May, 1973; Keon S. Chi, *The Politics of City-County Consolidation: A Case Study,* Georgetown College, 1975; and Andrew P. Grose, "Las Vegas-Clark County Consolidation: A Unique Event in Search of a Theory," in *Nevada Public Affairs,* Vol. XIV, No. 4, March, 1976.

25. Charles R. Cherrington, "Metropolitan Special Districts: The Boston Metropolitan District Commission," in Sweeney and Blair, *op. cit.,* pp. 127-42.

26. Winston W. Crouch, "Expanding the Role of the Urban County: Los Angeles Experiment," in *ibid.,* pp. 107-8.

27. Bollens and Schmandt, *op. cit.,* p. 300.

28. For further details, see Municipality of Metropolitan Toronto, *Metropolitan Toronto, 1953-1963: A Decade of Progress,* Toronto, 1963; Albert Rose, *Governing Metropolitan Toronto: A Social and Political Analysis, 1953-1971,* University of California Press, 1972; Harold Kaplan, *Urban Political Systems: A Functional Analysis of Metro Toronto,* Columbia University Press, 1967; and Frank Smallwood, *Metro Toronto: A Decade Later,* Bureau of Municipal Research, Toronto, 1963.

29. See Edward Sofen, *The Miami Metropolitan Experiment,* Anchor Books, 1966; Aileen Lotz, "Metropolitan Dade County," in Advisory Commission on Intergovernmental Relations, *op. cit.,* pp. 6-16; Dade County Metropolitan Study Commission, *Report and Recommendations,* Miami, 1971; and Aileen Lotz, "Strong Mayor Plan Defeated in Dade," *National Civic Review,* 61 (June, 1972), 303-4.

30. Richard Burton, "The Metropolitan State," *City,* 5 (Fall, 1971), 44-48.

31. *Ibid.*

32. John V. Lindsay, "Chartering 'National Cities'," *Current,* 131 (July-August, 1971), pp. 9-11.

33. Sweeney and Blair, *op. cit.,* p. 80.

Chapter 19

The Prospect of Local Government

From the discussion in the preceding chapters, it is clear that the performance of local government seldom achieves the promise expected by its most ardent supporters. On the other hand, its performance has far exceeded that envisioned by the prophets of doom who have predicted its demise. The paradoxical position of local government in the last part of the twentieth century was pointed out in Chapter 1. Although the services rendered are increasingly important, citizen attention is centered largely on the problems and performance of higher levels of government.

This final chapter focuses on the role of local government in the foreseeable future without attempting to write science-fiction. Barring unexpected developments, that role will continue to be important, for local governments do provide services and make policies that shape the communities in which Americans live, work, and play. Although these policies were largely limited to housekeeping functions in the past, local governments are now called upon to determine and achieve goals of social policy. Ecology and consumer protection are simply two of the newer "quality of life" concerns of local governments. This larger role envisions their continuing and increasingly successful struggle to ameliorate the effects of certain dilemmas resulting from conflicts between theory and practice. Roscoe Martin described these efforts as the "permanent preoccupation of a democracy which is always striving but never quite achieving."[1]

Heinz Eulau and Kenneth Prewitt, both political scientists, have drawn an analogy between local government and a labyrinth. In their words, "The labyrinth has walls that serve as boundaries but are more or less porous; it has major arteries and places of assembly but also byways, detours, nooks, and crannies."[2] One's journey through the labyrinth takes more or less time, depending on the continuities and discontinuities in the journey occasioned by what is known or unknown about the terrain.

RURAL-URBAN VALUES

The transformation of our nation from rural-agrarian to urban-industrial has been sufficiently documented in previous chapters. However, the romanticized myth of small, responsive democratic communities as the backbone of our governmental system remains almost intact. The trends of urbanization and suburbanization of our population seem certain to continue in the foreseeable future, but the agrarian myth is almost as destined to persist.

The general shibboleths surrounding rural government and democracy cast considerable doubt about big units of local government. These charges assess big government (300,000 or more population) as being (1) more impersonal and less human, (2) less subject to popular control, (3) more subject to political control, (4) out of touch with local conditions, (5) less flexible, (6) more bureaucratic, and, as a result, (7) less democratic than small government. Roscoe Martin recognized that there was much virtue in local rural government but believed a thorough reappraisal must assess its performance as at least one step this side of perfection. He concluded that the conditions of government in rural America are less favorable for democracy than is true for urban areas. He described rural government as "too picayune, too narrow in outlook, too limited in horizon, too self-centered in interests, to challenge the imagination or to enlist the support of the voter."[3]

Both rural and urban local governments have similar problems in challenging and enlisting citizen support. In many rural units, the problem exists because of small size, and it exists in our larger urban areas becase the citizenry is so large as to be difficult to reach and enlist the support of all the groups within it.

Unless current trends change, population within metropolitan areas will continue to be distributed somewhat along economic and racial lines. The description provided by William Whyte, journal editor, in 1958 has held largely true. He viewed the city as becoming a place of extremes—a place for the very rich, or the very poor, or the slightly odd. In pleasant tree-shaded neighborhoods, there were still islands of middle-class stability, but for young couples on the way up these were neighborhoods of the past in which an ethnic group of older citizens still lived.[4]

The racial composition of population growth in the central cities of our ten largest SMSAs in a recent decade is shown in Table 23. Only one of these cities—Los Angeles—had an increasing white population, while Washington showed a net loss of nearly 40 percent and St. Louis and Detroit each lost approximately 30 percent of their white citizenry. All ten central cities, on the other hand, showed increases in black citizens. Three cities—Boston, New York and Los Angeles—had increases of more than 50 percent, while only two cities—Pittsburgh and St. Louis—had increases of less than 20 percent. In many central cities, the result has been continuing residential segregation and polarization among the citizenry. More recent population estimates have shown a continuation of these trends.

TABLE 23
RACIAL COMPOSITION OF POPULATION GROWTH
IN TEN LARGEST SMSA CENTRAL CITIES, 1960-70

Central City	White Population Percent Change	Black Population Percent Change
New York	-9.3	53.2
Los Angeles – Long Beach	4.7	51.7
Chicago	-18.6	35.7
Philadelphia	-12.9	23.5
Detroit	-29.1	37.0
San Francisco – Oakland	-17.2	39.7
Washington, D.C.	-39.4	30.6
Boston	-16.5	65.8
Pittsburgh	-18.0	4.2
St. Louis	-31.6	18.6

Source: Bureau of Census, *United States Summary, General Demographic Trends for Metropolitan Areas, 1960-1970*, Government Printing Office, 1970, p. 34.

To some persons, Thomas Jefferson's words, penned in his *Notes on Virginia* in 1782, still reflect life in big cities. Jefferson wrote, "The mobs of great cities add just so much to the support of pure government, as sores do to the strength of the human body." Today, there is no question that rural America remains important, but no one can seriously doubt that our culture and politics are dominated by our urban communities. The small communities that once produced the leadership for our states and nation now face serious problems of their own, just as do the large urban centers. Thus, the basic problems differ more in degree than in kind as local government strives to become a more positive force in achieving richer, fuller lives for its citizens.

A sobering thought is planted by Edward Banfield. He believes that even if we could afford to throw the existing cities away and build new ones from the start, matters would not be essentially different because the people moving into the new cities would take the same old problems with them. The present problems in the cities, he feels, will eventually disappear or dwindle into relative unimportance, but they will not be "solved" by programs of the sort undertaken in recent years.[5]

TOO MANY, TOO LITTLE

As noted in Chapter 2, the Commission on Intergovernmental Relations coined the illuminating phrase "too many local governments, not enough local government." The existence of about 78,000 local governmental units seems to substanitate the first part of the indictment. The combination of state reluctance to grant certain powers to local communities and the failure of many local units to exercise powers they have been granted also gives credence to the second part. A recent study concluded that American institutions of local government are under severe and increasing strain. While they were reasonably well designed to meet the simpler needs of earlier times, they are poorly suited to cope with new burdens placed on all governments by the complex conditions of modern life. "Adaptation to change has been so slow, so limited, and so reluctant that the future role—even the continued viability—of these institutions· is now in grave doubt."[6]

The superstructure of local government in the United States is indeed complicated. The typical citizen lives under several layers of local government, including, in most cases, a county, a municipality, a school district, and one or more nonschool special districts. The citizens of Whitehall Borough in Allegheny County, Pennsylvania, pay taxes or user charges in support of services or benefits received from seventeen different governmental or quasi-governmental units. They are:

> Borough of Whitehall, population 16,607
> Baldwin-Whitehall School District
> Baldwin-Whitehall Schools Authority
> Pleasant Hills Sanitary Authority
> South Hills Regional Planning Commission
> South Hills Area Council of Governments
> City of Pittsburgh
> Allegheny County Sanitary Authority
> Allegheny County Soil and Water Conservation District
> Allegheny County Criminal Justice Commission
> Allegheny County Port Authority
> Allegheny County
> Western Pennsylvania Water Company
> Southwestern Pennsylvania Regional Planning Commission
> Air Quality Control Region
> Commonwealth of Pennsylvania
> United States of America.[7]

Such a patchwork pattern is both uneconomical and confusing to the citizen who tries to perform his civic responsibilities of maintaining an interest and participating in the affairs of his community. However, this condition will not be easily overcome because certain groups and interests, for example, employee organizations and pressure groups, support and encourage this patchwork pattern.

Many prescriptions have been made for simplifying the structure of local government. Of these, only one—the move for consolidation of small school districts—has achieved wide acceptance. Because of this success, many students of local government are now more optimistic concerning the consolidation of other local governmental jurisdictions in the future.

Consolidation of counties has been widely advocated as a desirable step in local reorganization, and many states have constitutional or statutory provisions authorizing the voluntary consolidation of contiguous counties. The progress of voluntary county consolidation, however, has been extremely slow. Since the beginning of the present century, there have been only two consolidations.[8]

While the movement toward school district consolidation has been proceeding for several decades, it may be expected to continue in general at least in the near future. However, eight states actually have had a slight increase in school districts in very recent years. And decentralization, if taken far enough, will produce more school districts.

One other type of consolidation of local governmental units that is widely urged pertains to city-county consolidation in one-county metropolitan areas. Its slow progress in this area was noted in Chapter 18 and needs no elaboration at this point. However, it seems reasonable to predict that a limited but increasing number of such consolidations will take place in future years as solutions continue to be sought for the governmental problems of our urban areas.

A more promising development in local government is the growing use of functional consolidation. This device involves the cooperation of two or more local governmental units in the performance of a common service. Although it has no effect on the number of local governments, it does do away with some duplication, waste, and inefficiency in the provision of certain services. Functional consolidations, in the form of interjurisdictional agreements, are widely employed in metropolitan areas, and offer promise for more cooperative relations among rural governments as well.

One other unit of local government figures prominently in most proposals for changing our local governmental structure. There has been widespread advocacy of the abolition of the rural township that exists in sixteen states. The tradition of the township is still strong, and such a change will take a number of years to effect. However, evidence points to the transfer of most township functions to other local units if not to their actual dissolution. A small decline in the number of townships has been under way recently.

Without question the large number of existing local governmental units could be sharply decreased and result in more efficient and economical government without a loss in representativeness and responsiveness. Movements to consolidate or to dissolve small units should be encouraged. However, the large number of units can be indicted too harshly. The incorporation of new municipalities in urban areas can actually assist rather than hinder the development of areawide policies. While it is difficult to obtain cooperation among local planning agencies for regional planning purposes, it is even more difficult to extract the same degree of cooperation from a number of landowners residing in an unincorporated area. There is much merit in proposals to limit future incorporations in urban areas, but incorporation of reasonable units of local government should be allowed to continue.

LEADERSHIP

Another dilemma confronting American local governments is the growing need for increased active and energetic leadership, which means a break with the long tradition of weak local government. Americans have long harbored a suspicion of strong government and some disposition toward the old adage "that government is best which governs least." The continuing need for giving local government vigorous leadership has been commented on previously. The role of the chief executive—whether elected or appointed—is peculiarly that of being the one person who is able to serve the interests of all the citizens. Local legislators, even when elected at large, often seem to represent segments of the citizenry rather than the whole.

In an excellent statement concerning leadership in local government, Stephen Bailey believes that local communities have too often been treated as problems in administrative mechanics:

> Like the human body, the local community is a functioning organism. It lives and breathes, grows and decays, aspires and doubts. Its viability depends not only upon the satisfactory functioning of its economic and administrative muscle, but upon the character of its will and vision; in short, upon its leadership.[9]

In a prescription of obligations of local leadership, Bailey lists four basic responsibilities that it must perform. The first is to identify the resources of the community—both public and private—that can serve as partners in making the community a more desirable place. These include creative and alert individuals, private capital—both local and nonlocal—and federal and state governmental agencies and policies. The second responsibility is to find and utilize the "permanent forces" of the community. These forces are identified as the most common and most ubiquitous long-range interests of the community. The third obligation is to use self-restraint in the exercise of power. This seeming paradox occurs because a democratic leader should combine the resolve to move with an equal resolve to safeguard the rights of those who appear to block the way. The fourth responsibility of leadership is vision so that tomorrow is not merely anticipated but is created.[10] As Bailey sees it, "The main job of local government, like the main job of a housewife, is not to dust under the bed; it is to raise a decent family." He urges local governments to become effective instruments of social policy by dreaming dreams about the future, and helping those dreams come true.[11]

A further aspect of the leadership dilemma is the controversy over the increasing replacement of amateur public employees with professionally trained public servants. Some persons view this advance of civil service and merit systems with alarm and consider the new class of employees as "bureaucrats" rather than public servants. Competence needs not be purchased at the price of responsiveness, and few would argue that the Jacksonian tenets concerning public office are adequately valid in the last decades of the twentieth century. However, the problems of strong employee unions are only beginning to be faced by local governments.

Students aspiring to careers in local public service and the colleges and universities educating them will continue to be plagued with the problem of generalist versus specialist programs of study. There are important roles for both generalist and specialist in the conduct of local affairs, and the generalists, except for the elected executives and legislators, probably will increasingly rise to policy positions after exercising administrative specialist functions.

AN INFORMED CITIZENRY

General consensus among researchers of local government in the United States holds that three principal requisites are needed for good government. The first two—good structure and honest and competent personnel—have been discussed in the preceding two sections. The third requisite is an informed, interested, and active citizenry, which is our concern in this section. Actually a close relationship exists among the three conditions. If the third is present, the first two also will likely exist. If the citizenry is not active and informed, the first two conditions may deteriorate to a degree that the community is not well governed.

The problem of citizen apathy and inertia has been discussed in Chapter 6. No community is confronted with complete citizen indifference because some persons are always concerned with government and its activities, particularly with respect to their interests. The greater the citizen abdication of responsibilities, the greater the influence over the many that will be exercised by the few. If the theory of the citizen's role in local government were faithfully carried out in practice, as Robert Wood points out, it would "demand so much of his time, so great a communion with his neighbors, so high a competence in public affairs, as to be nearly all consuming."[12]

There is, however, a middle ground between stark indifference and inaction on the one hand, and constant participation and concern on the other. The prepositional trilogy about government "of, by, and for" the people advocated by Abraham Lincoln is still of significant value in our local communities. The first condition above—indifference and inaction—represents government "for" the people at its extreme just as the second—constant participation and concern—represents the "by" the people theme. There remains the third preposition—"of" the people—which is the basis for the middle-ground concept. This implies that the citizens select persons to act for and represent them for a definite term of office. Then these agents are either re-elected for another term or replaced by other persons who are the choice of a majority of the citizens voting in that election. This is the essence of representative democracy where the people retain the power of direction through delegated authority.

To many thoughtful scholars and practitioners of local government, one of our most serious problems concerns the alienation of the citizen from the local political process. In part, this estrangement results from the appeal of national and international problems and concerns. A second and probably more serious reason is based on the commuting of many citizens—those residing in one governmental unit and working in another. These daylight citizens cannot participate in the affairs of the community where they work because they are not citizens, and the affairs of their dormitory communities seem to be operating satisfactorily and hence they do not participate there either. Accordingly, they become alienated from the local political and governmental process and become consumers rather than stockholders in their local governments.

The frequent indifference of the citizen toward his local government is often abetted by the poor "track-record" of the local mass media in reporting local news. Even the newswatcher in a metropolitan area will hear more about developments abroad and nationally than he will hear about his own area. The large daily newspapers similarly seem to slight local developments for national and international events. Grass-roots reform groups are thwarted in their efforts because of the expenses of running candidates for local office or qualifying a local initiative measure. Alienation thus often does not come from local citizen inaction or inattention but rather from the obstacles placed in the way of enlightened public participation.

Although a more active citizenry is a desirable community goal, some evidence supports the belief that what in part appears to be citizen apathy and inertia is really citizen satisfaction. When community crises occur, electorates do become aroused to meet the situations requiring community action and decision. Some persons support the "crisis" policy of active citizen participation as a proper functioning of the local electorate. While meeting crises satisfactorily is to be commended, preventive rather than corrective community action is more laudable. Such action spares the community the divisive effects often emanating from crises and the necessity for patching over the misunderstandings inevitably accompanying them.

Most listings of current problems of local government are statements of service needs and lags. There are many financial and administrative problems involved in providing new and extended services to citizens, but the more basic problem is to cultivate more enlightened civic leadership and more understanding support for such leadership. Two writers have issued a stirring appeal for a more active citizenry in these words:

> If the ordinary citizen would simply raise his sights to what his city, his county, his school district, and his state could be if everyone cared just a little more about the common good—and would then bestir himself a bit toward the fulfillment of that vision—there is hardly any limit to what could be accomplished.[13]

RELATIONS WITH HIGHER PUBLIC LEVELS

Democratic local government in a federal system faces two perplexing problems. These concern the distribution of powers and functions among the governmental levels and the pattern of representation for comprising legislative bodies at higher levels. Both these problems are of great importance to local governments, and vitally affect the future of our miniature republics.

The substitution of the concept of a "marble-cake" federalism for the outmoded view of the three-tier layercake in describing our federal system was discussed in Chapter 4. This newer approach is more realistic, recognizing that aspects of functions rather than entire functions are assigned to the three governmental levels. There is increasing intergovernmental activity in service areas once considered the responsibilities of local governments and private agencies, and local governments are being encouraged to undertake new functions and programs with financial assistance from higher public levels. As the budgets and activities of local governments continue to grow, only the most pessimistic observers of our governmental scene continue to predict their demise.

A concern has emerged over the role that local government units will assume in the future. Some persons view local governments only as administrative units to carry out the policies and programs of their creating state governments. Others see the policy role of local governments as expanding and making them even stronger political communities. In all probability, both roles will be maintained in the years ahead. In fields where the state enacts social policy, the local community will administer those within its boundaries. There will be other fields of social policy where the state will not act and where the local community will be called upon to initiate, enact, and enforce policy. Also, local communities likely will play an increasing role in shaping policies enacted by the state.

The second problem—the pattern of representation of local governments in higher legislative bodies is less serious than earlier before the general reapportionment of both Congress and state legislatures in compliance with the ''one man, one vote'' judicial principle. The progress of achieving this principle has been substantial. Recent studies reveal an increasing urban voice in both Congress and state legislatures.

If metropolitan government becomes a wider reality, probably problems just as acute as those pertaining to representation in higher bodies will develop in these areas between claimants for representation plans based on population and those supporting representation rooted in existing local governmental units. A problem also remains in patterns of representation in councils of governments, which still typically base representation on constituent units.

PROVISION OF ADEQUATE SERVICES

As noted in Chapter 18, the failure to provide adequate services has been described by Luther Gulick as the most obvious governmental failure in our big urban regions. Discussing the inadequacy of various remedial measures that have been attempted, Gulick concluded that

> Many of the heralded ''solutions'' have only made matters worse. In fact, conditions are generally deteriorating, and deteriorating fast, even with respect to the services where dramatic ''solutions'' have been adopted. Traffic, slums, commuter services, schools, water supplies, water and air pollution, urban crime, noise and dirt—one has only to mention these to recognize the facts.[14]

The need for more adequate services in rural and smaller urban communities also has been noted in Chapters 15 and 16. Thus, the problem of providing the necessary and essential services under existing financial limits is common to most governmental units. The hub of the problem has been aptly stated in these words:

> The difficulty of pricing public goods results because consumer-voter-taxpayers do not reveal their preferences. If they were to make known their true demand for public goods, the proper quantity and quality could be produced and the appropriate benefit tax levied.[15]

While citizens can vote for changes in services and taxes, the method is slow and produces incomplete results. As a further alternative, residents can move into another community but such extreme action is usually taken only if large-scale incentives are offered by a rival area.[16] And sometimes potential movers lack sufficient financial resources to find suitable housing elsewhere.

While it is not feasible to take up major service needs and discuss the problems they present and the difficulties inherent in ameliorating them individually, it seems most likely that heavy service demands will continue in our local communities. It is also probable that citizens will increasingly turn to their local governments for help in meeting these needs and will come to depend more upon government for such services. As this occurs, local governments will be forced to work cooperatively to an extent far exceeding current intergovernmental arrangements. Working together to solve mutual concerns and to meet common needs conceivably could pave the way for a new breakthrough in cooperative relations among local governments and serve as a testing ground for and a means to produce more effective local leadership in both metropolitan areas and less urban and rural communities.

AND IN CONCLUSION

Great changes have taken place in American local government during this century. The "shame of the cities" era of local government, with its graft, corruption, and inefficiency has been replaced by honest, competent administration in most local governments. The limited role of government in earlier years has been replaced by positive actions to advance and improve the amenities of community life. The tools and techniques needed to improve local governments are known and are receiving increasing adoption and use.

Heinz Eulau and Kenneth Prewitt conclude their study of local government in the San Francisco Bay area with this fitting statement:

> We take it for granted that the institutions of representative democracy in the United States will withstand the challenges of the new technological age, adapt to them, and control them. We do not take it for granted that these institutions will always work in the ways set forth by democratic theory.[17]

While the problems of democratic governance cannot be wished away by slogans of sovereignty or participatory democracy, Eulau and Prewitt believe that even "muddling through" will be enlightened by theory tested in the crucible of empirical research.

Any attempt to prophesy the future course of American local government in detail would require a nonexistent crystal ball. However, a general prediction may be ventured with considerable confidence. Barring unforeseen developments, it seems reasonable to predict that the future of American local governments is bright. They have made great strides in satisfying citizen demands and in providing a satisfying environment within local communities. Even more important, their record is one of continuing improvement—one deserving citizen support and understanding in the years ahead.

NOTES

1. Roscoe C. Martin, *Grass Roots*, University of Alabama Press, 1957, p. 79.
2. Heinz Eulau and Kenneth Prewitt, *Labyrinths of Democracy: Adaptations, Linkages, Representation and Policies in Urban Politics*, Bobbs-Merrill, 1973, pp. 611-612.
3. Martin, *op. cit.*, pp. 91-2.
4. William H. Whyte, Jr., "Introduction" in Fortune Magazine, *The Exploding Metropolis*, Doubleday, 1958, pp. viii-ix.
5. Edward C. Banfield, *The Unheavenly City Revisited*, Little, Brown, 1974, p. 279.
6. Committee for Economic Development, *Modernizing Local Government*, New York, 1966, p. 8.
7. Advisory Commission on Intergovernmental Relations, *Regional Decision Making: New Strategies for Substate Districts*, Substate Regionalism and the Federal System, Vol. I, Government Printing Office, 1973, p. 3.
8. In 1919, James County, Tennessee, consolidated with Hamilton (Chattanooga) County and in 1932 the counties of Campbell and Milton, Georgia, were merged with Fulton (Atlanta) County.
9. Stephen K. Bailey, "Leadership in Local Government," *Yale Review*, 45 (Summer, 1956), 563.
10. *Ibid*, pp. 566-72.
11. *Ibid.*, pp. 564-5.
12. Robert C. Wood, *Suburbia, Its People and Their Politics*, Houghton Mifflin, 1958, p. 97.
13. Henry A. Turner and John A. Vieg, *The Government and Politics of California*, McGraw-Hill, 1960, p. 266.
14. Luther H. Gulick, *The Metropolitan Problem and American Ideas*, Knopf, 1962, p. 3.
15. Werner Z. Hirsch, "Urban Government Services and Their Financing," in Hirsch (ed.), *Urban Life and Form*, Rinehart & Winston, 1962, p. 134.
16. *Ibid.*, p. 135.
17. Eulau and Prewitt, *op. cit.*, p. 613.

Suggested Readings Index

(Also see entries in Notes at end of each chapter.)

Chapter 1. TRADITION AND VALUES OF LOCAL GOVERNMENT

Bridenbaugh, Carl, *Cities in the Wilderness, The First Century of of Urban Life in America, 1625-1742* (New York: Ronald, 1938).

Gittell, Raymond G., *History of American Political Thought* (New York: Appleton-Century, 1928), Chap. XVIII.

Green, Constance M., *American Cities in the Growth of the Nation* (New York: Harper & Row, 1965).

Herson, Lawrence J. R., "The Lost World of Municipal Government," *American Political Science Review*, 51 (June, 1957), 330-44.

Long, Norton E., *The Unwalled City, Reconstituting the Urban Community* (New York: Basic Books, Inc., 1972).

Maass, Arthur (ed.), *Area and Power: A Theory of Local Government* (New York: The Free Press, 1959).

Mumford, Lewis, *The City in History* (New York: Harcourt, Brace and World, 1961).

Pranger, Robert J., "The Status of Democratic Values and Procedures in a Changing Urban America," *Western Political Quarterly*, 21 (September, 1968), 496-507.

Chapter 2. TYPES AND NUMBERS OF LOCAL GOVERNMENT

Advisory Committee on Local Government, *Local Government, A Report to the Commission on Intergovernmental Relations* (Washington: Government Printing Office, 1955).

Chamber of Commerce of the United States, *Modernizing Local Government* (Washington: 1967).

Dahl, Robert A. and Edward R. Tufts, *Size and Democracy* (Stanford, Calif.: Stanford University Press, 1973).

Drury, James W., "Townships Lose Ground," *National Municipal Review*, 44 (January, 1955), 10-13.

Editorial Research Reports, *Local Government Modernization* (Washington: Editorial Research Reports, 1967).

Havard, W. C. and Alfred Diamant, "The Need for Local Government Reform in the United States," *Western Political Quarterly*, 9 (December, 1956), 967-95.

Institute for Local Self Government, *Special Districts or Special Dynasties?* (Berkeley: 1970).

Lowe, Jeanne R., *The Near Side of Federalism, Improving State and Local Government* (New York: Ford Foundation, 1972).

Chapter 3. STATE–LOCAL RELATIONS

California Council on Intergovernmental Relations, *Allocation of Public Service Responsibilities* (Sacramento: 1970).

California Council on Intergovernmental Relations, *State Services for Local Government* (Sacramento: 1970).

Campbell, Alan K. (ed.), *The States and the Urban Crisis* (Englewood Cliffs: Prentice-Hall, Inc., 1970).

Elazar, Daniel J., *American Federalism: A View from the States* (New York: Crowell, 1972).

Feld, Richard D. and Carl Grafton, *The Uneasy Partnership, The Dynamics of Federal, State and Urban Relations* (Palo Alto: National Press Books, 1973).

Kresky, Edward M., "Local Government," in National Municipal League, *Salient Issues of Constitutional Revision* (New York: 1961), 150-62.

McCarthy, David J., Jr., *Local Government Law* (St. Paul: West Publishing Co., 1975).

Chapter 4. FEDERAL–LOCAL RELATIONS

Advisory Commission on Intergovernmental Relations, *Annual Report* (Washington: Government Printing Office), annually.

Advisory Commission on Intergovernmental Relations, *Sub-State Regionalism in the Federal System*, Vol. I and II (Washington: Government Printing Office, 1973).

Department of Housing and Urban Development, *The Model Cities Program, A Comparative Analysis of the Planning Process in Eleven Cities* (Washington: Government Printing Office, 1970).

Fox, Douglas M., *The New Urban Politics, Cities and the Federal Government* (Pacific Palisades: Goodyear, 1972).

Martin, Roscoe C., *The Cities and the Federal System* (New York: Atherton Press, 1965).

United States Commission on Civil Rights, *Making Civil Rights Sense Out of Revenue Sharing Dollars* (Washington: U.S. Commission on Civil Rights, 1975).

Warren, Roland L. (ed.), *Politics and the Ghettos* (New York: Atherton Press, 1969).

Willner, William and John P. Nichols, *Revenue Sharing* (Washington: Pro Plan International Ltd., Inc., 1973).

Chapter 5. POLITICS AND ELECTIONS IN LOCAL GOVERNMENT

Banfield, Edward C. and James Q. Wilson, *City Politics* (Cambridge: Harvard University Press, 1963).
Bollens, John C. and Grant B. Geyer, *Yorty: Politics of a Constant Candidate* (Pacific Palisades, Calif.: Palisades Publishers, 1973).
Callow, Alexander B., Jr. (ed.), *The City Boss in America* (New York: Oxford University Press, 1976).
Childs, Richard S., *Civic Victories* (New York: Harper, 1952).
Hahn, Harlan (ed.), *People and Politics in Urban Society* (Beverly Hills: Sage Publications, 1972).
Milbrath, Lester W., *Political Participation* (Chicago: Rand McNally, 1965).
Royko, Mike, *Boss, Richard J. Daley of Chicago* (New York: The New American Library, 1971).
Wirt, Frederick M. *et al., On the City's Rim: Politics and Policy in Suburbia* (Lexington, Mass.: D.C. Heath, 1972).

Chapter 6. CITIZEN ACTION AND CONTROL

Banfield, Edward C., *Political Influence* (New York: Free Press, 1961).
Bollens, John C. and Dale Rogers Marshall, *A Guide to Participation* (Englewood Cliffs, N.J.: Prentice-Hall, 1973).
Eyestone, Robert, *The Threads of Public Policy: A Study of Policy Leadership* (Indianapolis: Bobbs-Merrill, 1971).
Gans, Herbert J., *The Levittowners: Ways of Life and Politics in a New Suburban Community* (New York: Random House, 1967).
Hahn, Harlan (ed.), *People and Politics in Urban Society* (Beverly Hills, Calif.: Sage Publications, 1972).
Hertel, Michael M., *Irvine Community Associations* (Claremont, Calif.: Claremont Urban Research Center, 1971).
Janovitz, Morris, *The Community Press in an Urban Setting* (New York: Free Press, 1952).
Prewitt, Kenneth, *The Recruitment of Political Leaders: A Study of Citizen-Politicians* (Indianapolis: Bobbs-Merrill, 1971).

Chapter 7. COUNTY GOVERNMENT

Advisory Commission on Intergovernmental Relations, *Profile of County Government* (Washington: Government Printing Office, 1971).
"How Shall We Organize Our Counties?", *The American County*, 35 (March, 1970), 11-22.
Bollens, John C., *American County Government, with an Annotated Bibliography* (Beverly Hills: Sage Publications, 1969).

Duncombe, Herbert S., *County Government in America* (Washington: National Association of Counties, 1966).

Gladfelter, Jane, *California's Emergent Counties* (Sacramento: County Supervisors' Association of California, 1968).

Martin, Roscoe C., *Grass Roots* (University, Ala.: University of Alabama Press, 1957).

Murphy, Thomas P., *Metro-Politics and the Urban County* (Washington: National Press, 1970).

National Municipal League, *Model County Charter* (New York: National Municipal League, 1956).

Chapter 8. MUNICIPAL GOVERNMENT

Bollens, John C. and John C. Reis, *The City Manager Profession, Myths and Realities* (Chicago: Public Administration Service, 1969).

Booth, David A., *Council-Manager Government in Small Cities* (Washington: International City Managers' Association, 1968).

Carrell, Jeptha J., *Power Structure and City Characteristics of Council-Manager Cities* (Kansas City: Community Studies, Inc., 1964).

International City Management Association, *Municipal Year Book* (Washington: annual).

Loveridge, Ronald, *City Managers in Legislative Politics* (Indianapolis: Bobbs-Merrill, 1970).

Saltzstein, Alan L., "City Managers and City Councils: Perceptions of the Division of Authority," *Western Political Quarterly*, 27 (June, 1974), 275-88.

Zimmerman, Joseph F., *The Massachusetts Town Meeting: A Tenacious Institution* (Albany: Graduate School of Public Affairs, 1967).

Chapter 9. GOVERNMENT OF SPECIAL DISTRICTS

Campbell, Roald F. *et al.*, *The Organization and Control of American Schools* (Columbus, Ohio: Charles E. Merrill, 1965).

Government Research Center, *Government by Special Districts* (Lawrence: University of Kansas, 1969).

Portland State Research Bureau, *Voter Participation in Special Districts* (Portland: 1965).

Scott, Stanley and John C. Bollens, "Special Districts in California Local Government," *Western Political Quarterly*, 3 (June, 1950), 233-43.

Scott, Stanley and John Corzine, *Special Districts in the San Francisco Bay Area: Some Problems and Issues* (Berkeley: Institute of Governmental Studies, 1963).

Smith, Robert G., *Public Authorities, Special Districts and Local Government* (Washington: National Association of Counties, 1964).

Waters, Harry and William Raines, *Special Districts in Kentucky* (Frankfort: Kentucky Legislative Research Commission, 1968).

Chapter 10. THE LEGISLATIVE PROCESS

Blair, George S. and Houston I. Flournoy, *Legislative Bodies in California* (Belmont, Calif: Dickenson, 1967).

Bromage, Arthur W., *Councilmen at Work*, (Ann Arbor: George Wahr Publishing Co., 1954).

Eulau, Heinz, *Policy Making in American Cities: Comparisons in a Quasi-Longitudinal, Quasi-Experimental Design* (New York: General Learning Press, 1971).

Eulau, Heinz and Kenneth Prewitt, *Labyrinths of Democracy: Adaptations, Linkage, Representation, and Policies in Urban Politics* (Indianapolis: Bobbs-Merrill, 1973).

Eyestone, Robert, *The Threads of Public Policy: A Study in Policy Leadership* (Indianapolis: Bobbs-Merrill, 1971).

Loveridge, Ronald, *City Managers in Legislative Politics* (Indianapolis: Bobbs-Merrill, 1971).

Prewitt, Kenneth, *The Recruitment of Political Leaders: A Study of Citizen-Politicians* (Indianapolis: Bobbs-Merrill, 1970).

Williams, Oliver P. and Charles R. Adrian, *Four Cities: A Study in Comparative Policy Making* (Philadelphia: University of Pennsylvania Press, 1963).

Chapter 11. THE EXECUTIVE FUNCTION

Bancroft, Raymond L., "America's Mayors and Councilmen: Their Problems and Frustrations," *Nation's Cities,* 12 (April, 1974), 14-24.

Banfield, Edward C. (ed.), *Urban Government, A Reader in Administration and Politics*, rev. ed. (New York: Free Press, 1969).

International City Management Association, *Municipal Year Book,* annual (Washington: International City Management Association).

Bellush, Jewel, "A Bicentennial Resolution: Let the Mayor Be," *National Civic Review*, 64 (October, 1975), 459-63.

National Municipal League, *Best Practice with the Council-Manager Plan* (New York: 1972).

Nolting, Orin F., *Progress and Impact of the Council-Manager Plan* (Chicago: Public Administration Service, 1969).

Ries, John C., *Executives in the American Political System* (Belmont, Calif.: Dickenson, 1969).

Stillman, Richard J. II, *The Rise of the City Manager, A Public Professional in Local Government* (Albuquerque: University of New Mexico Press, 1974).

Chapter 12. THE JUSTICE PROCESS

Abraham, Henry J., *The Judicial Process* (New York: Oxford University Press, 1962).

Bayley, David H. and Harold Mendelsohn, *Minorities and the Police* (New York: Free Press, 1969).

Bell, Derrick A., Jr., "Racism in American Courts: Cause for Black Disruption or Despair?" *California Law Review*, 61 (January, 1973), 165-203.

Bent, Alan E., *The Politics of Law Enforcement* (Lexington, Mass.: D. C. Heath, 1974).

Doig, Jameson W. (ed.), "The Police in a Democratic Society, A Symposium," *Public Administration Review*, 28 (Sept.-Oct. 1968), 393-430.

Goldsmith, Jack and Sharon S. Goldsmith (eds.), *The Police Community: Dimensions of an Occupational Subculture* (Pacific Palisades, Calif.: Palisades Publishers, 1974).

Piliavin, Irving, *Police-Community Alienation: Its Structural Roots and a Proposed Remedy* (Andover, Mass.: Warner Modular Publications, 1973), Module 14.

Saunders, Charles B., Jr., *Upgrading the American Police* (Washington: Brookings Institution, 1970).

Skolnick, Jerome H., *Justice Without Trial: Law Enforcement in Democratic Society* (New York: Wiley, 1966).

Chapter 13. THE ADMINISTRATIVE PROCESS

Connery, Robert H. and William V. Farr, *Unionization of Municipal Employees*, Proceedings of the Academy of Political Science, Vol. 30, No. 2, 1970.

Dale, Ernest, *Management: Theory and Practice* (New York: McGraw Hill, 1969), 2nd ed.

Hatry, Harry P. and John F. Cotton, *Program Planning for State, County, City* (Washington: George Washington University, 1967).

Hawley, Willis D. and David Rogers (eds.), *Improving the Quality of Urban Management* (Beverly Hills: Sage Publications, 1974).

Nigro, Felix A., *Management-Employee Relations in the Public Service* (Chicago: Public Personnel Association, 1969).

Rogers, David, *The Management of Big Cities* (Beverly Hills: Sage Publications, 1971).

Saso, Carmen D., *Coping with Public Employee Strikes: A Guide for Public Officials* (Chicago: Public Personnel Association, 1970).

Zagoria, Sam (ed.), *Public Workers and Public Unions* (Englewood Cliffs: Prentice-Hall, 1972).

Chapter 14. LOCAL GOVERNMENT FINANCE

Advisory Commission on Intergovernmental Relations, *City Financial Emergencies: The Intergovernmental Dimension* (Washington: Government Printing Office, 1973).

Advisory Commission on Intergovernmental Relations, *Financing Schools and Property Tax Relief - A State Responsibility* (Washington: Government Printing Office, 1973).

Clark, Terry N., "Community Structure, Decision Making, Budget Expenditures and Urban Renewal in 51 American Communities," *American Sociological Review*, 33 (August, 1968), 576-93.

Crecine, John P. (ed.), *Financing the Metropolis: Public Policy in Urban Economics* (Beverly Hills: Sage Publications, 1970).

"Financing Our Urban Needs," *Nation's Cities*, 7 (March, 1969), 19-49.

Lyden, Fremont J. and Ernest G. Miller (eds.), *Planning, Programming, Budgeting: A Systems Approach to Management* (Chicago: Markham, 1968).

International City Managers' Association, *Municipal Finance Administration* (Chicago: International City Managers' Association, 1962), 6th ed.

State-Local Finances Project, *Planning, Programming, Budgeting for City, State, County Objectives* (Washington: George Washington University, 1967-68).

Chapter 15. LIFE-STYLE SERVICES

Bloomberg, Warner and Henry Schmandt (eds.), *Power, Poverty, and Urban Policy* (Beverly Hills: Sage Publications, 1968).

California Council on Intergovernmental Relations, *Serrano v. Priest, The Decision, The Implications, and the Alternatives for Funding* (Sacramento: September, 1972).

Committee for Economic Development, *Improving the Public Welfare System* (New York: 1970).

Gittell, Marilyn (ed.), *Educating an Urban Population* (Beverly Hills: Sage Publications, 1967).

Jenks, Christopher *et al., Inequality, A Reassessment of the Effect of Family and Schooling in America* (New York: Basic Books, 1976).

Kosa, John *et al.* (eds.), *Poverty and Health, A Sociological Analysis* (Cambridge: Harvard University Press, 1969).

Public Health Service, *Expenditures for Personal Health Service: National Trends and Variations, 1953-1970* (Washington: Government Printing Office, 1973).

Raab, Earl (ed.), *Major Social Problems* (New York: Harper & Row, 1973).

Chapter 16. SYSTEM-MAINTENANCE SERVICES

American Public Works Association, *Refuse Collection Practices* (Chicago: Public Administration Service, 1966), 3rd ed.

American Public Works Association, *Street and Urban Road Maintenance* (Chicago: Public Administration Service, 1963).

Barnett, James H., *A Study of Police and Fire Department Integration in Selected Cities of North America* (Grand Forks: Bureau of Governmental Affairs, University of North Dakota, 1973).

Creighton, Roger L., *Urban Transportation Planning* (Urbana: University of Illinois Press, 1970).

Downing, Paul F., *The Economics of Urban Sewage Disposal* (New York: Praeger, 1969).

Elgin, Duane *et al., City Size and the Quality of Life* (Washington: Government Printing Office, 1974).

Hanus, Jerome J., *Public Works Department: Organization and Management*, Urban Data Service, Vol. 2, April, 1970.

Muth, Richard, *Cities and Housing, The Spatial Pattern of Urban Residential Land Use* (Chicago: University of Chicago Press, 1969).

Chapter 17. PLANNING AND LAND-USE CONTROLS

Bolan, Richard S. and Ronald L. Nuttall, *Urban Planning and Politics* (Lexington, Mass.: D. C. Heath, 1975).
Brussat, William K., *The County's Role in Planning for Regional Problems* (Washington: Government Printing Office, 1966).
Burchell, Robert W. and David Listokin (eds.), *Future Land Use: Energy, Environmental and Legal Constraints* (New Brunswick, N.J.: Center for Urban Policy Research, Rutgers University, 1975).
Derthick, Martha, *New Towns In-Town* (Washington: The Urban Institute, 1972).
Fainstein, Susan and Norman Fainstein, "City Planning and Political Values," *Urban Affairs Quarterly,* 6 (March, 1971), 341-62.
McCarthy, David J., Jr., *Local Government Law* (St. Paul: West Publishing Co., 1975).
Ranney, David C., *Planning and Politics in the Metropolis* (Columbus, Ohio: Charles E. Merrill, 1969).
Scott, Mel, *American City Planning* (Berkeley: University of California Press, 1969).

Chapter 18. METROPOLITAN AREAS AND THEIR GOVERNMENTS

Canty, Donald (ed.), *The New City* (New York: Frederick Praeger, 1969).
Connery, Robert H. and D. Caraley (eds.), *Governing the City, Challenges and Options for New York*. Proceedings of the Academy of Political Science, Vol. 29, No. 4, 1969.
Fox, Douglas M. (ed.), *The New Urban Politics, Cities and the Federal Government*, (Pacific Palisades, Calif., Goodyear Publishing Co., 1972).
Harrigan, John J., *Political Change in the Metropolis* (Boston: Little, Brown, 1976).
Havard, William C., Jr. and Floyd Corty, *Rural-Urban Consolidation: The Merger of the Governments in the Baton Rouge Area* (Baton Rouge: Louisiana State University Press, 1964).
Hawley, Willis D. and David Rogers (eds.), *Improving the Quality of Urban Management*, Urban Affairs Annual Reviews, Vol. 8 (Beverly Hills: Sage Publications, 1974).
Murphy, Thomas P. and John Rehfuss, *Urban Politics in the Suburban Era* (Homewood, Ill.: Dorsey Press, 1976).
Wilson, James Q. (ed.), *The Metropolitan Enigma, Inquiries into the Nature and Dimensions of America's Urban Crisis* (Cambridge, Mass.: Harvard University Press, 1968).

Chapter 19. THE PROSPECT OF LOCAL GOVERNMENT

Bollens, John C. and Dale Rogers Marshall, *A Guide to Participation* (Englewood Cliffs, N.J.: Prentice-Hall, 1973).

Chamber of Commerce of the United States, *Modernizing Local Government* (Washington: 1967).

Clark, Terry N. (ed.), *Comparative Community Politics* (New York: Halstead Press Division, John Wiley & Sons, 1974).

Committee for Economic Development, *Reshaping Government in Metropolitan Areas* (New York: 1970).

Gimlin, Hoyt, *Local Government Modernization* (Washington: Editorial Research Reports, 1967).

Martindale, Don and R. G. Hanson, *Small Town and the Nation, Conflict of Local and Translocal Forces* (Westport, Conn.: Greenwood Publishing Corp., 1971).

U.S. Congress, Committee on Government Operations, *Unshackling Local Government*. House Report 1270, 90th Congress, 2nd session. (Washington: Government Printing Office, 1968).

Wood, Robert C., *The Necessary Majority: Middle America and the Urban Crisis* (New York: Columbia University Press, 1972).

Index